44 0425353 0

KT-150-887

WITHDRAWN

SPSS® Base 10.0 Applications Guide

University of
Hertfordshire

Learning and Info
Hatfield
...llege L...

For more information about SPSS® software products, please visit our WWW site at *http://www.spss.com* or contact

Marketing Department
SPSS Inc.
233 South Wacker Drive, 11th Floor
Chicago, IL 60606-6307
Tel: (312) 651-3000
Fax: (312) 651-3668

UNIVERSITY OF HERTFORDSHIRE
HATFIELD CAMPUS LRC
HATFIELD AL10 9AD 329956
BIB
013 017 901 9
CLASS
300.28542 SPS
LOCATION
SLC
BARCODE
4404253530
T

SPSS is a registered trademark and the other product names are the trademarks of SPSS Inc. for its proprietary computer software. No material describing such software may be produced or distributed without the written permission of the owners of the trademark and license rights in the software and the copyrights in the published materials.

The SOFTWARE and documentation are provided with RESTRICTED RIGHTS. Use, duplication, or disclosure by the Government is subject to restrictions as set forth in subdivision (c)(1)(ii) of The Rights in Technical Data and Computer Software clause at 52.227-7013. Contractor/manufacturer is SPSS Inc., 233 South Wacker Drive, 11th Floor, Chicago, IL, 60606-6307.

General notice: Other product names mentioned herein are used for identification purposes only and may be trademarks of their respective companies.

TableLook is a trademark of SPSS Inc.
Windows is a registered trademark of Microsoft Corporation.
ImageStream® Graphics & Presentation Filters, copyright © 1991-1999 by INSO Corporation. All Rights Reserved.
ImageStream Graphics Filters is a registered trademark and ImageStream is a trademark of INSO Corporation.

SPSS® Base 10.0 Applications Guide
Copyright © 1999 by SPSS Inc.
All rights reserved.
Printed in the United States of America.

No part of this publication may be reproduced, stored in a retrieval system, or transmitted, in any form or by any means, electronic, mechanical, photocopying, recording, or otherwise, without the prior written permission of the publisher.

1 2 3 4 5 6 7 8 9 0   03 02 01 00 99

ISBN 0-13-017901-9

Preface

SPSS® 10.0 is a comprehensive system for analyzing data. SPSS can take data from almost any type of file and use them to generate tabulated reports, charts, and plots of distributions and trends, descriptive statistics, and complex statistical analyses.

SPSS makes statistical analysis accessible for the casual user and convenient for the experienced user. The Data Editor offers a simple and efficient spreadsheet-like facility for entering data and browsing the working data file. High-resolution, presentation-quality charts and plots are integral parts of the Base system. Much of the output from the Base system and Tables option takes the form of flexible pivot tables that you can modify quickly and copy directly into other applications. The Viewer makes it easy to organize and manage your tables and charts using a familiar tree structure. When you have questions about an item in a dialog box, a statistic in your output, or the steps needed to accomplish a task, help is only a click or two away. With the Draft Viewer, you can create simple text output instead of interactive pivot tables.

This manual, the *SPSS Base 10.0 Applications Guide,* will give you ideas of how to approach your data, identify possible problems, remedy them, and interpret the results. A companion book, the *SPSS Base 10.0 User's Guide,* documents the graphical user interface of SPSS for Windows. Beneath the menus and dialog boxes, SPSS uses a command language that can be used to create and run production jobs. Dialog boxes can "paste" commands into a syntax window, where they can be modified and saved; a few features of the system can be accessed only via command syntax. Complete command syntax is documented in the *SPSS Syntax Reference Guide Release 10.0,* which is included on the CD version of the software and is available for purchase separately in print.

SPSS Options

The SPSS family of products includes add-on enhancements to the SPSS Base system, which are available on several computer platforms. Contact your local SPSS office or sales representative about availability of the following options:

- **SPSS Regression Models**™ provides techniques for analyzing data that do not fit traditional linear statistical models. It includes procedures for probit analysis, logistic regression, weight estimation, two-stage least-squares regression, and general nonlinear regression.

- **SPSS Advanced Models**™ focuses on techniques often used in sophisticated experimental and biomedical research. It includes procedures for general linear models (GLM), variance components analysis, loglinear analysis, actuarial life tables, Kaplan-Meier survival analysis, and basic and extended Cox regression.
- **SPSS Tables**™ creates a variety of presentation-quality tabular reports, including complex stub-and-banner tables and displays of multiple response data.
- **SPSS Trends**™ performs comprehensive forecasting and time series analyses with multiple curve-fitting models, smoothing models, and methods for estimating autoregressive functions.
- **SPSS Categories**® performs optimal scaling procedures, including correspondence analysis.
- **SPSS Conjoint**™ performs conjoint analysis.
- **SPSS Exact Tests**™ calculates exact p values for statistical tests when small or very unevenly distributed samples could make the usual tests inaccurate.
- **SPSS Missing Value Analysis**™ describes patterns of missing data, estimates means and other statistics, and imputes values for missing observations.
- **SPSS Maps**™ turns your geographically distributed data into high-quality maps with symbols, colors, bar charts, pie charts, and combinations of themes to present not only what is happening but where it is happening.

Compatibility

The SPSS Base 10.0 system is designed to operate on computer systems running Windows 95, Windows 98, or Windows NT 4.0.

Serial Numbers

Your serial number is your identification number with SPSS Inc. You will need this serial number when you call SPSS Inc. for information regarding support, payment, or an upgraded system. The serial number was provided with your Base system. Before using the system, please copy this number to the registration card.

Registration Card

Don't put it off: *fill out and send us your registration card.* Until we receive your registration card, you have an unregistered system. Even if you have previously sent a card to us, please fill out and return the card enclosed in your Base system package. Registering your system entitles you to:

- Technical support services
- New product announcements and upgrade announcements

Customer Service

If you have any questions concerning your shipment or account, contact your local office, listed on page vi. Please have your serial number ready for identification when calling.

Training Seminars

SPSS Inc. provides both public and onsite training seminars for SPSS. All seminars feature hands-on workshops. SPSS seminars will be offered in major U.S. and European cities on a regular basis. For more information on these seminars, call your local office, listed on page vi.

Technical Support

The services of SPSS Technical Support are available to registered customers of SPSS. Customers may contact Technical Support for assistance in using SPSS products or for installation help for one of the supported hardware environments. To reach Technical Support, see the SPSS home page on the World Wide Web at *http://www.spss.com*, or call your local office, listed on page vi. Be prepared to identify yourself, your organization, and the serial number of your system.

Additional Publications

Individuals worldwide can order manuals directly from the SPSS World Wide Web site at *http://www.spss.com/Pubs*. For telephone orders in the United States and Canada, call SPSS Inc. at 1-800-253-2565. For telephone orders outside of North America, contact your local SPSS office, listed on page vi.

Individuals in the United States can also order these manuals by calling Prentice Hall at 1-800-947-7700. If you represent a bookstore or have a Prentice Hall account, call 1-800-382-3419. In Canada, call 1-800-567-3800.

Tell Us Your Thoughts

Your comments are important. Please send us a letter and let us know about your experiences with SPSS products. We especially like to hear about new and interesting applications using the SPSS system. Write to SPSS Inc. Marketing Department, Attn: Director of Product Planning, 233 South Wacker Drive, 11th Floor, Chicago, IL 60606-6307.

Contacting SPSS

If you would like to be on our mailing list, contact one of our offices, listed on page vi, or visit our WWW site at *http://www.spss.com*. We will send you a copy of our newsletter and let you know about SPSS Inc. activities in your area.

SPSS Inc.
Chicago, Illinois, U.S.A.
Tel: 1.312.651.3000
www.spss.com/corpinfo
Customer Service:
1.800.521.1337
Sales:
1.800.543.2185
sales@spss.com
Training:
1.800.543.6607
Technical Support:
1.312.651.3410
support@spss.com

SPSS Federal Systems
Tel: 1.703.527.6777
www.spss.com

SPSS Argentina srl
Tel: +5411.4814.5030
www.spss.com

SPSS Asia Pacific Pte. Ltd.
Tel: +65.245.9110
www.spss.com

SPSS Australasia Pty. Ltd.
Tel: +61.2.9954.5660
www.spss.com

SPSS Belgium
Tel: +32.162.389.82
www.spss.com

SPSS Benelux BV
Tel: +31.183.651777
www.spss.com

SPSS Brasil Ltda
Tel: +55.11.5505.3644
www.spss.com

SPSS Czech Republic
Tel: +420.2.24813839
www.spss.cz

SPSS Danmark A/S
Tel: +45.45.46.02.00
www.spss.com

SPSS Finland Oy
Tel: +358.9.524.801
www.spss.com

SPSS France SARL
Tel: +01.55.35.27.00 x03
www.spss.com

SPSS Germany
Tel: +49.89.4890740
www.spss.com

SPSS Hellas SA
Tel: +30.1.72.51.925/72.51.950
www.spss.com

SPSS Hispanoportuguesa S.L.
Tel: +34.91.447.37.00
www.spss.com

SPSS Hong Kong Ltd.
Tel: +852.2.811.9662
www.spss.com

SPSS India
Tel: +91.80.225.0260
www.spss.com

SPSS Ireland
Tel: +353.1.496.9007
www.spss.com

SPSS Israel Ltd.
Tel: +972.9.9526700
www.spss.com

SPSS Italia srl
Tel: +39.51.252573
www.spss.it

SPSS Japan Inc.
Tel: +81.3.5466.5511
www.spss.com

SPSS Kenya Limited
Tel: +254.2.577.262/3
www.spss.com

SPSS Korea KIC Co., Ltd.
Tel: +82.2.3446.7651
www.spss.co.kr

SPSS Latin America
Tel: +1.312.651.3539
www.spss.com

SPSS Malaysia Sdn Bhd
Tel: +60.3.7873.6477
www.spss.com

SPSS Mexico SA de CV
Tel: +52.5.682.87.68
www.spss.com

SPSS Norway
Tel: +47.22.40.20.60
www.spss.com

SPSS Polska
Tel: +48.12.6369680
www.spss.pl

SPSS Russia
Tel: +7.095.125.0069
www.spss.com

SPSS Schweiz AG
Tel: +41.1.266.90.30
www.spss.com

SPSS Sweden AB
Tel: +46.8.506.105.68
www.spss.com

SPSS BI (Singapore) Pte. Ltd.
Tel: +65.324.5150
www.spss.com

SPSS South Africa
Tel: +27.11.807.3189
www.spss.com

SPSS Taiwan Corp.
Taipei, Republic of China
Tel: +886.2.25771100
www.sinter.com.tw/spss/

SPSS (Thailand) Co., Ltd.
Tel: +66.2.260.7070, +66.2.260.7080
www.spss.com

SPSS UK Ltd.
Tel: +44.1483.719200
www.spss.com

Contents

1
Overview of Data Analysis in SPSS

The meaning of data analysis varies from person to person and application to application. To some, it involves simply the display of descriptive statistics, a graph, or the results of a statistical computation. To others, it involves a series of steps, each of which may suggest further analyses and problems to investigate. SPSS is a comprehensive statistical software system that aids the data analysis process at any level, with procedures ranging from data listings, tabulations, and descriptive statistics to complex statistical analyses. Integrated with the statistical procedures are graphics for screening data, understanding and interpreting analyses, and communicating results.

This manual is organized by procedure, with examples of each and descriptions of how a statistician might interpret the output. This overview is a guide to the kinds of problems the data analyst needs to solve and the features of the SPSS Base system designed to help deal with those problems. Thus, it serves in part as a guide to the examples that follow, indicating which might be of particular interest to you as you design and carry out an analysis.

The examples in this manual illustrate only the SPSS Base system, not the many options that provide advanced and specialized statistical procedures, and they touch on only the default and commonly used features of the Base system. The emphasis is on understanding the basics and obtaining results you can trust. Further, although the examples use real data, there is no claim made that these data are reliable samples or that the results shown have any meaning for a real population. Obtaining a true random sample, or one whose relation to the population is understood, is critical to any study, but it is not a subject for this book.

The examples begin with shorthand instructions for carrying out the analyses using data distributed with the SPSS Base system. See Appendix B for information about the data files. Also installed with your SPSS system is a tutorial that illustrates how to navigate among and use the various windows and features that SPSS provides. A few minutes with this tutorial will make your subsequent work quicker and more rewarding. Finally, you can get help at many points in your work with SPSS. For example, this manual defines statistics operationally; by clicking with the right mouse button on a statistic name in a dialog box or in your output and choosing *What's This?* if a menu appears, you can obtain a definition of any statistic the software calculates.

Preliminaries

Data. SPSS allows you to read many kinds of data files or to enter data directly into the SPSS Data Editor. Whatever the structure of your original data file, data in the Data Editor are presented in the rectangular arrangement required by SPSS and most data analysis systems: rows **(cases)** and columns **(variables)**. A case contains information for one unit of analysis, such as a person, an animal, a business, or a jet engine. Variables are the information collected for each case, such as height, weight, profit, or fuel consumption. You can assign descriptive labels to the names of your variables and to the individual values of each variable (such as 1=Asia, 2=Europe, and so on), and you can choose whether to display the labels or the names in your output.

Figure 1.1   Data View in the Data Editor

Double-click on the variable name to edit labels, formats, and missing values

Each column is a variable

Each row is a case

country	populatn	density	urban	religion	lifeexpf	lifeexpm	literacy
Afghanistan	20500	25.0	18	Muslim	44	45	29
Argentina	33900	12.0	86	Catholic	75	68	95
Armenia	3700	126.0	68	Orthodox	75	68	98
Australia	17800	2.3	85	Protstnt	80	74	100
Austria	8000	94.0	58	Catholic	79	73	99
Azerbaijan	7400	86.0	54	Muslim	75	67	98
Bahrain	600	828.0	83	Muslim	74	71	77
Bangladesh	125000	800.0	16	Muslim	53	53	35
Barbados	256	605.0	45	Protstnt	78	73	99
Belarus	10300	50.0	65	Orthodox	76	66	99
Belgium	10100	329.0	96	Catholic	79	73	99
Bolivia	7900	6.9	51	Catholic	64	59	78

Data often contain missing values for answers omitted on a survey, results from a contaminated section of an experiment, or results of impossible calculations. When you do not supply a value for a case, SPSS supplies a system-missing value. You may choose, however, to assign a special code (like 9 for a 7-point scale item) to indicate that no response was given. If you do this, you need to define the missing value in the Data Editor so that SPSS knows to exclude the value from calculations (except when you specifically want it to be included).

See the *SPSS Base User's Guide* (henceforth just *User's Guide*) for information on labeling, missing values, data formats, and other data definition features.

Output. The results of your analyses appear in the SPSS Viewer. Most Base system procedures produce **pivot tables**, which you can edit in many ways to display the results in a way that emphasizes the relationships most important to your analysis. When the examples in this manual use pivot table edits, you will see the pivot symbol 🔧 as the shorthand that describes the specifications. To edit a table, double-click anywhere on the table to activate it. To hide a column or row, Ctrl-Alt-click on the label that defines the column or row (or right-click on the label and choose *Select Data Cells and Label* from the context menu that pops up) and then choose *Hide* from the View menu. To change a column's width, drag its right-hand boundary within the label area. To pivot the table, choose *Pivoting Trays* from the Pivot menu, and drag one of the icons from one tray to the other, or reverse the order of multiple icons in one dimension. If you left-click an icon, the element of the table the icon represents is highlighted.

See the *User's Guide* for more information about editing tables and working in the Viewer.

Transformations. This applications guide contains many examples of transformations used to prepare data for analysis. The word **transformations** describes a powerful set of functions, arithmetic operators, and other statements that operate on data values, one case at a time. For example, transformations are used to:

- Derive new variables, as in total = quiz1 + quiz2 + 2*final.
- Reexpress data, as in log_wt = LG10 (weight).
- Revise coding, as in religion (7, 8, 11, 12 = 0).

For more information on other transformations you can perform, see the *User's Guide*.

Case selection and sorting. You can use data values, functions, and operators to select a subset of cases for analysis, such as gender = 'male' and age > 21. The Select Cases dialog box (on the Data menu of the Data Editor) also allows you to choose a random sample or a range of cases to list or analyze. Select the *If condition is satisfied* option, click the *If* button, and define your selection criteria. Split File enables you to stratify analyses, for example, to run the same analysis separately for each value of *region*. See the *User's Guide* for these and other operations that limit or reorganize the cases in your file.

Data Screening

It is very unusual for real data to arrive without problems. In large studies, the process of data screening consumes considerably more time and effort than the primary analysis of interest. The first step is to identify recording or data entry errors and to examine how appropriately the data meet the assumptions of the intended analysis.

This section suggests some steps you can take to screen your data. Of course, exact instructions of what to do depend on the size of your study, its intended goals, and the problems encountered.

Identifying outliers and rogue values. The first step in cleaning data is usually to find values outside the reasonable range for a variable and to determine whether they are real outliers or errors.

- Use Frequencies to count the occurrence of each unique value (that is, when the variable does not have hundreds of unique values as Social Security numbers do). You may find typos or unexpected values and codes. Also, look for missing values that appear as valid values.

- For quantitative variables, use histograms in the Frequencies or Explore procedure and boxplots and stem-and-leaf diagrams in the Explore procedure. Notice the information on outliers in the Explore plots.

- For large data sets, scan minimum and maximum values displayed in procedures like Descriptives and Means (see Table 1.2 on p. 8). You might find codes that are outside your coding scheme or codes for missing values (like 999) that are being treated as data.

- Use Case Summaries to list data. You can choose a grouping variable to list the cases by category. You might also find it useful to sort your data by a variable of interest before listing. By default, only the first 100 cases in your file are listed; you can raise or lower that limit. To list just selected cases, first use Select Cases from the Data menu. You might compute standardized scores and select cases with values larger than 3.

Often, some outliers are better identified when you study two or more variables together.

- For categorical data, crosstabulations may reveal unlikely or undesirable combinations, such as a person who never visited your store but gave it a rating.

- Use bivariate scatterplots (from the Graphs menu) to reveal unusual combinations of values in numerical data. Consider a scatterplot matrix to display combinations of values between multiple variables.

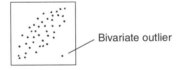 Bivariate outlier

- The Mahalanobis distance and leverage statistics in Regression are useful for identifying outliers among a set of quantitative variables.

Assessing distributional assumptions. Data distributions may not be as advertised; often, they are not normal and probably not symmetric. Using Regression to predict one variable from another will yield poor results if the variables are highly skewed. By trying a transformation such as

log_pop = LG10(populatn)

you may find that the logged values remedy the problem.

To check distributions, you can:

- Use Frequencies or the Graphs menu to generate histograms with normal curves overlaid.

Population

Log of Population

- Use the Explore procedure or P-P plots from the Graphs menu to generate normal probability plots. You can also use probability plots to compare the distribution of a variable to a number of standard distributions besides the normal.
- For larger data sets, compare the values of the mean, 5% trimmed mean, and median. If they differ markedly, the distribution is skewed.
- As a formal test of normality, try the Kolmogorov-Smirnov test or the Shapiro-Wilk test in Explore.

If you plan an analysis that compares means of groups, you may encounter more problems. For example, if you plan to use body weight in an analysis of variance, the probabilities in the output may be distorted if the distribution within groups differs widely from normal or if the spread of the distributions across the groups varies greatly (that is, the assumption of equal variances is violated). Use boxplots to identify skewed distributions and vastly different spreads across the groups. In the boxplots below, notice how a log transformation improves the within-group distributions of the variable *population*.

Population by Region

Log of Population by Region

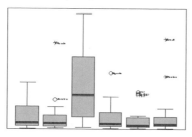 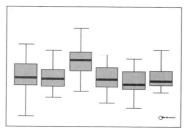

Use the following strategies to detect and deal with distribution problems across groups:

- Perform Levene's test of homogeneous (or equal) variances in Explore or One-Way ANOVA.
- Use the suggestion for a power transformation to stabilize cell variances provided with the spread-versus-level plot in Explore.

Descriptive Statistics

Descriptive statistics may be all you need for your current study, or they may be an early step in exploring and understanding a new set of data. Before deciding what you want to describe (the location or center of the distribution, its spread, and so on), you should consider what *types of variables* are present. That is, what do you know about the values of the variables?

Unordered categories. Examples of unordered categories include the variable *region* with codes 1 to 6 representing Africa, Latin America, and so on, or the string variable *religion* with values Buddhist, Catholic, Muslim, and others.

Ordered categories. Examples of ordered categories include the seven categories of the variable *polviews* that range from *Extremely liberal* to *Extremely conservative*.

Counts. The number of new cases of AIDS or children per family are examples of values that are counts.

Measurements. Values measured on a scale of equal units, such as height in inches or centimeters, are measurements. These values are *continuous*—you could record the *age* of a subject as 35 years or as 35.453729 (including days, hours, minutes, and seconds).

For many statistical purposes, counts are treated as measured variables. Arithmetic calculations like averages and differences make sense for both measurements and counts but not for the codes of unordered categorical variables. Numeric variables are called **quantitative variables** if it makes sense to do arithmetic on their values.

The most common statistical descriptors are appropriate for quantitative variables. In particular, means and standard deviations are appropriate for quantitative variables that follow a normal distribution. Often, however, real data do not meet this assumption of normality because the distribution is skewed or contains outliers, gaps, or other problems.

Descriptive Statistics for Normally Distributed Data

The statistics in Table 1.1 assume at least a quantitative variable with a symmetric distribution. Because these statistics can be very misleading for distributions that depart widely from the normal, use graphics wherever possible to display the distribution.

The *Groups* column in this and the following tables indicates whether the statistic is computed for the sample as a whole *(Sample)*, for subgroups of cases within the sample determined by a single grouping variable *(Groups)*, or for subgroups determined by combinations of grouping variables *(Crossed)*. (Statistical texts often call grouping variables *factors*, and their values *levels*; in that vocabulary, *crossed* means "for all combinations of levels of multiple factors.") You can also use the Split File feature on the Data menu of the Data Editor to stratify the cells further, although with Split File, you cannot get statistics across the sample as a whole.

Table 1.1   Descriptive statistics for normally distributed data

	Groups	Mean	SD	Std Error of Mean	Variance	Skewness	Kurtosis	95% C.I.
Frequencies	Sample	✓	✓	✓	✓	✓	✓	
Descriptives	Sample	✓	✓	✓	✓	✓	✓	
Explore	Groups	✓	✓	✓	✓	✓	✓	✓
Case Summaries	Crossed	✓	✓	✓	✓	✓	✓	
Means	Crossed	✓	✓	✓	✓	✓	✓	
One-Sample T-Test	Sample	✓	✓	✓				
Independent T-Test	Two	✓	✓	✓				
Paired T-Test	Sample	✓	✓	✓				
One-Way ANOVA	Groups	✓	✓	✓				✓
GLM Univariate	Crossed	✓						
Correlations	Sample	✓	✓					
Regression (Linear)	Sample	✓	✓					
Nonparametric Tests	Sample	✓	✓					
Discriminant Analysis	Groups	✓	✓					
Factor Analysis	Sample	✓	✓					

Always use graphics to ensure that the variables you are summarizing with these statistics have approximately normal distributions:

- Histogram with normal curve from Frequencies
- Stem-and-leaf plot from Explore
- Boxplot from Explore

Other statistics of interest are z scores and means ordered by size, both available from the Descriptives procedure.

Descriptive Statistics for Any Quantitative Variable or Numeric Variable with Ordered Values

The statistics in Table 1.2 can be used to describe any quantitative variable whether or not its distribution is normal, and they may be useful descriptors for values that code ordered categories (for example, 1 = *strongly disagree*, 2 = *disagree*, . . . and 5 = *strongly agree*).

Table 1.2   Descriptive statistics, normality not required

	Groups	Median	Min.	Max.	Range	Percentiles	Quartiles	Cum.%	Sum
Frequencies	Sample	✓	✓	✓	✓	✓	✓	✓	✓
Descriptives	Sample		✓	✓	✓				✓
Explore	Groups	✓	✓	✓	✓	✓	✓		
Case Summaries	Crossed	✓	✓	✓	✓				✓
Means	Crossed	✓	✓	✓	✓				✓
One-Way ANOVA	Groups		✓	✓					✓
Nonparametric Tests	Sample	✓	✓	✓			✓		

Graphics useful for understanding these distributions are the same as those for normally distributed numeric data: histograms, stem-and-leaf plots, and boxplots. The Explore procedure offers several robust estimators and other aids to understanding distributions that may deviate from the normal:

- 5% trimmed mean
- M-estimators
- Tukey's hinges

In Explore, you can request the five largest and five smallest values within each group, along with their respective case labels.

Descriptive Statistics for Variables with Unordered Categories

Frequency counts and percentages are useful for describing numeric and string variables with unordered categories.

Table 1.3   Descriptive statistics for categories

	Groups	Counts	Percents	Valid Percents
Frequencies	Sample	✓	✓	✓
Crosstabs	Crossed	✓	✓	

The Case Processing Summary that accompanies each output table also contains counts and percentages of valid and missing cases.

The most useful graphic for studying the distribution of variables with unordered categories is the bar chart, available from the Frequencies procedure or the Graphs menu.

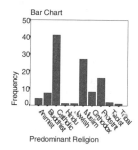

Tests for Comparing Means

The T Test and GLM Univariate procedures test hypotheses about means of quantitative variables. The purpose is to draw conclusions about population parameters based on statistics observed in the sample. These tests are available from the Compare Means and the General Linear Model menus.

When the data come from markedly non-normal distributions, a nonparametric test may be more appropriate. Rather than using the data as recorded, several of the tests use ranks (SPSS converts your data into ranks as part of the computations). Be aware, however, of using nonparametric procedures to rescue bad data. If you have data that violate distributional assumptions for a *t* test or an analysis of variance, you should consider transformations before retreating to nonparametrics. While the nonparametric test statistics drop the assumption of normality, they do have assumptions similar to their parametric counterparts. For example, the Mann-Whitney test assumes the distributions have the same shape. Also, if *in fact* the populations do differ, a nonparametric procedure may require a larger sample to prove it than a normal theory test would require.

T Tests for One, Paired, and Two Samples

SPSS provides three types of *t* tests for comparing means, depending on what you are comparing.

Use the **Independent-Samples T Test** procedure to test whether the mean of a single variable for subjects in one group differs from that in another group. For example, does the average cholesterol level for a treatment group differ from that for a control group?

The Mann-Whitney rank sum test is the nonparametric analog for the two-sample *t* test. It is used to test that two samples come from identically distributed populations—that is, there is no shift in the center of location (not the mean, because the distribution might be skewed). The test is not completely distribution-free because it assumes that the populations have the same shape. Thus, the groups may differ with respect to center of location, but they should have the same variability and skewness. Other nonparametric tests for two independent samples are the Moses test of extreme reactions, the Kolmogorov-Smirnov test, and the Wald-Wolfowitz runs test.

Use the **Paired-Samples T Test** procedure (also known as a dependent t test) to test whether the mean of casewise differences between two variables differs from 0. A typical study design for this test could include a *before* and an *after* measure for each subject. The before and after measures are stored as separate variables.

As nonparametric analogs to the paired t test, SPSS provides the sign test and the Wilcoxon signed-rank test. For each pair of observations, the sign test uses only the direction of the differences (positive or negative), while the Wilcoxon signed-rank test begins by ranking the differences without considering the signs, restoring the sign to each rank, and finally summing the ranks separately for the positive and negative differences.

Use the **One-Sample T Test** procedure to test whether the mean of a single variable differs from a hypothesized value. If the average IQ in your country supposedly is 100 and the average IQ for a sample of your co-workers is 127.5, use One-Sample T Test to see if you can conclude that your co-workers are smarter than the average person.

One-Way and Univariate Analysis of Variance

Analysis of variance is an extension of the two-samples t test to more than two groups. This analysis examines the variability among the sample means relative to the spread of the observations within each group. The null hypothesis is that the samples of values come from populations with equal means.

For a one-way analysis of variance (one-way ANOVA), groups or cells are defined using the levels of a single grouping factor that has two or more levels. In GLM Univariate analysis of variance, cells are defined using the cross-classification of two or more factors. For example, if study subjects are grouped by *gender* (male, female) and *city* (Los Angeles, Chicago, New York), six cells are formed: LA males, LA females, Chicago males, Chicago females, NY males, and NY females. The total variation in the dependent measure is separated into components for *gender*, *city*, and the interaction between the two.

The SPSS Base system provides three procedures for analysis of variance:

Table 1.4   Analysis-of-variance procedures

Means	One-way ANOVA table, test of linearity, eta
One-Way ANOVA	ANOVA table, post-hoc range tests and pairwise multiple comparisons, contrasts to test relations among cell means
GLM Univariate	Factorial ANOVA table, covariates

In some situations, a covariate (or in the language of regression, an *independent* variable) may add additional variability to the measure under study (the *dependent* variable). An analysis of covariance adjusts or removes the variability in the dependent variable due to the covariate. For example, if cholesterol is the measure studied for groups of people in treatment and control groups, age might be a useful covariate for subjects with varying ages. This is because cholesterol is known to increase with age; therefore, using it as a covariate removes unwanted variability.

The Kruskal-Wallis test is the nonparametric analog for a one-way ANOVA. It is just like the Mann-Whitney test for two independent samples except that it sums the ranks for each of *k* groups. SPSS also provides a median test where, for each group, the number of cases with values larger than the overall median and the number less than or equal to the median form a two-way frequency table. The Friedman test is a nonparametric extension of the paired *t* test to more than two variables.

Testing Relationships

In selecting a statistic to measure the relation among variables, you need to identify what types of variables you are investigating. If the values are categories, you will find an appropriate measure in the Crosstabs procedure. If the values are from a quantitative distribution that can be considered normal, you may want to use a linear model in Regression or a Pearson correlation in the Bivariate Correlations procedure. If normality is too strong an assumption to make, you might consider the Spearman correlation.

Measures of Association for Categorical Variables

For two-way tables of frequency counts formed by crossing two categorical variables, Crosstabs offers 22 tests of significance and measures of association. Each is appropriate for a particular table structure (rows by columns), and a few assume that categories are ordered.

Table Structure	Test
2 x 2	Pearson chi-square, likelihood-ratio chi-square, Fisher's exact test, Yates' corrected chi-square, McNemar's test, relative risk, and the odds ratio
R x C	Pearson and likelihood-ratio chi-squares, Phi, Cramér's *V*, contingency coefficient, symmetric and asymmetric lambdas, Goodman and Kruskal's tau, and uncertainty coefficient (the last three are predictive measures)
R x C with ordered categories	gamma, Spearman's rho, Kendall's tau-*b* and tau-*c*, and Somers' *d* (a predictive measure)
R x R	Cohen's kappa measure of agreement

Correlation and Regression for Quantitative Variables

A correlation coefficient is a measure of the linear relationship between two quantitative variables. A simple regression is another method for the same problem. A correlation matrix displays statistics for many variables pair by pair; while a multiple regression characterizes the linear relation between one variable and a set of variables.

Pearson correlations are available in the Bivariate, Partial, Regression, and Crosstabs procedures. If you want to test that a statistic differs from 0 (that is, that there is no linear relation between the two variables), the data should follow a normal distribution. When the data do not follow a normal distribution, the Spearman correlation is available in the Bivariate and Crosstabs procedures. The computations of this statistic replace each data value by its rank order (adjustments are made for ties).

Regression quantifies the linear relation between variables when the values of one variable are affected by changes in the values of the other variables. The equation of a straight line is the simplest form of a linear relation:

y = a + bx

Scatterplots are useful for assessing how appropriate a straight line is for summarizing the relationship. The following is a plot from the regression chapter that uses data from 85 countries. Values of female life expectancy are plotted on the y (vertical) axis and literacy on the x (horizontal) axis. The line is the *line of best fit*, estimated using the Regression procedure.

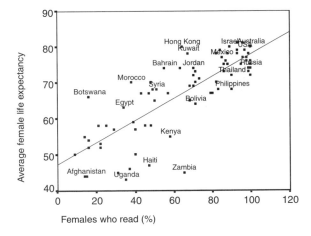

To write the equation of the straight line as a statistical model, add a term for random error (ε) because the points do not all fall on the line:

$$y = \beta_0 + \beta_1 x + \varepsilon$$

The Regression procedure is used to estimate β_0 (the intercept) and β_1 (the slope of the line) and to evaluate the fit of the line. At each x, the values of y should follow a normal distribution centered around the point on the line for that x. The values of x are ordered—they even could be simply 1 for male and 2 for female. You can include more than two independent variables in a regression:

$$y = \beta_0 + \beta_1 x_1 + \ldots + \beta_p x_p + \varepsilon$$

In applications, a researcher may not know just which set of p variables to include in a multiple regression model and may want to separate the important variables from those that do not contribute to the prediction. The Regression procedure provides several strategies for entering (or removing) variables one at a time in a stepwise manner. For example, one method begins at the first step by selecting the independent variable that has the largest Pearson correlation with the dependent variable. At each subsequent step, the variable that most improves the fit is added.

The screening process continues through all stages of an analysis. After you fit a regression model to your data, you should study residuals, predicted values, and diagnostics. The latter are useful for identifying outliers and departures from the assumptions necessary for the analysis. For example, this caseplot of a diagnostic named *DfFit* against the number of each case shows that more countries in the fourth interval tend to have extreme values of the diagnostic than do countries in the other intervals; and thus, the estimated model may be sensitive to their values. For this display, the countries are sorted by geographical region.

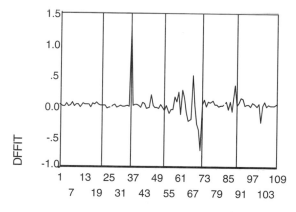

Sequence number

Identifying Groups

Cluster analysis, discriminant analysis, and factor analysis are useful for identifying groups. Cluster analysis is a multivariate procedure for detecting groupings in data. In both the k-means and hierarchical procedures, the clusters can be groups of cases. The hierarchical procedure can also be used to form groups of variables rather than cases. Clustering is a good technique to use when you suspect that the data may not be homogeneous and you want to see if distinct groups exist or you want to classify the data into groups. In other words, you can begin with no knowledge of group membership.

Classification can also be a goal for discriminant analysis. For this procedure, however, you begin with cases in known groups, and the analysis finds linear combinations of the variables that best characterize the differences among the groups (these functions can be used to classify new cases). Variables can be entered into the function in a stepwise manner—thus, a subset of variables that maximizes group differences is identified.

Factor analysis is appropriate for quantitative variables for which you want correlations. You can study the correlations of a large number of variables by grouping the variables into factors. The variables within each factor are more highly correlated with variables in their factor than with variables in other factors. You can also interpret each factor according to the meaning of the variables and summarize many variables with only a few factors. The scores from the factors can be used as data for t tests, regression, and so on.

2 Using Frequencies to Obtain Detailed Data Descriptions

The Frequencies procedure provides many statistics for describing data, although not all are appropriate for a given variable. These examples introduce:

- Frequency counts and percentages for numeric and string variables with unordered categories.
- Cumulative percentages for quantitative variables (or variables with ordered categories).
- Robust statistics such as the median, quartiles, and percentiles for quantitative variables that may or may not follow a normal distribution.
- Descriptors such as the mean and standard deviation for variables that do meet the assumption of normality (at least symmetry).
- Bar charts to represent variables with unordered or ordered categories and histograms to represent quantitative variables.

The examples in this chapter use data from the *world95* file. Each case has information about a country, including the region where it is located, the predominant religion, female life expectancy, average daily calorie intake, and population.

Example 1: Counts, percentages, cumulative percentages, and a bar chart. The default display summarizes each distinct value of variables with values that are numeric category codes, short string characters, and numbers from a quantitative distribution. This example also shows a bar chart for each variable and shows how categories in both the chart and the default display can be ordered by their codes or by ascending or descending frequency counts.

Example 2: Descriptive statistics, percentiles, quartiles, and a histogram. For the quantitative variable *calories* (average daily calorie consumption), dialog box selections include the mean, standard deviation, standard error of the mean, and minimum and maximum values. The 10th and 90th percentiles and the quartiles (the 25th, 50th, and 75th percentiles) are requested, as is a histogram of calorie values with a normal curve superimposed.

Example 3: Using data transformations to improve estimates. The mean and standard deviation can be misleading when the distribution is highly skewed. Often, the desired symmetry is achieved by transforming the data. In this example, statistics are estimated for the data as recorded and after log transforming each value. The difference between the estimates is remarkable. This example also shows how to suppress the frequency table.

Example 1
Counts, Percentages, Cumulative Percentages, and a Bar Chart

By default, for each value of a numeric or string variable, the Frequencies procedure reports the number of times the value occurs (the frequency, or count), the percentage of the total sample size for each count, and the cumulative percentage. Frequency counts and percentages can help describe data from any distribution. By scanning the values found for each variable, you can identify measurement, recording, or coding errors—or values that are correct but depart markedly from others in the sample.

In this example, the default display summarizes variables with these types of values:

- Numeric codes identify unordered categories—*region*, with codes 1 to 6 representing Africa, Latin America, and so on. Each code has a value label that is printed in the output.
- String values identify categories—*religion*, with values Buddhist, Catholic, Muslim, and so on.
- Numbers from a quantitative distribution—*lifeexpf*, with female life expectancy ranging from 43 to 82 years.

This example also shows a bar chart for each variable and shows how categories in both the chart and the default display can be ordered by their codes or by ascending or descending frequency counts.

To produce this output, from the menus choose:

Analyze
  Descriptive Statistics
    Frequencies...

Click *Reset* to restore the dialog box defaults, and then select:

▶ Variable(s): region, religion, lifeexpf

Charts...
  Chart Type
  ⊙ Bar charts

Region or economic group

		Frequency	Percent	Valid Percent	Cumulative Percent
Valid	OECD	21	19.3	19.3	19.3
	East Europe	14	12.8	12.8	32.1
	Pacific/Asia	17	15.6	15.6	47.7
	Africa	19	17.4	17.4	65.1
	Middle East	17	15.6	15.6	80.7
	Latn America	21	19.3	19.3	100.0
	Total	109	100.0	100.0	
Total		109	100.0		

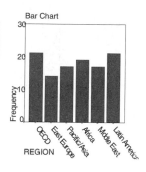

Bar Chart

Region or economic group. In the first column, SPSS lists the value labels for the variable *region*. The *Frequency* column contains the count or number of times each category occurs. In this sample, of 109 countries (cases), 21 have code 1 for OECD (Organization for Economic Cooperation and Development), 14 have code 2 for East Europe, . . . and 21 have code 6 for Latin America. The percentage of the total sample size for each count is reported in the *Percent* column. Countries in the East Europe category make up 12.8% of the sample; those in the Middle East, 15.6%. These percentages are useful descriptors because no *region* values are missing. When data are missing, use the percentages reported in the *Valid Percent* column. For the percentage calculations here, SPSS uses the number of values present instead of the total number of cases in the sample.

For unordered categories such as these, focus on the *Frequency*, *Percent*, or *Valid Percent* columns, and use the *Cumulative Percent* column for quantitative variables or variables with ordered categories.

If you want to display data values instead of their labels, from the Edit menu choose *Options* and then *Output Labels*. Then select *Values* under Pivot Table Labeling. Use this same dialog box to specify whether variable labels or short variable names are used in table titles.

Bar Chart. For each category in the bar chart, the height of its bar is the count reported in the *Frequency* column in the table for region or economic group. The bars are ordered by their codes. Options for alternative orders are described in "Ordering Categories in Reports and Bar Charts" on p. 20. You can also display the scale as percentages instead of frequency counts.

Predominant religion

		Frequency	Percent	Valid Percent	Cumulative Percent
Valid	Animist	4	3.7	3.7	3.7
	Buddhist	7	6.4	6.5	10.2
	Catholic	41	37.6	38.0	48.1
	Hindu	1	.9	.9	49.1
	Jewish	1	.9	.9	50.0
	Muslim	27	24.8	25.0	75.0
	Orthodox	8	7.3	7.4	82.4
	Protstnt	16	14.7	14.8	97.2
	Taoist	2	1.8	1.9	99.1
	Tribal	1	.9	.9	100.0
	Total	108	99.1	100.0	
Missing		1	.9		
	Total	1	.9		
Total		109	100.0		

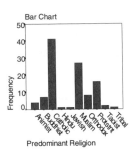

Bar Chart

Predominant religion. For the short string variable *religion*, SPSS sorts the categories alphabetically. Because the counts for Animist, Hindu, Jewish, Taoist, and Tribal are small, you may need to exclude these categories from some analyses and displays. Because *religion* was left blank for one country (see *Missing* at the bottom of the first column), the values in the *Percent* and *Valid Percent* columns differ slightly. SPSS uses the total 109 to compute the percentage and 108 to compute the valid percentage. The values in *Cumulative Percent* are computed using the valid percentages but are of little interest for this variable with unordered categories.

Bar Chart. The categories in the bar chart follow the same order as those in the table for predominant religion. The sparse categories are apparent here.

Average female life expectancy

		Frequency	Percent	Valid Percent	Cumulative Percent
Valid	43	1	.9	.9	.9
	44	2	1.8	1.8	2.8
	45	2	1.8	1.8	4.6
	46	1	.9	.9	5.5
	47	1	.9	.9	6.4
	50	2	1.8	1.8	8.3
	52	2	1.8	1.8	10.1
	53	1	.9	.9	11.0
	54	1	.9	.9	11.9
	55	2	1.8	1.8	13.8
	57	2	1.8	1.8	15.6
	58	4	3.7	3.7	19.3
	59	1	.9	.9	20.2
	63	1	.9	.9	21.1
	64	1	.9	.9	22.0
	65	2	1.8	1.8	23.9
	66	1	.9	.9	24.8
	67	5	4.6	4.6	29.4
	68	5	4.6	4.6	33.9
	69	2	1.8	1.8	35.8
	70	5	4.6	4.6	40.4
	71	1	.9	.9	41.3
	72	3	2.8	2.8	44.0
	73	3	2.8	2.8	46.8
	74	5	4.6	4.6	51.4
	75	9	8.3	8.3	59.6
	76	5	4.6	4.6	64.2
	77	6	5.5	5.5	69.7
	78	9	8.3	8.3	78.0
	79	7	6.4	6.4	84.4
	80	7	6.4	6.4	90.8
	81	7	6.4	6.4	97.2
	82	3	2.8	2.8	100.0
	Total	109	100.0	100.0	
Total		109	100.0		

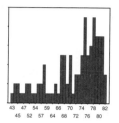

Average female life expectancy

Average female life expectancy. The quantitative variable *lifeexpf* has 33 distinct values ranging from 43 to 82 years. One country reports 43 years; four countries, 58 years; nine countries, 75 years; and so on. The **cumulative percent** is the sum of the values in the *Valid Percent* column up to and including the current percentage.

In Example 2, SPSS reports specific percentiles, but you can also read percentiles from the values here and use them to make descriptive statements for any quantitative variable or variable with ordered categories. For example, using the cumulative percentage value 10.1% at 52 years, you can say that for roughly 10% of the countries in this sample, female life expectancy is 52 years or less. Using the value 90.8% at 80 years, you can say that in 10% of the countries, females are expected to live 80 or more years. Similarly, looking for 25%, 50%, and 75%, you can say that the first, second, and third quartiles are, respectively, 66, 74, and 78 years; the 50th percentile (74 years) represents the median life expectancy.

In which countries do females live the longest? To find out, choose *Select Cases* on the Data menu (specify *lifeexpf* > = 80), and then use the Summarize procedure to list the country names—you will find Australia, Canada, France, Finland, Greece, Hong Kong, Iceland, Israel, Italy, Japan, the Netherlands, New Zealand, Norway, Spain, Sweden, Switzerland, and the U.K.

Bar Chart. The frequency values in the bar chart are the same as those reported in the table for average female life expectancy (for example, four countries have 58 years of life expectancy). Notice that a bar chart displays a bar with counts for each unique data value in the sample. A histogram presents a smoother picture of the distribution of a quantitative variable such as *lifeexpf* because the values are collected into intervals (or bins) before they are counted. (A histogram is displayed in Example 2.)

The distribution of the life expectancy variable does not look like a normal distribution because it is not symmetric. It is called **left-skewed** because the distribution has a long tail extending to the left.

Ordering Categories in Reports and Bar Charts

By default, SPSS orders the categories for *region* by its codes; those for the string variable *religion*, alphabetically; and those for life expectancy in ascending numeric order. The Frequencies procedure has options for alternative orders: descending order of the data values (numerically or alphabetically) or ascending or descending order of the counts in the categories. In this example, descending counts are used to order the categories of the variable *region*. The results of ordering affect the table and the bar chart.

To produce this output, in the Frequencies dialog box, click *Reset* to restore the defaults, and then select:

▶ Variable(s): region

Charts...
    Chart Type
    ⊙ Bar charts

Format...
    Order by
    ⊙ Descending counts

Region or economic group

		Frequency	Percent	Valid Percent	Cumulative Percent
Valid	OECD	21	19.3	19.3	19.3
	Latin America	21	19.3	19.3	38.5
	Africa	19	17.4	17.4	56.0
	Pacific/Asia	17	15.6	15.6	71.6
	Middle East	17	15.6	15.6	87.2
	East Europe	14	12.8	12.8	100.0
	Total	109	100.0	100.0	
Total		109	100.0		

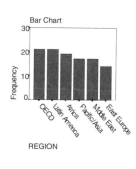

Bar Chart

Region or economic group. Compare this table with the table for *region* on p. 17, where Latin America was listed last and East Europe, second.

Bar Chart. The bars in the chart are now ordered by the count within each bar rather than by the category code in the data.

Example 2
Descriptive Statistics, Percentiles, Quartiles, and a Histogram

The Frequencies procedure optionally provides more than a dozen summary statistics. Many require that the data follow a normal distribution (or at least that the shape of the variable's histogram be symmetric). In particular, the mean, standard deviation, variance, standard error of the mean, skewness, and kurtosis should be used with caution unless you have screened the data well and know that the distribution is fairly symmetric and has no extreme outliers or subpopulations. A descriptive statistic is called **robust** if the calculations are insensitive to violations of the assumption of normality. This category includes the median, mode, minimum and maximum values, range, first and third quartiles (25th and 75th percentiles), and any specific percentiles that you request.

In this example, the dialog box selections for the quantitative variable *calories* (average daily calorie intake) are:

- The mean, median, standard deviation, standard error of the mean, and minimum and maximum values.
- The 10th and 90th percentiles and the quartiles (the 25th, 50th, and 75th percentiles).
- A histogram of the values, using the sample mean and standard deviation to draw a normal curve on top of the histogram. (A histogram is more appropriate than a bar chart for a quantitative variable.)
- Suppression of the default frequency table.

To produce this output, in the Frequencies dialog box, click *Reset* to restore the defaults, and then select:

▶ Variable(s): calories

☐ Display frequency tables (deselect)

Statistics...
    Percentile Values
    ☑ Quartiles   ☑ Percentiles (enter 10 and 90)
    Central Tendency
    ☑ Mean   ☑ Median
    Dispersion
    ☑ Std. deviation ☑ Minimum ☑ Maximum ☑ S.E. mean

Charts...
    Chart Type
    ◉ Histograms
       ☑ With normal curve

Statistics

	N		Mean		Median	Std. Deviation	Minimum	Maximum	Percentiles				
	Valid	Missing							10.00	25.00	50.00	75.00	90.00
	Statistic	Statistic	Statistic	Std. Error	Statistic	Statistic	Statistic	Statistic	Statistic	Statistic	Statistic	Statistic	Statistic
Daily calorie intake	75	34	2753.83	65.57	2653.00	567.83	1667	3825	2030.00	2247.00	2653.00	3236.00	3566.00

Statistics. This is the default layout for summary statistics. To obtain the layout shown in the next table:

 Double-click the table. If the pivoting trays are not visible, from the Pivot Table menus choose:

Pivot
    Pivoting Trays

Drag *Statistics* from the column tray to the row tray; then, drag *Variables* to the top of the column tray.

Statistics

		Daily calorie intake	
		Statistic	Std. Error
N	Valid	75	
	Missing	34	
Mean		2753.83	65.57
Median		2653.00	
Std. Deviation		567.83	
Minimum		1667	
Maximum		3825	
Percentiles	10.00	2030.00	
	25.00	2247.00	
	50.00	2653.00	
	75.00	3236.00	
	90.00	3566.00	

Statistics. The number of valid cases shows that 75 countries reported average daily calorie consumption for the people in their countries. This information is *Missing* for 34 countries. The *Mean* calorie intake is 2753.8 calories. The **mean** is the arithmetic average. How much do you have to eat in order to consume 2754 calories? A typical meal at McDonald's, for example, has 1170 calories (510 calories in a Big Mac sandwich, 450 for french fries, and 210 for a medium Coca-Cola).

The *Median* for the sample is 2653 calories. In a sample with an odd number of cases, the **median** is the middle observation when the data values are ordered from smallest to largest. When the sample size is even, the median is the average of the two middle values. More simply, just remember that half of the values in the sample are larger and half are smaller.

The mean and median are called **measures of central tendency** because they describe the center, middle, or most typical value in a sample. For a **symmetric distribution** (each half is a mirror image of the other), these measures coincide. The sample mean and median differ by approximately 100 calories. Does this mean that the distribution is not symmetric? To find out, consider the dispersion of the values.

The smallest (**minimum***)* calorie intake is 1667 calories; the largest (**maximum**), 3825. What can you say about the spread of data between the two extremes? Are the values clustered around the mean or spread out across the range? The **standard deviation** (*Std. Deviation*) is commonly used as a measure of dispersion or variation. It measures the amount by which each calorie value differs from the mean.

To compute the standard deviation, SPSS calculates the difference between each calorie value and the mean, squares the differences (this eliminates the effect that some differences are negative and others are positive), and finds the average of the squared values. For theoretical reasons, 74 $(n - 1)$ is used to compute the average, not $75(n)$. Finally, SPSS computes the square root of this quantity, resulting in a measure with the same units as *calories* (not squared units). The formula can be written as

$$s = \sqrt{\frac{\sum_{i=1}^{75} (c_i - \bar{c})^2}{74}}$$

where s is the standard deviation, c_i is the calorie value of the ith country, and $\bar{c}$ is the mean calorie value. If the square root step is omitted, the statistic is called the **variance**.

For this sample, the standard deviation is 567.83. If you know that the distribution of *calories* is normal, you can state that roughly 95% of the observations should fall into the interval formed by the mean plus or minus two standard deviations: $2754 - (2 \times 568)$ to $2754 + (2 \times 568)$, or 1618 to 3890 calories. This theoretical interval exceeds the range of our calorie values, indicating that the sample standard deviation is larger than that for a normal distribution.

While the standard deviation measures the dispersion of the sample data, the **standard error of the mean** is used to assess the precision with which the population mean is estimated from the sample. (Some call this statistic the standard deviation of the sampling distribution of the mean—conceptually, the values of the distribution are the means of an infinitude of samples of size n drawn randomly from the same population). It is the sample standard deviation divided by the square root of the sample size. For this sample, the standard error is 65.6 (568 / 8.66). The standard error can be used to construct a confidence interval such that 95% of the intervals constructed in the same way (from many random samples of the same size) will include the population mean: $2754 \pm (2 \times 66)$ results in an interval from 2622 to 2886 calories.

The median is just one robust statistic that divides the set of data values into two or more equal parts; percentiles and quartiles are others. Just as the calculation of the median depends on the position of the ordered sample values rather than the exact value of every observation in the sample (such as the mean), so does the calculation of the percentiles and quartiles:

- **Percentiles** are values above and below which a specified percentage of cases fall (for example, the 25th percentile is the value below which 25% of the cases fall and above which 75% of the cases fall).

- The **first quartile**, or 25th percentile, is the median of all of the values to the left of the median.

- The **second quartile** is the median.

- The **third quartile**, or 75th percentile, is the median of all of the values to the right of the median.

In this sample, the daily calorie intake for 10% of the countries is below 2030 calories, while it is above 3566 calories for another 10% (using the 90th percentile: 100–90). The countries in the central 50% of the distribution (between the first and third quartiles) consume between 2247 and 3236 calories daily.

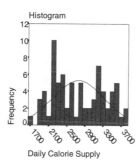

Histogram. SPSS uses the sample mean and standard deviation to construct the normal curve superimposed on the histogram of calorie values. Notice that the bars on the left and right tend to be taller than the curve, while those in the middle are shorter. Thus, the tails of the sample distribution are higher than those of a normal distribution, agreeing with the conclusion reached earlier about the size of the standard deviation.

Example 3
Using Data Transformations to Improve Estimates

Means and standard deviations are useful descriptors for data that follow a normal distribution, but they can be misleading when the distribution is highly skewed, has outliers, or is a mixture of subgroups.

What if, for example, you want to estimate the average population? Does the sample mean provide a good estimate? In the chart on the left on p. 27, you can see that the shape of the histogram of the population values is not symmetric—it has a long tail on the right side. If you ask SPSS to compute the log of each population value and draw a histogram of the transformed values (see the chart on the right on p. 27), the histogram is much more symmetric than that for the data as recorded.

In this example, the estimates of the mean for the raw and transformed population values differ markedly (an average of more than 47 million people versus 13 million), and the confidence interval for the transformed data is considerably shorter than that for the data as recorded.

Figure 2.1   Means and confidence intervals before and after transformation

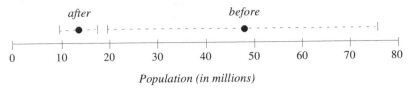

Figure 2.1 displays means from the output that follows. The *before* statistics are computed using population values; the *after* (transformation) values are computed using logarithms of the population values and transforming the results back to the original units. The discussion of the Statistics table on p. 27 describes how to construct the confidence intervals shown in the figure. Notice that even though the confidence interval for the raw data is very wide, it does not include the sample median (the median is 10.4 million people).

To produce this output, use Compute from the Transform menu to compute the log of each population value (log_pop = LG10(populatn)). In the Frequencies dialog box, click *Reset* to restore the dialog box defaults, and then select:

▶ Variable(s): populatn, log_pop

Statistics...
   Central Tendency
   ☑ Mean   ☑ Median
   Dispersion
   ☑ S.E. mean
   Distribution
   ☑ Skewness   ☑ Kurtosis

Charts...
   Chart Type
   ⊙ Histograms
      ☑ With normal curve

Format...
   ☑ Suppress tables with more than 10 categories

 Double-click the Statistics table. Then, from the Pivot Table menus choose:

Pivot
 Transpose Rows and Columns

Drag *Statistics* from the row tray to the column tray.

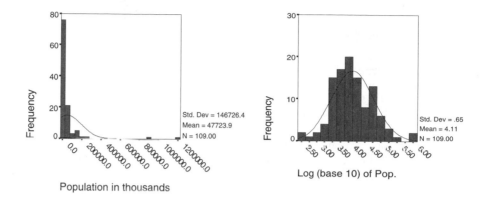

Population in thousands

Histogram (Population in thousands). Even if you ignore the two countries at the right with extremely large populations (India with over 900 million people and China with more than one billion), this histogram is very right-skewed. If you see a distribution that is this skewed, be wary of using the variable in analyses that assume the data are from a normal distribution.

Histogram (Log (base 10) of Population). This histogram displays population values in log units. While not perfect, it certainly is more symmetric than that for the untransformed data.

Statistics

		Population in thousands		Log (base 10) of Population	
		Statistic	Std. Error	Statistic	Std. Error
N	Valid	109		109	
	Missing	0		0	
Mean		47723.88	14053.84	4.1140	6.266E-02
Median		10400.00		4.0170	
Skewness		6.592	.231	.250	.231
Kurtosis		46.651	.459	.584	.459

Statistics. The mean and median of the untransformed population values differ markedly (more than 47 million people versus 10 million). Remember that both statistics are measures of central tendency. With respect to the median, 50% of the countries have more people and 50% have fewer. If you display the table, you will see that 79% of the countries have a population smaller than the mean. The estimate of the mean is very sensitive to the extreme values in the right tail of the distribution.

Skewness measures the symmetry of the sample distribution; **kurtosis** measures its peakedness. (Is the center, or peak, much shorter or taller than that of a normal distribution? Also, are both tails shorter or longer?) These measures are centered at 0; however, even for samples from a normal distribution, these values fluctuate around 0. So, how large or how small does either statistic have to be for you to reject normality? The ratio of each statistic to its standard error can be used as a test of normality (that is, you can reject normality if the ratio is less than –2 or greater than +2). A large positive value for skewness indicates a long right tail; an extreme negative value, a long left tail. A large positive value for kurtosis indicates that the tails of the distribution are longer than those of a normal distribution; a negative value for kurtosis indicates shorter tails (becoming like those of a box-shaped uniform distribution). Because skewness and kurtosis statistics are sensitive to anomalies in the distribution, you should study them in conjunction with a histogram, boxplot, or stem-and-leaf diagram.

For the values of population in this sample, the ratio of skewness to its standard error is 28.5, indicating as shown in the histogram (*Population in thousands*) on p. 27 that the distribution is extremely right-skewed. The ratio for kurtosis (101.6) indicates tails much longer than those for a normal distribution.

The mean (4.114) and median (4.017) for the log-transformed data are much closer in size than they were for the raw data above. The ratios for the skewness and kurtosis statistics divided by their standard errors are now 1.1 and 1.3, respectively (or 0.250 / 0.231 and 0.584 / 0.459). Considering that these values are less than +2 and that the shape of the histogram is fairly symmetric, you can use the results in log units to compute an estimate of average population. The mean of the sample in log units is 4.114. Using a calculator to raise 10 to this power ($10^{4.114}$), the estimate of the mean in the original units is 13,001.70, or roughly 13 million people.

To construct a 95% **confidence interval for the mean**, compute

$$\text{Mean} \ \pm \ t_{0.975}(df) \times \text{Std. Error}$$

where the value of t is found in a table for percentiles of the t distribution. The table is entered using $(n - 1)$ or 108 degrees of freedom.

Or, you can obtain the same results using the Explore procedure. To compute confidence intervals for the raw data and the log values, use the following equations:

$$47,723.881 \ \pm \ 1.99 \times 14,053.837 \quad \text{or} \quad 47,723.881 \ \pm \ 27,967.22$$
$$4.114 \ \pm \ 1.99 \times 0.063 \quad \text{or} \quad 4.114 \ \pm \ 0.125$$

The first interval ranges from almost 20 million people to over 75 million (19,756.5 to 75,691.1). The second ranges from 3.989 to 4.239 and, transforming these endpoints ($10^{3.989}$ and $10^{4.239}$), the interval is much shorter, extending from almost 10 million people to a little more than 17 million (9,749.9 to 17,338). These are the values plotted in Figure 2.1.

3

Using Descriptives to Obtain Basic Statistics and Z Scores

Descriptives is not a procedure to use for a first look at your data because most of its statistics require that the data follow a normal distribution. Here, an assumption is made that you have screened your data, hopefully by using graphics, and know that the distributions are fairly symmetric. The statistics illustrated in this chapter (except for z scores) are introduced in Chapter 2.

Example 1: A ranking of means. Default statistics are requested for variables that are items from a survey about favorite types of music. Listing them in order of their means provides a ranking of music preferences. The Split File feature is used to repeat the analysis for subsets of the cases—the preferences of college graduates are found to differ from the sample as a whole. This example uses the *gss 93 subset* data file.

Example 2: Selecting statistics and requesting z scores. The variables are population size, birth rate, daily calorie intake, and percentage of urban population for a sample of countries. Statistics are added and deleted from the default set. A listing of the data with their corresponding z scores is restricted to the 10% of the countries (cases) with values that differ most from the mean. This example uses the *world95* data file.

Example 1
A Ranking of Means

What type of music do people like best? The 1993 General Social Survey conducted by the National Opinion Research Center includes the responses of subjects to questions about music preferences. Each subject rated each of 11 types of music (country, rap, classical, heavy metal, and so on) on a 1 to 5 scale labeled, respectively, *Like it very much*, *Like it*, *Mixed feelings*, *Dislike it*, *Dislike it very much*. Sample means are one way to measure the typical response to each item. Descriptives has an option for ordering the variables by the size of their means (the default is the order in which you specify them). Thus, the order of the variables provides a ranking of music preferences.

These data are not ideal for the normal theory statistics in Descriptives because their numeric codes represent only five ordered categories and most of the distributions are right-skewed, except those for *opera*, *rap*, and *hvymetal,* which are left-skewed (see the bar charts from the Frequencies procedure in Figure 3.1). After examining percentiles

and medians, you can see that the order of the means for theses variables provides a
fairly reasonable ranking despite the distributional problems.

Figure 3.1   Music preferences

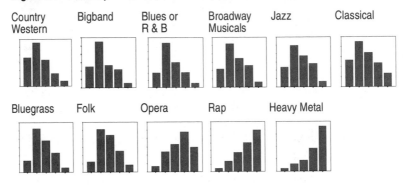

To produce this output, from the menus choose:

Analyze
  Descriptive Statistics
    Descriptives...

Click *Reset* to restore the dialog box defaults, and then select:

▶ Variable(s): bigband, blugrass, country, blues, musicals, classicl, folk, jazz, opera,
rap, hvymetal

Options...
  Display Order
    ⊙ Ascending means

Descriptive Statistics

	N	Minimum	Maximum	Mean	Std. Deviation
Country Western Music	1468	1	5	2.32	1.09
Bigband Music	1337	1	5	2.45	1.09
Blues or R & B Music	1434	1	5	2.51	1.03
Broadway Musicals	1412	1	5	2.60	1.09
Jazz Music	1451	1	5	2.62	1.11
Classical Music	1425	1	5	2.66	1.22
Bluegrass Music	1335	1	5	2.66	1.02
Folk Music	1414	1	5	2.76	1.04
Opera	1410	1	5	3.49	1.13
Rap Music	1431	1	5	3.93	1.12
Heavy Metal Music	1423	1	5	4.13	1.11
Valid N (listwise)	1106				

Descriptive Statistics. For each variable, N is a tally of how many values are present: 1468 people responded to the country western music question; 1335, to the bluegrass music question; and so on. Interestingly, considerably more people skipped the bluegrass music question than any other question. At the bottom of the table, SPSS uses *Valid N* to report the number of cases (respondents) that have no values missing for this set of 11 variables. Cases with no missing values are **listwise complete**.

The responses to all 11 questions range from 1 (minimum) to 5 (maximum). The means for the 11 variables range from 2.32 to 4.13. The smallest ordered mean (2.32) is closest to code 2 (*Like it*), and the largest mean (4.13) is closest to code 4 (*Dislike it*). So, country music, big band music, and possibly blues and rhythm & blues are favored; while rap, heavy metal, and possibly opera tend to be disliked. The standard deviations are fairly constant, ranging from 1.09 to 1.22.

Using Split File to Check Preferences within Strata

The following question should be asked more frequently: Is the sample homogenous, or are there differences among subpopulations or groups of subjects? Let's explore whether music preference differs by education. For the variable *degree2*, a code of 0 means *No college degree*, and a code of 1 means *College degree*. In the Split File dialog box (from the Data menu), select *Compare groups*, based on *degree2*, and then repeat the steps for the Descriptives procedure, outlined at the beginning of this example.

Descriptive Statistics

	N	Minimum	Maximum	Mean	Std. Deviation
Classical Music	344	1	5	2.06	.98
Broadway Musicals	339	1	5	2.26	.94
Bigband Music	324	1	5	2.30	.96
Blues or R & B Music	339	1	5	2.35	.97
Jazz Music	342	1	5	2.37	1.04
Folk Music	344	1	5	2.56	.94
Country Western Music	342	1	5	2.72	1.04
Bluegrass Music	315	1	5	2.78	.95
Opera	332	1	5	3.14	1.17
Rap Music	336	1	5	4.03	1.04
Heavy Metal Music	337	1	5	4.15	.99
Valid N (listwise)	281				

Descriptive Statistics. The biggest difference in preference between the college and non-college graduates is that the college graduates favor classical music over the other types. Classical music is ranked first for them but sixth for the sample as a whole. The other switch is that the college graduates rank country and western music seventh, while it was first for the complete sample. (Additional tables, for the *No college degree* and missing-value groups, are not shown here.)

Example 2
Selecting Statistics and Requesting Z Scores

Descriptives optionally provides *z* **scores** (also called **standard scores**) for quantitative variables. These scores are transformations of the data values to standard deviation units and indicate the relative position of each value within its distribution. For each variable that you specify, SPSS subtracts the variable's sample mean from each value and then divides the difference by the sample standard deviation.

$$z_i = \frac{x_i - \bar{x}}{s}$$

The mean *z* score is always 0, and the standard deviation is 1. For example, if in your sample, the average age is 40 years and the standard deviation is 15, the *z* score for a 40-year-old is 0. The age corresponding to a *z* score of 1 (one standard deviation unit) is 55 years; a score of 2, 70 years; a score of –1, 25 years; a score of –2, 10 years; and so on.

What countries have large (or small) populations? Birth rates? When variables are measured in different units (population, birth rate, percentage urban, and calories per day), a *z* score transformation places the variables on a common scale, making it easier to compare their values. The distribution of scores has the same shape as the original distribution, so they are *not* a remedy for problem data.

In this example, you request descriptive statistics and *z* scores (standardized values), using data from the *world95* file. Each case has information about a country, including the percentage of the population living in cities (*urban*), average daily calorie consumption (*calories*), number of births per 1000 people per year (*birth_rt*), and population in log base 10 units (*log_pop*). Because *z* scores are most useful for data that follow a normal distribution (or at least a symmetric distribution), population is analyzed in log units. (See Chapter 2, Example 3, where the success of a log transformation for symmetrizing the distribution of population values is demonstrated.)

The default set of statistics is displayed in Example 1. Here, you omit the minimum and maximum values and add a request for skewness to check whether any of the distributions are markedly asymmetric. When you request that standardized values (*z* scores) be saved as variables, they are added as variables to the right side of the Data Editor.

To produce this output, in the Descriptives dialog box, click *Reset* to restore the dialog box defaults, and then select:

▶ Variable(s): urban, calories, birth_rt, log_pop

☑ Save standardized values as variables

Options...
    Dispersion
        ☐ Minimum (deselect)   ☐ Maximum (deselect)
    Distribution
        ☑ Skewness

 From the Pivot Table menus choose:

Pivot
    Transpose Rows and Columns

Descriptive Statistics

		People living in cities (%)	Daily calorie intake	Birth rate per 1000 people	Log (base 10) of Population	Valid N (listwise)
N	Statistic	108	75	109	109	74
Mean	Statistic	56.53	2753.83	25.923	4.1140	
Std. Deviation	Statistic	24.20	567.83	12.361	.6542	
Skewness	Statistic	-.308	.170	.446	.250	
	Std. Error	.233	.277	.231	.231	

Descriptive Statistics. The birth rate and population variables each have 109 values, *urban* has 108, and *calories* has only 75 (34 of its values are missing). From the four means, it's easy to see that the variables are measured in very different units, making it hard to determine what's large and what's small in a display of data values.

The ratio of skewness to its standard error is used to test the symmetry of the distribution (that is, to reject the hypothesis that the distribution is symmetric if the ratio is less than –2 or greater than +2). The hypothesis of symmetry is not rejected for any of the four variables here. (See the Statistics table on p. 27 for more information about the skewness statistic.) However, such a test should be used in conjunction with a graphical display such as a boxplot or a histogram.

Notice that the layout of this table differs from that in the table on p. 30. Here, Transpose Rows and Columns on the Pivot menu was used to reformat the table.

Notes

Contents	Variables Created or Modified	ZURBAN	Zscore: People living in cities (%)
		ZCALORIE	Zscore: Daily calorie intake
		ZBIRTH_R	Zscore: Birth rate per 1000 people
		ZLOG_POP	Zscore: Log (base 10) of Population

Notes. To see how SPSS names the new variables containing *z* scores, open Notes in the Viewer or scroll to the right side of the Data Editor. The scores in the Data Editor are easier to read if you set width to 6 and decimal places to 2 in the Define Variable dialog box.

Viewing the Data and Corresponding Z Scores

In this example, the listing for each variable is restricted to the countries (cases) with the largest 10% or 11% of the values. If the data follow a normal distribution, approximately 10% of the values will fall outside the interval mean ±1.6 standard deviations. The Select Cases command on the Data menu is used to make this restriction:

ABS(zurban) > 1.6 I ABS(zcalorie) > 1.6 I ABS(zbirth_r) > 1.6 I ABS(zlog_pop) > 1.6

The Case Summaries procedure is used to list the original variables and the corresponding *z*-score variables.

Case Summaries

	COUNTRY	People living in cities (%)	Daily calorie intake	Birth rate per 1000 people	Log (base 10) of Population	Zscore: People living in cities (%)	Zscore: Daily calorie intake	Zscore: Birth rate per 1000 people	Zscore: Log (base 10) of Population
1	Afghanistan	18	.	53.0	4.31	-1.59	.	2.19	.30
2	Bahrain	83	.	29.0	2.78	1.09	.	.25	-2.04
3	Bangladesh	16	2021	35.0	5.10	-1.67	-1.29	.73	1.50
4	Barbados	45	.	16.0	2.41	-.48	.	-.80	-2.61
5	Belgium	96	.	12.0	4.00	1.00	.	-1.13	-.17
6	Brazil	75	2751	21.0	5.19	.76	.00	-.40	1.65
7	Burkina Faso	15	2288	47.0	4.00	-1.72	-.82	1.71	-.17
8	Burundi	5	1932	44.0	3.78	-2.13	-1.45	1.46	-.51
9	Cambodia	12	2166	45.0	4.00	-1.84	-1.04	1.54	-.17
10	China	26	2639	21.0	6.08	-1.26	-.20	-.40	3.01
11	Ethlopia	12	1667	45.0	4.74	-1.84	-1.91	1.54	.96
12	Gambia	23	.	46.0	2.98	-1.39	.	1.62	-1.73
13	Greece	63	3825	10.0	4.02	.27	1.89	-1.29	-.15
14	Iceland	91	.	16.0	2.42	1.42	.	-.80	-2.59
15	India	26	2229	29.0	5.96	-1.26	-.92	.25	2.82
16	Indonesia	29	2750	24.0	5.30	-1.14	-.01	-.16	1.81
17	Ireland	57	3778	14.0	3.56	.02	1.80	-.96	-.85
18	Kuwait	96	3195	28.0	3.26	1.63	.78	.17	-1.31
19	Oman	11	.	40.0	3.28	-1.88	.	1.14	-1.28
20	Russia	74	.	13.0	5.17	.72	.	-1.05	1.62
21	Rwanda	6	1971	49.0	0.00	-2.09	-1.38	1.87	-.29
22	Singapore	100	3198	16.0	3.46	1.80	.78	-.80	-1.00
23	Somalia	24	1906	46.0	3.82	-1.34	-1.49	1.62	-.44
24	Tanzania	21	2206	46.0	4.47	-1.47	-.96	1.62	.55
25	USA	75	3671	15.0	5.42	.76	1.62	-.88	1.99
26	Uganda	11	2153	49.0	4.30	-1.88	-1.06	1.87	.28
27	Zambia	42	2077	46.0	3.96	-.60	-1.19	1.62	-.24

Case Summaries. The z score for Afghanistan's birth rate is 2.19—that is, its birth rate of 53 is more than two standard deviations (2.19) above the average birth rate for this sample. Eighteen percent of this country's people live in cities (*urban* =18). This percentage is well below the sample mean (z score = –1.59). China's population is more than 3 standard deviations (3.01) above the sample mean. India follows, with a z score of 2.82. At the other extreme, Barbados' population is more than 2 1/2 standard deviations (–2.61) *below* the sample mean. For the countries in this sample, the daily calorie intake for Ethiopia is the smallest (z score = –1.91 for 1667 calories). Ethiopia is also very rural—its z score for *urban* is –1.84 (12% of its population live in cities).

The z score for *calories* has only four scores outside the 1.6 limit set with Select Cases. Its sample size is smaller (75 versus 109 or 108 for the other variables); and its tails are heavier than those of a normal distribution (see "Statistics" on p. 23), so the standard deviation is also larger.

Thus, a quick scan of the z scores for a group of variables makes it easy to spot cases with unusual values. For the same reason, you may find it convenient to use z scores to plot two variables with different scales on the same axis.

4 Using Explore to Screen and Describe Subpopulations

No matter what your goals are—simple description or preparation for a complicated analysis later—you need to carefully scrutinize your data. The examples in Chapter 2 and Chapter 3 featured statistics and graphics useful for describing variables and estimating parameters for the complete sample. This chapter illustrates many of the same statistics but applies them to strata or groups of cases. The first two examples present statistics and features for screening and describing within-group distributions. The last two explain tests and features for assessing normality, determining if variances differ significantly across groups, and identifying a transformation that stabilizes variances across groups.

These examples use data from the *world95* file. Each case has information about a country including average female life expectancy (in years), population (in thousands of people), population in log base 10 units (*log_pop*), the region where the country is located, and its name. Population is included as a variable because its distribution is very asymmetric. In later examples, results are compared for population and the log of population. The variable *region* is a **factor**—its numeric codes classify the 109 countries into six groups. The values of factors can be numbers or short strings. The names of the countries, stored in the variable *country*, are used to label extreme values in boxplots and in a list of extreme values (see Example 2).

Example 1: Descriptive statistics, boxplots, and stem-and-leaf diagrams. Within each of six groups of countries, the distribution of female life expectancy values is explored. The groups are defined by geographical region and economics. From boxplots and stem-and-leaf diagrams, it is easy to see that, across the groups, there is considerable variation in median life expectancy and in spread. Default descriptive statistics are displayed for each group. A robust rule for identifying outliers is defined and a 5% trimmed mean is introduced for minimizing the influence of outliers on the estimate of central tendency.

Example 2: M-estimators, percentiles, and identification of extreme values. When the data are not normally distributed and no transformation magically fixes the problem, M-estimators may be useful for estimating the center of each group's distribution, and percentiles can characterize their spreads. The five smallest and five largest values within each group are reported, along with their respective country names.

Example 3: Shapiro-Wilk and Lilliefors tests of normality and normal probability plots. The focus in this example switches from description, estimation, and outlier identification to preparation for hypothesis testing and model building. More specifically, are the within-group data samples from a normal distribution? For the six groups in the previous examples, test results are reported for population as recorded and for log transformed values of population. Normal probability plots and detrended normal probability plots are introduced for characterizing how the data depart from normality.

Example 4: Levene test for equal variances and a spread-versus-level plot to identify a variance stabilizing transformation. Results of the Levene test indicate that the variances of the six groups of population values differ significantly, while those for the log transformed values are not found to differ. The spread-versus-level diagnostic plot suggests that population values should be analyzed in log units in order to remove an unwanted relationship between the spread and level of each group.

Example 1
Descriptive Statistics, Boxplots, and Stem-and-Leaf Diagrams

There are many ways to describe data; however, not all are appropriate for a given sample. Means and standard deviations are useful for data that follow a normal distribution but are poor descriptors when distributions are highly skewed or have outliers, subgroups, or other anomalies. These normal theory statistics are introduced in Chapter 2, along with additional measures like skewness, kurtosis, and confidence intervals. The median, quartiles, and percentiles for quantitative variables that may or may not follow a normal distribution are also defined in that chapter. Here, you revisit these descriptors for subgroups within the sample and add the 5% trimmed mean and interquartile range.

During the process of selecting a statistic appropriate for describing your data, you should scan graphical displays. Data analysts use univariate graphical displays not only to communicate concise and clear summaries of their data in talks and papers but also during data screening to gain an understanding of what the data are and to identify problems that might hinder later analyses. Every data analyst has his or her favorite story about distorted results because a researcher skipped data screening. For example, in one study where the researchers hoped to estimate the average property tax, renters were not excluded—a bar of zeros well-separated from the other values in a stem-and-leaf diagram would have raised a hard-to-ignore flag. Then there was the researcher who forgot to identify '99' as the missing value code for a variable measuring the weekly frequency of sexual intercourse. Or, the researcher who reported a misleading estimate of the mean because he failed to recognize the need for transforming a highly skewed distribution (see Chapter 2, Example 3 to learn how a transformation can improve an estimate).

For univariate views of each group in the sample, the Explore procedure provides boxplots (or box-and-whisker displays), stem-and-leaf diagrams, and histograms. No one is best for all data. Often you need to view more than one display in order to understand the data, detect problems, and validate whether one or more descriptors is appropriate for the data at hand. In Explore, the within-group histograms are like those introduced in Chapter 2, so they are omitted here.

It is often useful to examine both a boxplot and a stem-and-leaf display. A boxplot clearly indicates the range in which the central 50% of the observations fall but can mask gaps or separations in the distribution and also hide the existence of multiple outliers. In a stem-and-leaf diagram, gaps and bimodal distributions are exposed and the leading digits of each outlier are reported.

How does female life expectancy vary by region? The goal in this example is to describe how average female life expectancy differs across the six groups of countries defined by codes stored in the variable *region*.

To produce this output, from the menus choose:

Analyze
  Descriptive Statistics
    Explore...

Click *Reset* to restore the dialog box defaults, and then select:

▶ Dependent List: lifeexpf
▶ Factor List: region
▶ Label Cases by: country

Double-click the Descriptives table, and from the menus choose:

Pivot
  Transpose Rows and Columns

Pivot
  Pivoting Trays

Drag the statistics from the column tray to the row tray. Then select the following columns and hide them: *Africa*, *East Europe*, and *Middle East*. (To select a column, Ctrl-Alt-click the column title. To hide the selected column, from the View menu choose *Hide*.)

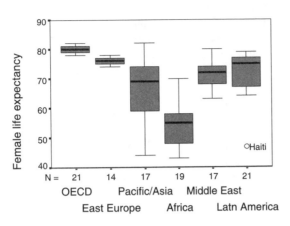

Boxplot. Although this is not the first output listed in the Viewer, move down and open it for an overview of the within-group distributions. This display, designed by John Tukey, is sometimes called a **box-and-whisker plot**. For each group of countries (cases), the horizontal line in the middle of the box marks the median of the sample. Thus, for example, the median life expectancy for females in OECD countries is around 80 years, while in Latin American countries it is roughly 75 years. The edges of each box, called **hinges**, mark the 25th and 75th percentiles. (These percentiles are calculated a little differently than ordinary percentiles.) It is easiest to think that the median splits the ordered batch of numbers in half, and the hinges split the remaining halves in half again—that is, the central 50% of the data values fall within the range of the box. The length of the box (the difference between the values of the hinges) is called the **hspread** and corresponds to the interquartile range. The hspread for the OECD countries is very short (maybe two or so years), while that for the Pacific/Asia countries is considerably longer—it extends from 59 to 74 or 75 years. The **whiskers** (vertical lines extending up and down from each box) show the range of values that fall within 1.5 hspreads of the hinges (1.5 hspreads can be longer than a whisker).

It is easy to see from the display that the medians and spreads of the six groups of countries vary greatly. In addition, notice that the shapes of the distributions differ. The median life expectancy for the Latin American countries falls toward the top of its box, indicating that the distribution is left-skewed, while that for the OECD and Eastern European groups is more centered as occurs for symmetric distributions.

Figure 4.1   Annotated sketch of a boxplot

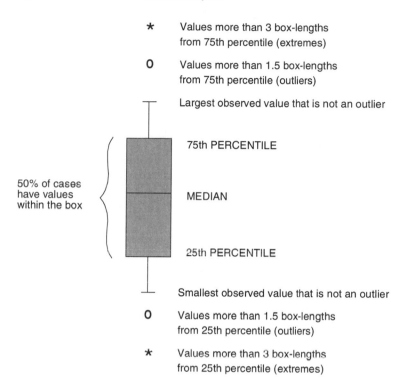

In addition to providing a succinct summary of where the bulk of the values are concentrated and the shape of each distribution, the boxplot is constructed to flag outliers. Cases that have values more than 3 hspreads below the lower hinge or above the upper hinge are marked by an asterisk (*) and called **extreme values** or "far outside values," while cases that have values between 1.5 and 3 hspreads outside the hinges are marked by an open circle (o) and called **outliers** or "outside values." See Figure 4.1 for a summary of these definitions.

In this example, Haiti is an outlier among the Latin American countries because its average female life expectancy is considerably lower than that for the other countries in its group.

Descriptives

			Average female life expectancy		
			Region or economic group		
			OECD	Pacific/Asia	Latn America
Mean		Statistic	80.10	67.41	71.76
		Std. Error	.26	2.64	1.61
95.0% Confidence Interval for Mean	Lower Bound	Statistic	79.56	61.81	68.40
	Upper Bound	Statistic	80.63	73.01	75.13
5% Trimmed Mean		Statistic	80.11	67.90	72.69
Median		Statistic	80.00	69.00	75.00
Variance		Statistic	1.39	118.51	54.59
Std. Deviation		Statistic	1.18	10.89	7.39
Minimum		Statistic	78	44	47
Maximum		Statistic	82	82	79
Range		Statistic	4	38	32
Interquartile Range		Statistic	2.00	17.50	10.50
Skewness		Statistic	-.201	-.682	-1.959
		Std. Error	.501	.550	.501
Kurtosis		Statistic	-.827	-.300	5.391
		Std. Error	.972	1.063	.972

Descriptives (after pivoting). Females in the 21 OECD countries tend, on the average, to live 80.1 years; those in the 17 Pacific/Asia countries, 67.41 years; and those in 21 Latin American countries, 71.76 years. The sample sizes are from the Case Processing Summary (not shown here) printed at the beginning of the output. The median for the Latin American countries is 75 (more than 3 years older than the mean). In left-skewed distributions, the median is larger than the mean. To test that the distribution is skewed, look at the ratio of skewness to its standard error (that is, reject the hypothesis that the distribution is symmetric if the ratio is less than -2 or greater than $+2$). For the Latin American countries, this ratio is $-1.959 / 0.501 = -3.91$, so the hypothesis that the distribution is symmetric is rejected.

The **interquartile range** is the difference between the 25th and 75th percentile. For example, for the Pacific/Asia countries the interquartile range is 17.5 years. See Example 2 for its 25th and 75th percentiles ($76 - 58.5 = 17.5$). The middle 50% of the life expectancy values for this group fall between 58.5 and 76 years. The length of the Pacific/Asia box in the boxplot on p. 40 differs slightly—that is, Tukey computes the percentiles as 59 and 74 years, so the length of the box is $74 - 59 = 15$ years. The interquartile range for the OECD countries is much shorter. It is 2 years, the same as its box length.

If the values in your sample are from a normal distribution, the sample mean provides the best estimate of the population mean. If, however, there are outliers or departures from normality, look at the *5% trimmed mean* (and/or the robust estimates in Example 2). You should be concerned if the estimates differ markedly. For example, in Example 3, the estimate of average population size for OECD countries is 33.1 million people; the 5% trimmed mean is 22.7 million, and the median is 10.4 million. All three statistics estimate the center of the distribution. In this case, the problem is remedied by log transforming the data.

The **5% trimmed mean** is computed by ordering the values within each group from smallest to largest, **trimming** (deleting) 5% from the top and 5% from the bottom of each group, and then computing the usual mean for the observations that remain. Thus, unusual values in the tails of the distribution do not affect the size of the mean, and the trimmed estimate uses more data values (more information) than the median.

The sample size for the Latin American group is 21, and 5% of this is 1.05. So, for the 5% trimmed mean estimate, roughly one observation is trimmed from each end (the SPSS formula allows fractional observations to be trimmed). In Example 2, Figure 4.3, the shortest life expectancy for this group is 47 years (Haiti) and the longest is 79 years (Costa Rica). So ignoring the fractional trimming, an estimate of the trimmed mean is

$$\frac{21 \times 71.76 - 47 - 79}{21 - 2} = 72.68 \text{ years}$$

(The sample size times the mean is the sum of all 21 life expectancies.) The values of the second-to-smallest and largest are 64 and 78 years. If 5% of each of these values is excluded (and 90% of the sample size is used in the denominator), the estimate with fractional trimming is

$$\frac{1506.96 - 47 - 79 - 0.05 \times 64 - 0.05 \times 78}{0.9 \times 21} = \frac{1373.86}{18.9} = 72.69 \text{ years}$$

This estimate falls between the sample mean and median.

```
Average female life expectancy Stem-and-Leaf Plot for
REGION: OECD

 Frequency    Stem &  Leaf

     2.00      78 .  00
     5.00      79 .  00000
     5.00      80 .  00000
     7.00      81 .  0000000
     2.00      82 .  00

Stem width:     1
Each leaf:      1 case(s)


Average female life expectancy Stem-and-Leaf Plot for
REGION: Pacific/Asia

 Frequency    Stem &  Leaf

     1.00       4 .  4
     4.00       5 .  2389
     4.00       6 .  5889
     6.00       7 .  223489
     2.00       8 .  02

Stem width:    10
Each leaf:      1 case(s)


Average female life expectancy Stem-and-Leaf Plot for
REGION: Latn America

 Frequency    Stem &  Leaf

     1.00 Extremes    (=<47)
     1.00       6 .  4
     5.00       6 .  77779
     3.00       7 .  003
    11.00       7 .  55567788889

Stem width:    10
Each leaf:      1 case(s)
```

Stem-and-Leaf plots. In a way, a **stem-and-leaf diagram** is similar to a histogram because the data values are collected into intervals and displayed as bars (turned on their side). However, from a stem-and-leaf diagram, you can recover more information about the digits of each number and also see if any values are identified as outliers.

In a stem-and-leaf display, the digits of each number are separated into a stem and a leaf, and each part is listed under its respective head. For example, the number 36.85 could be split as 3 and 685, or 36 and 85, or 368 and 5. To see how a number is split, it helps first to read the maximum value for each group in the Descriptives table. For example, for OECD, the maximum value of average female life expectancy is 82 years; for Pacific/Asia, 82 years; and for Latin America, 79 years. Look for these values at the bottom of each stem-and-leaf display. For OECD, the digits are not separated: the stem is 82 years, and the leaf is 0 (as in 82.0). For Pacific/Asia, the stem is 8 and the leaf is 2 (notice that leaf next to 2 is 0—for the value 80). For Latin America, the stem is 7 and the leaf is 9. In the same row, 10 other countries have a stem of 7, but their leaves range from 5 to 8 (for 75 to 78). The *Frequency* count to the left of this stem is 11. That is, 11 countries are represented in this last row of the display.

For these data, there is one leaf for each case (country) in the sample. For larger samples, SPSS may let a leaf represent more than one case. If so, SPSS reports the number of cases per leaf. For larger numbers, only the leading digits are used; the others are ignored. For example, for a sample of calorie values ranging from 1667 to 3825, only the 16 and 38 are used—the thousands digit (1 and 3) are stems, the hundreds digits (6 and 8) are leaves, and the 67 and 25 are ignored.

Why, since values of life expectancy are displayed in each diagram, does the stem for OECD include both the tens digit and the units digit and the other stems just the tens digit? SPSS uses an algorithm that looks at the variability of the values in the batch, and tries to form a scale for the stems that best displays the shape of the distribution when the leaves are added.

The values of the stems in the OECD diagram and the Pacific/Asia diagram increase in equal increments (78 through 82 and 4 through 8). For Latin America, there are two stems for the 60's and two for the 70's. The leaves with values 0, 1, 2, 3, and 4 belong in the first bar for each pair; and those with digits 5, 6, 7, 8, and 9, in the second. The algorithm allows a single stem to be split into as many as five bars. The following is part of a display where a '1' stem is split into five bars:

```
1  *  000000011111
1  t  23
1  f  4555
1  s  6667
1  .  889
```

The letter "t" between the stem and leaves labels bars for the digits 2 and 3; the letter "f", for 4's and 5's; the letter "s" for 6's and 7's; and the period (.) for 8's and 9's.

Why does the diagram appear as though SPSS used an old-fashioned typewriter to construct it? Because the leaves need to be printed in a monospaced font to ensure that, say, leaves that are 1's fill the same horizontal space as 8's. The shape of the distribution would be misrepresented if the font for the digits in the leaves varied in width.

The shape of the stem-and-leaf displays for OECD and Pacific/Asia is fairly symmetric, while that for Latin America is left-skewed. This agrees with observations regarding the boxplot on p. 40 and skewness on p. 42.

Outliers. In the *Leaf* column of the diagram for Latin America, 47 years is enclosed within parentheses and *Extremes* is printed instead of a stem value. This is how outliers are identified (that is, values that stand markedly apart from the others in the batch). For your data, there may be one or more outliers at either end of the distribution. Notice that while the stems for the bulk of the data fall along an equal interval scale, the scale stops for the extremes (there is no stem position for numbers in the 50's). The rule for identifying outliers is the same as for the boxplot. A value is an outlier if it falls below the lower hinge minus 1.5 times the hspread (1.5 * 10 years = 15 years) or above the upper hinge plus 15 years. In Example 2, the hinges for the Latin American countries are 67 and 77 years; so the lower limit is 67 − 15 = 52 years, and the upper limit is 82 years.

In the past, some data analysts identified outliers as values that are more than two or three standard deviations from the mean. This rule may work fine for well-behaved data from a normal distribution, but the boxplot and stem-and-leaf rule works better across a spectrum of distributions from real-world applications.

Example 2
M-Estimators, Percentiles, and Identification of Extreme Values

Often, data do not arrive looking as though a computer just generated them from a normal distribution. Theoretically, such well-behaved values should have the same mean and median. So what do you do when this is far from true for your data? Look at the values of outliers: Are they recording errors that can be corrected? Will a log, square root, or reciprocal transformation of each data value tame the outliers and make the distribution more symmetric? (This last question is addressed in Example 4.) If these remedies are not satisfactory, consider using one of the M-estimators introduced in this section to estimate the center of each group's distribution and using percentiles to characterize the spread of values.

Trimmed means, introduced in the last example, and M-estimators are called **robust** estimators because their calculations are insensitive to departures from normality. The usual sample mean can change considerably if you alter the smallest or largest values in the sample. For example, take a sample of 20 or so observations from a normal distribution with mean 0 and standard deviation 1. Say the largest value is 2.5. Change this value to 250 or 25 and watch the mean increase. The median, however, will not change because it is not influenced by how large a particular outlier is. The 5% trimmed mean also remains unchanged if the largest (or smallest) observation is modified. Sadly, many of the advanced analyses users' needs are based on normal theory so means cannot be forgotten.

In computing the usual mean, every observation has the same weight, whether it is in the middle or in the tails of the distribution. Let's say each observation has a weight of 1. For the 5% trimmed mean, the central 90% of the ordered observations have a weight of 1, and the 5% in each tail have a weight of 0. The median can be viewed as a 50% trimmed mean. When the sample size is odd, the weight of the middle observation is 1 and the weight for all others is 0; for an even sample size, the weight is 1 for each member of the middle pair.

M-estimators provide a scheme for assigning weights to cases, but instead of weights that dramatically drop from 1 to 0 when the observations reach a certain distance from the center, the weights decrease smoothly (or in a stagewise manner) as an observation's distance from the center increases.

M-estimators are one class among the seven dozen or so robust estimators found in the statistical literature. SPSS provides four M-estimators (named after the statisticians who introduced them): Huber, Tukey's biweight, Hampel, and Andrews. The weights for these estimators are defined in terms of residuals (that is, a standardized distance that measures how far each observation is from center of its distribution) rather than for the data values. The residual is

$$\frac{\text{value for } i\text{th case} - \text{current estimate of location}}{\text{estimate of spread}}$$

where the spread estimate, known as **MAD**, is the median of the absolute deviations from the sample median. (First compute the median, then find the difference between it and each value, and finally, ignoring the sign, find the median of the differences.) The computations are done iteratively—that is, they are repeated several times, each time inserting the most recent estimate from the M-estimator results.

Each M-estimator has a Ψ function that is used to construct a weight for each residual. Hampel's M-estimator is displayed in Figure 4.2.

Figure 4.2   Hampel psi function

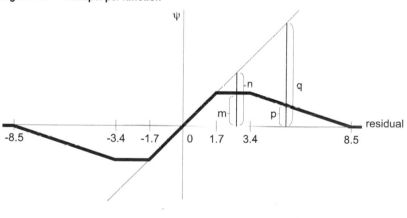

for |residual| < 1.7   the weight is 1
      1.7 < |residual| < 3.4   the weight is m/n
      3.4 < |residual| < 8.5   the weight is p/q
      8.5 < |residual| the weight is 0

The weight of each observation is the ordinate (height) of the psi function divided by the observation's residual. The ordinate to the 45-degree line that extends through the origin is the size of the residual, making it easy to visually compare the numerator and denominator of each weight. For residuals between 0 and 1.7 (they are close to the center of the distribution), the height of the psi function and the 45-degree line are the same, so the weight is 1. For residuals smaller than –8.5 or larger than 8.5, the height of the psi function is 0, so the weight is 0. For residuals between 1.7 and 8.5, the weights decrease as the residual becomes larger.

The Huber psi function differs from Hampel's in that it does not redescend (the horizontal line between 1.7 and 3.4 extends to the right for large residuals and to the left for extreme negative values); and also, instead of 1.7, the horizontal line begins at 1.339. Andrews' psi function is based on a sine function, so there is no abrupt change in the assignment of weights as there is for the Hampel four-piece function. Tukey's biweight, due to Beaton and Tukey, also is constructed to have a smooth psi function and to have weights equal 1 for a reasonable range near 0.

So which estimator is best? There is no one clear answer. The robust estimators described here are designed for symmetric distributions and, for the most part, have been evaluated using samples of computer-generated data from smooth, continuous distributions with tails longer than those of a normal distribution. Some statisticians feel that real distributions often are asymmetric, lumpy (exhibit digit preferences), and have few unique values (relative to generated data). When used on asymmetric distributions, the Huber and trimmed means tend to produce estimates closer to the population mean and the redescending estimators (Hampel, biweight, Andrews) closer to the population median. Look at several estimates and compare them with the sample mean and median. Do they differ? Look at graphs to see if you can understand why. When the distribution is asymmetric, be sure to explore the effect of a transformation.

In this example, you continue with the distributions illustrated in Example 1. You now request M-estimators, percentiles, and a list of the five smallest and largest values for each subpopulation.

To produce this output, in the Explore dialog box, click *Reset* to restore the dialog box defaults, and then select:

▶ Dependent List: lifeexpf
▶ Factor List: region
▶ Label Cases by: country

Display
⊙ Statistics

Statistics...
☐ Descriptives (deselect)	☑ M-estimators
☑ Outliers	☑ Percentiles

 To hide footnotes, select them and choose *Hide* from the View menu.

M-Estimators

	Region or economic group	Huber's M-Estimator	Tukey's Biweight	Hampel's M-Estimator	Andrews' Wave
Average female life expectancy	OECD	80.14	80.13	80.13	80.13
	East Europe	76.00	76.00	76.00	76.00
	Pacific/Asia	68.54	68.46	67.97	68.45
	Africa	53.78	53.41	53.57	53.42
	Middle East	71.71	71.80	71.66	71.80
	Latn America	73.53	73.93	73.49	73.93

M-Estimators. In this example, for the OECD group of countries, the M-estimators are essentially the same (80.13 or 80.14 years). In Example 1, the mean life expectancy for females is 80.1 years; the 5% trimmed mean, 80.11 years; and the median, 80 years. From the graphical displays, you saw nothing unusual about the shape of this distribution, so the strong agreement among the estimates is not surprising. However, the shape of the Latin American distribution is left-skewed (its mean is 71.76 years; 5% trimmed mean, 72.69 years; and median, 75 years). The values of the M-estimators differ by less than half a year and fall between the mean and median, but closer to the median than the mean.

Percentiles

		Region or economic group	Percentiles						
			5	10	25	50	75	90	95
Weighted Average(Definition 1)	Average female life expectancy	OECD	78.00	78.20	79.00	80.00	81.00	81.80	82.00
		East Europe	74.00	74.50	75.00	76.00	77.00	77.50	.
		Pacific/Asia	44.00	50.40	58.50	69.00	76.00	80.40	.
		Africa	43.00	44.00	46.00	55.00	58.00	68.00	.
		Middle East	63.00	64.60	68.00	72.00	74.50	78.40	.
		Latn America	48.70	64.60	67.00	75.00	77.50	78.00	78.90
Tukey's Hinges	Average female life expectancy	OECD			79.00	80.00	81.00		
		East Europe			75.00	76.00	77.00		
		Pacific/Asia			59.00	69.00	74.00		
		Africa			48.00	55.00	58.00		
		Middle East			68.00	72.00	74.00		
		Latn America			67.00	75.00	77.00		

Percentiles. This table displays the estimates of six percentiles for each group. The 25th percentile is Q1, the first quartile; the 50th, the median; and the 75th, Q3, the third quartile. The 5th, 10th, 90th, and 95th percentiles for the OECD group of countries show that the spread of life expectancies is small—these percentiles are, respectively, 78, 78.2, 81.8, and 82 years.

More interesting are the percentiles for the Latin American group of countries. Five percent of the countries should have a value below the 5th percentile (48.7 years) and 95% above it. For this sample of 21 countries, 5% is 1.05 countries—thus the 5th percentile falls some place between the 1st and 2nd ordered value. In Figure 4.3, you can see that the lowest life expectancy is 47 years and the second lowest is 64 years, so 48.7 years is close to the lowest. There are five ways of defining just where this point is. (By default, SPSS uses the weighted average method—you can access other methods with the PERCENTILES subcommand).

The 10th percentile is 64.6 years. Using this value, you could report that 10% of the countries in the Latin American group have an average female life expectancy of 64 years or less or that for 90%, it is greater than 64.6 years. From the 90th percentile, you could report that in 10% of the countries, life expectancy is 78 or more years. Notice that the 75th percentile is 77.5 years. However, because four of the values immediately above 77.5 are 78, you might say that in 25% of the countries, life expectancy is 78 or more years. Some data analysts, however, are uncomfortable reporting percentages when they are considerably larger than the count being described (25% is larger than five countries).

As stated in the description for the boxplot on p. 40, although the usual percentiles and Tukey's hinges both estimate the 1st and 3rd quartiles, their computational formulas differ. Part of the difference arises because not all sample sizes are like 20, where the ordered observations are separated easily into four sets of exactly five observations each.

The following discusses how to compute the 75th percentile for the Latin American life expectancies displayed in Figure 4.3 (the sample size is 21):

Percentiles. First, locate where to split the ordered observations by adding 1 to the sample size and multiplying by 0.75:

$$(n + 1) \times p = 22 \times 0.75 = 16.5$$

or halfway between the 16th and 17th ordered observations. The 16th is 77 years (Uruguay); the 17th, 78 years (Chile). The fractional difference between 16 and 17 is 0.5. Now, to get the 75th percentile, adjust the data values by this fractional difference:

$$77 \times (1 - 0.5) + 78 \times 0.5 = 77.5$$

Tukey's hinges. Begin by finding d:

$$d = \frac{\text{greatest integer less than } \frac{(n + 3)}{2}}{2} = \frac{12}{2} = 6$$

Next compute L as:

$$L = n + 1 - d = 21 + 1 - 6 = 16$$

The 16th ordered value is 77 years (Uruguay). If 16 had a fractional part, continue as shown for the percentiles.

Figure 4.3   Ordered values of female life expectancy

order	cumulative percent	country	lifeexpf	percentile	Tukey's hinge
1		Haiti	47		
	——5%——			48.7	
2		Bolivia	64		
	——10%——			64.6	
3		Nicaragua	67		
4		Guatemala	67		
5		Peru	67		
	——25%——			67	
6		Brazil	67		67
7		El Salvador	69		
8		Honduras	70		
9		Domincan R.	70		
10		Ecuador	73		
11	——50%——	Argentina	75	75	75
12		Colombia	75		
13		Paraguay	75		
14		Venezuela	76		
15		Mexico	77		
16		Uruguay	77		77
	——75%——			77.5	
17		Chile	78		
18		Cuba	78		
19		Panama	78		
	——90%——			78	
20		Barbados	78		
	——95%——			78.9	
21		Costa Rica	79		

Extreme Values

Region or economic group				Case Number	COUNTRY	Value
Average female life expectancy	OECD	Highest	1	94	Switzerland	82
			2	38	France	82
			3	21	Canada	81
			4	70	Netherlands	81
			5	93	Sweden	.
		Lowest	1	82	Portugal	78
			2	54	Ireland	78
			3	30	Denmark	79
			4	11	Belgium	79
			5	42	Germany	.
	Pacific/Asia	Highest	1	57	Japan	82
			2	47	Hong Kong	80
			3	89	Singapore	79
			4	96	Taiwan	78
			5	86	S. Korea	74
		Lowest	1	1	Afghanistan	44
			2	19	Cambodia	52
			3	8	Bangladesh	53
			4	76	Pakistan	58
			5	50	India	59
	Latn America	Highest	1	26	Costa Rica	79
			2	77	Panama	78
			3	9	Barbados	78
			4	23	Chile	78
			5	28	Cuba	78
		Lowest	1	45	Haiti	47
			2	12	Bolivia	64
			3	79	Peru	67
			4	15	Brazil	67
			5	44	Guatemala	.

Extreme Values. When *Outliers* is selected in the Statistics dialog box, SPSS reports the five largest and five smallest values for each group along with their respective case labels. (When no case-labeling variable is specified, SPSS reports the order of the case in the data file.)

Cases (countries) listed here may or may not be outliers—they simply have the smallest and largest values within their group. To identify a value as an outlier, use the outlier identification schemes available with boxplots or stem-and-leaf diagrams, and then learn the identity of the case from this panel.

In the OECD group, the highest value of female life expectancy is 82 years in both France and Switzerland. Although not shown here, a note by Sweden indicates that additional countries (not listed) have a life expectancy of 81 years. In the OECD group, Portugal and Ireland have the lowest values (78 years).

In the stem-and-leaf diagram for the Latin American group, a life expectancy of 47 years is identified as an outlier. Here you see that this case is Haiti.

Example 3
Shapiro-Wilk and Lilliefors Tests of Normality and Normal Probability Plots

The focus in this example shifts from estimation and description to preparation for hypothesis testing and model building. An important assumption in analysis of variance and other classical statistical procedures is that the within-group data are samples from normal populations with the same variance. Normality is addressed in this example, equality of variance in the next. Often, however, when both normality and equality of variance have been violated, a transformation simultaneously solves both problems. Therefore, in both Example 3 and Example 4, results are shown for population as recorded (for each country in the *world95* data file) and again after log transforming each data value. The first variable is named *populatn*, the second *log_pop*. (Chapter 2, Example 3 demonstrated the success of log transforming population for symmetrizing the distribution of the sample; here, within-group distibutions are studied.)

In screening data for analysis, many data analysts use boxplots and stem-and-leaf diagrams to check for outliers and study the effect of transformations on distributional shape. To actually test the hypothesis that the data are from a normal distribution, SPSS provides the Shapiro-Wilk and the Lilliefors tests. The latter is a modification of the Kolmogorov-Smirnov test for use when the mean and variance is not known and sample estimates are used. SPSS also provides normal probability and detrended normal probability plots for graphically assessing departures from normality.

Before showing test results and normal probability plots for *populatn* and *log_pop*, boxplots and descriptive statistics for each variable are shown.

To produce this output, in the Explore dialog box, click *Reset* to restore the dialog box defaults, and then select:

▸ Dependent List: populatn, log_pop
▸ Factor List: region
▸ Label Cases by: country

Plots...
   ☑ Normality plots with tests

Descriptive
   ☐ Stem-and-leaf (deselect)

 On the Descriptives table, from the Pivot Table menus choose:

Pivot
 Transpose Rows and Columns

Then hide the *East Europe*, *Africa*, and the *Middle East* columns, and the *95% Confidence Interval*, *Variance*, *Minimum*, *Maximum*, *Range*, and *Interquartile Range* rows.

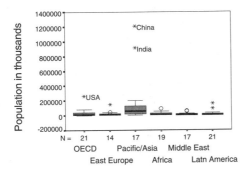

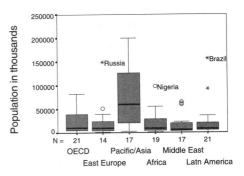

Boxplots (*populatn* and *populatn* edited). China's and India's populations are so large that too little space remains to show the other distributions clearly. You can edit the chart, making the maximum slightly smaller than the USA's population. After editing the *populatn* chart, it is now easy to see that the distributions are very right-skewed (each median falls below the middle of its box), and there are several other extreme values and outliers in addition to China, India, and the USA.

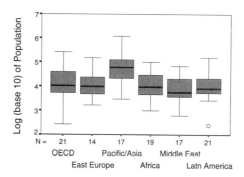

Region or economic group

Boxplot. The distributions in the boxplot of *log_pop* are a great improvement over those for the untransformed values. The median is closer to middle of box, so the distributions are more symmetric. Notice that the spreads of the six groups are now more similar and there is only one outlier.

Descriptives

		Population in thousands			Log (base 10) of Population		
		Region or economic group			Region or economic group		
		OECD	Pacific/Asia	Latn America	OECD	Pacific/Asia	Latn America
Mean	Statistic	33085.10	179126.12	21928.86	4.1157	4.7230	3.9738
	Std. Error	12470.77	82323.91	8031.90	.1398	.1700	.1286
5% Trimmed	Statistic	22724.22	131912.35	15816.40	4.1361	4.7176	3.9909
Median	Statistic	10400.00	59400.00	7000.00	4.0170	4.7700	3.8970
Std. Deviation	Statistic	57148.25	339430.18	36806.78	.6406	.7008	.5894
Skewness	Statistic	3.470	2.599	3.020	-.388	.253	-.280
	Std. Error	.501	.550	.501	.501	.550	.501
Kurtosis	Statistic	13.602	5.964	9.516	1.483	-.007	1.892
	Std. Error	.972	1.063	.972	.972	1.063	.972

Descriptives (after pivoting and hiding East Europe, Africa, and the Middle East—and also hiding the 95% confidence interval, variance, minimum, maximum, range, and interquartile range). For the OECD group, the average population size is 33 million (33085.10); the 5% trimmed mean, 22.7 million; and the median, 10.4 million (10400). The mean is more than three times larger than the median. Not surprisingly, the ratios of the skewness statistics to their standard errors for all three groups exceed 2.0, so the hypothesis of symmetry is rejected.

Statistics for the logarithm of population are displayed in the last three columns of this table. There is little variation among the mean, 5% trimmed mean, and median here. The ratios of each skewness statistic to its standard error are well within a range where the hypothesis of symmetry is not rejected.

Tests of Normality

	Region or economic group	Kolmogorov-Smirnov			Shapiro-Wilk		
		Statistic	df	Sig.	Statistic	df	Sig.
Population in thousands	OECD	.283	21	.000	.545	21	.010
	East Europe	.343	14	.000	.571	14	.010
	Pacific/Asia	.383	17	.000	.536	17	.010
	Africa	.239	19	.005	.743	19	.010
	Middle East	.264	17	.003	.706	17	.010
	Latn America	.300	21	.000	.559	21	.010
Log (base 10) of Population	OECD	.140	21	.200	.950	21	.388
	East Europe	.207	14	.108	.952	14	.577
	Pacific/Asia	.115	17	.200	.970	17	.780
	Africa	.106	19	.200	.968	19	.716
	Middle East	.135	17	.200	.954	17	.496
	Latn America	.124	21	.200	.949	21	.379

Tests of Normality. The test results agree with the graphical displays—for all six groups, both the Kolmogorov-Smirnov and Shapiro-Wilk tests strongly reject the hypothesis of normality for population as recorded, but they do not reject normality for population in log units. Rather than having a *yes* or *no* answer about normality, some data analysts are more concerned about how the distribution may depart from that of a normal distribution. They prefer to study graphical displays.

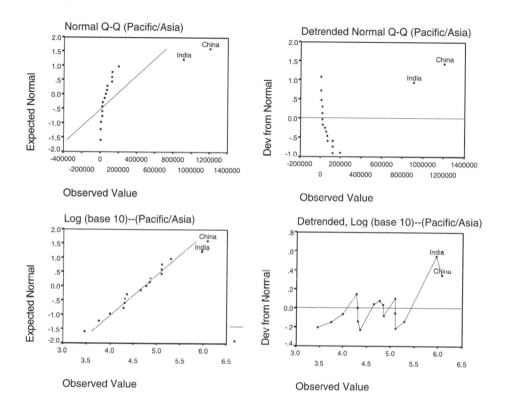

Normal probability and detrended normal probability plots. Each observation in a **normal probability plot** is plotted against the corresponding quantile of a standard normal distribution (that is, its expected z score)—the observed data values are plotted on the horizontal axis and the "expected" values under normality on the vertical axis. Notice that for each size sample, there is a set of expected values. For example, for a sample of size 4, the expected values are $-1.03, -0.30, 0.30,$ and 1.03; for a sample of size 20, the expected values are $-1.87, 1.41, -1.13, \ldots, 1.13, 1.41,$ and 1.87; and so on.

The points on the line displayed in the plot pair each expected normal score (vertical axis) with the corresponding z score for the data on the horizontal axis—that is, the point coordinates, for example, are $(-1.5, -1.5), (0,0), (1.5, 1.5),$ and so on. If the data are from a normal distribution, the plotted values should fall roughly around the line. But when do the points deviate enough from the line to cause worry? Some feel this is an art form and use the detrended normal probability plot as an aid to characterize how the values depart from a normal distribution.

In the normal probability plot for the Pacific/Asia region (top left), the points definitely do not cluster along the line, and China and India (at the far right) stand apart from the other values in the batch. In the plot for the log transformed values (bottom left), the configuration of points does cluster fairly well along the line.

A **detrended normal probability plot** is helpful for detecting patterns of how the points depart from normality. In this display, the difference between the usual z score for each case and its expected score under normality are plotted against the data values (the scale on the vertical axis remains in standardized units).

In the detrended normal plot for population (top right), China and India stand apart from the other 15 values as they did in the normal probability plot to the left. Here, since the plot line is horizontal, the vertical plot scale enlarges, magnifying the view of the configuration. The plotted points dip below the line only once—there obviously is not a random scatter along the line. In the detrended normal plot for log transformed population (bottom right), the trail of 17 points moves above and below the line seven or more times. And, since the vertical scale is in standardized units, notice that most of the points fall within a band between –0.2 and +0.2. If you ignore China in the detrended plot for the untransformed data, the remaining points fall between –1.0 and +1.2. Thus, the log transformed data cluster around the line much more closely than the untransformed values, and their pattern of scatter is more like that for data from a normal distribution.

Example 4
Levene Test for Equal Variances and a Spread-versus-Level Plot

One of the assumptions for a classical analysis of variance is that the data in each cell come from populations with the same variance. Many data analysts use the **Levene test** to test this assumption because it is fairly robust to departures from normality. The computations of the Levene test based on means use the deviation (with sign discarded) from each case to its group mean as data in an analysis of variance. Older tests for homogeneity of variance based on the ratios of sample variances are heavily dependent on the data being from a normal population and are used infrequently today.

Often when variances are unequal, the within-cell distributions also are skewed. When this occurs, a transformation of the data may remedy the problem. In the 1960's, Box and Cox suggested a diagnostic tool to help you decide whether transforming the data will result in greater homogeneity among cell variances. The tool determines whether there is a relationship between cell means and standard deviations (the size of each cell mean should be independent of the size of its standard deviation). Box and Cox use the slope (b) from the regression of the log of mean deviations from the group means on the log of the cell means to construct a **power transformation** for the data of the form:

$$y^{(1-b)}$$

Thus, the power transformation raises each data value to a specified power. Following are some commonly used transformations with their power and slope:

Transformation	Power	Slope b
square	2	−1
none	1	0
square root	1/2	1/2
logarithm	0	1
reciprocal of the square root	−1/2	3/2
reciprocal	−1	2

SPSS provides a robust version of this diagnostic tool, naming it the **spread-versus-level plot**. SPSS uses the log of the interquartile range as the measure of spread instead of deviations from the mean; and the log of the median instead of the log of the mean. If there is no relation between the spread (variability) and level (typical value or median) of a variable, the points should cluster around the horizontal line (that is, the slope is 0).

This diagnostic tool should be regarded as a suggestion for a possible transformation and not as an exact rule. For example, if the power reported in your output is 0.329, try a square root transformation because 0.329 is close to 0.5, the power for square root. Notice that the value you get is an *estimate* from a sample (and for small sample sizes, it may be a poor estimate). You may want to try several transformations and select one for your analysis based on a visual assessment of the shape of the distributions in the within-group boxplots or stem-and-leaf diagrams, and also the result of the Levene test. Also consider what transformations are commonly used in your subject area for similar measurements.

To produce this output, in the Explore dialog box, click *Reset* to restore the dialog box defaults, and then select:

▶ Dependent List: populatn, log_pop
▶ Factor List: region
▶ Label Cases by: country

Plots...
    Boxplots
    ⊙ None

    Descriptive
    ☐ Stem-and-leaf (deselect)

    Spread vs. Level with Levene Test
    ⊙ Power estimation

Test of Homogeneity of Variance

		Levene Statistic	df1	df2	Sig.
Population in thousands	Based on Mean	8.771	5	103	.000
	Based on Median	3.252	5	103	.009
	Based on Median and with Adjusted df	3.252	5	18.339	.028
	Based on Trimmed Mean	5.181	5	103	.000
Log (base 10) of Population	Based on Mean	.317	5	103	.902
	Based on Median	.264	5	103	.932
	Based on Median and with Adjusted df	.264	5	99.227	.931
	Based on Trimmed Mean	.324	5	103	.897

Test of Homogeneity of Variance. For population as recorded, the Levene test based on means, which tests for equality of group variances, is highly significant ($F = 8.771$, p value < 0.0005). For population in log units, the hypothesis of equal variances is not rejected ($F = 0.317$, p value $= 0.902$).

The other modifications of the Levene test based on the median, the median with adjusted degrees of freedom, and the trimmed mean make the test more robust for different types of data. For example, the Levene test based on the median or trimmed mean is robust for very heavy-tailed distributions, such as a Cauchy distribution.

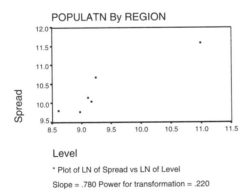

POPULATN By REGION

Level

* Plot of LN of Spread vs LN of Level

Slope = .780 Power for transformation = .220

Spread versus Level plot (*populatn* by *region*). On the vertical axis of this plot, for each of the six groups, the log (natural log or base e logarithm) of the interquartile range is plotted against the log of the median. The plot point in the upper right corner is Pacific/Asia; on the vertical axis, 11.579 is the natural log of its interquartile range (106,800); and on the horizontal axis, 10.992 is the log of its median (59,400). The Pacific/Asia point stands apart from the others. The next largest plot point (9.250, 10.679) is the OECD group.

SPSS reports that the slope through these six points is 0.780, so $(1 - b)$, the suggested power for a transformation, is 0.220. This value falls between 0 (a log transform) and 0.5 (a square root transform). You might examine results for both. (For the log transform, it makes no difference whether you use log base e or log base 10.) Be sure to examine the configuration of points because one or two outliers in such a small sample can exert great influence on the slope. Here, cover Pacific/Asia with your hand and check whether the slope of an imaginary line through the remaining five points is positive; you will find that it is.

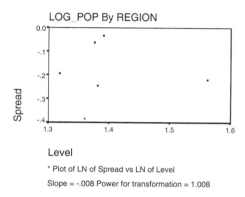

LOG_POP By REGION

Level

* Plot of LN of Spread vs LN of Level

Slope = -.008 Power for transformation = 1.008

Spread versus Level plot (*log_pop* by *region*). The six group medians and interquartile ranges used to construct this plot were computed for population values in log (base 10) units. The point for Pacific/Asia again stands at the right side of the plot. In log units, its median is 4.7738, so the natural log of this value (1.563) is plotted on the horizontal axis. Its interquartile range is 0.8022, so −0.220 is the vertical axis value.

The slope through these points is −0.008 and, thus, suggests a power of $(1 - (-0.008))$ or 1.008. This is very close to 1, indicating that no transformation is needed. This agrees with observations regarding distributional shape as viewed via boxplots, skewness/SE tests, and the Levene test.

A Shortcut for Checking How Well a Transformation Works

Because of the suspicion that a log transformation would help symmetrize the within-group distributions and stabilize their spreads, in Example 3 and Example 4, you showed plots and test results for both population as recorded and population in log units. The Compute dialog box under Transform on the Data Editor was used to request the transformation.

Instead of going to the Data Editor, you can ask Explore to draw a spread-versus-level plot after executing one of six built-in transformations (square root, natural log, reciprocal, reciprocal of a square root, square, and cube). This is the *Transformed* feature available in the Explore Plots dialog box under Spread vs. Level with Levene Test. If you select *Transform* and *Natural log* (base *e* logarithm) and rerun this example, SPSS outputs the following plot with results for *populatn* (the median and the interquartile range of the log transformed data are plotted).

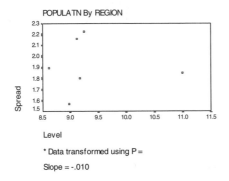

POPULATN By REGION

Spread

Level

* Data transformed using P =

Slope = -.010

Pacific/Asia is the point at the far right. The log base *e* of its median population (59,400) is 10.992; the interquartile range is computed by finding the difference between the 25th and 75th percentiles in log units. Notice that this configuration of plot points is the same as that on p. 61.

The slope through these points is –0.01 or almost 0, indicating little relation between spread and level.

5

Using Crosstabs to Obtain Crosstabulations and Measures of Association

Sometimes, simply describing crosstabulations and their percentages may be all you need for a report or a paper. At other times, sophisticated analyses are needed to understand relationships between categorical variables. Or, you may want to use tables as a data-screening tool for cross-variable edit checks to uncover errors. A 2×2 table of *gender* (*male, female*) against *hysterectomy* (*yes, no*), for example, might uncover males coded as *yes* hysterectomy (or vice versa).

After creating your table, you may want to report a measure of association between the two table variables or test whether the variables are independent. No single measure summarizes all types of association. The following examples illustrate the use of several measures of association. Throughout the examples, other table features will be introduced, such as percentages, expected values, residuals, and even how to use Select Cases to eliminate codes for unwanted categories. If the measure you want is in a later example, you may need to skim earlier examples for these features.

The examples in this chapter use data (*gss 93 subset*) from the 1993 General Social Survey conducted by the National Opinion Research Center. The examples are structured as follows:

Example 1: An R x C table with the chi-square test of independence. A two-way frequency table with five rows and four columns is formed for to compare religious preference and geographical region. The chi-square test of independence is defined, but two categories have too few subjects for a valid test.

Example 2: Requesting percentages, expected values, and residuals—and omitting categories. An association is identified between religious preference and region of the country. After the table is pivoted, cellwise results are interpreted. Other measures for the general $R \times C$ table with unordered categories are introduced in a subsection, including the phi coefficient, the contingency coefficient, Cramér's *V*, lambda, Goodman and Kruskal's tau, and the uncertainty coefficient.

Example 3: Tests within layers of a multiway table. The variables *marital*, *life*, and *sex* form a multiway table with *sex* as the layer variable. Separate results are studied within each layer. Of concern is the fact that small expected values are found for males who find life dull and that these same cells have large standardized residuals.

Example 4: The relative risk and odds ratio for a 2 x 2 table. This example illustrates the use of the odds ratio to investigate whether home owners are more likely than renters to vote. Relative risk is also defined. Other tests and measures for 2×2 tables displayed in a subsection include the chi-square test for equality of proportions, Fisher's exact test, and Yates' continuity correction.

Example 5: The kappa measure of agreement for an R x R table. For this table structure, the row and column categories are the same as those that occur when two raters judge each subject. Here, the agreement between the educational level of a person's mother and that of his or her father is found to be greater than that expected by chance alone. Percentages of the total table count are requested.

Example 6: Measures of correlation and association for R x C tables with ordered categories. Results are displayed for measures based on correlations and measures based on concordant pairs. Correlation-based measures include the Spearman correlation coefficient, the Pearson correlation, and the linear-by-linear association chi-square. Measures based on concordant and discordant pairs of cases include Kendall's tau-*b*, Kendall's tau-*c*, and Goodman and Kruskal's gamma. Somers' *d* and eta are displayed in a subsection.

Example 1
An R x C Table with the Chi-Square Test of Independence

Does religious preference vary by region of the country? Regional differences in religious preference are found in many parts of the world such as India, the former Yugoslavia, and Ireland. Is religious preference independent of geographical region in the United States?

In this example, the variables *relig* and *region4* (from the *gss 93 subset* file) are used as table variables to form a table with five rows and four columns. The five religions are *Protestant*, *Catholic*, *Jewish*, *None*, and *Other*; the regions are *Northeast*, *Midwest*, *South,* and *West*. This table structure is called a general $R \times C$ table with no ordering across categories of its variables. Numbers code the categories of both table variables, but SPSS uses their respective labels in the output. The **Pearson chi-square** statistic is requested for testing the independence of table rows and columns—that is, testing the premise that religious preference and region are independent of each other. Sometimes this task is expressed as testing equality of proportions across rows (or columns).

To produce this output, from the menus choose:

Analyze
  Descriptive Statistics
    Crosstabs...

Click *Reset* to restore the dialog box defaults, and then select:

▶ Row(s): relig
▶ Column(s): region4

Statistics...

  ☑ Chi-square

Case Processing Summary

	Cases					
	Valid		Missing		Total	
	N	Percent	N	Percent	N	Percent
Religious Preference * Region	756	50.4%	744	49.6%	1500	100.0%

Case Processing Summary. This panel describes the number of cases used in each table you request. The total number of cases in the *gss 93 subset* file is 1500, and for 756 of these cases, the values of both *relig* and *region4* are *Valid*. One or both values are missing for the remaining 744 cases. Thus, only half of the sample is used (50.4%). With so many values missing, you should be concerned that the results might be biased. For example, people from certain groups may feel uncomfortable about stating their religion, so they omit the question. Using the Frequencies procedure to check the number of missing values, you find that *relig* has fairly complete data but that *region4* has many missing values.

Religious Preference * Region Crosstabulation

Count

		Region				Total
		Northeast	Midwest	South	West	
Religious Preference	Protestant	54	140	206	80	480
	Catholic	55	56	28	43	182
	Jewish	10	1	1	3	15
	None	12	20	8	24	64
	Other	5	4	4	2	15
Total		136	221	247	152	756

Religious Preference by Region Crosstabulation. In this sample of 756 people, 480 are *Protestant*, 15 are *Jewish*, 15 are *Other*, and so on. These counts are totals of the cell frequencies in their respective rows. The counts along the bottom are totals for each column. The row and column totals are known as **marginals** because they summarize the counts within each table variable independently of the other variable. The cell counts in the body of the table result from crosstabulating the two table variables. For example, in the upper left corner there are 54 Protestants who live in the Northeast, 140 who live in the Midwest, and so on. These counts are the **observed** number for each cell.

Chi-Square Tests

	Value	df	Asymptotic Significance (2-tailed)
Pearson Chi-Square	109.104[1]	12	.000
Likelihood Ratio	105.926	12	.000
Linear-by-Linear Association	4.261	1	.039
N of Valid Cases	756		

1. 8 cells (40.0%) have expected count less than 5. The minimum expected count is 2.70

Chi-Square Tests. The null hypothesis for the Pearson chi-square test is that the row and column variables are independent of each other. By definition, two table variables are **independent** if the probability that a case falls in a specific cell is the product of its marginal probabilities. Using the probability that a subject is Protestant ($480/756$) and the probability that a subject lives in the Northeast ($136/756$), the probability for a case falling in the upper left cell is

$$\frac{480 \times 136}{756^2} = 0.114$$

This probability is used to estimate the number of cases expected (under the hypothesis of independence) in each cell. The expected count is then compared with the observed count. To compute the **expected** number of cases, multiply the probability by the total sample size. This result is the row total multiplied by the column total divided by the total sample size, or 86.3 cases expected for this cell (in Example 2, SPSS computes expected values for all cells).

The difference between the observed count of 54 and the expected count of 86.3 is large. Does this gap support the variables' independence? For an overall test of independence, the Pearson chi-square statistic repeats this process of comparing the observed number of cases with the number expected for each cell. After subtracting the expected count from the actual observed count for each cell, SPSS constructs the statistic by squaring the difference and dividing the result by the expected count. Thus, for the Pearson chi-square statistic, these quantities are summed across all cells:

$$\chi^2 = \sum_i \sum_j \frac{(o_{ij} - e_{ij})^2}{e_{ij}}$$

When the resulting chi-square statistic is large, the null hypothesis of independence is rejected. To define large, the sample statistic is compared to a critical point on the theoretical chi-square distribution that depends on the number of rows and columns in the table. This latter information is labeled df for **degrees of freedom**. For an $R \times C$ table, the degrees of freedom are the number of rows minus 1.0 times the number of columns minus 1.0, or $(r - 1)(c - 1)$. For this table, df $= (5 - 1)(4 - 1)$, or 12.

The computed chi-square statistic for this table is 109.1 and has an associated probability (p value) or **significance level** of less than 0.0005 (the probability is not 0). Conventionally, if this probability is small enough (less than 0.05 or 0.01), the hypothesis of independence is rejected. Using these numbers alone, you could report that there is an association between religious preference and region.

However, if certain assumptions are not met, this probability can be distorted or misleading. Many researchers use the guideline that no cell has an expected value less than 1.0 and not more than 20% of the cells have expected values less than 5 (in 2×2 tables, some say that no cell has an expected value less than 5).

SPSS reports the *minimum expected count*, the number of *cells with expected count < 5*, and the *% of cells with expected count < 5*. In this table, the minimum expected count is 2.7, and eight cells (40%) have expected counts < 5. Clearly, the guideline is violated. The statistics are discussed further in Example 2.

What should you do? Can you see a way to make the table less sparse? A total of 15 people are in the *Other* category. Because it is probably a mixture of religions, you can justify deleting it. The *Jewish* category also has very few subjects. If you delete it, however, you should be careful to indicate that any conclusions are restricted to the *Protestant, Catholic,* and *None* groups.

In Example 2, you will omit the *Jewish* and *Other* categories and request features useful for describing results.

Example 2
Requesting Percentages, Expected Values, and Residuals—and Omitting Categories

In Example 1, concern was expressed that the probability associated with the chi-square test was not valid because 40% of the cells had expected counts less than 5. This example uses Select Cases to omit the *Other* and *Jewish* categories for the *relig* factor and revisit the table. The smallest expected value for this modified table is 10.7, so you are able to report results of the chi-square test of independence, finding that region and religious preference (now restricted to *Protestant, Catholic,* and *None*) are associated. Percentages of row totals and adjusted standardized residuals are used to describe what cells depart most from the hypothesis of independence.

In the subsection at the end of this example, additional measures for $R \times C$ tables with variables that have unordered categories are displayed.

To produce this output, use Select Cases from the Data menu to select cases with *relig* not equal to 3 and *relig* not equal to 5 (relig ~= 3 & relig ~= 5). In the Crosstabs dialog box, click *Reset* to restore the dialog box defaults, and then select:

▶ Row(s): region4
▶ Column(s): relig

Statistics...

☑ Chi-square

Nominal

☑ Contingency coefficient   ☑ Phi and Cramér's V
☑ Lambda   ☑ Uncertainty coefficient

Cells...

Counts
☑ Expected

Percentages
☑ Row

Residuals
☑ Adj. standardized

 On the Region by Religious Preferences Crosstabulation, drag *Statistics* on the row tray to the left of *Region*.

To hide the footnotes in the Directional Measures table, select them and choose *Hide* from the View menu.

Region * Religious Preference Crosstabulation

			Religious Preference			
			Protestant	Catholic	None	Total
Region	Northeast	Count	54	55	12	121
		Expected Count	80.0	30.3	10.7	121.0
		% of Region	44.6%	45.5%	9.9%	100.0%
		Adjusted Residual	-5.5	5.7	.5	
	Midwest	Count	140	56	20	216
		Expected Count	142.8	54.1	19.0	216.0
		% of Region	64.8%	25.9%	9.3%	100.0%
		Adjusted Residual	-.5	.3	.3	
	South	Count	206	28	8	242
		Expected Count	160.0	60.7	21.3	242.0
		% of Region	85.1%	11.6%	3.3%	100.0%
		Adjusted Residual	7.7	-5.9	-3.7	
	West	Count	80	43	24	147
		Expected Count	97.2	36.9	13.0	147.0
		% of Region	54.4%	29.3%	16.3%	100.0%
		Adjusted Residual	-3.4	1.3	3.6	
Total		Count	480	182	64	726
		Expected Count	480.0	182.0	64.0	726.0
		% of Region	66.1%	25.1%	8.8%	100.0%

Region by Religious Preference Crosstabulation. This is the default layout when two or more results are requested for each table cell.

Region * Religious Preference Crosstabulation

			Religious Preference			Total
			Protestant	Catholic	None	
Count	Region	Northeast	54	55	12	121
		Midwest	140	56	20	216
		South	206	28	8	242
		West	80	43	24	147
	Total		480	182	64	726
Expected Count	Region	Northeast	80.0	30.3	10.7	121.0
		Midwest	142.8	54.1	19.0	216.0
		South	160.0	60.7	21.3	242.0
		West	97.2	36.9	13.0	147.0
	Total		480.0	182.0	64.0	726.0
% of Region	Region	Northeast	44.6%	45.5%	9.9%	100.0%
		Midwest	64.8%	25.9%	9.3%	100.0%
		South	85.1%	11.6%	3.3%	100.0%
		West	54.4%	29.3%	16.3%	100.0%
	Total		66.1%	25.1%	8.8%	100.0%
Adjusted Residual	Region	Northeast	-5.5	5.7	.5	
		Midwest	-.5	.3	.3	
		South	7.7	-5.9	-3.7	
		West	-3.4	1.3	3.6	

Region by Religious Preference Crosstabulation (after pivoting). After pivoting the previous table, each type of result is placed in a separate panel.

The counts and totals for the religion categories are the same as those in Example 1, except that *Jewish* and *Other* are omitted here.

The *Expected Count* for each cell is defined in "Chi-Square Tests" on p. 66. Notice that none of these expected counts is less than 5.

The entry in each row in the *% of Region* panel is the *Count* divided by its row total ($54/121 = 0.446$). Percentages are useful for describing differences among categories, especially when there is variation in the marginal totals. Across all four regions (see *Total*), 66.1% of the sample is *Protestant*; 25.1%, *Catholic*; and 8.8%, *None*. The profile for the *Midwest* (64.8%, 25.9%, and 9.3%) departs little from the total percentages. The departure for the other groups is greater. In this sample, the number of Protestants and Catholics in the Northeast is very similar (44.6% versus 45.5%), but in the South, there are considerably more Protestants (85.1% versus 11.6%). Many more people in the West report *None* as their preference (16.3%) than those in the South (3.3%).

The numerator of each **adjusted residual** (or adjusted deviate) is the difference between the observed count for that cell and its expected count. The denominator is an estimate of the residual's standard error normalized to have variance of 1 when the data are from a multinominal distribution. In other words, read the values roughly as *z* scores (look for values well below -2 or above $+2$) to identify cells that depart markedly from the model of independence. The most extreme residual (7.7) is for Protestants from the South—if the table variables were independent, you would expect many fewer Protestants in this cell. At the same time, you would expect many more Catholics in the South (notice that the sign of its deviate, -5.9, is negative). In the Northeast, the residuals -5.5 and 5.7 indicate that the sample has fewer Protestants and more Catholics than expected under independence. For the people with no religious preference (*None*), the South has fewer than expected (-3.7), while the West has more (3.6).

Chi-Square Tests

	Value	df	Asymptotic Significance (2-tailed)
Pearson Chi-Square	81.464[1]	6	.000
Likelihood Ratio	82.835	6	.000
Linear-by-Linear Association	.933	1	.334
N of Valid Cases	726		

1. 0 cells (.0%) have expected count less than 5. The minimum expected count is 10.67

Chi-Square Tests. In Example 1, the validity of the test results was questioned because the table had too many cells with small expected values. In this example, SPSS reports that the minimum expected count is 10.7, so you are able to study the test results. The null hypothesis that the table variables are independent is rejected (Pearson chi-square = 81.5 with 6 degrees of freedom and p value < 0.0005). Thus, there is a significant association between religious preference and region of the country. The chi-square test, however, provides little information about how the variables are related or how strong the relation is (the adjusted residuals described on p. 70 do provide useful information). Also notice that the size of the chi-square depends not only on the differences between the observed and expected counts but also on the sample size. Try making a file with 100 or even 10 copies of the data and watching how the chi-square statistic increases with the sample size.

The **likelihood-ratio chi-square** is also highly significant. It is an alternative to the Pearson chi-square and is used as a test statistic for loglinear models. For large samples, the likelihood-ratio and Pearson chi-square statistics are approximately the same. The **linear-by-linear association chi-square** is a function of the Pearson correlation coefficient and is appropriate only for quantitative variables. For this example, ignore this statistic because the variables have unordered categories.

The output for the symmetric and directional measures is discussed in the following section.

More Measures for Table Variables with Unordered Categories

When there is no ordering across the categories of the table variables, SPSS provides several additional measures that fall into two groups: those based on the chi-square statistic and those based on the idea of **proportional reduction in error** (PRE). The chi-square-based measures are the phi coefficient, coefficient of contingency, and Cramér's V; the PRE measures are lambda, Goodman and Kruskal's tau, and the uncertainty coefficient.

In constructing the chi-square-based measures, an attempt was made to make them range from 0 to 1 (but not all do) and to minimize the influence of the sample size and degrees of freedom. Thus, these measures are more useful than the usual chi-square statistic for comparing tables with varying sample sizes and dimensions, but they are more difficult to interpret.

The PRE measures indicate the reduction in prediction error that is obtained when one table factor is used to predict the other. That is, they measure the gain in predicting one categorical table factor when the value of the second factor is known, relative to when it is not known.

Symmetric Measures

		Value	Approx. Sig.
Nominal Measures	Phi	.335	.000
	Cramer's V	.237	.000
	Contingency Coefficient	.318	.000
N of Valid Cases		726	

Symmetric Measures. Phi, Cramér's V, and the contingency coefficient are scaled differently, but all are 0 if (and only if) the Pearson chi-square test is 0. The probability associated with the Pearson chi-square is used to test the hypothesis that each measure is 0. Here, the observed significance level is very small, so this hypothesis is rejected. Cramér's V is always less than or equal to 1.0, but phi can exceed 1. For a 2×2 table, phi and Cramér's V are the same and equal the Pearson correlation coefficient. The contingency coefficient ranges from 0 to 1, but generally does not reach the upper limit of 1.

Directional Measures

			Value	Asymptotic Std. Error	Approx. T	Approx. Sig.
Nominal Measures	Lambda	Symmetric	.062	.020	3.019	.003
		Region Dependent	.091	.021	4.133	.000
		Religious Preference Dependent	.004	.042	.096	.924
	Goodman and Kruskal tau	Region Dependent	.039	.008		.000
		Religious Preference Dependent	.077	.016		.000
	Uncertainty Coefficient	Symmetric	.052	.011	4.734	.000
		Region Dependent	.042	.009	4.734	.000
		Religious Preference Dependent	.068	.014	4.734	.000

Directional Measures. Lambda, Goodman and Kruskal's tau, and the uncertainty coefficient range from 0 to 1, where 0 means that knowledge of the independent variable is no help in predicting the dependent variable, and 1 means that knowing the independent variable perfectly identifies the categories of the dependent variable. SPSS declares each variable in turn as dependent and computes the measure. The choice of whether a variable is dependent or independent depends on the nature of your problem. Notice that both lambda and the uncertainty coefficient have a symmetric form created by summing the numerators and denominators of the two forms and then calculating the ratio.

Here, when religious preference is used to predict region, lambda indicates that there is a 9.1% reduction in error. When the prediction is in the opposite direction (using region to predict religion), the reduction is almost nonexistent (0.4%). The approximate significance, or p value, indicates that the former reduction is highly significant (< 0.0005) and that the latter is not (0.924). Notice that for these data, the reduction is not impressively large (all measures are well under 10%), yet they are highly significant (p values $\le$ 0.003). So, in a practical sense, a highly significant measure may not be very important.

The *Asymptotic Std. Error* can be used to form an approximate 95% confidence interval for the estimated parameter. For example, an interval for lambda when region is predicted from religious preference is $0.091 \pm 2*0.021$, or 0.049 to 0.133. The *Approx. T* statistic is the ratio of the statistic to its estimated asymptotic standard error under the null hypothesis that the parameter is 0. (Thus, the t value is *not* the ratio of the statistic to the value in the *Asymptotic Std. Error* column).

Example 3
Tests within Layers of a Multiway Table

SPSS displays multiway tables as a set of two-way tables. If you specify a row, a column, and a layer variable (control variable), SPSS forms one two-way subtable or panel for each value of the layer variable (or combination of values for two or more control variables).

Is the relationship between marital status and view of life the same for males and females? The intention in this example is to show how to request a multiway frequency table and to explore or describe its subtables. This is a preliminary look at the question of whether a possible association between marital status and view of life is the same for males and females. If you want to study relationships among more than two table variables, you should use the General Loglinear Analysis procedure, available in the Advanced Statistics option. It allows you to model the cell counts by using information about the association between marital status and life, between life and sex, and between marital status and sex (that is, search for interactions that explain the counts from among every possible interaction).

In this example, *sex* is a layer factor for a table of *marital* status (*married*, *widowed*, *divorced*, or *never married*) against *life* (*exciting*, *routine*, or *dull*). Tests, measures, and cellwise results (counts and statistics) are printed for two tables: one two-way table for males; the other, for females. However, cells with small expected values still remain, so you will examine their components of chi-square (standardized residuals) and expected values.

The variable *marital* also has a category for separated, but its counts are sparse (only 7 males and 18 females). You can use the Select Cases feature to omit this category.

To produce this output, use Select Cases from the Data menu to select cases with *marital* not equal to 4 (marital ~= 4). In the Crosstabs dialog box, click *Reset* to restore the dialog box defaults, and then select:

▶ Row(s): marital
▶ Column(s): life
▶ Layer 1 of 1: sex

Statistics...

☑ Chi-square

Cells...

Counts
☑ Expected

Percentages
☑ Row

Residuals
☑ Standardized   ☑ Adj. standardized

On the Marital Status by Is Life Exciting or Dull by Respondent's Sex Crosstabulation, drag *Statistics* on the row tray to the right of *Respondent's Sex*.

Chi-Square Tests

Respondent's Sex		Value	df	Asymptotic Sig. (2-tailed)
Male	Pearson Chi-Square	27.506[1]	6	.000
	Likelihood Ratio	23.450	6	.001
	Linear-by-Linear Association	.610	1	.435
	N of Valid Cases	418		
Female	Pearson Chi-Square	11.578[2]	6	.072
	Likelihood Ratio	10.426	6	.108
	Linear-by-Linear Association	.047	1	.829
	N of Valid Cases	553		

1. 3 cells (25.0%) have expected count less than 5. The minimum expected count is 1.00
2. 0 cells (.0%) have expected count less than 5. The minimum expected count is 6.44

Chi-Square Tests. The minimum expected count for the females is 6.4 and for the males, 1.0. Three of the cells in the *male* subtable have expected values less than 5.0 (25% of the cells). This exceeds the guideline of no more than 20% of the cells. Let's examine the results carefully. First, ignore the results for the linear-by-linear association chi-square because the categories are not ordered. For the females, you cannot reject the hypothesis of independence (chi-square = 11.578 with p value = 0.072). For the males, however, the chi-square test is highly significant (chi-square = 27.5, p value < 0.0005). This last result is questionable because of the small expected values. The concern is that the cells with small expected values make large contributions to the size of the chi-square statistic (discussed on p. 76). That is, you do not want to reject the hypothesis of independence because of a few sparse cells.

Marital Status * Is Life Exciting or Dull * Respondent's Sex Crosstabulation

	Respondent's Sex			Is Life Exciting or Dull			Total
				Dull	Routine	Exciting	
Count	Male	Marital Status	married	6	121	121	248
			widowed	4	14	4	22
			divorced	6	25	19	50
			never married	3	39	56	98
		Total		19	199	200	418
	Female	Marital Status	married	15	120	130	265
			widowed	13	40	36	89
			divorced	4	49	46	99
			never married	8	40	52	100
		Total		40	249	264	553
Expected Count	Male	Marital Status	married	11.3	118.1	118.7	248.0
			widowed	1.0	10.5	10.5	22.0
			divorced	2.3	23.8	23.9	50.0
			never married	4.5	46.7	46.9	98.0
		Total		19.0	199.0	200.0	418.0
	Female	Marital Status	married	19.2	119.3	126.5	265.0
			widowed	6.4	40.1	42.5	89.0
			divorced	7.2	44.6	47.3	99.0
			never married	7.2	45.0	47.7	100.0
		Total		40.0	249.0	264.0	553.0
% of Marital Status	Male	Marital Status	married	2.4%	48.8%	48.8%	100.0%
			widowed	18.2%	63.6%	18.2%	100.0%
			divorced	12.0%	50.0%	38.0%	100.0%
			never married	3.1%	39.8%	57.1%	100.0%
		Total		4.5%	47.6%	47.8%	100.0%
	Female	Marital Status	married	5.7%	45.3%	49.1%	100.0%
			widowed	14.6%	44.9%	40.4%	100.0%
			divorced	4.0%	49.5%	46.5%	100.0%
			never married	8.0%	40.0%	52.0%	100.0%
		Total		7.2%	45.0%	47.7%	100.0%
Standardized Residual	Male	Marital Status	married	-1.6	.3	.2	
			widowed	3.0	1.1	-2.0	
			divorced	2.5	.2	-1.0	
			never married	-.7	-1.1	1.3	
	Female	Marital Status	married	-1.0	.1	.3	
			widowed	2.6	.0	-1.0	
			divorced	-1.2	.7	-.2	
			never married	.3	-.7	.6	
Adjusted Residual	Male	Marital Status	married	-2.5	.6	.5	
			widowed	3.2	1.5	-2.9	
			divorced	2.7	.4	-1.5	
			never married	-.8	-1.8	2.1	
	Female	Marital Status	married	-1.4	.1	.6	
			widowed	2.9	.0	-1.5	
			divorced	-1.4	1.0	-.3	
			never married	.3	-1.1	.9	

Marital Status by Is Life Exciting or Dull by Respondent's Sex Crosstabulation. The three cells with an *Expected Count* less than 5 are *widowed*, *divorced*, and *never married* men who find life dull (the observed counts in these cells are, respectively, 4, 6, and 3). The *Dull* category for the males is sparse—only 19 of the 418 men sampled view life as dull.

The contribution of each cell to the Pearson chi-square statistic is printed in the table of **standardized residuals**. Chi-square is the sum of the squares of these values. The standardized residuals for the three questionable cells are 3, 2.5, and −0.7. Squaring these values results in 9, 6.25, and 0.49 with a sum of 15.74. In the table on p. 75, the chi-square for males is 27.5, so the contribution from the other nine cells is smaller (27.5 − 15.74 = 11.76). This is a researcher's worst-case scenario: the contribution of three sparse cells causes the test results to be highly significant.

If the results had not been clouded by the sparseness of the *Dull* category, you could continue to describe why these data depart from the model of independence by using the adjusted residuals or deviates. Look at the values for males in the *Exciting* column. More never married men than expected find life exciting (2.1) and many fewer widowed men find it exciting (−2.9). To go even further, you might add that among the men who describe life as dull, there are many fewer married men (−2.5) and considerably more widowed and divorced men (3.2 and 2.7).

Example 4
The Relative Risk and Odds Ratio for a 2 x 2 Table

Are home owners more likely to vote than renters? To answer this question, you want to construct a 2×2 table with the two variables, home ownership and voted or did not vote.

The *gss 93 subset* data file contains variables *dwelown* (own or rent dwelling) and *vote92* (voted or did not vote), which you can use for the analysis. As often happens with items on a questionnaire, additional values are coded. For example, *dwelown* uses code 3 for *other* and code 8 for *don't know*, while *vote92* uses code 3 for *not eligible* and code 4 for *refused*. Select the cases with *dwelown* less than 3 and *vote92* less than 3.

From the menus choose:

Data
  Select Cases...

▶   Select *If condition is satisfied* and click *If*.

▶   Enter (dwelown < 3 & vote92 < 3) as the condition and click *Continue*.

In the Crosstabs dialog box, click *Reset* to restore the dialog box defaults, and then select:

▸ Row(s): dwelown
▸ Column(s): vote92

Cells...

Percentages
☑ Row

 On the Homeowner or Renter by Voting in 1992 Election Crosstabulation, drag *Statistics* on the row tray to the left of *Homeowner or Renter*.

Homeowner or Renter * Voting in 1992 Election Crosstabulation

| | | | Voting in 1992 Election | | Total |
			voted	did not vote	
Count	Homeowner or Renter	owns home	509	135	644
		pays rent	167	140	307
	Total		676	275	951
% of Homeowner or Renter	Homeowner or Renter	owns home	79.0%	21.0%	100.0%
		pays rent	54.4%	45.6%	100.0%
	Total		71.1%	28.9%	100.0%

Homeowner or Renter by Voting in 1992 Election Crosstabulation. In the sample, there are 644 home owners and 307 renters—of these, 509 home owners and 167 renters voted. In terms of percentages, 79% of the home owners voted and 54.4% of the renters voted.

The crosstabulation seems to support the notion that home owners are more likely to vote, but you'd like some statistical assurance. Moreover, how much more likely is a home owner to vote? Two commonly used statistics to answer questions like these are the odds ratio and the relative risk.

In the Crosstabs dialog box, select:

Statistics...

☑ Risk

Cells...

Counts
☐ Observed (deselect)

Percentages
☐ Row (deselect)

Risk Estimate

	Value	95% Confidence Interval	
		Lower	Upper
Odds Ratio for Homeowner or Renter (owns home / pays rent)	3.161	2.356	4.241
For cohort Voting in 1992 Election = voted	1.453	1.302	1.622
For cohort Voting in 1992 Election = did not vote	.460	.379	.558
N of Valid Cases	951		

The **relative risk** is the ratio of event probabilities for the subgroups of interest. The relative risk of voting in your example is the ratio of the probability that a home owner votes to the probability that a renter votes. You can estimate the relative risk by dividing the proportion of voting home owners by the proportion of voting renters, or $79.0\%/54.4\% = 1.453$. Likewise, the relative risk of not voting is the ratio of the probability that a home owner does not vote to the probability that a renter does not vote. Your estimate of this relative risk is $21.0\%/45.6\% = .460$. Given these results, you can estimate that a home owner is 1.453 times as likely to vote as a renter, or .460 times as likely as a renter not to vote.

The **odds ratio** is the ratio of the event odds for the subgroups of interest. The **odds** of an event is the ratio of the probability that the event occurs to the probability that the event does not occur. You can estimate the odds that a home owner votes by dividing the proportion of voting home owners by the proportion of nonvoting home owners, or $79.0\%/21.0\% = 3.77$. Likewise, the estimate of the odds that a renter votes is $54.4\%/45.6\% = 1.19$. You can estimate the odds ratio by dividing the odds that a home owner votes by the odds that a renter votes, or $3.77/1.19 = 3.161$. The odds ratio is also equivalent to the ratio of the event-relative risks. Thus, the odds ratio in the example is the ratio of the relative risk of voting to the relative risk of not voting, or $1.453/.460 = 3.16$.

What does all this mean about the odds ratio? It means that it is very difficult to interpret, because it is a ratio of ratios. The relative risk is easier to interpret, so the odds ratio in and of itself is not very helpful. However, there are certain commonly occurring situations in which the estimate of the relative risk is not very good and the odds ratio can be used to approximate the relative risk.

The odds ratio should be used as an approximation to the relative risk when the following conditions are met:

• The probability of the event is small (<0.1). This condition guarantees that the odds ratio will make a good approximation to the relative risk. In this example, the event is that a person votes.

• The design of the study is **case-control**. This condition signals that the estimate of the relative risk will likely not be good. A case-control study is retrospective, most often used when the event of interest is unlikely, or when the design of a prospective experiment is impractical or unethical.

These conditions are not met in the example of home owner versus renter voting habits, because the probability that a randomly selected person votes is greater than 10%.

If, however, you want to study the relationship between smoking and lung cancer, then the conditions for using the odds ratio are met. The event of interest, contracting lung cancer, is a low-probability event. Moreover, your study should be of the case-control design.

This is because good prospective design calls for you to take a sample of smokers and a sample of nonsmokers and then count how many in each group contract lung cancer in 40 years. This is highly impractical because lung cancer is still a fairly rare disease, and you would be required to follow the 40-year medical history of thousands upon thousands of patients to obtain useful results.

A case-control study simply calls for you to take a sample of lung cancer patients (cases), and a sample of healthy patients (controls), and ask each patient whether they are a smoker or a nonsmoker.

Other Measures for 2 x 2 Tables

In the past, researchers often used the chi-square test of equal proportions to analyze a 2×2 table. Now, many prefer the relative risk and the odds ratio approximation to the relative risk because they are more interpretable than the chi-square statistic.

When chi-square is selected for a 2×2 table, SPSS also reports Yates' correction for continuity and Fisher's exact test.

In the Crosstabs dialog box, select:

Statistics...

   ☑ Chi-square
   ☐ Risk (deselect)

In the 2×2 table, the chi-square test can be used to test the **equality of proportions**. For the data in this example, the null hypothesis might be that the proportion of home owners who vote equals that for renters (that is, do the sample values 0.79 and 0.544 come from populations where the proportions are equal?).

Yates' continuity correction is intended to improve the approximation to the chi-square distribution when samples are small. However, many researchers feel that it is too conservative.

In the Chi-Square Tests table on p. 66, SPSS reported that 40% of the cells had expected counts of less than 5, indicating that the significance associated with the chi-square test might be suspect. This warning does not apply to Fisher's exact test because it counts all possible outcomes exactly, including the ones that produce an interaction greater than that observed.

Chi-Square Tests

	Value	df	Asymptotic Sig. (2-tailed)	Exact Sig. (2-tailed)	Exact Sig. (1-tailed)
Pearson Chi-Square	61.405^2	1	.000		
Continuity Correction[1]	60.212	1	.000		
Likelihood Ratio	59.320	1	.000		
Fisher's Exact Test[1]				.000	.000
Linear-by-Linear Association	61.340	1	.000		
N of Valid Cases	951				

1. Computed only for a 2x2 table
2. 0 cells (.0%) have expected count less than 5. The minimum expected count is 88.77

Chi-Square Tests. The conclusion from the chi-square test of equal proportions is that the proportion of home owners who vote (0.79) clearly differs from that for renters (0.544): chi-square = 61.405, 1 df, and p value < 0.0005. The results of the other tests are also highly significant and do not contradict these results.

For **Fisher's exact test**, assume that the marginal counts remain fixed at their observed values. The probability for the two-tailed test is found by evaluating the observed table and all other tables having the same marginal frequencies (attention is restricted to the probabilities less than or equal to those of the observed table). Here, the result agrees with that of the Pearson chi-square.

Example 5
The Kappa Measure of Agreement for an R x R Table

The table structure for the kappa statistic is square, $R \times R$, and has the same row and column categories because each subject is classified or rated twice. For example, doctor A and doctor B diagnose the same patients as schizophrenic, manic depressive, or behavior-disorder:

Table 5.1   Table structure for kappa statistic

		Doctor B		
		schizophrenic	depressive	other
	schizophrenic	a	b	c
Doctor A	depressive	d	e	f
	other	g	h	i

Notice that there need be no ordering across the categories of each table factor. **Kappa** is a measure of interrater agreement that tests if the counts in the diagonal cells (the subjects who receive the same rating—that is, cells a, e, and i) differ from those expected by chance alone.

Let
   p_o = the sum of the observed proportions in the diagonal cells
   p_e = the sum of the expected proportions in the same cells

then,

$$\kappa = \frac{p_o - p_e}{1 - p_e}$$

The numerator is the excess beyond chance, and the denominator is the maximum that this value could be. When all off-diagonal cells are empty, kappa achieves its maximum value, 1.0.

Kappa is a measure rather than a test. Its size is judged by using an asymptotic standard error to construct a *t* statistic (that is, measure divided by standard error) to test whether the measure differs from 0. Values of kappa greater than 0.75 indicate *excellent* agreement beyond chance; values between 0.40 to 0.75 indicate *fair* to *good*; and values below 0.40 indicate *poor* agreement.

How do the educational levels of a person's mother and father agree? In this example, you continue using the *gss 93 subset* data file and use kappa to measure the agreement between the level of education attained by each respondent's mother and his or her father. These table variables happen to have ordered categories, but this is not required for kappa. The category *Junior College* (code 2 in the data) is very sparse, so you can use Select Cases on the Data menu to omit it.

To produce this output, use Select Cases from the Data menu to select cases with *madeg* not equal to 2 and *padeg* not equal to 2 (madeg ~= 2 & padeg ~= 2). In the Crosstabs dialog box, click *Reset* to restore the dialog box defaults, and then select:

‣ Row(s): padeg
‣ Column(s): madeg

Statistics...

   ☑ Kappa

Cells...

   Percentages
   ☑ Total

On the Father's Highest Degree by Mother's Highest Degree Crosstabulation, drag *Statistics* on the row tray to the left of *Father's Highest Degree*.

Father's Highest Degree * Mother's Highest Degree Crosstabulation

			Mother's Highest Degree				
			LT High School	High School	Bachelor	Graduate	Total
Count	Father's Highest Degree	LT High School	355	139	14	1	509
		High School	74	297	15	3	389
		Bachelor	7	61	34	6	108
		Graduate	2	37	15	12	66
	Total		438	534	78	22	1072
% of Total	Father's Highest Degree	LT High School	33.1%	13.0%	1.3%	.1%	47.5%
		High School	6.9%	27.7%	1.4%	.3%	36.3%
		Bachelor	.7%	5.7%	3.2%	.6%	10.1%
		Graduate	.2%	3.5%	1.4%	1.1%	6.2%
	Total		40.9%	49.8%	7.3%	2.1%	100.0%

Father's Highest Degree by Mother's Highest Degree Crosstabulation. The educational levels of fathers and mothers are the same for 698 (355 + 297 + 34 + 12) of the 1072 respondents (this is 65.1% of the sample, or 33.1% + 27.7% + 3.2% + 1.1%). Are the counts along this diagonal greater than those expected by chance alone?

Symmetric Measures

		Value	Asymptotic Std. Error	Approx. T	Approx. Sig.
Other	Kappa	.434	.022	19.510	.000
N of Valid Cases		1072			

Symmetric Measures. The value of kappa is 0.434, indicating *fair* to *good* agreement between the parents' levels of education. The t statistic for testing that the measure is 0 is 19.5 with an approximate significance less than 0.0005. The *Asymptotic Std. Error* is used to construct a confidence interval for the measure. That is, a 95% interval for kappa extends from $0.434 - 2*0.022$ to $0.434 + 2*0.022$, or 0.390 to 0.478.

Example 6
Measures of Correlation and Association for R x C Tables with Ordered Categories

The measures in this example are used when both table variables have ordered categories. For example, children are categorized as sedentary, normal, or hyperactive; or side effects to a drug are categorized as none, minimal, moderate, or severe. The measures fall in two groups: those based on correlations and those based on concordant pairs. In the section at the end of this example, Somers' d and the eta coefficient are displayed—they are measures that incorporate the fact that one factor is dependent and the other independent. For eta, however, the categories of the independent variables need not be ordered.

The correlation-based measures are the Spearman correlation coefficient, the Pearson correlation, and the linear-by-linear association chi-square. For the **Spearman correlation coefficient**, the rank order of each data value is used in the computation of the Pearson correlation. The **linear-by-linear association chi-square** is simply the square of the usual Pearson correlation multiplied by the sample size minus 1. For the Pearson correlation, the assumption is that the data come from a bivariate normal population—often this is not the case for two-way table data. For the Spearman correlation, no assumptions are made about the nature of the population sampled.

The measures based on concordant pairs are Kendall's tau-*b*, Kendall's tau-*c*, and Goodman and Kruskal's gamma. To construct these measures, imagine examining the values of the two table factors (variables) for every pair of cases. If the values for one case are both larger (or smaller) than those for the other member of the pair, the pair is **concordant**. If the direction is reversed for the second factor, the pair is **discordant**. When the cases have the same values for one or both variables, the pair is **tied**. So, if the ranks of factor A tend to increase with those of factor B (the factors have a positive association), the majority of the pairs are concordant. If the ranks of factor A increase as the ranks of factor B decrease (the association is negative), the majority of pairs are discordant. When the number of concordant and discordant pairs is the same (or approximately the same), there is no association. The numerator of each measure involves the difference between the number of concordant (P) and discordant (Q) pairs. The measures differ in how ties are treated. Here are the formulas for **Kendall's tau-*b*** and **Kendall's tau-*c***:

$$\tau_b = \frac{P - Q}{\sqrt{(P + Q + T_X)(P + Q + T_Y)}} \qquad \tau_c = \frac{2m(P - Q)}{N^2(m - 1)}$$

where T_X is the number of pairs tied on X but not on Y, T_Y the number tied on Y but not on X, and m is the smaller of the number of rows and columns.

SPSS also provides **Somers' *d***, which is an asymmetric extension of **gamma**. Each table factor in turn is treated as the dependent variable. Here are the formulas for gamma and Somers' *d*:

$$G = \frac{P - Q}{P + Q}$$

$$d_Y = \frac{P - Q}{P + Q + T_Y}$$

A symmetric version of Somers' *d* is also printed. See the subsection at the end of this example.

Are a respondent's preferences for blues and jazz music correlated? How about classical and rap music? In this example, the focus is on how people feel about jazz, blues, classical, and rap music. Each of the table variables has five ordered categories indicating the respondent's preference for the type of music: *Like very much, Like it, Mixed feelings, Dislike it,* and *Dislike very much.*

To produce this output, use Select Cases from the Data menu to make sure that all cases in the data are selected. In the Crosstabs dialog box, click *Reset* to restore the dialog box defaults, and then select:

▶ Row(s): blues, classicl
▶ Column(s): jazz, rap

Statistics...

☑ Correlations

Ordinal

☑ Gamma   ☑ Somers' d
☑ Kendall's tau-b   ☑ Kendall's tau-c

Nominal by Interval
☑ Eta

Crosstab

Count

		Jazz Music					Total
		Like it very much	Like it	Mixed feelings	Dislike it	Dislike very much	
Blues or R & B Music	like very much	105	64	18	8	7	202
	like it	104	306	141	59	5	615
	mixed feelings	17	92	158	62	11	340
	dislike it	5	21	39	122	15	202
	dislike it very much	3	7	6	17	24	57
Total		234	490	362	268	62	1416

Crosstab (Blues or R & B Music by Jazz Crosstabulation). The heaviest concentration of responses occurs in the upper left corner of the table, where both types of music are liked. Few people like one type and dislike the other, as evidenced by the small counts in the off-diagonal cells in the lower left and upper right corners of the table.

Symmetric Measures (Blues or R & B Music * Jazz Music)

		Value	Asymptotic Std. Error	Approx. T	Approx. Sig.
Ordinal Measures	Kendall's tau-b	.490	.020	23.633	.000
	Kendall's tau-c	.447	.019	23.633	.000
	Gamma	.638	.023	23.633	.000
Other	Pearson's R	.556	.023	25.148	.000
	Spearman Correlation	.551	.022	24.854	.000
N of Valid Cases		1416			

Symmetric Measures (Blues or R & B Music by Jazz Music). Using the t statistic with its associated probability (approximate significance), you can conclude that each measure differs significantly from 0 (see "Symmetric Measures" on p. 83). Preferences for jazz and rhythm & blues are correlated: if a person likes one type of music, he or she may like the other. For each measure, use the Asymptotic standard error to construct a confidence interval. Pearson and Spearman correlations are described in more detail in Chapter 11.

Symmetric Measures (Classical Music * Rap Music)

		Value	Asymptotic Std. Error	Approx. T	Approx. Sig.
Ordinal Measures	Kendall's tau-b	.013	.023	.590	.555
	Kendall's tau-c	.012	.021	.590	.555
	Gamma	.018	.031	.590	.555
	Spearman Correlation	.015	.027	.572	.567
Other	Pearson's R	.014	.027	.519	.604
N of Valid Cases		1383			

Symmetric Measures (Classical Music by Rap Music). There appears to be no correlation between the respondents preferences for classical and rap music: the t statistics are very small (less than 1.0) and the associated probabilities are well above 0.05.

When One Factor Is Dependent and the Other Is Independent

Somers' *d* is a modification of gamma that includes the number of pairs not tied on the independent variable. It is appropriate when both table variables have ordered categories and the role of the independent and dependent variables is clear.

If the values of the dependent variable are quantitative and the independent factor has ordered or unordered categories, consider the **eta coefficient**. When squared, eta is interpreted as the proportion of the variability of the dependent variable that is explained by knowing the values of the independent variable. Eta-squared is sometimes called an effect-size statistic and is used in analysis of variance to measure the variability accounted for by the grouping factor.

Directional Measures

			Value	Asymptotic Std. Error	Approximate T	Approximate Significance
Ordinal Measures	Somers' d	Symmetric	.490	.020	23.633	.000
		Blues or R & B Music Dependent	.477	.020	23.633	.000
		Jazz Music Dependent	.503	.020	23.633	.000
Nominal by Interval Measures	Eta	Blues or R & B Music Dependent	.558			
		Jazz Music Dependent	.559			

Directional Measures. Each value of Somers' *d* indicates the proportionate excess of concordant pairs over discordant pairs among pairs not tied on the independent variable. When jazz is considered the independent variable, the statistics value is 0.477; when the role of the items is reversed, the value is 0.503. Either way, the result is significant (the probabilities are less than 0.0005). Here, however, you have no reason to consider one or the other as dependent.

If you view each variable in turn as a categorical variable for predicting the other variable (and making the considerable leap that this variable with five ordered values is quantitative), eta measures the success of the prediction. Using the respondents' preference for jazz as an independent variable to predict their preference for blues and rhythm & blues accounts for 55.8% of the variability of the later item. If the roles of the independent and dependent variables are reversed, eta is 55.9%.

6

Using Case Summaries to Obtain Cell Statistics and Data Listings

Often it is useful to look at descriptive statistics for cells or subgroups of cases. For smaller data sets, it may be desirable to list the cases that fall into each cell. With larger data sets, you can limit the output to display only the first *n* cases. The cells are defined by crosstabulating the levels of the grouping variables. You may want to divide the data into males and females, or you may further wish to break down the data by not only males and females, but also vegetarians and nonvegetarians.

Several statistics are available. The mean, standard deviation, variance, standard error of the mean, and skewness and kurtosis along with their standard errors assume that the data are normally distributed. The median, grouped median, minimum and maximum, range, sum, and number of cases are also available. Also in this chapter are the **First** and **Last** options—for each cell, they display, respectively, the first and last data values encountered in the data file (use Minimum and Maximum for the smallest and largest values, respectively).

Example 1 uses data from the 1993 General Social Survey. The variables recorded for the 1500 respondents include age, education (highest year of school completed), region of primary residence in the United States (Northeast, Midwest, South, West), marital status (married or not married), and voting history (voted or did not vote in 1992). The names of these variables are, respectively, *age*, *educ*, *region4*, *married*, and *vote92*. These data are stored in the file *gss 93 subset*.

Example 2 uses car data from the 1980's. European and Japanese six-cylinder cars are examined using *origin* (European or Japanese) as the grouping variable. The variables are time to accelerate from 0 to 60 miles per hour (in seconds), horsepower, and miles per gallon, respectively named, *accel*, *horse*, and *mpg*. These data are stored in the file *cars*.

Example 1: Cell statistics. The sample sizes, means, and standard deviations of age and education level are requested for cells defined by the grouping variables *region4*, *married*, and *vote92*.

Example 2: Listing cases and descriptive statistics. The car data contain information about four European cars and six Japanese cars. The time to accelerate, horsepower, and miles per gallon are displayed for each car and summarized for the European and the Japanese cars.

Example 1
Cell Statistics

The Case Summaries procedure can be used to explore your data when they are divided into cells based on certain factors. This example evaluates age and education level for married and unmarried people living in four different regions of the United States. Results are further stratified for people who voted in 1992 and those who did not. For exploratory purposes, this example requests the number of people who fall into each cell, as well as the average age, average education level, and standard deviations.

To produce this output, use Select Cases from the Data menu to select cases with *vote92* less than 3 (vote92 < 3). Then, from the menus choose:

Analyze
  Reports
    Case Summaries...

Click *Reset* to restore the dialog box defaults, and then select:

▶ Variables: age, educ

▶ Grouping Variables: region4, married, vote92

☐ Display cases (deselect)

Statistics...

  ▶ Statistics: Number of Cases

  ▶ Cell Statistics: Mean, Standard Deviation, Number of Cases

 From the Pivot Table menus choose:

Pivot
  Pivoting Trays

Drag *Statistics* from the row tray to the column tray.

To bold the totals, right-click the *Total* row label, and from the pop-up menu choose:

Select
  Data Cells and Labels

Then, from the Formatting toolbar, click the *B* (bold icon). If the Formatting toolbar is not displayed, from the View menu choose *Formatting Toolbar*.

Case Summaries

Region	Married?	Voting in 1992 Election	Age			Education Level		
			Mean	Std. Deviation	N	Mean	Std. Deviation	N
Northeast	Yes	Voted	49.02	14.20	61	13.75	2.66	61
		Did Not Vote	49.67	15.32	9	12.78	3.56	9
		Total	49.10	14.23	70	13.63	2.78	70
	No	Voted	50.35	16.67	37	13.70	3.37	37
		Did Not Vote	43.00	18.63	21	11.81	3.04	21
		Total	47.69	17.61	58	13.02	3.35	58
	Total	Voted	49.52	15.11	98	13.73	2.93	98
		Did Not Vote	45.00	17.71	30	12.10	3.18	30
		Total	48.46	15.80	128	13.35	3.05	128
Midwest	Yes	Voted	46.04	13.91	99	13.67	2.43	99
		Did Not Vote	38.00	11.39	22	12.41	3.02	22
		Total	44.58	13.80	121	13.44	2.58	121
	No	Voted	49.54	22.17	61	13.19	2.87	62
		Did Not Vote	39.50	21.26	32	12.28	2.28	32
		Total	46.09	22.27	93	12.88	2.71	94
	Total	Voted	47.38	17.54	160	13.48	2.61	161
		Did Not Vote	38.89	17.79	54	12.33	2.58	54
		Total	45.23	17.95	214	13.20	2.65	215
South	Yes	Voted	51.01	15.11	91	13.30	3.64	91
		Did Not Vote	41.46	15.46	39	11.00	3.78	39
		Total	48.15	15.78	130	12.61	3.82	130
	No	Voted	53.04	19.50	69	12.88	3.24	69
		Did Not Vote	51.59	22.07	39	10.18	2.98	39
		Total	52.52	20.37	108	11.91	3.39	108
	Total	Voted	51.89	17.11	160	13.12	3.47	160
		Did Not Vote	46.53	19.60	78	10.59	3.41	78
		Total	50.13	18.10	238	12.29	3.64	238
West	Yes	Voted	48.80	15.60	60	14.53	3.16	60
		Did Not Vote	44.50	11.25	14	12.93	3.66	10
		Total	47.99	14.92	74	14.12	3.22	73
	No	Voted	47.62	18.37	56	13.30	3.07	56
		Did Not Vote	54.12	24.33	17	11.31	3.05	16
		Total	49.14	19.93	73	12.86	3.15	72
	Total	Voted	48.23	16.93	116	13.94	3.17	116
		Did Not Vote	49.77	19.88	31	11.72	2.95	29
		Total	48.56	17.53	147	13.50	3.24	145
Total	Yes	Voted	48.61	14.72	311	13.74	3.03	311
		Did Not Vote	41.94	14.03	84	11.76	3.46	83
		Total	47.19	14.81	395	13.32	3.22	394
	No	Voted	50.28	19.55	223	13.21	3.11	224
		Did Not Vote	46.78	22.10	109	11.29	2.91	108
		Total	49.13	20.46	332	12.58	3.17	332
	Total	Voted	49.31	16.91	534	13.52	3.07	535
		Did Not Vote	44.67	19.12	193	11.49	3.16	191
		Total	48.08	17.63	727	12.99	3.22	726

Case Summaries. Many observations can be made about these results from the output table. The output table consists of five panels—one for each region, plus one at the bottom, where the values of region are collapsed into one sample. If you are primarily interested in who votes and who does not, you could focus on voters and nonvoters. The panel at the very bottom of the output table reveals that the average age of voters is 49.31, while the average age of nonvoters is 44.67. Among the married people sampled, 311 voted and 84 did not; among the unmarried, 224 voted and 109 did not. Voters and nonvoters also differ in average education level. The average education level of voters is higher than that of nonvoters in all four regions of the country. Overall, the average education level of voters is 13.52, and the average education level of nonvoters is 11.49.

The four regions of the country can be examined to determine which region had the highest percentage of voters. In the Northeast, 77% of the people sampled voted, and 23% did not. In the Midwest, 75% of the people sampled voted, and 25% did not. The people sampled in the South had the lowest percentage of voters (67%), while those sampled in the West had the highest percentage (79%). Overall, the people sampled in the West also had the highest average education level (13.50).

Notice that the *gss 93 subset* data consist of 1500 cases. The bottom panel of the output table reveals that only 727 cases were available for age and 726 for education level. More than half of the cases are missing. The region variable accounts for most of the missing values; it has 743 missing cases.

Example 2
Listing Cases and Descriptive Statistics

Sometimes it is desirable not only to obtain descriptive statistics for subgroups but also to list the cases that fall into each subgroup. This example examines car data containing information about 10 foreign cars. The case number of each car is listed, along with the country of origin (Japan or Europe), the time to accelerate from 0 to 60 miles per hour (in seconds), horsepower, and miles per gallon.

To produce this output, use Select Cases from the Data menu to select cases with *origin* equal to 2 or 3 and *cylinder* equal to 2 ((origin = 2 | origin = 3) & cylinder = 2). In the Case Summaries dialog box, click *Reset* to restore the defaults, and then select:

▸ Variables: accel horse mpg

▸ Grouping Variables: origin

☑ Display cases

    ☐ Limit cases to first 100 (deselect)

    ☑ Show only valid cases

    ☑ Show case numbers

Statistics...

    ▸ Statistics: Number of Cases

    ▸ Cell Statistics: Mean, Number of Cases

Case Summaries

			Case Number	Time to accelerate from 0 to 60 mph (sec)	Horsepower	Miles per gallon
Origin of car	Japanese	1	131	14	122	20
		2	218	16	108	19
		3	249	15	97	22
		4	341	11	132	33
		5	370	13	116	25
		6	371	14	120	24
		Total	Mean	13.55	115.83	23.88
			N	6	6	6
	European	1	219	17	120	17
		2	283	14	125	17
		3	285	16	133	16
		4	369	20	76	31
		Total	Mean	16.43	113.50	20.10
			N	4	4	4
	Total	Mean		14.70	114.90	22.37
		N		10	10	10

Case Summaries. Here, data for 10 makes of cars are grouped by the origin of the car (Japanese or European). The case numbers for the European cars are 219, 283, 285, and 369 and can be used to look up which European cars are listed. They are, respectively, Mercedes-Benz 280, Volvo 264GL, Peugeot 604SL, and Volvo Diesel. Of these four cars, the Volvo 264GL appears to accelerate the fastest (14 seconds), while the Peugeot 604SL has the most horsepower (133). The Volvo Diesel gets the best gas mileage by far (31 mpg).

The European cars can also be compared to the Japanese cars. On average, the Japanese cars accelerate faster, have more horsepower, and get better gas mileage.

The Case Summaries procedure is useful for exploring and comparing descriptive statistics for subgroups. Case Summaries also allows you to list cases. With large data sets, it is useful to display only the first 10 or first 100 cases. You can limit the number of cases that are displayed by selecting *Display cases* and *Limit cases to first*.

7 Using Means to Obtain Within-Cell Descriptive Statistics

Many of the descriptive statistics introduced in the Frequencies and Explore chapters are revisited here for cells or subgroups of cases defined by the cross-classification of levels of two or more grouping variables. (Notice that you can request statistics for dependent variables within subgroups of a *single* grouping variable but that this is better accomplished in Explore, where graphical displays are provided with the descriptors.)

More than a dozen statistics are available, including those that assume that the data follow a normal distribution (mean, standard deviation, variance, standard error of the mean, skewness, and kurtosis). The median, grouped median, and minimum and maximum values are also available. You may also find the **First** and **Last** options useful—for each cell, they display, respectively, the first and last data values encountered in the file (use Minimum and Maximum for the smallest and largest values).

The Means procedure optionally provides a one-way analysis of variance with the eta statistic, and also, when the levels of the independent variable are ordered, a test of linearity, multiple R, and R^2.

The examples in this chapter use data from the 1993 General Social Survey conducted by the National Opinion Research Center. Information available for 1500 or so respondents includes age, voting history (voted or did not vote in 1992), dwelling (owns or rents), education (no degree or college degree), income (coded from 1 to 21), and political views (categories ranging from *Extremely liberal* to *Extremely conservative*). The short names for these variables are, respectively, *age*, *vote92*, *dwelown*, *degree2*, *rincome91*, and *polviews*. Numbers are used to code all six variables, but the Means procedure does allow short strings for independent variables. These data are stored in the file *gss 93 subset*.

Example 1: Descriptive statistics for cells defined by three factors. Age and income are the dependent variables. The means of these variables, their standard errors, and sample sizes are requested for cells defined by the cross-classification of the variables *degree2*, *dwelown*, and *vote92*.

Example 2: A one-way analysis of variance with test of linearity. The analysis of variance illustrated in Chapter 9, Example 1 is repeated here. The problem is to test whether average age differs according to political view. Because the categories of *polviews* (the grouping variable), are ordered, a test of linearity is requested. The eta statistic is also requested.

Example 1
Descriptive Statistics for Cells Defined by Three Factors

In Chapter 5, Example 4, where the use of the odds ratio is described, home owners were found to be roughly three times more likely to vote than renters. A researcher interested in voting patterns would not stop with these results and would want to consider other factors. Are home owners older than renters and thus more settled and concerned about their community? Are they more secure financially? Does education make a difference?

In this example, the same cells are defined to compute the odds ratio, but *degree2* (does or does not have a college degree) is also used to stratify the cases further. In addition to counting the number of people who fall into each cell, you request their average age and average income score. While not a smooth continuous variable, *rincom91* has 21 ordered codes that serve to make the distribution of income more symmetric than the actual income values would be (that is, the lowest codes increase in increments of $1,000; middle values, in increments of $2,500; higher values, in increments of $10,000 and, finally, $15,000). This provides a quick, rough impression of whether any of the factors should be pursued more carefully.

The variable *degree2* is included to help clarify how independent (grouping) variables define cells. In the following SPSS dialog box instructions, *degree2* is selected as the independent variable for layer 1; *dwelown,* for layer 2; and *vote92,* for layer 3. This specifies that their levels are cross-classified. If all three variables were selected at layer 1, SPSS would report statistics for each of them separately (that is, they would not be crossed).

To produce this output, use Select Cases from the Data menu to select cases with *vote92* less than 3 and *dwelown* less than 3 (vote92 < 3 & dwelown < 3). Then, from the menus choose:

Analyze
  Compare Means
    Means...

Click *Reset* to restore the dialog box defaults, and then select:

▶ Dependent List: age, rincom91

▶ Independent List: degree2

Click *Next*.

▶ Independent List: dwelown

Click *Next*.

▶ Independent List: vote92

Options...

▶ Statistics: Standard Deviation, Number of Cases

▶ Cell Statistics: Std Error of Mean, Number of Cases

 Drag *Statistics* from the row tray to the column tray.

Report

DEGREE2	DWELOWN	VOTE92	AGE Mean	AGE Std. Error of Mean	AGE N	RINCOM91 Mean	RINCOM91 Std. Error of Mean	RINCOM91 N
No College degree	owns home	voted	52.26	.93	352	13.30	.38	210
		did not vote	46.38	1.57	123	11.00	.64	80
		Total	50.74	.81	475	12.67	.33	290
	pays rent	voted	40.73	1.47	129	10.60	.55	90
		did not vote	39.97	1.64	128	9.42	.60	74
		Total	40.35	1.10	257	10.07	.41	164
	Total	voted	49.17	.82	481	12.49	.32	300
		did not vote	43.11	1.15	251	10.24	.44	154
		Total	47.09	.67	732	11.73	.26	454
College degree	owns home	voted	46.66	1.15	154	15.97	.43	127
		did not vote	40.17	4.68	12	13.50	1.85	10
		Total	46.19	1.12	166	15.79	.42	137
	pays rent	voted	40.45	2.38	38	12.89	.90	35
		did not vote	31.58	2.15	12	15.40	1.38	10
		Total	38.32	1.94	50	13.44	.77	45
	Total	voted	45.43	1.04	192	15.30	.40	162
		did not vote	35.88	2.67	24	14.45	1.14	20
		Total	44.37	.99	216	15.21	.38	182
Total	owns home	voted	50.55	.74	506	14.31	.29	337
		did not vote	45.83	1.49	135	11.28	.61	90
		Total	49.56	.67	641	13.67	.27	427
	pays rent	voted	40.66	1.25	167	11.24	.48	125
		did not vote	39.25	1.52	140	10.13	.59	84
		Total	40.02	.97	307	10.79	.37	209
	Total	voted	48.10	.66	673	13.48	.26	462
		did not vote	42.48	1.08	275	10.72	.42	174
		Total	46.47	.57	948	12.72	.23	636

Report. Results here are separated into three panels: the first for respondents with no college degree, the second for those who do have a degree, and the last for both groups combined.

The last panel has the same cells as in the odds ratio example (Chapter 5, Example 4). In the column labeled *N*, you can see that 506 home owners voted and 135 did not. Among the renters, 167 voted, and 140 did not. In the table on p. 79, the counts are the same except for the voting home owners (509 versus 506 here). The difference is due to the fact that *degree2* is now included, and it has missing values. Notice that the cell sizes are considerably smaller for *rincom91* than for *age*.

On the average, the home owners are 49.56 years old and have an income score of 13.67, while the renters are almost 10 years younger (the total *pays rent* mean is 40.02) and have a lower income (10.79). Within each group, the difference between voters and nonvoters is less.

Overall, the college graduates are slightly younger than those without degrees (44.37 versus 47.09 years), but their income score is certainly higher (15.21 versus 11.73). Notice that the standard errors for these means, 0.38 and 0.26, are small).

Looking within the four groups formed by *degree2* and *dwelown*, the voters are older and have higher incomes than the nonvoters in each group, except for the college graduates who pay rent. In that group, the voters earn less than the nonvoters (12.89 versus 15.40). The sample size for the nonvoters, however, is 10, the smallest among all the cells.

Example 2
A One-Way Analysis of Variance with Test of Linearity

In Chapter 9, Example 1, significant age differences are identified among groups of people with differing political orientations. In Chapter 9, Example 3, the differences in age are defined more clearly: average age increases linearly across groups ordered from *Extremely liberal* to *Extremely conservative*. A test of a linear contrast verifies this.

The significant linear contrast indicates that the slope of a line through the ordered means differs from 0. Here, you repeat the same one-way analysis of variance, adding a **test of linearity** (to determine whether or not the means for the groups are located on a straight line).

To produce this output, use Select Cases on the Data menu to make sure all cases are selected. In the Means dialog box, click *Reset* to restore the dialog box defaults, and then select:

▶ Dependent List: age
▶ Independent List: polviews

Options...

▶ Statistics: Standard Deviation, Number of Cases

▶ Cell Statistics: Std Error of Mean, Number of Cases

Statistics for First Layer
☑Test for linearity

 On the Report table, drag *Statistics* from the row tray to the column tray.

Report

AGE

POLVIEWS	Mean	Std. Error of Mean	N
Extremely liberal	39.07	2.91	30
Liberal	45.27	1.25	162
Slightly liberal	42.06	1.18	192
Moderate	45.53	.76	527
Slightly conservative	44.43	1.06	247
Conservative	50.76	1.18	240
Extremely conservative	54.55	2.77	40
Total	45.84	.46	1438

Report. The average age for respondents in the seven political orientation groups ranges from 39.07 to 54.55 years. The analysis-of-variance table that follows tests whether there is a significant difference among these means.

Measures of Association

	R	R Squared	Eta	Eta Squared
Age of Respondent * Think of Self as Liberal or Conservative	.136	.018	.177	.031

Measures of Association. When squared, the eta statistic measures the variability in *age* accounted for by the grouping factor *polviews*. Eta is the ratio of the between-groups sum of squares to the total sum of squares (13556.868 / 431147.21). For this statistic, the categories of the grouping variable need not be ordered; therefore, it is often used in analysis of variance. Here, the categories of *polviews* explain 3.1% (0.031) of the variance of *age*.

Multiple R and R^2 are statistics used in linear regression, so they are appropriate only when the categories of the grouping variable are ordered. When there is only one independent variable, R is the simple correlation between *age* and *polviews* (expressed as the codes 1 through 7). R^2 is the square of this correlation value and ranges from 0 to 1. If there is no *linear* relation between the dependent and independent variable, R^2 is 0 or very small. If all the observations fall on the regression line, R^2 is 1.

For these data, both goodness-of-fit measures are pretty dismal. Be aware that when sample sizes are as large as these, it is easier to detect significance differences in an analysis of variance. While the differences in means here are highly significant, they are not very meaningful in a practical sense. In the Descriptives table on p. 124, notice that the age spread in all *polview* groups is great, ranging from 18 to 80 years.

Test of Linearity

It is possible for the overall trend in means across ordered categories to follow a line with a significant slope, and, at the same time, for some of the means to drift away from the line. For example, in addition to a significant linear effect, there could be a significant quadratic effect.

Figure 7.1   A linear and a quadratic pattern of means

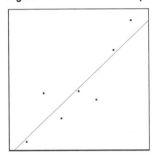 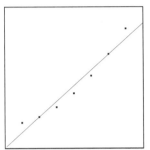

The means for the political groups in this example are shown on the left with the line of best fit. A hypothetical set of means that exhibits both a linear and a quadratic effect is displayed on the right. The quadratic effect for the data in the left plot is tested in Chapter 9, Example 3, and, not surprisingly, is found nonsignificant. There can be other types of departures. The ANOVA table that follows displays results for the test of linearity.

ANOVA Table

			Sum of Squares	df	Mean Square	F	Sig.
AGE * POLVIEWS	Between Groups	(Combined)	13556.868	6	2259.478	7.743	.000
		Linearity	7954.247	1	7954.247	27.258	.000
		Deviation from Linearity	5602.620	5	1120.524	3.840	.002
	Within Groups		417590.35	1431	291.817		
	Total		431147.21	1437			

ANOVA Table. The highly significant F of 7.743 (with a p value $< .0005$) indicates that there is a difference among the seven means. The lines labeled *Linearity* and *Deviation from Linearity* are included for the test of linearity.

The linearity sum of squares is obtained from a simple linear regression of *age* on *polviews* (coded 1 to 7)—that is, the sum of squares obtained by fitting a straight line. The F for linearity (27.258) is the same as that computed for the weighted linear contrast in Chapter 9, Example 3.

The *Deviation from Linearity* sum of squares is the difference between the between-groups sum of squares and the linearity sum of squares. The **test of linearity** is the deviation-from-linearity mean square (1120.524) divided by the within-groups mean square (291.817), or $F = 3.84$, with a p value of 0.002. Thus, you can reject the null hypothesis that the group means are located on a straight line.

A more intuitive way of understanding the F for the test of linearity is that the numerator sums of squares can be formed by:

- Taking the difference between each *age* group mean and the corresponding point on the estimated regression line for the group (called $\hat{y}$ or the predicted value of the *age* for each *polview* code).

- Squaring each difference and multiplying by its group size.

- Summing these quantities and dividing by $(k - 2)$ or $(7 - 2)$.

The denominator is the usual pooled-variance estimate from the analysis of variance (the within-groups mean square).

8 Using T Tests to Compare Means

SPSS provides *t* tests, including two-sample (independent), paired (dependent), and one-sample *t* tests. In Chapter 5, you tested hypotheses about the independence of factors in a two-way table. The data were counts. Here, you test hypotheses about means of quantitative variables. You test whether:

- The mean of a single variable for subjects in one group differs from that in another (an independent-samples *t* test).
- The mean of casewise differences between two variables differs from 0 (a paired *t* test).
- The mean of a single variable differs from an hypothesized value (a one-sample *t* test).

Diagrams of the data structures for these tests should make their uses more clear. In the following rectangles, imagine that the rows are cases and the columns are variables. Under each figure is the appropriate null hypothesis.

Figure 8.1   Organizing data for t tests

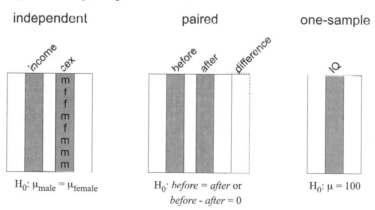

independent

H_0: $\mu_{male} = \mu_{female}$

paired

H_0: *before = after* or
before - after = 0

one-sample

H_0: $\mu = 100$

For the independent-samples *t* test, the values of the variable *income* are stored in a single column, and SPSS uses values of a grouping variable (*sex*) to separate the cases into two groups. SPSS provides three ways to define the groups: using two numbers, text values of a short string variable, or a cut point that separates the data values into two sets. For each case in a paired *t* test, SPSS computes the differences between values of two variables (columns) and tests if the average differs from 0. For the one-sample *t* test, values of a single variable are compared against a constant you specify.

Each hypothesis is an assertion or conjecture about the parameters (or parameter) of a population. Notice that the null hypothesis is usually set up to see whether it can be rejected. This—at first glance—backwards approach is not unique to statistics. In criminal proceedings, the assumption that the accused is not guilty is a null hypothesis. The criminal is assumed innocent unless his or her guilt is established beyond a reasonable doubt.

The examples in this chapter use data from the *world95* file. Each case has information about a country, including the percentage of the population living in cities, average daily calorie intake, climate, fertility, predominant religion, last year's increase in population, and female and male life expectancy.

Example 1: Two-sample t tests with numeric codes for climate. The default output is displayed for two tests—the pooled-variance *t* test is appropriate for one, the separate-variance test for the other. The variable in the first test is *urban,* percentage of the population living in the city, and the variable in the second test is *calories*. Countries in the temperate region form one group; countries in the tropical region form the other group.

Example 2: Two-sample t tests with short string values for religion. Average fertility is compared for Catholic and Muslim countries. Transpose Rows and Columns on the Pivot menu is used to alter the layout of test results.

Example 3: Two-sample t tests using a cut point to form groups. Measures of population growth are studied. A cut point of 1% on a variable measuring population increase is used to split the cases into two groups. Tests of five variables are requested and results for the separate-variance *t* tests (pooled-variance results are omitted) are displayed in a compact table. Because results of several tests are scanned simultaneously, the problem of multiple tests is discussed, and the level for confidence intervals is set to provide an overall 95% level. Some data are missing, so listwise deletion is requested in order to use the same cases for each test.

Example 4: Paired comparison (or dependent) t test. The variable female life expectancy is compared with male life expectancy. In order to have a homogeneous sample, the Select Cases feature is used to select a subset of cases from the *world95* file. Only the OECD (Organization for Economic Cooperation and Development) countries are used.

Example 5: A one-sample t test. The average birth-to-death ratio for the sample is tested against the hypothesized value of 1.25 (five births for every four deaths). The Split File feature is used to produce results within strata and collect them into one display. The level of the confidence interval is specified to allow for the fact that tests are carried out for several groups simultaneously.

Many of the features illustrated apply to all three types of tests (including maintaining the same sample size across tests when data are missing, adjusting probabilities as protection for the problem of multiple tests, specifying levels for confidence intervals, and manipulating pivot tables). Therefore, if the test in which you are interested appears in a later example, you may need to refer to an earlier example for an explanation of some features.

Multiple testing. SPSS allows you to request tests for several variables with one specification (and also to request tests using the Split File feature for each of several subpopulations or stratum within your sample). The p value (or significance) associated with the t test (regardless of whether the test is for two-groups, paired values, or one group) assumes you are making only one test. The probability of finding a significant difference by chance alone increases rapidly with the number of tests. So, we caution you against requesting tests for many variables (or subpopulations within the sample) and reporting only those that appear significant.

One solution to the multiple testing problem is to make a Bonferroni correction to the probability associated with each test by multiplying it by the number of tests executed. That is, if the printed probabilities for three tests are 0.001, 0.010, and 0.035, the adjusted probabilities would be 0.003, 0.030, and 0.105. Therefore, you would be unable to report that results for the third test are significant at the 5% level.

With respect to confidence intervals, you make the adjustment before SPSS computes the interval. In specifying the level of confidence, divide the alpha level by the number of comparisons made (for a 95% or 0.95 confidence interval, alpha is 0.05). For example, if you want the overall significance level for five intervals to be 95%, divide 0.05 by 5. This is 0.01, so you should request $(1 - 0.01)$ or a 99% interval in order to report intervals appropriate for all five tests at an overall 95% level.

Example 1
Two-Sample T Tests with Numeric Codes for Climate

One of the most common situations encountered in statistical practice is that of comparing means for two groups. For example, does the average response for the treatment group differ from that for the control group? Ideally, subjects are randomly assigned to the two groups, so that any differences in response are due to the treatment (or lack of) and not to other factors. This is not the case in this example because the countries are not randomly assigned to have one type of climate or another. In such situations, a researcher should explore carefully to ensure that differences in other factors are not masking or falsely enhancing the difference in means.

Does life for people in temperate zone countries differ from that in the tropics? In the latter region, do fewer people live in cities? And do they consume fewer calories than those in cooler regions? You use the *world95* data to test whether the average percentage of population living in cities differs for countries in temperate or tropical regions, and whether the average calorie intake differs in the two regions:

$$H_{o}: \mu_{\text{temperate}} = \mu_{\text{tropic}}$$

In other words, do the two sample means come from populations with equal means?

The data file has one case for each country with its percentage of city dwellers (*urban*), average daily calorie intake (*calories*), and a numeric code that identifies its climate (*climate*). The codes for *climate* range from 1 (desert) through 10 (arctic). The climate for countries in the region between the tropic of Cancer and the tropic of Capricorn is classified as tropical (code 5) and that for countries in the region between the tropic of Cancer and the Arctic Circle or between the tropic of Capricorn and the Antarctic Circle as temperate (code 8). Here are box-and-whisker displays of *urban* and *calories* for the two groups of countries:

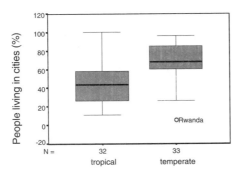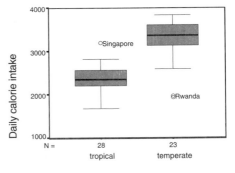

The horizontal line in the middle of each distribution marks the median of the *urban* or *calories* values. Even though a *t* test compares means, this display is still useful for checking whether the spreads of the two groups differ (to see if the equal variance assumption is violated) and whether there are outliers (extreme values) that influence the mean and inflate the standard deviation.

A data analyst likes to see that the median is approximately in the center of each box and that the spreads of the boxes (that is, the central 50% of each distribution) are similar. Here both variables have outliers—for *calories*, Singapore makes the mean for the *tropical* group larger than its median and Rwanda and Burundi pull the mean for the *temperate* group well below its median. Thus, the outliers serve to move the means closer together than medians, and their presence might make us fail to identify true differences. However, this does not happen in this example. It is possible for the reverse to be true—the presence of one or a few outliers can cause the means to differ more than the medians, making the test results appear more significant than the bulk of the data indicate.

To produce this output, from the menus choose:

Analyze
  Compare Means
    Independent-Samples T Test...

Click *Reset* to restore the dialog box defaults, and then select:

▶ Test Variable(s): urban, calories
▶ Grouping Variable: climate

Define Groups...
    ⊙ Use specified values:
    Group 1: 5
    Group 2: 8

 To hide the dimension label, *Predominant climate*, on the Group Statistics table, select it, and from the menus choose:

View
  Hide Dimension Labels

Group Statistics

		N	Mean	Std. Deviation	Std. Error Mean
People living in cities (%)	tropical	32	44.94	24.07	4.25
	temperate	33	66.36	23.29	4.05
Daily calorie intake	tropical	28	2374.93	308.81	50.00
	temperate	23	3216.65	529.42	110.39

Group Statistics. The average percentage of people living in cities for the 32 countries in the tropics is 44.94%. This is considerably lower than 66.36% for the 33 countries in the temperate zone. (In the Independent Samples Test (part 2) on p. 110, the difference in these two means is displayed with a confidence interval for the difference.) The standard deviations (*Std. Deviation*) for the two groups are quite similar (24.07 versus 23.29), as are the standard errors (*Std. Error Mean*).

The average daily calorie intake for the 28 countries in the tropics is 2374.93 calories, while the intake for the 23 countries in the temperate region averages 3216.65 calories. The standard deviation for the temperate countries (529.42) is 70% larger than for the tropical countries (308.81). The Rwanda and Burundi outliers inflate the temperate value.

Notice that the sample sizes for *urban* and *calories* differ. The test results for *urban* include 14 more countries than those for *calories*. In Example 3, the *listwise* option is used to maintain the same countries (cases) across tests.

The Independent Samples Test table has been broken into two tables so that it is easier to read. Each part is discussed separately.

Independent Samples Test

		Levene's Test for Equality of Variances		t-test for Equality of Means		
		F	Sig.	t	df	Sig. (2-tailed)
People living in cities (%)	Equal variances assumed	.046	.832	-3.648	63	.001
	Equal variances not assumed			-3.646	62.743	.001
Daily calorie intake	Equal variances assumed	5.180	.027	-7.082	49	.000
	Equal variances not assumed			-6.741	33.861	.000

Independent Samples Test (part 1). By default, when SPSS prints the Independent Samples Test table, it splits it into two panels. The first part is described here, the second part on p. 110.

Levene's Test for Equality of Variances is displayed first. Use it to test if the *spread* of the groups differs. The null hypothesis is that the two population variances (not the means) are equal. If the observed significance level for this test is low (for example, less than 0.05), you should use the separate-variance t test for means. Here the F statistic for *urban* is 0.046 with a significance (or p value) of 0.832 supporting the use of the pooled-variance t test. The F statistic for the **Levene test** is obtained by computing a one-way analysis of variance on the absolute deviations of each case from its group mean. Some older textbooks present Bartlett's equality of variances test, but it is sensitive to departures from normality.

The F statistic for *calories* is 5.180 with a significance of 0.027, indicating that the hypothesis of equal variances is rejected. Thus, it is not appropriate to use the pooled (*Equal variances assumed*) test for comparing means.

Two tests are computed for comparing group means. The first, labeled *Equal variances assumed* (often the first two-sample t test introduced in elementary textbooks), is called the **pooled-variance t test.** It assumes that the population variances for the two groups are equal—that is, that the distributions have the same shape. The second test, as its label *Equal variances not assumed* indicates, does not require equal variances and is called the **separate-variance t test.** Here are the formulas for the two statistics:

Pooled Variance

$$t = \frac{\bar{x}_1 - \bar{x}_2}{\sqrt{s_p^2 \left(\frac{1}{n_1} + \frac{1}{n_2} \right)}}$$

Separate Variance

$$t = \frac{\bar{x}_1 - \bar{x}_2}{\sqrt{\frac{s_1^2}{n_1} + \frac{s_2^2}{n_2}}}$$

where:

$\bar{x}_i$ = mean of group i
n_i = number of observations in group i
s_i^2 = sample variance in group i

$$s_p^2 = \frac{(n_1 - 1)s_1^2 + (n_2 - 1)s_2^2}{n_1 + n_2 - 2}$$

The degrees of freedom for the pooled tests are $(n_1 + n_2 - 2)$. The degrees of freedom for the separate-variance test are computed—the formula involves s_1, s_2, n_1, and n_2. To obtain one-tailed probabilities, divide the t probabilities by 2.

Which test should you use? Consider the results of the Levene test and scan graphical displays for similar shapes. Notice that as sample variances differ more, the degrees of freedom computed for the separate-variance test become smaller. In many situations, data transformations may remedy the problem. See the population variable in Chapter 4, Example 4.

Using the pooled-variance (*Equal variances assumed*) t test for *urban*, you determine that the sample means of 44.94% and 66.36% do not come from populations with equal means. The means differ markedly. The t statistic is –3.648 with 63 degrees of freedom (*df*) and has an associated probability (*Significance*) of 0.001. This probability is often called p value. From the size of the means, you conclude that countries in the temperate region have a significantly larger proportion of city dwellers than do countries in the tropical region.

Since, for *calories*, the Levene test was rejected, the separate-variance (*Equal variances not assumed*) t test should be used. The results are $t = 6.741$ with 33.861 degrees of freedom (*df*) and a p value (*Sig. (2-tailed)*) of < 0.0005 (be wary of saying a probability is 0). On the average, people in temperate countries consume more calories than those in tropical zones. Compare the degrees of freedom for the pooled- and separate-variance tests (49 versus 33.861). You pay a penalty for unequal variances—diminished degrees of freedom mean that your effective sample size decreases. Here, by using the separate-variance test, you have essentially decreased the sample size by 30%.

Independent Samples Test

		t-test for Equality of Means			
		Mean Difference	Std. Error Difference	95% Confidence Interval of the Mean	
				Lower	Upper
People living in cities (%)	Equal variances assumed	-21.43	5.87	-33.16	-9.69
	Equal variances not assumed	-21.43	5.88	-33.17	-9.68
Daily calorie intake	Equal variances assumed	-841.72	118.86	-1080.58	-602.87
	Equal variances not assumed	-841.72	124.87	-1095.52	-587.92

Independent Samples Test (part 2). In the Group Statistics table on p. 107, the means for the tropical and temperate regions are, respectively, 44.94% and 66.36% for *urban* and 2374.9 and 3216.7 for *calories*. The difference in these means (*Mean Difference*) is displayed here: –21.43% for *urban* and –841.72 for *calories*. The standard error for each difference (*Std. Error Difference*) is displayed in the next column. These standard errors are used to construct confidence intervals for the difference in means. This interval is labeled *95% Confidence Interval of the Mean*. In Chapter 2, Example 3, the steps for constructing a confidence interval are described.

Because of the results for the Levene test, use the *Equal variances assumed* standard error of the difference (5.87) for *urban* and the *Equal variances not assumed* value (124.87) for *calories*. The pooled-variance 95% confidence interval for the difference in *urban* means ranges from –33.16 to –9.69. (To make the interval more readable, place temperate first, writing the difference in means as 21.43% with an interval ranging from 9.69% to 33.16%.) Zero is not in the interval—if it were, you could not reject the null hypothesis of equal means. The separate-variance 95% confidence interval for the difference in *calorie* means ranges from –1095.52 to –587.92 (or 587.92 to 1095.52 for a mean difference of 841.72). Notice that when separate-variance estimates are necessary, there is a loss in precision—the interval that assumes equal variances is 30 units shorter than the one that does not.

Example 2
Two-Sample T Tests with String Values for Religion

Who tends to have more children? People in countries that are predominantly Catholic or Muslim? This example compares fertility rates (average number of children per family) for Catholic and Muslim countries. The grouping variable *religion* has string values 'Catholic' and 'Muslim'. The variable *religion* actually contains codes for ten religions, but no special processing is needed to omit the other codes—the Independent-Samples T Test allows you to enter strings directly for your groups of interest.

To produce this output, in the Independent-Samples T Test dialog box, click *Reset* to restore the dialog box defaults, and then select:

▶ Test Variable(s): fertIlty
▶ Grouping Variable: religion

Define Groups...
   Group 1: Catholic
   Group 2: Muslim

 To hide the dimension label, *Predominant religion*, on the Group Statistics table, select it, and from the menus choose:

View
  Hide Dimension Labels

On the Independent Samples Test table, from the menus choose:

Pivot
  Transpose Rows and Columns

Group Statistics

		N	Mean	Std. Deviation	Std. Error Mean
Fertility: average number of kids	Catholic	41	3.138	1.687	.263
	Muslim	26	5.204	1.514	.297

Group Statistics. In the 41 countries where Catholicism is the predominant religion, the average number of children is roughly 3.1; in the 26 Muslim countries, the average is 5.2 children. Could these sample means come from populations with equal means?

Independent Samples Test

		Fertility: average number of kids	
		Equal variances assumed	Equal variances not assumed
Levene's Test for Equality of Variances	F	.254	
	Sig.	.616	
t-test for Equality of Means	t	-5.081	-5.207
	df	65	57.564
	Sig. (2-tailed)	.000	.000
	Mean Difference	-2.066	-2.066
	Std. Error Difference	.407	.397
95% Confidence Interval of the Mean	Lower	-2.878	-2.861
	Upper	-1.254	-1.272

Independent Samples Test (after pivoting). Before looking at the *t* tests, check the results of the Levene test to see if the assumption of equal variances has been violated. Here, $F = 0.254$ with an associated probability (*Sig.*) of 0.616 indicates that the hypothesis of equal variances is not rejected. Therefore, you use the *Equal variances assumed t* test results, finding that the fertility averages do differ significantly ($t = -5.081$ with 65 degrees of freedom and significance < 0.0005).

The *Mean Difference* or average difference in the fertility rate is -2.066 children (on the average, families in Muslim countries tend to have two more children than families in Catholic countries). The confidence interval for this difference extends from -2.878 to -1.254 (or 1.254 to 2.878 children).

Example 3
Two-Sample T Tests Using a Cut Point to Form Groups

For each country in the *world95* data, the values of the variable *pop_incr* indicate how much the country's population has grown during the previous year, and the variable *b_to_d* contains the ratio of its birth rate to death rate. Somewhere you read that the ratio of births to deaths must exceed 1.25 (five or more births for every four deaths) for a population to grow. You wonder if countries with no growth or very little growth (for example, less than 1%) do indeed have significantly smaller birth-to-death ratios than those with large increases in population.

You specify 1.0 as a cut point to split the countries into two groups (those with less than a 1% increase in population and those with an increase of 1% or more), and then test if the average birth-to-death ratios differ for the two groups of countries. Additionally, you examine birth rates and death rates to see if countries with little increase in population differ from those with greater growth. In other words, are higher birth rates or lower death rates contributing to higher rates of population increase? Also, how about the fertility rates and population densities for the two groups?

Because you are exploring possible differences among five variables, you would like to use the same countries (that is, the same sample size) from test to test by excluding all data for any country that has one or more values missing across the five variables. This is called **listwise** deletion.

When results of five tests are viewed simultaneously, you need protection against multiple testing (see "Multiple testing" in the introduction of this chapter). Here you adjust the *t* test probabilities after they are displayed (see the discussion of the Independent Samples Test on p. 115) and specify 99% as the level for confidence intervals. Dividing alpha = 0.05 by 5, the number of variables tested, results in 0.01. Thus, you request a 99% interval $(1.0 - 0.01 = 0.99)$ in order to have five intervals simultaneously covered at the 0.05 level.

To produce this output, in the Independent-Samples T Test dialog box, click *Reset* to restore the dialog box defaults, and then select:

▸ Test Variable(s): b_to_d, birth_rt, death_rt, fertilty, density
▸ Grouping Variable: pop_incr

Define Groups...
⊙ Cut point: 1.0

Options...
Confidence Interval: 99

Missing Values
⊙ Exclude cases listwise

 To hide the dimension label, *Population increase (% per year)*, on the Group Statistics table, select it, and from the menus choose:

View
 Hide Dimension Labels

On the Independent Samples Test table, drag *Assumptions* from the row tray to the layer tray, then change the visible layer from *Equal variances assumed* to *Equal variances not assumed* (by clicking the arrow beside the *Assumptions* pivot icon).

Group Statistics

		N	Mean	Std. Deviation	Std. Error Mean
Birth to death ratio	>= 1.0	70	4.1891	2.0311	.2428
	< 1.0	37	1.3663	.3576	5.879E-02
Birth rate per 1000 people	>= 1.0	70	32.957	9.859	1.178
	< 1.0	37	13.216	1.734	.285
Death rate per 1000 people	>= 1.0	70	9.36	5.14	.61
	< 1.0	37	10.02	1.62	.27
Fertility: average number of kids	>= 1.0	70	4.499	1.720	.206
	< 1.0	37	1.792	.244	4.009E-02
Number of people / sq. kilometer	>= 1.0	70	167.251	542.120	64.796
	< 1.0	37	264.746	892.003	146.644

Group Statistics. The average birth-to-death ratio for the 37 countries with no population increase or a very small increase is 1.37, while the average ratio is 4.19 for the 70 countries whose population increased by 1% or more. In the Independent Samples Test figure below, you can see that there is a significant difference in these means.

Birth rate is the numerator of each birth-to-death ratio, and death rate is the denominator. The countries with fairly stable populations average 13 births per 1000 people; those that are growing average more than twice as many births (33). The average death rates for the two groups appear similar—9.4 versus 10 deaths per 1000 people. So, it appears that differences in the birth-to-death ratios are due more to birth rates than to death rates. The countries exhibiting growth, not surprisingly, have greater fertility (4.5 children per family versus 1.8 children), and their population is less dense (167 people per square kilometer versus 265 people). Notice, however, that the standard deviations of this last measure are large (542 and 892).

Independent Samples Test

Equal variances not assumed

	t-test for Equality of Means						
						99% Confidence Interval of the Mean	
	t	df	Sig. (2-tailed)	Mean Difference	Std. Error Difference	Lower	Upper
Birth to death ratio	11.301	76.823	.000	2.8228	.2498	2.1630	3.4825
Birth rate per 1000 people	16.283	76.810	.000	19.741	1.212	16.539	22.943
Death rate per 1000 people	-.993	91.177	.323	-.66	.67	-2.42	1.10
Fertility: average number of kids	12.931	74.145	.000	2.708	.209	2.154	3.261
Number of people / sq. kilometer	-.608	50.426	.546	-97.495	160.322	-526.660	331.671

Independent Samples Test. In order to display a compact table, the results for the Levene test and the *Equal variances assumed t* tests have been omitted. The *p* values (*Significance*) for the birth-to-death ratio, birth rate, and fertility are all highly significant (< 0.0005), while those for death rate and population density are not (0.323 and 0.546). Here you are scanning results for five tests simultaneously, so the discussion about "Multiple testing" in the introduction should be considered. The results that are nonsignificant here remain so, and the probabilities for significant results should be multiplied by 5 (the number of tests). How do you multiply 0 by 5.0? The probabilities printed as *.000* are known to be < 0.0005; so you would have to have more than 100 tests before the result of the multiplication could reach 0.05 and larger.

Confidence intervals. The birth-to-death ratio for the growing countries is more than 2.8 units larger than that for the more stable countries (that is, $4.1891 - 1.3663$). The 95% confidence interval for the difference in means (2.8) extends from 2.16 to 3.48. Zero (no difference in means) is not included in the interval, so you reject the hypothesis of equal means. Remember that, because of the multiple testing problem, you requested 99% intervals in order to cover intervals simultaneously for all five variables at the 95% level.

The results of the *t* tests for death rate and population density were not significant and correspondingly, 0 is included in each of their confidence intervals (2.42 to 1.10 and −526.7 to 331.7). The confidence interval for the difference in average birth rate for the two groups extends from 16.5 to 22.9 births and that for fertility extends from 2.2 to 3.3 children.

Example 4
Paired Comparison (or Dependent) T Test

In each two-sample *t* test above, SPSS split the values of a single variable into two groups, computed the average for each group, and compared the averages. For the **paired** (or **dependent**) *t* **test,** the means of two variables (columns) are compared. Often, the study design for this test involves measuring each subject twice: *before* and *after* some kind of treatment or intervention. The paired comparison *t* is used to test if the means of the two measures differ—or, equivalently, whether the average of the differences (of the two values for each case) differs from 0.

This test is also appropriate for a **matched pairs** design where subjects are matched on a variable that is related to the measure studied. The goal is to remove the variability in the measure of interest that is due to the matching variable. For example, in studying a new method for teaching language, you might match each student in the new method class with a student in the traditional program using their grade point average, SAT verbal score, or other measure related to classroom performance. At the end of the term, give both groups of students the same language exam. For each pair of matched students, use the paired *t* test to analyze the difference in their final exam scores. Enter the data for each pair as one case (one variable contains the final score for the experimental group, another variable the final score for his or her matched control). Be sure to give the variables unique names like *expfinal* and *confinal*. If the correlation between the experimental and control group values turns out to be low, the matching has not been effective.

Are females in OECD countries expected to live longer than males? In this example, you use a design where each case has two measures recorded in the same units. Each country (case) in the *world95* file contains a variable with female life expectancy and a variable with male life expectancy. Since the example focuses on a subset of the cases in the *world95* data, you use Select Cases on the Data menu of the Data Editor to request only the cases with code 1 for the variable *region*.

To produce this output, use Select Cases from the Data menu to select cases where *region* equals 1 (region = 1). Then, from the menus choose:

Analyze
  Compare Means
    Paired-Samples T Test...

Click *Reset* to restore the dialog box defaults, and then select:

Variable 1: lifeexpf
Variable 2: lifeexpm
▶ Move the pair to Paired Variables

Paired Samples Statistics

		Mean	N	Std. Deviation	Std. Error Mean
Pair 1	Average female life expectancy	80.10	21	1.18	.26
	Average male life expectancy	73.71	21	1.15	.25

Paired Samples Statistics. In the sample, females in the 21 OECD countries, on the average, are expected to live 80.1 years; the males, 73.7 years.

Paired Samples Correlations

		N	Correlation	Sig.
Pair 1	Average female life expectancy & Average male life expectancy	21	.724	.000

Paired Samples Correlations. The correlation between female and male life expectancy values is 0.724. The associated *p* value (*Sig.*) is very small (< 0.0005), indicating that the correlaton differs significantly from 0—there is a strong linear relation between the female and male values. In matched pairs or case-control designs, the higher the correlation, the greater the advantage in using a paired design rather than a design with two independent groups.

Paired Samples Test

		Paired Differences			95% Confidence Interval of the Difference				
		Mean	Std. Deviation	Std. Error Mean	Lower	Upper	t	df	Sig. (2-tailed)
Pair 1	Average female life expectancy - Average male life expectancy	6.38	.86	.19	5.99	6.77	33.819	20	.000

Paired Samples Test. The *Mean of the Paired Differences* between female and male life expectancy is 6.38 years (80.10 – 73.71). Look back at the sample means to see that it is the females who are expected to live longer. A *95% Confidence Interval of the Difference* extends from 5.99 years to 6.77 years. The *p* value *(Sig. (2-tailed))* associated with the *t* statistic of 33.8 is very small (< 0.0005), indicating that a difference of 6.38 years departs significantly from 0. Females do tend to live longer.

To calculate the *t* statistic by hand, first, for each country, compute the difference between female and male life expectancy; then compute the average of the differences and the standard deviation (SD) of the differences; and finally compute the *t*:

$$t = \frac{\text{average of differences}}{SD / \sqrt{n}}$$

Example 5
A One-Sample T Test

The goal in a **one-sample *t* test** is to test if the mean of a single sample differs from a hypothesized population value. For example, you read that in the U.S., the average IQ is 100 and you know that the average IQ for your coworkers is 127.5. Are your coworkers smarter than the average person in the U.S.? To answer this type of question in SPSS, request a one-sample *t* test to compare the mean of the sample IQ values with the constant 100.

Will countries that are predominantly Catholic maintain a stable population size? In Example 3, you introduced the variable *b_to_d* (the ratio of birth rate to death rate for each country in the *world95* data file) and indicated that for a population to remain stable in size, this ratio should not exceed 1.25 (five births for every four deaths).

This example will illustrate the Split File feature, showing how easy it is to produce results separately for strata within the data file. You ask the same question for countries that are predominantly Muslim and for countries that are Protestant.

The variable *religion* contains string codes that identify 10 religions. You want to request separate results for only three of these religions (*protstnt*, *catholic*, and *muslim*) and use Select Cases on the Data menu of the Data Editor to extract these three groups.

Next you use the Split File feature to stratify the analysis. By clicking *Compare Groups,* results for each group are collected within each output panel rather than displayed separately.

By requesting three tests simultaneously, you encounter the multiple testing problem described in the introduction to these examples. In Example 3, the problem was discussed because five variables were tested—here, you have three groups and use a Bonferroni correction as protection when requesting confidence intervals.

To produce this output, use Select Cases from the Data menu to select cases with *religion* equal to *protstnt, catholic,* or *muslim* (religion = 'Protstnt' | religion = 'Catholic' | religion = 'Muslim'). Use Split File from the Data menu to separate cases into three groups based on *religion*. (Move *religion* into Groups Based on.) Use the Compare groups option to display results in a single table. Then, from the menus choose:

Analyze
  Compare Means
    One-Sample T Test...

Click *Reset* to restore the dialog box defaults, and then select:

▸ Test Variable(s): b_to_d

Test Value: 1.25

Options...
  Confidence Interval: 98.3

One-Sample Statistics

Predominant religion		N	Mean	Std. Deviation	Std. Error Mean
Catholic	Birth to death ratio	41	2.9145	1.7519	.2736
Muslim	Birth to death ratio	27	5.1242	2.6109	.5025
Protstnt	Birth to death ratio	16	1.6526	.5548	.1387

One-Sample Statistics. The average birth-to-death ratios for countries that are predominantly Catholic, Muslim, and Protestant are, respectively, 2.91, 5.12, and 1.65. All are larger than the value 1.25 hypothesized for a stable population. But are any of them significantly larger?

One-Sample Test

Predominant religion		Test Value = 1.25					
		t	df	Sig. (2-tailed)	Mean Difference	95% Confidence Interval of the Difference	
						Lower	Upper
Catholic	Birth to death ratio	6.084	40	.000	1.6645	1.1116	2.2175
Muslim	Birth to death ratio	7.710	26	.000	3.8742	2.8414	4.9071
Protstnt	Birth to death ratio	2.903	15	.011	.4026	.1070	.6983

One-Sample Test. The p values *(Sig. (2-tailed))* are all less than 0.05, indicating that the average sample birth-to-death ratios are significantly larger than 1.25. But wait; you are scanning three tests at once. To make a Bonferroni correction that adjusts for the three tests, multiply each probability by 3. The probability for the Protestant group becomes 0.033 and that for the other groups becomes at most 0.0015 (see comments in "Independent Samples Test" on p. 115). Thus, for the Protestants, the null hypothesis that their average birth-to-death ratio equals 1.25 is rejected at the 0.05 level of significance, but it is not rejected at the 0.01 level.

The difference between the Protestant mean and 1.25 *(Mean Difference)* is smaller than the difference for the other groups. It is 0.4026 (1.6526 – 1.25). The confidence interval for this difference extends from 0.0292 to 0.7761—0 almost falls within the interval.

9 One-Way Analysis of Variance

In Chapter 8, Example 1, the two-sample t test was introduced for testing the hypothesis that a difference between two independent sample means is attributable to chance (that is, the samples come from populations with equal means). In this chapter, you use analysis of variance (ANOVA) to extend this comparison to means of more than two samples. The null hypothesis is

$$H_0: \mu_1 = \mu_2 = \ldots = \mu_k$$

where μ_i is the mean of group i. Since means are compared, *analysis of variance* may sound like a misnomer. If you look at how the F statistic is constructed for testing the hypothesis, the name becomes more clear:

$$F = \frac{\text{variation among the sample means}}{\text{variation within the samples}}$$

If the means are far apart, especially relative to the variation within each group, the size of the F statistic is large and the null hypothesis is rejected. Incidentally, if you use only two groups in an analysis of variance, the F statistic that results is the square of the t statistic from a two-sample t test.

Assumptions. First, explore your variables graphically in boxplots or within-group histograms to see if the distribution of values in each group is symmetric and free of gross outliers or other anomalies. Also, see if the spread of data across groups is fairly constant. More formally, check to see that:

- The k populations are normally distributed.
- The variances of the k populations are equal.
- The observations are independent.

Post hoc pairwise multiple comparisons and range tests. Simply stating that your ANOVA results are significant may not be enough information for a report—you probably want to indicate which particular means differ significantly from others. The One-Way ANOVA procedure provides more than a dozen methods for testing all pairwise differences in means and 10 multiple range tests for identifying subsets of means that are not different from each other.

Contrasts. To test other relations among means, One-Way ANOVA provides tests of linear, quadratic, and other polynomials across means of ordered groups. Also, the user may supply coefficients for contrasts to test specific relations among means (for example, comparing the means of two treatment groups against that of a control group).

The data and problem. For these examples, you use data from the 1993 General Social Survey conducted by the National Opinion Research Center. The respondents were asked to describe their political orientation according to categories labeled *Extremely liberal* to *Extremely conservative*. The data file is *gss 93 subset*.

Do people become more conservative politically as they age? To answer this question, ideally, individuals' views would be monitored from, for example, age 20 to 60. Or, alternatively, older people would be queried about their views now and when they were younger. Instead, here, you take a snapshot at one point in time and look at the average age for groups of people who identify themselves as *liberals*, *moderates*, *conservatives*, and so on.

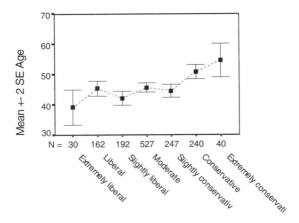

Think of Self as Liberal or Conservative

Example 1: A one-way analysis of variance with the Levene test. The result of the analysis of variance indicates that there are differences in average age for people grouped according to their political view.

Example 2: Post hoc pairwise multiple comparisons and range tests. The difference in average age is tested for every pair of political groups using the Bonferroni adjustment to significance levels and the Tukey method, which is based on the Studentized range distribution. Significant differences are identified for 10 of the 21 pairs. This, however, is not the most useful approach for describing results, because it ignores the fact that the groups are ordered.

Example 3: Tests of contrasts across group means. The seven political orientations are ordered from *Extremely liberal* to *Extremely conservative*, so a linear contrast is used to test if the slope of mean age across the ordered groups differs from 0—that is, is there a significant linear increase in average age as you move across groups ordered from liberal to conservative?

Example 1
A One-Way Analysis of Variance with the Levene Test

Analysis of variance is used to test if any differences exist among the means (average age) for the seven groups of people with different political views. An assumption for analysis of variance is that the groups' variances are equal, so the Levene homogeneity of variance test is requested for testing the assumption.

To produce the output, from the menus choose:

Analyze
  Compare Means
    One-Way ANOVA...

▶ Dependent List: age
▶ Factor: polviews

Options...

  Statistics
  ☑ Descriptive
  ☑ Homogeneity-of-variance

 On the Descriptives table, from the menus choose:

Pivot
  Transpose Rows and Columns

Descriptives

		Extremely liberal	Liberal	Slightly liberal	Moderate	Slightly conservative	Conservative	Extremely conservative	Total
		AGE							
		POLVIEWS							
N		30	162	192	527	247	240	40	1438
Mean		39.07	45.27	42.06	45.53	44.43	50.76	54.55	45.84
Std. Deviation		15.94	15.90	16.38	17.38	16.63	18.23	17.50	17.32
Std. Error		2.91	1.25	1.18	.76	1.06	1.18	2.77	.46
95% Confidence Interval for Mean	Lower Bound	33.12	42.80	39.73	44.05	42.35	48.44	48.95	44.94
	Upper Bound	45.02	47.74	44.39	47.02	46.52	53.08	60.15	46.74
Minimum		18	19	19	18	18	18	22	18
Maximum		80	86	89	89	87	89	86	89

Descriptives. These statistics for subpopulations are available in Explore and were de-scribed there. Here, for the seven groups ordered by political viewpoint, the average age increases from 39.07 years for the 30 *Extremely liberal* respondents to 54.55 years for the 40 *Extremely conservative* people. Notice that while the 95% confidence intervals for the central five means have a spread of 3 to 5 years, the age of the subjects in each group ranges from 18 or 19 years to well into the 80's. The confidence intervals for the average age in the two most extreme groups with much smaller sample sizes cover 11 or 12 years, and the spread of ages is considerable here, too.

Test of Homogeneity of Variances

	Levene Statistic	df1	df2	Sig.
AGE	2.348	6	1431	.029

Test of Homogeneity of Variances. This is the Levene test for equal variances introduced in Chapter 4, Example 4. The Levene statistic is 2.348 with a p value (*Sig.*) = 0.029. Thus, at the 0.05 level, the hypothesis of equal variances across the seven groups is re-jected; but, at the 0.01 level, it is not rejected.

A quick look at boxplots requested in Explore shows that the distribution of age for most of the groups is right-skewed. When the analysis was rerun using the square root of each age value (making the within-group distributions more symmetric), the results found Levene's $F = 1.54$ with a p value of 0.161. When the results of the ANOVA table shown on p. 125 were rerun using the square root values, the conclusions were the same as those shown here.

ANOVA

		Sum of Squares	df	Mean Square	F	Sig.
AGE	Between Groups	13556.87	6	2259.48	7.743	.000
	Within Groups	417590.35	1431	291.82		
	Total	431147.21	1437			

ANOVA. The layout of this table is standard in text books. The *F statistic* for testing if a difference exists between one or more means is 7.743 with a *p* value (*Sig.*) of less than 0.0005. A difference in means is identified. If the population age means *are* equal, it would be extremely unusual to find sample means that differ as much as these—an *F* ratio this large could be expected fewer than five times out of 10,000.

More formally than the introduction to the *F* statistic at the beginning of the chapter, the test statistic is

$$F = \frac{\text{Between-groups sum of squares} / (k-1)}{\text{Within-groups sum of squares} / (N-k)} \quad \text{or} \quad \frac{\text{Between mean square}}{\text{Within mean square}}$$

where *k* is the number of groups and N is the total sample size.

The **between-groups** estimate of variability in the numerator is computed by subtracting the mean of all the observations (the overall mean) from the mean of each group, squaring each difference, multiplying each square by the number of cases in its group, and adding the results for each group together. The total is called the *between-groups sum of squares*.

The **within-groups** estimate of variability uses the variances (the standard deviation squared) of each group. To calculate the *within-groups sum of squares*, multiply each group variance by the number of cases in the group minus 1, and add the results for all groups.

The numerator degrees of freedom (*df*) is (*k* – 1), and the denominator degrees of freedom is (N – *k*). For this sample, the latter is 1438 – 7 = 1431.

The *Mean Square* column reports each sum of squares divided by its respective degrees of freedom, and *F* is the ratio of the two mean squares. Note that while the test results are highly significant for detecting that some differences exist among the seven means, this is no measure of the group structure's contribution to the explanation of the variability of age. See R^2 and eta in Chapter 7.

Example 2
Post Hoc Pairwise Multiple Comparisons and Range Tests

The results in the ANOVA table in Example 1 clearly indicate a difference among the means, but they do not identify just which mean differs from another.

If you want to report for which pairs of means the means differ significantly, you might think of computing a two-sample t test for each pair. Do not do this. *The probability associated with the t statistic assumes that only **one** test is performed.* When several means are tested pairwise, the probability of finding one significant pair by chance alone increases rapidly with the number of pairs. If you use a 0.05 significance level to test that means A and B are equal and also to test that means C and D are equal, the overall acceptance region is now 0.95 * 0.95 or 0.9025. Thus, the acceptance region is roughly 90% and the critical region is 10% (instead of the desired 5%). For six pairs of means tested at the 0.05 significance level, the probability of a difference falling in the critical region is not 0.05 but

$$1 - 0.95^6 = 0.265$$

For 10 pairs, this probability increases to 0.40. The result of using the usual t test is to declare differences significant when they are not.

SPSS provides 20 multiple comparison procedures that provide protection from identifying too many differences as significant when they are not. There are two types of procedures: those that test the difference between each pair of means and those that identify homogeneous subsets of the means that are not different from each other. The latter are called **multiple range tests**. Two frequently used pairwise methods are Bonferroni and Tukey. The Tukey method also provides homogeneous subsets. When the number of comparisons is large, the Tukey procedure may be more sensitive in detecting differences; when the number of comparisons is small, the Bonferroni method may be more sensitive.

The Bonferroni method is easiest to explain: divide the observed significance level by the number of pairs tested. To report, for example, differences among 5 pairs of means as significant at the 5% level, the probability for the usual t test must be less than 0.05 / 5 or 0.01. For the seven political view groups, there are 21 pairs of means, so 0.05 / 21 = 0.00238. SPSS does these calculations for you. The Tukey procedure is based on the Studentized range distribution.

Both the Bonferroni and Tukey methods require the assumption that the group variances are equal. SPSS does provide four methods that allow unequal variances: their names are Games-Howell, Tamhane's T2, Dunnett's T3, and Dunnett's C.

The Scheffé method is usually viewed as too conservative because it provides protection for tests of every linear combination of means, not just pairwise differences. Recent theoretical and Monte Carlo (simulation) research indicates that the Student-Newman-Keuls and Duncan tests do not offer their stated protection levels, so we do not recommend using them. For more information on post hoc pairwise multiple comparisons and post hoc range tests, see the *SPSS Base User's Guide*.

To produce this output, in the One-Way ANOVA dialog box, click *Reset* to restore the defaults, and then select:

▸ Dependent List: age
▸ Factor: polviews

Post Hoc...

  Equal Variances Assumed
  ☑ Bonferroni
  ☑ Tukey

 The Multiple Comparisons table has been split into two tables for easier readability.

Multiple Comparisons

Dependent Variable: AGE
Bonferroni

(I) POLVIEWS	Mean Difference (I-J)	Mean Difference (I-J)	Std. Error	Sig.	95% Confidence Interval	
					Lower Bound	Upper Bound
Extremely liberal	Liberal	-6.20	2.401	1.000	-16.54	4.13
	Slightly liberal	-3.00	2.371	1.000	-13.20	7.21
	Moderate	-6.47	2.267	.922	-16.23	3.29
	Slightly conservative	-5.37	2.335	1.000	-15.42	4.69
	Conservative	-11.70*	2.339	.009	-21.76	-1.63
	Extremely conservative	-15.48*	2.917	.004	-28.04	-2.93
Liberal	Extremely liberal	6.20	2.401	1.000	-4.13	16.54
	Slightly liberal	3.21	1.289	1.000	-2.34	8.76
	Moderate	-.26	1.085	1.000	-4.93	4.41
	Slightly conservative	.84	1.221	1.000	-4.42	6.09
	Conservative	-5.49*	1.228	.034	-10.78	-.20
	Extremely conservative	-9.28*	2.133	.045	-18.46	-9.89E-02
Slightly liberal	Extremely liberal	3.00	2.371	1.000	-7.21	13.20
	Liberal	-3.21	1.289	1.000	-8.76	2.34
	Moderate	-3.47	1.018	.337	-7.85	.91
	Slightly conservative	-2.37	1.162	1.000	-7.37	2.63
	Conservative	-8.70*	1.170	.000	-13.73	-3.67
	Extremely conservative	-12.49*	2.099	.001	-21.52	-3.45
Moderate	Extremely liberal	6.47	2.267	.922	-3.29	16.23
	Liberal	.26	1.085	1.000	-4.41	4.93
	Slightly liberal	3.47	1.018	.337	-.91	7.85
	Slightly conservative	1.10	.931	1.000	-2.91	5.11
	Conservative	-5.23*	.941	.002	-9.28	-1.18
	Extremely conservative	-9.02*	1.981	.028	-17.54	-.49
Slightly conservative	Extremely liberal	5.37	2.335	1.000	-4.69	15.42
	Liberal	-.84	1.221	1.000	-6.09	4.42
	Slightly liberal	2.37	1.162	1.000	-2.63	7.37
	Moderate	-1.10	.931	1.000	-5.11	2.91
	Conservative	-6.33*	1.095	.001	-11.04	-1.62
	Extremely conservative	-10.12*	2.059	.011	-18.98	-1.26
Conservative	Extremely liberal	11.70*	2.339	.009	1.63	21.76
	Liberal	5.49*	1.228	.034	.20	10.78
	Slightly liberal	8.70*	1.170	.000	3.67	13.73
	Moderate	5.23*	.941	.002	1.18	9.28
	Slightly conservative	6.33*	1.095	.001	1.62	11.04
	Extremely conservative	-3.79	2.063	1.000	-12.67	5.09
Extremely conservative	Extremely liberal	15.48*	2.917	.004	2.93	28.04
	Liberal	9.28*	2.133	.045	9.89E-02	18.46
	Slightly liberal	12.49*	2.099	.001	3.45	21.52
	Moderate	9.02*	1.981	.028	.49	17.54
	Slightly conservative	10.12*	2.059	.011	1.26	18.98
	Conservative	3.79	2.063	1.000	-5.09	12.67

*. The mean difference is significant at the .050 level.

Multiple Comparisons (Bonferroni results). In the column labeled *Mean Difference (I-J)*, the difference in average age is reported for every pair of groups. In the first panel, you can read differences in average age for the *Extremely liberal* group—on the average, the *Extremely conservative* folks are 15.48 years older than the *Extremely liberal* group, the *Conservative* people are 11.7 years older, and so on. Looking back at the group means in the Descriptives table on p. 124, 54.55 − 39.07 = 15.48 and 50.76 − 39.07 = 11.69.

The difference in means for each pair is printed twice. The first entry in the first panel is the pair *Extremely liberal* with *Liberal*; results for the same pair are reported at the beginning of the second panel, but the labels are reversed. Notice that the groups are reordered by the size of their means.

The asterisks (*) printed by the differences for the *Conservative* and *Extremely conservative* groups indicate that their average age differs significantly from that of the *Extremely liberal* group (at the 0.05 level). That is, differences of 11.7 and 15.48 years are significant. The adjusted *p* values for these differences are printed in the column labeled *Sig.* (they are 0.009 and 0.004, respectively). The *95% Confidence Interval* for the average difference in age between the *Extremely liberal* and *Conservative* groups extends from −21.76 to −1.63 (or 1.63 years to 21.76 years); the interval for the difference with the *Extremely conservative* group from 2.93 to 28.04 years. Zero is not included in either interval.

Reading down the column, you see that *Conservative* and *Extremely conservative* groups differ significantly from all the other groups.

Multiple Comparisons

Dependent Variable: AGE
Tukey HSD

	(J) POLVIEWS	Mean Difference (I-J)	Std. Error	Significance	95% Confidence Interval Lower Bound	95% Confidence Interval Upper Bound
Extremely liberal	Liberal	-6.20	2.401	.529	-16.22	3.81
	Slightly liberal	-3.00	2.371	.974	-12.88	6.89
	Moderate	-6.47	2.267	.404	-15.92	2.99
	Slightly conservative	-5.37	2.335	.666	-15.10	4.37
	Conservative	-11.70*	2.339	.007	-21.45	-1.94
	Extremely conservative	-15.48*	2.917	.003	-27.65	-3.32
Liberal	Extremely liberal	6.20	2.401	.529	-3.81	16.22
	Slightly liberal	3.21	1.289	.575	-2.16	8.58
	Moderate	-.26	1.085	1.000	-4.79	4.26
	Slightly conservative	.84	1.221	.999	-4.25	5.93
	Conservative	-5.49*	1.228	.026	-10.61	-.37
	Extremely conservative	-9.28*	2.133	.034	-18.17	-.39

*. The mean difference is significant at the .050 level.

Multiple Comparisons (Tukey results). For these data, the results for the Bonferroni and Tukey methods are the same with respect to pairs of means that differ significantly, so only the first two panels are shown here. Notice that the *p* values and confidence intervals do differ somewhat.

AGE

Tukey HSD[a]

POLVIEWS	N	1	2	3
		Subset for alpha = .050		
Extremely liberal	30	39.07		
Slightly liberal	192	42.06		
Slightly conservative	247	44.43	44.43	
Liberal	162	45.27	45.27	
Moderate	527	45.53	45.53	
Conservative	240		50.76	50.76
Extremely conservative	40			54.55
Significance		.157	.177	.764

Means for groups in homogeneous subsets are displayed.

a. Uses Harmonic Mean Sample Size = 87.689

AGE (Homogeneous subsets). This panel is printed because the Tukey method also has a multiple range procedure (the panel is printed for the Waller-Duncan, Student-Newman-Keuls, Tukey, Tukey's *b,* Duncan, Scheffé, Hochberg's GT2, Gabriel, R-E-G-W *F,* and R-E-G-W *Q* multiple range methods). Subsets of means that do not differ from one another are identified. The first subset here, for the Tukey method, has five means ranging from 39.07 to 45.53 years; the second has four means, from 44.43 to 50.76 years; and the third has two means (50.76 and 54.55 years). These tests are based on a test statistic that uses percentiles of the Studentized range. Notice that the groups are reordered by the size of their means.

According to this range test, the *Conservative* group is not significantly older than the liberal, moderate, or slightly conservative groups, but these three pairs do have significant pairwise differences. Why? Because, for the sample size estimate in the multiple range calculations, the harmonic mean of the counts in all seven groups is used; and for each pairwise test, only the counts for the two groups in that pair are used. That is, these three particular pairwise tests are based on larger sample sizes than the range tests; therefore, it is easier to detect significance.

Example 3
Tests of Contrasts across Group Means

Contrasts are used to test relationships among means. A contrast is a linear combination of means μ_i with coefficients α_i

$$\alpha_1 \mu_1 + \alpha_2 \mu_2 + \ldots + \alpha_k \mu_k = 0$$

where $\alpha_1 + \alpha_2 + \ldots + \alpha_k = 0$

You can select the coefficients to test:

- **Pairwise comparisons.** For example, is there a difference between two particular means?

- **A linear combination of means meaningful to the study at hand.** For example, in a study of absorbed grams of fat in samples of three types of oil, you could contrast the means of the oils high in unsaturated fat against those high in saturated fat:

    $-1 \cdot (\text{peanut oil}) + 2 \cdot (\text{lard}) - 1 \cdot \text{corn oil}$

    Notice the coefficients $(-1, 2, -1)$ sum to 0. Or, if you have three treatment groups $(T_1, T_2, \text{and } T_3)$ and one control group (C), you can contrast all three treatment groups against the control group:

    $1 \cdot T_1 + 1 \cdot T_2 + 1 \cdot T_3 - 3 \cdot C$

- **Linear, quadratic, and other increases (or decreases) across a set of ordered means.** You might test a linear increase in average sales for three groups of people: people with *no* training, those with *moderate* training, and those with *extensive* training.

How do you specify coefficients for these contrasts? Many experimental design texts table coefficients for linear and quadratic contrasts for three means, four means, and so on. SPSS provides them automatically when you select *Polynomial* in the Contrasts dialog box. This example illustrates a linear and a quadratic contrast. If you have your own coefficients, such as $(1, -2, 1)$ for the saturated and unsaturated fats or $(1, 1, 1, -3)$ for the three treatment groups against a control group, enter each coefficient at the bottom of the One-Way ANOVA Contrasts dialog box.

SPSS assumes that the first coefficient you specify corresponds to the smallest code of the factor variable, the second coefficient to the next largest factor value, . . . and the last coefficient corresponds to the largest value. For most applications, the coefficients should sum to 0. When polynomials are requested, the group code is used as the metric.

The test statistic for a contrast is similar to that for a two-sample *t* test: the result of the contrast (the relation among means, such as mean A minus mean B) is the numerator of the test statistic, and an estimate of the within-group variability (the pooled-variance estimate or error term from the analysis of variance) is part of the denominator. The null hypothesis is that the contrast is 0.

Is there a linear increase in average age across the seven ordered political categories? A quadratic change?

To produce this output, from the One-Way ANOVA dialog box, click *Reset* to restore the defaults, and then select:

▶ Dependent List: age
▶ Factor: polviews

Contrasts...
   ☑ Polynomial   ▼ Degree: Linear

Then repeat this run, selecting *Quadratic* instead of *Linear*.

ANOVA

				Sum of Squares	df	Mean Square	F	Sig.
AGE	Between Groups	(Combined)		13556.9	6	2259.478	7.743	.000
		Linear Term	Unweighted	6213.073	1	6213.073	21.291	.000
			Weighted	7954.247	1	7954.247	27.258	.000
			Deviation	5602.620	5	1120.524	3.840	.002
	Within Groups			417590	1431	291.817		
	Total			431147	1437			

ANOVA (linear test only). The lines labeled *Between Groups*, *Within Groups*, and *Total* are the same as in the ANOVA table on p. 125. The request for the linear polynomial added the results labeled *Unweighted*, *Weighted*, and *Deviation*. Unweighted results are printed when group sizes are unequal.

What is the difference between weighted and unweighted sums of squares? For the *unweighted sum of squares*, the group means all have the same weight even if the group sample sizes vary greatly (it is as though you, by hand, construct the numerator of the test statistic by simply multiplying each mean by the appropriate coefficient). This means that each observation in a group with lots of cases has less weight than an observation in a cell with a small sample size. For the *weighted sums of squares*, all observations have the same weight (thus, the means have different weights).

The weighted sum of squares here is 7954.25. If you request a regression analysis with *age* as the dependent variable and *polviews* (with codes 1 through 7) as the independent variable, the sum of squares due to regression is 7954.25. The between-groups sum of squares minus the weighted sum of squares is the *Deviation Sum of Squares*.

Here we think each cell mean has equal importance, so the *Unweighted* results are used. The null hypothesis is that the linear contrast is 0—that is, there is no linear effect. The F statistic to test the contrast is 21.291, with a p value less than 0.0005. There is a significant linear increase in average age as you move across from very liberal to very conservative groups. Imagine fitting a line through the ordered means that has a significant slope and yet the means do not fit tightly along the line—they move away from the line in places. See Chapter 7 for a test of linearity for these means.

ANOVA

				Sum of Squares	df	Mean Square	F	Significance
AGE	Between Groups	(Combined)		13556.87	6	2259.48	7.743	.000
		Linear Term	Unweighted	6213.07	1	6213.07	21.291	.000
			Weighted	7954.25	1	7954.25	27.258	.000
			Deviation	5602.62	5	1120.52	3.840	.002
		Quadratic Term	Unweighted	445.49	1	445.49	1.527	.217
			Weighted	1856.49	1	1856.49	6.362	.012
			Deviation	3746.13	4	936.53	3.209	.012
	Within Groups			417590.35	1431	291.82		
	Total			431147.21	1437			

ANOVA (linear and quadratic results). When the quadratic polynomial contrast is requested, results are reported for both linear and quadratic contrasts. The results in this table are exactly like those in the table on p. 132, except three lines are added for the quadratic results: Unweighted and Weighted Sums of Squares and the Deviation Sum of Squares. The Quadratic Deviation sum of squares is the Linear Deviation sum of squares minus the quadratic weighted sum of squares (5602.62 − 1856.49 = 3746.13).

The unweighted quadratic contrast is not significant ($F = 1.527$ with a p value of 0.217). Thus, there is a significant linear increase across the seven ordered means, and a quadratic component is not part of the change across the groups.

10 Univariate Analysis of Variance

The GLM Univariate procedure replaces the Simple Factorial ANOVA procedure found in previous versions of the software. The Univariate procedure is much more powerful than Simple Factorial ANOVA. You can estimate random and mixed effects models (including univariate repeated measures models), perform post-hoc tests on cell means, analyze ANCOVA and regression models, and test custom hypotheses using syntax.

A general linear model (GLM) is a general model that encompasses both analysis of variance (ANOVA) and regression. For the theory underlying the models illustrated here, see the books and articles referenced in the examples.

Among the choices available in the GLM procedures is the sum-of-squares method. Various standard methods are commonly used for calculating the sums of squares that are used in determining the F statistic. The Type III sum-of-squares method is the one most often used and is the default in SPSS. This chapter also contains an example using Type IV so that you can see the differences in the data structure. Information on the methods of calculating sums of squares can be found in the Help system and in the *SPSS Base User's Guide*.

The use of the dialog boxes is described in the *SPSS Base User's Guide*. Many standard analyses are available through the dialog boxes. In some of the examples here, we extend the procedures and show you how to customize them when necessary by adding syntax commands to specify custom analyses.

Since the examples are not presented in order of difficulty, you may want to turn directly to the ones that interest you. This chapter includes the following examples:

Example 1: Regression with two independent variables. This study considers the effects of outdoor temperature and insulation thickness on the amount of heating oil consumed in individual homes. Because both predictors (temperature and insulation thickness) are measured on continuous scales, they are entered as covariates. A model with only covariates entered as predictors is a regression model. Residual plots are used to check assumptions about the data.

Example 2: Two-way analysis of variance (ANOVA). In stores, often the shelf location of a product has an effect on sales, as does the size of the store. The data for this example include weekly sales totals classified by four types of shelf location and three store sizes. The results of the analysis indicate that the shelf location and the store size each affect the sales, but the interaction between location and store size is not a significant effect.

Example 3: Univariate ANOVA: A randomized complete block design with two treatments. The effects on the volume of baked bread of all possible combinations of three fats and three surfactants in the dough are investigated. Flour samples from four different sources are used as blocking factors. The *fat*surfactant* interaction effect is shown to be significant using the default method (Type III sums of squares). After the interaction is found to be significant, custom contrast coefficients are discussed to find out which combinations of levels of the factors are different.

Example 4: Univariate ANOVA: A randomized complete block design with empty cells. This study provides another look at bread baking, this time with some combinations of fats and surfactants not available. This creates empty cells in the design and illustrates the difference in data that calls for the Type IV sum-of-squares method.

Example 5: Analysis-of-covariance model and nesting using the interaction operator. This study investigates the effects of three types of fertilizer on the final height of tomato plants. The initial height of each plant affects its final height, and the model uses this information by including the initial height as a covariate. A nested model is studied by using an interaction effect instead of syntax.

Example 6: A mixed-effects nested design model. A study involving machines and the strains on their glass cathode supports investigates the effects of the four randomly selected heads mounted on each machine. (Heads are nested within machines, since the same head is not used on different machines.) The *head* effect is treated as a random factor. The ANOVA statistics indicate that the machines are not significantly different, but there is an indication that the heads on the same machine may be different. The differences between machines are not significant, but for two of the machines, the differences between head types are significant.

Example 7: Univariate repeated measures analysis using a split-plot design. This experiment was intended to determine the effect of a person's anxiety rating on test performance in four successive trials. The data are set up to be studied as subsections of the whole data set (the "whole plot"). The *anxiety* effect is determined to be not significant, but the *trial* effect is significant.

Example 1
Regression Model with Two Independent Variables

How does the consumption of home heating oil depend on temperature and the thickness of attic insulation? The data for this example are taken from Berenson and Levine (1992). Fifteen similar homes built by one developer in various locations around the United States were evaluated in the study. The builders recorded the amount of oil consumed in January, the average outside temperature (in degrees Fahrenheit), and the number of inches of attic insulation in each home. The data are shown in Figure 10.1.

Figure 10.1   Oil consumption data

Case	Avg. Temperature	Insulation (inches)	Oil Consumed in January (gallons)
1	40	3	275.3
2	27	3	363.8
3	40	10	164.3
4	73	6	40.8
5	64	6	94.3
6	34	6	230.9
7	9	6	366.7
8	8	10	300.6
9	23	10	237.8
10	63	3	121.4
11	65	10	31.4
12	41	6	203.5
13	21	3	441.1
14	38	3	323.0
15	58	10	52.5

First, consider the scatterplot matrix in Figure 10.2 to see how the data are distributed. The chart was created by using the Graph menu, with regression lines added in the Chart Editor window.

Figure 10.2   Scatterplot matrix of the oil consumption data

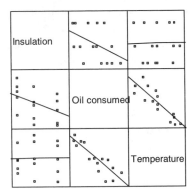

From the scatterplots, you can see a definite negative relationship between temperature and oil consumed and a less well-defined negative relationship between insulation and oil consumed. There is no apparent relation between insulation and temperature. We will use the GLM Univariate procedure to examine the following model:

$$y = \beta_0 + \beta_1 x_1 + \beta_2 x_2 + \varepsilon$$

or

$$\text{oil consumed} = \beta_0 + \beta_1 \text{temperature} + \beta_2 \text{insulation} + \varepsilon$$

This model uses temperature and insulation to predict the amount of heating oil consumed. The two predictor variables in this example are entered as covariates, creating a regression model. To produce the output for this model, from the menus choose:

Analyze
  General Linear Model
    Univariate...

▶ Dependent Variable: oil
▶ Covariate(s): tempf insu

Model...
    ⊙ Custom
      ▶ Model (Main effects): insu tempf

Options...
    Display
        ☑ Observed power
        ☑ Parameter estimates
        ☑ Residual plot

The tests from the output are shown in Figure 10.3.

Figure 10.3   Tests of between-subjects effects

Dependent Variable: Oil consumed (gallons)

Source	Type III Sum of Squares	df	Mean Square	F	Sig.	Noncent. Parameter	Observed Power[1]
Corrected Model	228014.626[2]	2	114007.313	168.471	.000	336.942	1.000
Intercept	480653.404	1	480653.404	710.272	.000	710.272	1.000
INSU	49390.202	1	49390.202	72.985	.000	72.985	1.000
TEMPF	176938.161	1	176938.161	261.466	.000	261.466	1.000
Error	8120.603	12	676.717				
Total	939175.680	15					
Corrected Total	236135.229	14					

[1]. Computed using alpha = .05
[2]. R Squared = .966 (Adjusted R Squared = .960)

The table contains rows for the components of the model that contribute to the variation in the dependent variable. The row labeled *Corrected Model* contains values that can be attributed to the regression model, aside from the intercept. *INSU* and *TEMPF* are the effects in the model. *Error* displays the component attributable to the residuals, or the unexplained variation. *Total* shows the sums of squares of all of the dependent values.

Corrected Total (sum of squared deviations from the mean) is the sum of the component due to the model and the component due to the error.

Most of the columns in this table are equivalent to those in the ANOVA table in Linear Regression (see Chapter 12). The sums of squares and degrees of freedom are given for each effect listed in the *Source* column. The mean square is the sums of squares divided by the degrees of freedom, and the *F* statistic is the mean square divided by the error mean square. Its significance (*p* value) is given in the *Sig.* column. In the last two columns, the noncentrality parameter is used in calculating the observed power, which gives the probability that the *F* test will detect the differences between groups equal to those implied by the sample differences. The 1.000 value, which is greater than or equal to 0.9995, indicates that population effects of the magnitude seen in this sample would be detected nearly every time with a sample of this size.

In Figure 10.3, the *F* statistic for the corrected model, 168.471, is highly significant ($p < 0.0005$), indicating rejection of the simultaneous test that each coefficient is 0. Footnote 2 shows that R^2 is 0.966 and adjusted R^2 is 0.960. Thus, about 96% of the variation in oil consumption is explained by this model.

Figure 10.4   Parameter estimates

Dependent Variable	Parameter	B	Std. Error	t	Sig.	95% Confidence Interval Lower Bound	95% Confidence Interval Upper Bound	Noncent. Parameter	Observed Power[1]
Oil consumed (gallons)	Intercept	562.151	21.093	26.651	.000	516.193	608.109	26.651	1.000
	INSU	-20.012	2.343	-8.543	.000	-25.116	-14.908	8.543	1.000
	TEMPF	-5.437	.336	-16.170	.000	-6.169	-4.704	16.170	1.000

[1]. Computed using alpha = .05

The parameter estimates are shown in Figure 10.4. From the estimates in the column labeled *B*, the model for estimating the value of oil consumption is

oil consumption $= 562.151 - 20.012\,\text{insulation} - 5.437\,\text{temperature}$

You could use this model to predict the January oil consumption of a house in a given temperature zone, for different values of insulation within the studied range of 3 to 10 inches.

Diagnostics

The matrix scatterplot of residuals is shown in Figure 10.5. The plots are useful for checking assumptions about the data.

Figure 10.5   Residuals plots

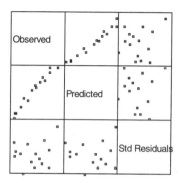

Model:Intercept+INSU+TEMPF

The plot of predicted versus observed values (left middle plot) is close to a straight line, which indicates a good fit. The standardized residuals versus the predicted values (middle lower plot) shows some tendency to increase variability as the dependent variable increases (heteroscedasticity). See Chapter 12 for a more detailed discussion of analyzing various plots in regression analysis.

Example 2
Two-Way Analysis of Variance (ANOVA) with Equal Sample Sizes

When the independent (predictor) variables are categorical, you can enter them in the GLM Univariate procedure as factors. Consider a supermarket chain that is interested in various effects on weekly sales. Does the sales volume of a particular product depend on its shelf location? If it does, is the size of the store a significant factor? And is there any interaction between the shelf location and the size of the store? Berenson and Levine (1992) consider this problem, with sample sizes equal for each combination of shelf location and size. The data are shown in Figure 10.6. You can see that there are two entries for weekly sales for small stores and shelf location A, and there are two entries for each of the other combinations.

Figure 10.6   Weekly sales data

Store Size	Shelf Location			
	A	B	C	D
Small	45	56	65	48
	50	63	71	53
Medium	57	69	73	60
	65	78	80	57
Large	70	75	82	71
	78	82	89	75

In the SPSS data file used for this study, variables include weekly sales (*sales*), shelf location (*location*), and store size (*size*). One case was entered for each value of weekly sales. The two predictor variables in this study, *location* and *size*, are categorical, which means that they should be entered as factors in the GLM Univariate procedure. For this example, assuming that these variables include all of the categories of interest to the supermarket chain makes them **fixed** factors.

To produce the output, from the menus choose:

Analyze
 General Linear Model
  Univariate...

▸ Dependent Variable: sales
▸ Fixed Factor(s): location size

Model...
  ⊙ Custom
  ▸ Model (Main effects): location size
  ▸ Model (Interaction): location*size

Plots...
  ▸ Horizontal Axis: size
  ▸ Separate Lines: location (Click *Add*)

Options...
  ▸ Display Means for: location*size

  Display
   ☑ Observed power

 Double-click on the table labeled *Shelf location * Store size* and, in the row dimension, drag the *Shelf location* icon to the right of the *Store size* icon.

The tests displayed in the output are shown in Figure 10.7.

Figure 10.7   Tests of between-subjects effects

Dependent Variable: Weekly sales

Source	Type III Sum of Squares	df	Mean Square	F	Sig.	Noncent. Parameter	Observed Power[1]
Corrected Model	3019.333[2]	11	274.485	12.767	.000	140.434	1.000
Intercept	108273	1	108273	5035.938	.000	5035.938	1.000
LOCATION	1102.333	3	367.444	17.090	.000	51.271	1.000
SIZE	1828.083	2	914.042	42.514	.000	85.027	1.000
LOCATION * SIZE	88.917	6	14.819	.689	.663	4.136	.183
Error	258.000	12	21.500				
Total	111550	24					
Corrected Total	3277.333	23					

[1.] Computed using alpha = .05
[2.] R Squared = .966 (Adjusted R Squared = .960)

The *location*size* interaction term is not significant ($p = 0.689$), so the location and size effects will be assumed to be consistent across levels of the other factor. Since the design is balanced, main-effect estimates are the same here as they would be if the model was refitted without the interaction. Some statisticians would prefer to fit the main-effects-only model anyway, with the interaction sums of squares and degrees of freedom going into the error term. In this case, it would make no difference in the main effects tests—we see that there is indeed a location effect as well as a size effect.

Estimated Marginal Means and Profile Plots

To further explore the interaction effects, look at the table of estimated marginal means in Figure 10.8 and the profile plot of the same values in Figure 10.9.

Figure 10.8   Estimated marginal means

LOCATION * SIZE

Dependent Variable: SALES

SIZE	LOCATION	Mean	Std. Error	95% Confidence Interval	
				Lower Bound	Upper Bound
Small	A	47.500	3.279	40.356	54.644
	B	59.500	3.279	52.356	66.644
	C	68.000	3.279	60.856	75.144
	D	50.500	3.279	43.356	57.644
Medium	A	61.000	3.279	53.856	68.144
	B	73.500	3.279	66.356	80.644
	C	76.500	3.279	69.356	83.644
	D	58.500	3.279	51.356	65.644
Large	A	74.000	3.279	66.856	81.144
	B	78.500	3.279	71.356	85.644
	C	85.500	3.279	78.356	92.644
	D	73.000	3.279	65.856	80.144

Figure 10.9   Estimated marginal means of weekly sales

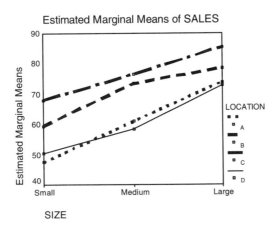

Each line in the chart represents one type of shelf location for the product. You can see that shelf location C produces the highest estimates of weekly sales and that shelf locations A and D produce the lowest. Because the lines are almost parallel, it is apparent that the differences between the shelf locations do not change much with the size of the store. The parallelism in this chart indicates that there is little or no interaction between the two factors. This conclusion reinforces the previous statements about the F test.

Example 3
Univariate ANOVA: A Randomized Complete Block Design with Two Treatments

How is the volume of baked bread affected by different combinations of fats and surfactants in the dough? This example uses data from Chapter 12 in Milliken and Johnson (1984). The data are in the SPSS file *fat surfactant*. The object of the experiment was to study differences in the specific volume of bread baked with different combinations of ingredients. The doughs were mixed using each of the nine possible combinations of three fats and three surfactants. (Surfactants are often used either to reduce surface tension of a liquid so it absorbs flour and other ingredients better or as containers of emulsifiers to promote a better mix of oil and water.) In statistical terminology, the fats and surfactants are called **treatments**.

Flour is a major ingredient of bread, but differences in flour were not the focus of this experiment. However, the bakers were concerned that differences between fats and surfactants in one batch of flour might not hold for flour from a different source. Therefore, four flours of the same type but from different sources were used in order to **randomize** unsuspected sources of variation in the effects of the two treatments among the flour sources. To create a **complete block design**, all combinations of the treatments were randomly assigned within each block (source) of flour. Because all possible levels of each factor are represented, this is a **fixed-effects model**. Random effects are illustrated in "Mixed-Effects Nested Design Model" on p. 165. Figure 10.10 shows the results of the current experiment.

Figure 10.10   Fats, surfactants, flour, and volume of bread

Fat	Surfactant	Flour			
		1	2	3	4
	1	6.7	4.3	5.7	-
1	2	7.1	-	5.9	5.6
	3	-	5.5	6.4	5.8
	1	-	5.9	7.4	7.1
2	2	-	5.6	-	6.8
	3	6.4	5.1	6.2	6.3
	1	7.1	5.9	-	-
3	2	7.3	6.6	8.1	6.8
	3	-	7.5	9.1	-

Notice that there are empty cells in the data (indicated by hyphens) due to an ineffective yeast container. Thus, the number of trials for each combination (subclass) across a row varies. However, all nine possible *fat*surfactant* treatment combinations were observed at least once. Therefore, estimation of the *fat*surf* interaction is not affected by the empty cells.

The SPSS data file *fat surfactant* uses four variables: *fat* (fat), *surf* (surfactant), *flour* (flour), and *spvol* (specific volume). The dependent variable is *spvol*, and the factors are *fat*, *surf*, and *flour*. Each specific volume is represented by one case in the data file. Empty data cells have no case. The *fat* and *surf* factors each have three levels and *flour* has four.

To produce the output in this example, from the menus choose:

Analyze
  General Linear Model
    Univariate...

▶ Dependent Variable: spvol
▶ Fixed Factor(s): fat surf flour

Model...
    ⊙ Custom
    ▶ Model: flour fat surf fat*surf

Options...
    ☑ Observed power

In this model, the *fat* factor and the *surf* factor are the main effects of interest, and the *flour* factor serves as a randomized blocking effect to reduce experimental error. Both main effects, *fat* and *surf*, and their interaction are in the model. The blocking effect, *flour*, is also entered. The intercept is included by default. The model does not include interactions between the blocking effect and the treatment effects.

Following Milliken and Johnson's approach, since all *fat*surfactant* treatment combinations are observed at least once, and since some of the same treatment combinations are observed in each block, the test hypotheses for Type III sums of squares are of interest for this design. Because the default method in SPSS is Type III sums of squares, the method was not changed in the Model dialog box.

Figure 10.11   Tests of between-subjects effects

Dependent Variable: SPVOL

Source	Type III Sum of Squares	df	Mean Square	F	Sig.	Noncent. Parameter	Observed Power[1]
Corrected Model	22.520^{2}	11	2.047	12.376	.000	136.137	1.000
Intercept	1016.981	1	1016.981	6147.938	.000	6147.938	1.000
FLOUR	8.691	3	2.897	17.513	.000	52.538	1.000
FAT	10.118	2	5.059	30.583	.000	61.165	1.000
SURF	.997	2	.499	3.014	.082	6.028	.491
FAT * SURF	5.639	4	1.410	8.522	.001	34.088	.986
Error	2.316	14	.165				
Total	1112.960	26					
Corrected Total	24.835	25					

1. Computed using alpha = .05
2. R Squared = .907 (Adjusted R Squared = .833)

The analysis-of-variance table is shown in Figure 10.11. The first column of the table, labeled *Source,* lists the effects in the model, and the second column shows the *Type III Sum of Squares* for each effect. The degrees of freedom for each sum of squares is presented in the column labeled *df.* The *Mean Square* column shows the mean square of each effect, which is calculated by dividing the sum of squares by its degrees of freedom. The *F* column shows the *F* statistic for each effect, and its corresponding significance is shown in the next column. In a fixed-effects model, the *F* statistic is calculated by dividing the mean square by the mean square error term at the bottom of the *Mean Square* column. The next to last column presents the estimated *Noncentrality Parameter* under the alternative hypothesis for each *F* test. It is used in determining the observed power under the alternative hypothesis. The *Observed Power* in the last column is evaluated based on the fixed-effect assumptions. Its value ranges from 0 to 1 and indicates the strength of the *F* test for each effect. The power gives the probability that the *F* test will detect the differences between groups equal to those implied by the sample differences.

In this example, the F value for the interaction effect *fat*surfactant* is 8.522. The p value 0.001 is significant at the conventional level, $\alpha = 0.05$. Thus, in further analysis, the surfactant effect should be compared at each level of fat, and the fat effect should be compared at each level of surfactant.

Estimated Marginal Means and Profile Plots

To study the *surf* effect at each level of fat, the estimated population marginal means of the dependent variable *spvol* at the cell combinations of surfactant and fat are useful, as are plots of the estimated marginal means.

To produce the output in this section, recall the GLM Univariate dialog box and make the following additional selections:

Options...
  Estimated Marginal Means
  ▸ Display means for: fat*surf

Plots...
  ▸ Horizontal Axis: fat
  ▸ Separate Lines: surf (Click *Add*)

The estimated population marginal means are the predicted cell means from the model. The population marginal means estimates[1] for the surfactant and fat combination are the average of the estimated population cell means over the *flour* factor in the model. The cells that are involved in the calculation are those that have at least one observation.

Figure 10.12   Estimated marginal means of spvol for fat*surfactant

fat * surfactant

Dependent Variable: SPVOL

fat	surfactant	Mean	Std. Error	95% Confidence Interval	
				Lower Bound	Upper Bound
1	1	5.536	.240	5.021	6.052
	2	5.891	.239	5.378	6.404
	3	6.123	.241	5.605	6.641
2	1	7.023	.241	6.505	7.541
	2	6.708	.301	6.064	7.353
	3	6.000	.203	5.564	6.436
3	1	6.629	.301	5.984	7.274
	2	7.200	.203	6.764	7.636
	3	8.589	.300	7.945	9.233

---

1. In calculating the estimated marginal means, SPSS uses the modified definition based on Searle, Speed, and Milliken (1980). Because the estimated marginal means in Milliken and Johnson use another definition of means, the values shown in SPSS output may be different from theirs.

The list of the estimated population marginal means and their standard errors is displayed in Figure 10.12. The table shows, for example, that with fat 2 and surfactant 1, the volume of bread predicted from this model is 7.023 units, and with the same fat (fat 2) and surfactant 3, the predicted volume is 6.0 units.

The same information can be shown graphically. Figure 10.13 shows a profile plot of the estimated population marginal means of the dependent variable *spvol* at each level of fat, with a separate line drawn for each type of surfactant.

Figure 10.13   Estimated population marginal means of spvol

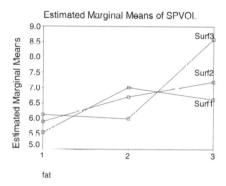

The plot indicates that when surfactant was fixed at level 2, the volume increased with the fat level. At level 1 of surfactant, the volume increased from fat level 1 to level 2 but decreased at fat level 3. On the other hand, the volume at level 3 of surfactant decreased slightly from fat level 1 to level 2 and increased sharply at fat level 3.

Custom Hypothesis Testing

The crossed lines in the profile plot indicate that the surfactant levels do not vary in the same way for all fats in the study. This means that custom hypotheses are needed. This section provides some theory and discusses how to customize your analysis by using syntax commands that are not available in the dialog boxes. You may want to skip this section.

To determine whether there is a significant difference among the levels of surfactant at each level of fat, you can specify three custom hypotheses. Each one tests the surfactant levels for one level of fat. To specify each of these three custom hypotheses, the LMATRIX subcommand is used. The LMATRIX subcommand can be used to customize the hypothesis by specifying the coefficients of the L matrix in the general linear hypothesis $LB = 0$, where B is the vector of parameters. In this example, the mathematical model can be written as

$$\text{spvol}_{ijkl} = \mu + \text{flour}_i + \text{fat}_j + \text{surf}_k + \text{fat*surf}_{jk} + \text{error}_{ijkl}$$

where μ denotes the overall mean, flour_i denotes the effect of the ith level of flour (i = 1, 2, 3, 4), fat_j denotes the jth level of fat (j = 1, 2, 3), surf_k denotes the kth effect of surfactant (k = 1, 2, 3), fat*surf_{jk} denotes the (j,k)th interaction effect of fat and surfactant, and error_{ijkl} denotes the random effect of the lth bread in the ith level of flour at the (j,k)th fat and surfactant treatment combination. The values of μ, flour_i, fat_j, surf_k, and fat*surf_{jk} are free parameters that are to be estimated from the data. The vector of parameter **B** is the column vector that consists of all of the above parameters.

$$\begin{aligned}
\text{B}' = (&\mu, \text{flour}_1, \text{flour}_2, \text{flour}_3, \text{flour}_4, \\
&\text{fat}_1, \text{fat}_2, \text{fat}_3, \text{surf}_1, \text{surf}_2, \text{surf}_3, \\
&\text{fat*surf}_{11}, \text{fat*surf}_{12}, \text{fat*surf}_{13}, \\
&\text{fat*surf}_{21}, \text{fat*surf}_{22}, \text{fat*surf}_{23}, \\
&\text{fat*surf}_{31}, \text{fat*surf}_{32}, \text{fat*surf}_{33})
\end{aligned}$$

To set up the custom hypothesis, the coefficients of the **L** matrix in the expression **LB** must be specified.

$$\begin{aligned}
\text{LB} = l_1\mu + \\
&l_2\text{flour}_1 + l_3\text{flour}_2 + l_4\text{flour}_3 + l_5\text{flour}_4 \\
&l_6\text{fat}_1 + l_7\text{fat}_2 + l_8\text{fat}_3 \\
&l_9\text{surf}_1 + l_{10}\text{surf}_2 + l_{11}\text{surf}_3 \\
&l_{12}\text{fat*surf}_{11} + l_{13}\text{fat*surf}_{12} + l_{14}\text{fat*surf}_{13} \\
&l_{15}\text{fat*surf}_{21} + l_{16}\text{fat*surf}_{22} + l_{17}\text{fat*surf}_{23} \\
&l_{18}\text{fat*surf}_{31} + l_{19}\text{fat*surf}_{32} + l_{20}\text{fat*surf}_{33}
\end{aligned}$$

where

$$\text{L} = (l_1, l_2, l_3, l_4, l_5, l_6, l_7, l_8, l_9, l_{10}, l_{11}, l_{12}, l_{13}, l_{14}, l_{15}, l_{16}, l_{17}, l_{18}, l_{19}, l_{20})$$

To compare level 1 of surfactant with its level 3 at fat 1, the **L** coefficients (l_9 and l_{12}) associated with the parameters that involve surfactant 1 (surf_1) and the combination of surfactant 1 at fat 1 (fat*surf_{11}) are set to 1, while the **L** coefficients (l_{11} and l_{14}) associated with the parameters that involve surfactant 3 (surf3) and the combination of surfactant 3 at fat 1 (fat*surf_{13}) are set to -1. All other **L** coefficients that do not associate with the above parameters are irrelevant and are set to 0. The expression **LB** that corresponds to comparing surfactant 1 with 3 at fat 1 is

$$\text{LB} = (\text{surf}_1 - \text{surf}_3) + (\text{fat*surf}_{11} - \text{fat*surf}_{13})$$

Notice that the first part of the above expression compares the main effect of surfactant 1 with surfactant 3 and that the second part specifies the surfactant comparison at fat 1. Similarly, the **LB** expression that corresponds to comparing surfactant 2 with 3 at fat 1 is

$$\mathbf{LB} = (\text{surf}_2 - \text{surf}_3) + (\text{fat*surf}_{12} - \text{fat*surf}_{13})$$

Testing the above two expressions together provides a custom hypothesis test to study the effects of surfactant at fat 1.

To produce the custom hypotheses in SPSS, from the menus choose:

Analyze
  General Linear Model
    Univariate...

▶ Dependent Variable: spvol
▶ Fixed Factor(s): fat surf flour

Model...
    ⊙ Custom
    ▶ Model: flour fat surf fat*surf

Paste

The pasted syntax is

```
UNIANOVA SPVOL BY FAT SURF FLOUR
  /METHOD - SSTYPE(3)
  /CRITERIA = ALPHA(.05)
  /DESIGN = FLOUR FAT SURF FAT*SURF.
```

The METHOD and CRITERIA subcommands give default specifications. They are not necessary and are not shown in the syntax below.

To specify the custom hypothesis, add an LMATRIX subcommand. The label *Surfactant Difference at Fat 1* is specified within the apostrophes. It is used to identify this custom hypothesis in the output. Next, the effects of SURF and FAT*SURF related to this custom hypothesis are specified, each of them followed by the values of the coefficients of **L** associated with it. For example, the values following the SURF effect are 1, 0, and −1. They are the **L** coefficients associated with the parameters surf_1, surf_2, and surf_3 in the **LB** expression, respectively. The values for all *fat*surf* coefficients that would come after these are set to 0.

```
UNIANOVA SPVOL BY FAT SURF FLOUR
 /LMATRIX 'Surfactant Difference at Fat 1'
  SURF 1 0 -1 FAT*SURF 1 0 -1 0 0 0 0 0 0;
  SURF 0 1 -1 FAT*SURF 0 1 -1 0 0 0 0 0 0
 /DESIGN = FLOUR FAT SURF FAT*SURF.
```

Similarly, the LMATRIX subcommands for studying the effects of surfactants for fat 2 and the effects of surfactants for fat 3 can be specified as follows:

```
UNIANOVA SPVOL BY FAT SURF FLOUR
/LMATRIX 'Surfactant Difference at Fat 2'
   SURF 1 0 -1 FAT*SURF 0 0 0 1 0 -1 0 0 0;
   SURF 0 1 -1 FAT*SURF 0 0 0 1 -1 0 0 0
/LMATRIX 'Surfactant Difference at Fat 3'
   SURF 1 0 -1 FAT*SURF 0 0 0 0 0 0 1 0 -1;
   SURF 0 1 -1 FAT*SURF 0 0 0 0 0 0 0 1 -1
/DESIGN = FLOUR FAT SURF FAT*SURF.
```

The custom hypothesis labeled *Surfactant Difference at Fat 2* is the custom hypothesis for studying the effects of surfactants at fat 2; the one labeled *Surfactant Difference at Fat 3* is the custom hypothesis for studying the effects of surfactants at fat 3. Notice that the values of the coefficients of **L** following the FAT*SURF effect are 0, 0, 0, 1, 0, and -1 (for the one with coefficients 1, 0, and -1 for SURF). The first three zeros represent the **L** coefficients associated with the parameters fat*surf$_{11}$, fat*surf$_{12}$, and fat*surf$_{13}$. Since the effects of surfactants at fat 2 are being studied, the **L** coefficients associated with parameters related to fat 1 are set to 0. Similarly, in the last LMATRIX subcommand, there are two sets of three zeros for fat 1 and fat 2. The results of the three custom hypotheses are displayed in Figure 10.14, with captions added to identify them.

Figure 10.14   Custom hypothesis test results

Univariate Test Results

Dependent Variable: SPVOL

Source	Type III Sum of Squares	df	Mean Square	F	Sig.	Noncentrality Parameter	Observed Power
Contrast	.488	2	.244	1.475	.262	2.950	.262
Error	2.316	14	.165				

Surfactant Difference at Fat1

Univariate Test Results

Dependent Variable: SPVOL

Source	Type III Sum of Squares	df	Mean Square	F	Sig.	Noncentrality Parameter	Observed Power
Contrast	1.831	2	.915	5.534	.017	11.067	.764
Error	2.316	14	.165				

Surfactant Difference at Fat2

Univariate Test Results

Dependent Variable: SPVOL

Source	Type III Sum of Squares	df	Mean Square	F	Sig.	Noncentrality Parameter	Observed Power
Contrast	3.817	2	1.909	11.539	.001	23.077	.977
Error	2.316	14	.165				

Surfactant Difference at Fat3

The resulting F statistics show that there are statistically significant effects of surfactant on the dependent variable *spvol* at fat 2 and fat 3. The effect of surfactant on *spvol* is not significant at fat 1.

Example 4
Univariate ANOVA: A Randomized Complete Block Design with Empty Cells

How is the volume of baked bread affected by different combinations of fats and surfactants in the dough when data for some of the *fat*surfactant* combinations are not available? This example uses the data from Chapter 15 in Milliken and Johnson (1992). In "Univariate ANOVA: A Randomized Complete Block Design with Two Treatments" on p. 145, we studied the effect of the combining three different fats with each of three surfactants on the specific volume of bread. All combinations of fats and surfactants were included at least once. Here, we have deleted some of the data. The Type III sum-of-squares method is no longer appropriate because there are empty cells in the design. The data, with some treatment combinations removed, are shown in Figure 10.15.

Figure 10.15   Fat and surfactant combinations missing

Fat	Surfactant	Flour 1	2	3	4	
1	1	6.7	4.3	5.7	-	
	2	7.1	-	5.9	5.6	
	3	-	-	-	-	
2	1	-	5.9	7.4	7.1	Data missing across two rows
	2	-	-	-	-	
	3	6.4	5.1	6.2	6.3	
3	1	7.1	5.9	-	-	
	2	7.3	6.6	8.1	6.8	
	3	-	7.5	9.1	-	

Notice that all data in the treatment combinations (fat 1 and surfactant 3) and (fat 2 and surfactant 2) were removed. They are treated as missing data in this example. Figure 10.16 illustrates the treatment combinations available for hypothesis testing.

Figure 10.16   Treatment combinations available

Fat	Surfactant 1	2	3
1	Data available	Data available	
2	Data available		Data available
3	Data available	Data available	Data available

Since some of the treatment combinations are empty, the test hypotheses for Type III sums of squares are not suitable for this set of data; they may not have meaningful interpretations. Instead, the test hypotheses for Type IV sums of squares are more suitable here. The Type IV sum-of-squares method is designed to construct test hypotheses that are meaningful in the presence of empty cells in the model. Type IV hypotheses compare the levels of one treatment by averaging over one or more common levels of the other treatments. Such a hypothesis is constructed by using contrasts of available treatment combinations. The next section considers all of the Type IV hypotheses for fat.

Constructing Hypotheses

The mathematical model for the design considered in this example can be written as

$$\text{spvol}_{ijkl} = \mu + \text{flour}_i + \mu_{jk} + \text{error}_{ijkl}$$

where μ denotes the overall mean, flour_i denotes the effect of the ith level of flour ($i = 1, 2, 3, 4$), μ_{jk} denotes the effect of the treatment combination of the jth level of fat and kth level of surfactant, and error_{ijkl} denotes the random effect of the lth bread in the ith level of flour at the (j,k)th fat and surfactant treatment combination. The treatment combination effect can then be written as

$$\mu_{jk} = \text{fat}_j + \text{surf}_k + \text{fat*surf}_{jk}$$

where fat_j denotes the jth level of the effect of fat ($j = 1, 2, 3$), surf_k denotes the kth level of the effect of surfactant ($k = 1, 2, 3$), and fat*surf_{jk} denotes the (j,k)th interaction effect of fat and surfactant. The means μ_{13} and μ_{22} do not exist because there is no data available. Thus, any hypothesis that involves these two treatment combinations cannot be tested. Using Figure 10.16, all possible meaningful Type IV hypotheses are illustrated in Figure 10.17.

Figure 10.17 All possible Type IV hypotheses for fat

Hypothesis		
$H_{10}:$	$\mu_{11} = \mu_{21}$	$\text{fat}_1 - \text{fat}_2 + \text{fat*surf}_{11} - \text{fat*surf}_{21} = 0$
$H_{20}:$	$\mu_{21} = \mu_{31}$	$\text{fat}_2 - \text{fat}_3 + \text{fat*surf}_{21} - \text{fat*surf}_{31} = 0$
$H_{30}:$	$\mu_{12} = \mu_{32}$	$\text{fat}_1 - \text{fat}_3 + \text{fat*surf}_{12} - \text{fat*surf}_{32} = 0$
$H_{40}:$	$\mu_{23} = \mu_{33}$	$\text{fat}_2 - \text{fat}_3 + \text{fat*surf}_{23} - \text{fat*surf}_{33} = 0$
$H_{50}:$	$\mu_{11} + \mu_{12} = \mu_{31} + \mu_{32}$	$(\text{fat}_1 - \text{fat}_3) + 0.5(\text{fat*surf}_{11} + \text{fat*surf}_{12} - \text{fat*surf}_{31} - \text{fat*surf}_{32}) = 0$
$H_{60}:$	$\mu_{21} + \mu_{23} = \mu_{31} + \mu_{32}$	$(\text{fat}_2 - \text{fat}_3) + 0.5(\text{fat*surf}_{21} + \text{fat*surf}_{23} - \text{fat*surf}_{31} - \text{fat*surf}_{33}) = 0$

Analysis

To produce the output in this section, first modify the data in the *fat surfactant* file. You can save it under a new name. Then, from the menus choose:

Analyze
  General Linear Model
    Univariate...

▶ Dependent Variable: spvol
▶ Fixed Factor(s): flour fat surf

Model...
  ⊙ Custom
    ▶ Model: flour fat surf fat*surf
  Sum of squares: Type IV

Options...
  ☑ Observed power

The results of the analysis of variance are shown in Figure 10.18.

Figure 10.18   Analysis-of-variance table using Type IV sums of squares

Tests of Between-Subjects Effects

Dependent Variable: Specific Volume

Source	Type IV Sum of Squares	df	Mean Square	F	Sig.	Noncent. Parameter	Observed Power[1]
Corrected Model	20.244[2]	9	2.249	11.815	.000	106.339	1.000
Intercept	830.754	1	830.754	4363.845	.000	4363.845	1.000
FLOUR	7.773	3	2.591	13.609	.001	40.820	.007
FAT	5.046	2	2.523	13.252	.001	26.504	.984
SURF	2.500	2	1.250	6.566	.013	13.133	.810
FAT * SURF	5.400	2	2.700	14.183	.001	28.367	.989
Error	2.094	11	.190				
Total	930.510	21					
Corrected Total	22.338	20					

1. Computed using alpha = .05
2. R Squared = .906 (Adjusted R Squared = .830)

The analysis-of-variance table shows that the effects are significant with $p = 0.001$. The effects *surf* and *fat*surf* are also significant with $p = 0.013$ and $p = 0.001$, respectively.

Contrast Coefficients

To understand the Type IV hypothesis testing for fat in this example, you can look at the contrast coefficients shown in the contrast coefficients table for fat. As in "Univariate ANOVA: A Randomized Complete Block Design with Two Treatments" on p. 145, customized contrast coefficients are available using syntax commands but not in the dialog boxes. To obtain a contrast coefficients table for each effect in the model, recall the GLM Univariate dialog box, paste the syntax, and add a PRINT=TEST(LMATRIX) subcommand.

```
unianova spvol by flour fat surf
 /method = sstype(4)
 /print = test(lmatrix) opower
 /design = flour fat surf fat*surf.
```

The output contains tables of contrast coefficients for each effect in the design. The table for fat is shown in Figure 10.19. The first column indicates the parameters in the model. For example, *[FAT=1]* represents the parameter for fat_1, *[FAT=1]*[SURF=1]* represents the parameter for $fat*surf_{11}$, and so on. The next two columns, labeled *L6* and *L7*, indicate the two hypotheses on the fat effect that are being tested together in the analysis-of-variance table shown in Figure 10.18.

Figure 10.19   Contrast coefficients

FAT[1]

Parameter	Contrast	
	L6	L7
Intercept	.000	.000
[FLOUR=1]	.000	.000
[FLOUR=2]	.000	.000
[FLOUR=3]	.000	.000
[FLOUR=4]	.000	.000
[FAT=1]	1.000	.000
[FAT=2]	.000	1.000
[FAT=3]	-1.000	-1.000
[SURF=1]	.000	.000
[SURF=2]	.000	.000
[SURF=3]	.000	.000
[FAT=1] * [SURF=1]	.500	.000
[FAT=1] * [SURF=2]	.500	.000
[FAT=2] * [SURF=1]	.000	.500
[FAT=2] * [SURF=3]	.000	.500
[FAT=3] * [SURF=1]	-.500	-.500
[FAT=3] * [SURF=2]	-.500	.000
[FAT=3] * [SURF=3]	.000	-.500

The default display of this matrix is the
transpose of the corresponding L matrix.
Based on Type IV Sums of Squares.

1. The estimable function is not unique

Hypotheses L6 and L7 correspond to hypotheses H_{50} and H_{60} in Figure 10.17. Hypotheses H_{10} to H_{40} can be tested using the LMATRIX subcommand to set up custom hypotheses. For example, to test hypotheses H_{10} and H_{20} together, the following syntax can be used:

```
unianova spvol by flour fat surf
/method = sstype(4)
/LMATRIX = 'H10 and H20'
    fat 1 -1  0  fat*surf  1  0 -1  0   0   0   0;
    fat 0  1 -1  fat*surf  0  0  1  0  -1   0   0
/design = flour fat surf fat*surf.
```

The univariate results of the above custom hypothesis for H_{10} and H_{20} are shown in Figure 10.20.

Figure 10.20   Univariate test results for custom hypotheses

Test Results

Dependent Variable: Specific Volume

Source	Type IV Sum of Squares	df	Mean Square	F	Sig.	Noncent. Parameter	Observed Power[1]
Contrast	3.307	2	1.654	8.687	.005	17.374	.908
Error	2.094	11	.190				

1. Computed using alpha = .050

SPSS automatically chooses meaningful Type IV hypotheses for you. However, other sets of hypotheses, such as the ones for H_{10} and H_{20}, may be more appropriate for your study. When there are situations where other sets of Type IV hypotheses are possible, SPSS reminds you by displaying a message saying that the Type IV testable hypothesis is not unique in the tests of between-subjects effects table (see Figure 10.18). You can set up your own Type IV hypotheses by using the LMATRIX subcommand.

Example 5
Analysis of Covariance (ANCOVA) and Nesting Using the Interaction Operator

Do different types of fertilizers have different effects on the height of tomato plants? The data in this example are taken from Searle (1987). They are stored in SPSS file *tomato* and shown in Figure 10.21.

Figure 10.21   Tomato plant growth

Fertilizer	Final height	Initial height
1	74	3
1	68	4
1	77	5
2	76	2
2	80	4
3	87	3
3	91	7

The dependent variable is the height of tomato plants at 10 weeks (*height*). The factor of interest is the type of fertilizer used after transplanting (*fert*). Three varieties of fertilizer were applied. Since there was variation in the initial heights of the plants at the time of transplantation, the initial value (*initial*) is entered as a covariate in order to determine whether the type of fertilizer makes a difference in the final height for plants of equal initial height.

Testing Assumptions: Homogeneity of Regression Slopes

To be able to compare final height means for the three types of fertilizer without having to condition on a particular value of the covariate, you must be able to assume that the regression of final height on initial height is the same for all three types of fertilizer. This assumption of equality (homogeneity) of regression slopes can be tested by fitting a model containing main effects of *fert* and *initial*, as well as the *fert*initial* interaction. The interaction term provides the test of the null hypothesis of equal slopes.

To produce the output in this section, from the menus choose:

Analyze
  General Linear Model
    Univariate...

▶ Dependent Variable: height
▶ Fixed Factors(s): fert
▶ Covariate(s): initial

Model...
  ⊙ Custom
    ▶ Model: fert initial fert*initial

Options...
  ▶ Display Means for: location*size

  Display
    ☑ Observed power

Figure 10.22   Tests of between-subjects effects

Dependent Variable: Final Height

Source	Type III Sum of Squares	df	Mean Square	F	Sig.	Noncent. Parameter	Observed Power[1]
Corrected Model	330.500[2]	5	66.100	1.763	.515	8.813	.085
Intercept	2932.423	1	2932.423	78.198	.072	78.198	.512
FERT	30.396	2	15.198	.405	.743	.811	.060
INITIAL	18.000	1	18.000	.480	.614	.480	.061
FERT * INITIAL	1.750	2	.875	.023	.977	.047	.051
Error	37.500	1	37.500				
Total	44055.000	7					
Corrected Total	368.000	6					

[1]. Computed using alpha = .05

[2]. R Squared = .898 (Adjusted R Squared = .389)

The results are shown in Figure 10.22. The interaction term, *FERT*INITIAL*, shows no evidence of violation of the equal slopes assumption: the *F* value is 0.023, with a significance level of 0.977. The homogeneity of regressions assumption is not rejected, and you can proceed to estimate the effects of fertilizer type on final height given initial height. (Of course, such a small sample provides little power to detect much; these data are being used simply to illustrate the steps involved in this type of analysis.)

Analysis-of-Covariance Model

To produce the analysis-of-covariance results, recall the GLM Univariate dialog box, or from the menus choose:

Analyze
  General Linear Model
    Univariate...

▶ Dependent Variable: height
▶ Fixed Factors(s): fert
▶ Covariate(s): initial

Model...
  ⊙ Full factorial

Options...
  Estimated Marginal Means
  ▶ Display Means for: fert

  Display
      ☑ Parameter estimates
      ☑ Observed power

Figure 10.23   Tests of between-subjects effects

Dependent Variable: Final Height

Source	Type III Sum of Squares	df	Mean Square	F	Sig.	Noncent. Parameter	Observed Power[1]
Corrected Model	328.750[2]	3	109.583	8.376	.057	25.127	.584
Intercept	3796.875	1	3796.875	290.207	.000	290.207	1.000
INITIAL	18.750	1	18.750	1.433	.317	1.433	.138
FERT	243.187	2	121.594	9.294	.052	18.588	.600
Error	39.250	3	13.083				
Total	44055.000	7					
Corrected Total	368.000	6					

[1]. Computed using alpha = .05

[2]. R Squared = .893 (Adjusted R Squared = .787)

The ANCOVA results are shown in Figure 10.23. In the *F* and *Sig.* columns, there is some evidence of a *fert* effect: the *F* value is 9.294, with a significance of 0.052. Using the default Type III sums of squares, the test for the covariate is a test of the common or pooled within-cells regression of final height on initial height. This regression coefficient estimate appears in the parameter estimates table as the *B* coefficient for *INITIAL* (see Figure 10.24).

Figure 10.24   Parameter estimates

Dependent Variable	Parameter	B	Std. Error	t	Sig.	95% Confidence Interval Lower Bound	95% Confidence Interval Upper Bound	Noncent. Parameter	Observed Power[1]
Final Height	Intercept	82.750	5.814	14.234	.001	64.248	101.252	14.234	1.000
	[FERT=1]	-14.750	3.463	-4.259	.024	-25.771	-3.729	4.259	.801
	[FERT=2]	-8.500	4.177	-2.035	.135	-21.792	4.792	2.035	.297
	[FERT=3]	0[2]	.	.	.	.	.	.	.
	INITIAL	1.250	1.044	1.197	.317	-2.073	4.573	1.197	.138

[1]. Computed using alpha = .05

[2]. This parameter is set to zero because it is redundant.

In the GLM parameterization, the intercept parameter estimate gives the estimated value of the last category of *fert* (*FERT=3*) when the covariate is equal to 0. The *FERT=1* and *FERT=2* coefficients subtract the level 3 predicted value from the levels 1 and 2 predicted values, respectively. Adding one of these coefficients to the intercept estimate gives the estimated value for that level of *fert*, again when the covariate is equal to 0.

Estimated Marginal Means

The estimated marginal means table (see Figure 10.25) displays the estimated means and standard errors for each level of *fert* when the covariate is at its mean value (which, for this data set, is 4).

Figure 10.25   Estimated marginal means

Fertilizer

Dependent Variable: Final Height

Fertilizer	Mean	Std. Error	95% Confidence Interval	
			Lower Bound	Upper Bound
1	73.000	2.088	66.354	79.646
2	79.250	2.763	70.458	88.042
3	87.750	2.763	78.958	96.542

These means can be calculated by using values from the *B* column in Figure 10.24. The level 1 estimated marginal mean is

$$82.75 - 14.75 + 4 \times 1.25 = 73$$

For level 2,

$$82.75 - 8.5 + 4 \times 1.25 = 79.25$$

and for level 3,

$$82.75 + 0 + 4 \times 1.25 = 87.75$$

The 0 in the level 3 equation is from the aliased coefficient for *FERT=3*. This version of adjusted means is based on the definitions given in Searle, Speed, and Milliken (1980). In unbalanced designs, these estimated means usually differ from the adjusted means given by the **PMEANS** subcommand in the MANOVA procedure by a constant amount. Although both give the same results for all contrasts among covariate adjusted means, the GLM estimated marginal means (*EMMEANS*) definition is more consistent with the statistical literature.

A Nested Model Using the Interaction Operator

Finally, had there been evidence of **heterogeneity** or inequality of regressions, you could estimate a model incorporating separate slopes. The separate slopes estimates could be reconstructed from parameter estimates from the interaction model originally fitted, since this is the same overall model as the separate slopes model, but there are easier ways to obtain the individual slope estimates. If you were to specify the nesting of *initial* within *fert* explicitly, you would have to use syntax. However, due to the parameterization used in GLM, many nested models can be specified using the crossing or interaction operator in the Model dialog box. Specifying the main effect of *fert* and the interaction of *fert*initial* without the main effect *initial* fits the same nested model as one with *fert* and *initial-within-fert* effects, and the *FERT*INITIAL* parameter estimates will give the simple slope estimates within each level of *fert*.

To obtain these separate slope estimates, recall the GLM Univariate dialog box, or from the menus choose:

Analyze
  General Linear Model
    Univariate...

▶ Dependent Variable: height
▶ Fixed Factors(s): fert
▶ Covariate(s): initial

Model...
    ⊙ Custom
    ▶ Model: fert fert*initial (initial is removed)
    ☐ Include intercept in model (deselect)

Options...
    ☑ Parameter estimates
    ☑ Observed power

The tests of between-subjects effects (ANOVA table) are not of much interest at this point (see Figure 10.26).

Figure 10.26   Tests of between-subjects effects

Dependent Variable: Final Height

Source	Type III Sum of Squares	df	Mean Square	F	Sig.	Noncent. Parameter	Observed Power[1]
Model	44017.500[2]	6	7336.250	195.633	.055	1173.800	.989
FERT	3521.963	3	1173.988	31.306	.130	93.919	.300
FERT * INITIAL	20.500	3	6.833	.182	.899	.547	.054
Error	37.500	1	37.500				
Total	44055.000	7					

[1.] Computed using alpha = .05

[2.] R Squared = .999 (Adjusted R Squared = .994)

The *FERT*INITIAL* effect tests the null hypothesis that all slopes are equal to 0 (a hypothesis already rejected if an interaction between the factor and the covariate is assumed). The *fert* effect tests the null hypothesis that all three estimated means in the separate slopes model are equal to 0 when the covariate is set to 0.

Figure 10.27   Parameter estimates

Parameter Estimates

Dependent Variable	Parameter	B	Std. Error	t	Sig.	95% Confidence Interval		Noncent. Parameter	Observed Power[1]
						Lower Bound	Upper Bound		
Final Height	[FERT=1]	67.000	17.678	3.790	.164	-157.616	291.616	3.790	.234
	[FERT=2]	72.000	13.693	5.258	.120	-101.987	245.987	5.258	.320
	[FERT=3]	84.000	11.659	7.205	.088	-64.144	232.144	7.205	.428
	[FERT=1] * INITIAL	1.500	4.330	.346	.788	-53.519	56.519	.346	.053
	[FERT=2] * INITIAL	2.000	4.330	.462	.725	-53.019	57.019	.462	.055
	[FERT=3] * INITIAL	1.000	2.165	.462	.725	-26.510	28.510	.462	.055

[1.] Computed using alpha = .05

The parameter estimates table (see Figure 10.27) displays the estimated simple slopes (the three *FERT*INITIAL* coefficients in the *B* column). Suppressing the intercept term produces *FERT* coefficients that give estimated values for the *fert* means when *initial* is 0. Therefore, each *FERT* coefficient and the corresponding *FERT*INITIAL* coefficient can be combined into a separate prediction equation for that level of the fertilizer factor. For example, for *FERT=1*, using values in the *B* column, the equation would be

$$\hat{Y}_1 = 67 + 1.5(initial)$$

Example 6
Mixed-Effects Nested Design Model

Do strain readings of glass cathode supports from five different machines depend on the various heads installed in the machine? An engineer studied the strain readings of glass cathode supports from five different machines, as described by Hicks (1982). Each machine has its own four heads mounted. Since four heads are mounted on each machine, and the types of heads are not interacting with different machines, heads are said to be **nested within** machines. The four types of heads that are mounted on a machine can be chosen from many possible heads. Therefore, the four heads are considered as a random sample that might be used on a given machine. Four strain readings were taken from each head in each machine. The results of this experiment are shown in Figure 10.28.

Figure 10.28   Strain readings of glass cathode supports

Head	Machine				
	A	**B**	**C**	**D**	**E**
1	6, 2, 0, 8	10, 9, 7, 12	0, 0, 5, 5	11, 0, 6, 4	1, 4, 7, 9
2	13, 3, 9, 8	2, 1, 1, 10	10, 11, 6, 7	5, 10, 8, 3	6, 7, 0, 3
3	1, 10, 0, 6	4, 1, 7, 9	8, 5, 0, 7	1, 8, 9, 4	3, 0, 2, 2
4	7, 4, 7, 9	0, 3, 4, 1	7, 2, 5, 4	0, 8, 6, 5	3, 7, 4, 0

The SPSS data file *glass strain* contains three variables: *strain*, *machine*, and *head*. One case is entered for each strain reading. The variable *strain* is the dependent variable, *machine* is a factor with five levels, and *head* is a random factor with four levels within each level of *machine*.

To indicate a factor that is random, move it to the Random Factor(s) list. To specify a nested design, you must use syntax.

To produce the output in this example, from the menus choose:

Analyze
  General Linear Model
    Univariate...

▶ Dependent Variable: strain
▶ Fixed Factor(s): machine
▶ Random Factor(s): head

Model...
    ⊙ Custom
    ▶ Model: machine

Options...
    ☑ Observed power

Paste

In the syntax window, at the end of the DESIGN subcommand, type in the nested factor for *head-within-machine*, HEAD(MACHINE). The modified syntax is

```
UNIANOVA STRAIN BY MACHINE HEAD
  /RANDOM HEAD
  /METHOD = SSTYPE(3)
  /INTERCEPT = INCLUDE
  /CRITERIA = ALPHA(.05)
  /PRINT = OPOWER
  /DESIGN MACHINE HEAD(MACHINE).
```

Run the command by clicking the Run Current tool.

Note that this nested model has no interaction effect because the head factor is not crossed with the five machine levels. It is a **mixed-effects model** in which the machine factor is a fixed effect and the head factor is a random effect. The *head-within-machine* effect is also treated as random because it contains a random factor. If you specify a random factor, all effects that contain the random factor are automatically random.

Figure 10.29   Tests of between-subjects effects

Source		Type III Sum of Squares	df	Mean Square	F	Sig.	Noncent. Parameter	Observed Power[a]
Intercept	Hypothesis	2020.05	1	2020.05	107.117	.000	107.117	1.000
	Error	282.875	15	18.858[b]				
MACHINE	Hypothesis	45.075	4	11.269	.598	.670	2.390	.156
	Error	282.875	15	18.858[b]				
HEAD(MACHINE)	Hypothesis	282.875	15	18.858	1.762	.063	26.437	.869
	Error	642.000	60	10.700[c]				

a. Computed using alpha = .050

b. MS(HEAD(MACHINE))

c. MS(Error)

Univariate tests are shown in Figure 10.29. The table displays the appropriate error terms for a mixed-effects model. These error terms are used in the F tests to determine whether the effects are significant. In fact, the appropriate error term for the F test is usually a linear combination of the mean squares in the model. When a random factor is specified, each of these combinations of mean squares is calculated and used automatically.

The linear combination of the mean squares that is used as the error term in testing each effect in the model is displayed in footnotes at the bottom of the analysis-of-variance table. For example, to test the *machine* effect, the mean square $MS(HEAD(MACHINE))$ is used as the error term, and the F statistic for the *machine* effect is

$$\frac{11.269}{18.858} = 0.598$$

You can see that the error term for *MACHINE* is the same as the mean square for *HEAD(MACHINE)*.

Footnote c indicates that to test the *head-within-machine* effect, the error mean square $MS(ERROR)$ is used as the error term; the F statistic for the *head-within-machine* effect is

$$\frac{18.858}{10.7} = 1.762$$

From the table in Figure 10.29, the *machine* effect is not significant, but the *head-within-machine* effect is significant at the 0.10 alpha level ($p = 0.0625$). This result suggests that there may be differences in glass strain between heads on the same machine.

Composition of Error Terms in a Mixed-Effects Model

To see how SPSS determines the appropriate error term in a mixed-effects model, look at the expected mean square components of each effect in the model. These components are shown in Figure 10.30.

Figure 10.30   Expected mean square components

Expected Mean Squares[a,b]

Source	Variance Component		
	Var(HEAD(MACHINE))	Var(Error)	Quadratic Term
Intercept	4.000	1.000	Intercept, MACHINE
MACHINE	4.000	1.000	MACHINE
HEAD(MACHINE)	4.000	1.000	.
Error	.000	1.000	.

a. For each source, the expected mean square equals the sum of the coefficients in the cells times the variance components, plus a quadratic term involving effects in the Quadratic Term cell.

b. Expected Mean Squares are based on the Type III Sums of Squares.

The **expected mean square** of an effect in the model is the expectation of the mean squares of that effect in the model. It is usually a linear combination of variance components of the random effects and quadratic terms of the fixed effects in the model. In Figure 10.30, each row represents the linear combination of variance components involved in the expected mean square of the effect in the model.

The expected mean square for the *head-within-machine* effect involves only two variance terms: the variance of the *head-within-machine* effect itself and the variance of error. The coefficient for the variance of *HEAD(MACHINE)* is 4, and the coefficient for the variance of error is 1. This means that the expected mean square for *HEAD(MACHINE)* is

4 Var(HEAD(MACHINE)) + 1 Var(Error)

For the *machine* effect, in addition to the linear combination of the variance components—$4\text{Var}(\text{HEAD}(\text{MACHINE})) + 1\text{Var}(\text{Error})$—a quadratic term that involves the fixed effect *machine* is also included. Therefore, the expected mean square of the *machine* effect is

$$(4\text{Var}(\text{HEAD}(\text{MACHINE})) + 1\text{Var}(\text{Error}) + Q(\text{MACHINE}))$$

where *Q(MACHINE)* represents the quadratic term involving the *machine* effect.

Testing the *machine* effect is equivalent to testing whether the quadratic term of *MACHINE* is 0. If $Q(\text{MACHINE}) = 0$, the expected mean square of the *machine* effect is the same as the expected mean square of *HEAD(MACHINE)*. Therefore, the mean square for *HEAD(MACHINE)* is an appropriate error term for testing the *machine* effect. In the univariate tests table (see Figure 10.29), the error term for *MACHINE* has a footnote to indicate the relationship. You can see that the values across the row for the *MACHINE* error term are the same as the values in the *HEAD(MACHINE)* hypothesis row.

Similarly, testing the *head-within-machine* effect is equivalent to testing whether the variance of *HEAD(MACHINE)* is 0. Since the expected mean square of *HEAD(MACHINE)* when $\text{Var}(\text{HEAD}(\text{MACHINE})) = 0$ is the same as the variance of error, the mean square of error is an appropriate error term for testing the *head-within-machine* effect.

Contrast Coefficients

To detect which machine contains heads that are significantly different, five sets of custom hypotheses (one for each machine) are needed. In each of the five sets of custom hypotheses, the heads within the same machine will be compared. Comparing four heads implies three contrasts. Notice that the degrees of freedom for *HEAD(MACHINE)* is 15, which means that 15 contrasts are involved in this hypothesis. You can partition the hypothesis for *HEAD(MACHINE)* into five parts; each part represents one comparison of heads within a machine with three contrasts. To display all 15 contrasts for testing *HEAD(MACHINE)*, you must use syntax. Click the Dialog Recall tool and select the GLM Univariate dialog box. Click the *Paste* button and add the subcommand PRINT=TEST(LMATRIX) as well as the HEAD(MACHINE) effect.

```
UNIANOVA strain BY machine head
 /PRINT TEST(LMATRIX) OPOWER
 /RANDOM head
 /DESIGN machine HEAD(MACHINE).
```

Run the command by clicking the Run Current tool. SPSS displays matrices showing all of the contrast coefficients. The part of the matrix with nonzero coefficients for *HEAD(MACHINE A)* has the following entries:

[HEAD=1]([MACHINE=A])	1.000	.000	.000
[HEAD=2]([MACHINE=A])	.000	1.000	.000
[HEAD=3]([MACHINE=A])	.000	.000	1.000
[HEAD=4]([MACHINE=A])	-1.000	-1.000	-1.000

To specify the custom hypothesis for comparing the heads in machine A, the coefficients for the first three contrasts (columns) in the contrast coefficients matrix for *HEAD(MACHINE)* are used. Similarly, the coefficients for the second three contrasts in the contrast matrix are used for machine B, and so on. The remaining coefficients in the table are all equal to 0. The following syntax shows the five custom hypotheses using the **LMATRIX** subcommand:

```
UNIANOVA STRAIN BY MACHINE HEAD
  /RANDOM HEAD
  /DESIGN MACHINE HEAD(MACHINE)
  /LMATRIX= "HEAD(MACHINE A)"
    HEAD(MACHINE) 1 0 0 -1 0 0 0 0 0 0 0 0 0 0 0 0 0 0 0 0;
    HEAD(MACHINE) 0 1 0 -1 0 0 0 0 0 0 0 0 0 0 0 0 0 0 0 0;
    HEAD(MACHINE) 0 0 1 -1 0 0 0 0 0 0 0 0 0 0 0 0 0 0 0 0
  /LMATRIX= "HEAD(MACHINE B)"
    HEAD(MACHINE) 0 0 0 0 1 0 0 -1 0 0 0 0 0 0 0 0 0 0 0 0;
    HEAD(MACHINE) 0 0 0 0 0 1 0 -1 0 0 0 0 0 0 0 0 0 0 0 0;
    HEAD(MACHINE) 0 0 0 0 0 0 1 -1 0 0 0 0 0 0 0 0 0 0 0 0
  /LMATRIX= "HEAD(MACHINE C)"
    HEAD(MACHINE) 0 0 0 0 0 0 0 0 1 0 0 -1 0 0 0 0 0 0 0 0;
    HEAD(MACHINE) 0 0 0 0 0 0 0 0 0 1 0 -1 0 0 0 0 0 0 0 0;
    HEAD(MACHINE) 0 0 0 0 0 0 0 0 0 0 1 -1 0 0 0 0 0 0 0 0
  /LMATRIX= "HEAD(MACHINE D)"
    HEAD(MACHINE) 0 0 0 0 0 0 0 0 0 0 0 0 1 0 0 -1 0 0 0 0;
    HEAD(MACHINE) 0 0 0 0 0 0 0 0 0 0 0 0 0 1 0 -1 0 0 0 0;
    HEAD(MACHINE) 0 0 0 0 0 0 0 0 0 0 0 0 0 0 1 -1 0 0 0 0
  /LMATRIX= "HEAD(MACHINE E)"
    HEAD(MACHINE) 0 0 0 0 0 0 0 0 0 0 0 0 0 0 0 0 1 0 0 -1;
    HEAD(MACHINE) 0 0 0 0 0 0 0 0 0 0 0 0 0 0 0 0 0 1 0 -1;
    HEAD(MACHINE) 0 0 0 0 0 0 0 0 0 0 0 0 0 0 0 0 0 0 1 -1.
```

The results of the custom hypotheses are shown in Figure 10.31. A caption was inserted at the bottom of each table to identify the contrast.

Figure 10.31   Contrasts for head-within-machine

Univariate Test Results

Dependent Variable: STRAIN

Source	Type III Sum of Squares	df	Mean Square	F	Sig.	Noncentrality Parameter	Observed Power
Contrast	50.188	3	16.729	1.563	.208	4.690	.391
Error	642.000	60	10.700				

HEAD(MACHINE A)

Univariate Test Results

Dependent Variable: STRAIN

Source	Type III Sum of Squares	df	Mean Square	F	Sig.	Noncentrality Parameter	Observed Power
Contrast	126.187	3	42.062	3.931	.013	11.793	.806
Error	642.000	60	10.700				

HEAD(MACHINE B)

Univariate Test Results

Dependent Variable: STRAIN

Source	Type III Sum of Squares	df	Mean Square	F	Sig.	Noncentrality Parameter	Observed Power
Contrast	74.750	3	24.917	2.329	.083	6.986	.558
Error	642.000	60	10.700				

HEAD(MACHINE C)

Univariate Test Results

Dependent Variable: STRAIN

Source	Type III Sum of Squares	df	Mean Square	F	Sig.	Noncentrality Parameter	Observed Power
Contrast	6.500	3	2.167	.202	.894	.607	.086
Error	642.000	60	10.700				

HEAD(MACHINE D)

Univariate Test Results

Dependent Variable: STRAIN

Source	Type III Sum of Squares	df	Mean Square	F	Sig.	Noncentrality Parameter	Observed Power
Contrast	25.250	3	8.417	.787	.506	2.360	.209
Error	642.000	60	10.700				

HEAD(MACHINE E)

Using $\alpha = 0.10$, you can see that there are significant differences between heads in machine B and machine C.

Example 7
Univariate Repeated Measures Analysis Using a Split-Plot Design Approach

Does the anxiety rating of a person affect performance on a learning task? An experiment was conducted to study the effect of anxiety on a learning task. Twelve subjects were assigned to one of two anxiety groups according to their anxiety measurement scores. The subjects were given four sets of trials, called blocks of trials. The criterion (score) is the number of errors in each block of trials. The data are taken from Winer, Brown, and Michels (1991) and are shown in Figure 10.32.

Figure 10.32   Error scores by students in two anxiety groups

		Score			
Subject	Anxiety Group	Trial 1	Trial 2	Trial 3	Trial 4
1	1	18	14	12	6
2	1	19	12	8	4
3	1	14	10	6	2
4	1	16	12	10	4
5	1	12	8	6	2
6	1	18	10	5	1
7	2	16	10	8	4
8	2	18	8	4	1
9	2	16	12	6	2
10	2	19	16	10	8
11	2	16	14	10	9
12	2	16	12	8	8

The SPSS file *anxiety* contains the four variables *subject, anxiety, score,* and *trial*. Each value of *score* is represented by one case in the data file, as shown in Figure 10.33.

Figure 10.33   Data structure

	subject	anxiety	tension	score	trial	va
1	1	1	1	18	1	
2	1	1	1	14	2	
3	1	1	1	12	3	
4	1	1	1	6	4	
5	2	1	1	19	1	
6	2	1	1	12	2	
7	2	1	1	8	3	
8	2	1	1	4	4	
9	3	1	1	14	1	
10	3	1	1	10	2	

There are two sizes of experimental units in the data: the subjects, which are the larger experimental units, and the blocks of trials within each subject, which are the smaller experimental units. The *anxiety* effect is considered as the whole-plot treatment, since it is applied to the subjects, the larger experimental unit. Historically, statistical studies divided an agricultural plot into subplots, and the names **whole plot** and **subplot** have carried over into fields of study other than agriculture. The *trial* effect is considered as the subplot treatment, since it is applied to the blocks of trial within each subject, the smaller experimental units.

When people perform the same type of task more than once, there is often a change from one trial to the next, so that performance on one trial is correlated with performance on previous trials. These tendencies can be expressed by saying that there are nonzero correlations among the blocks of trials within the same subject, with higher correlations for blocks that are closer in time. Usually, a split-plot design assumes that these correlations are 0 or at least remain constant over all the blocks within the same subject. In this example, the covariances among the blocks of trials within the same subject are temporarily assumed to be 0.

In this example, the model uses a split-plot design. The *anxiety* effect is the whole plot treatment, and the *subject-within-anxiety* effect, designated as *SUBJECT(ANXIETY)*, serves as the replication term in testing the *anxiety* effect. It should be entered as a random factor. The *trial* effect has four levels. It is the subplot treatment. The *trial*anxiety* effect is the interaction effect between the *anxiety* effect and the *trial* effect.

To produce the output shown in this example, from the menus choose:

Analyze
  General Linear Model
    Univariate

▸ Dependent Variable: score
▸ Fixed Factor(s): trial anxiety
▸ Random Factor(s): subject

Model...
  ⊙ Custom
    ▸ Model: anxiety trial trial*anxiety

Options...
  Display
      ☑ Observed power

Paste

In the syntax window, on the DESIGN subcommand, insert the *subject-within-anxiety* effect—SUBJECT(ANXIETY)—after ANXIETY. The resulting syntax is

```
UNIANOVA score BY trial anxiety subject
  /RANDOM subject
  /METHOD = SSTYPE(3)
  /CRITERIA = ALPHA(.05)
  /PRINT = OPOWER
  /DESIGN anxiety SUBJECT(ANXIETY) trial trial*anxiety.
```

To run the command, click the Run Current tool. The analysis-of-variance table is shown in Figure 10.34.

Figure 10.34   Tests of between-subjects effects

Source		Type III Sum of Squares	df	Mean Square	F	Sig.	Noncent. Parameter	Observed Power[a]
Intercept	Hypothesis	4800.00	1	4800.00	280.839	.000	280.839	1.000
	Error	170.917	10	17.092[b]				
ANXIETY	Hypothesis	10.083	1	10.083	.590	.460	.590	.107
	Error	170.917	10	17.092[b]				
SUBJECT(ANXIETY)	Hypothesis	170.917	10	17.092	6.652	.000	66.519	1.000
	Error	77.083	30	2.569[c]				
TRIAL	Hypothesis	991.500	3	330.500	128.627	.000	385.881	1.000
	Error	77.083	30	2.569[c]				
TRIAL*ANXIETY	Hypothesis	8.417	3	2.806	1.092	.368	3.276	.265
	Error	77.083	30	2.569[c]				

a. Computed using alpha = .050

b. MS(SUBJECT(ANXIETY))

c. MS(Error)

Notice from the footnote for the error term of the *anxiety* effect (footnote *c*) that the mean square of the *subject-within-anxiety* effect is used as the error term in testing the *anxiety* effect. The *F* statistic is 0.590, which is not significant. Both the *trial* effect and the *trial*anxiety* effect use the error mean square as the error term. The *F* statistic for the *trial* effect is 128.627, which is significant with $p = 0.0001$. The *F* statistic for the *trial*anxiety* effect is 1.092, which is not significant.

Expected Mean Squares

The expected mean squares table is shown in Figure 10.35.

Figure 10.35   Expected mean squares components

Expected Mean Squares[1,2]

Source	Variance Component		
	Var(SUBJECT(ANXIETY))	Var(Error)	Quadratic Term
Intercept	4.000	1.000	Intercept, ANXIETY, TRIAL, TRIAL * ANXIETY
ANXIETY	4.000	1.000	ANXIETY, TRIAL * ANXIETY
SUBJECT(ANXIETY)	4.000	1.000	.
TRIAL	.000	1.000	TRIAL, TRIAL * ANXIETY
TRIAL * ANXIETY	.000	1.000	TRIAL * ANXIETY
Error	.000	1.000	

[1] For each source, the expected mean square equals the sum of the coefficients in the cells times the variance components, plus a quadratic term involving effects in the Quadratic Term cell.

[2] Expected Mean Squares are based on the Type III Sums of Squares.

In addition to the variance components, there is a quadratic term associated with each of the fixed effects and other fixed effects containing the effect. For the *anxiety* effect, the other fixed effect that contains it and involves the quadratic term is the higher-order interaction effect *trial*anxiety*. This higher interaction effect is assumed to be 0 when testing the *anxiety* effect. For the *trial* effect, the higher-order interaction effect *trial*anxiety* is the effect that contains it and involves the quadratic term. This effect is assumed to be 0 when testing the *trial* effect. Since there are no other effects in the model that contain the *trial*anxiety* effect, the quadratic term for *trial*anxiety* consists only of itself.

11 Bivariate and Partial Correlations

A correlation coefficient measures the strength of a linear association between two variables. The Correlate submenu provides three items for correlations, but only two are explained in this chapter: Bivariate and Partial. The usual Pearson product-moment correlation is the default for the first item, with Kendall's tau-*b* and Spearman's rho rank-order coefficients available as options. Both Pearson correlations and partial correlations are provided on the second item. Partial correlations measure the linear association between two variables after the effects of one or more variables are removed.

Correlations. The **Pearson correlation coefficient**, *r*, measures the strength of a *linear* relationship between two quantitative variables. Examples of some relations are:

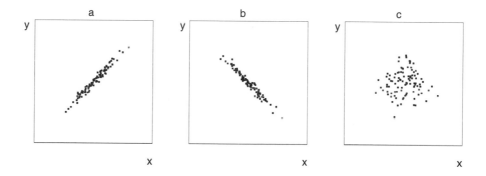

The correlations in these figures are, respectively,

- Positive (close to +1).
- Negative (close to –1).
- No relation (close to 0).

The values of the coefficient are not expressed in units of the data, but range from –1 to 1. While scatterplots provide a picture of the relation, the value of the correlation is the same if you switch the *y* (vertical) and *x* (horizontal) measures.

The formula is

$$r = \sum_{i=1}^{N} \frac{(x_i - \bar{x})(y_i - \bar{y})}{(N-1)s_x s_y}$$

where N is the sample size and s_x and s_y are the standard deviations of the two variables.

The discussion about data screening in the introduction to the Regression procedure (see Chapter 12) applies to correlations, too. In particular, see Figure 12.4, which illustrates the importance of scanning scatterplots, because the same correlation coefficient can result from very different configurations of data values. Note that a test that the slope (b) of the regression line is 0 is the same as a test that the correlation is 0, because the relation between the slope and the correlation is

$$r = b\frac{s_x}{s_y}$$

Normality is assumed when testing hypotheses about these correlations.

Before reporting correlations, you should examine a scatterplot for each pair of variables. Look for:

- Outliers.
- A need for a transformation to improve linearity.
- The presence of subpopulations that might mask a relationship or, conversely, falsely enhance it.

To compute the **Spearman rank correlation coefficient**, SPSS uses the rank order of each data value in the formula for the Pearson correlation coefficient (adjustments are made if there are ties). Like the Pearson correlation coefficient, the values of this statistic range between −1 and +1. However, the assumption of normality is not required, so this measure is appropriate for variables with ordered codes as well as quantitative variables.

Partial correlations can reveal variables that enhance or suppress the relation between two particular variables. For example, if each Sunday for a year, you were to count the number of ants in the kitchen at a beach cabin and the number of cars passing the house in a five-minute interval, a scatterplot of the ants against the cars would look like plot *a* above, and the correlation would be close to 1. Are the cars bringing the ants? Does this sound silly? A third variable, temperature, is ignored. When the weather is hot, the ants flourish and lots of people flock to the beach; when it is cool, the numbers of both the cars and ants diminish. If the linear effect of temperature is controlled, the relationship between ants and cars disappears.

The **partial correlation** of variables *A* and *B* after removing the effect of variable *C* (or "controlling" for variable *C*) is estimated as follows:

- Regress variable *A* on *C*.
- Regress variable *B* on *C*.
- For each case, compute the residuals for each of the regression equations.
- Compute the usual Pearson correlation between the two sets of residuals.

The residuals represent variables *A* and *B* with the effect of variable *C* removed.

Missing data. Often when you want to examine correlations among several variables, one or more data values may be missing. By default, for Bivariate, SPSS treats the calculation for each pair of variables as a separate problem, using all cases with complete data for the pair. Thus, the correlation for variables *A* and *B* might use data from 30 cases, the correlation for variables *A* and *C*, 20 cases. This is the Exclude cases **pairwise** method for handling missing data. As an option, you can select the **listwise** method to include only those cases complete on variables *A*, *B*, and *C*. If you include a fourth variable *D* and it has values missing for cases different from those for variables *A*, *B*, and *C*, the sample size for the *AB* correlation is reduced further with the listwise method.

Why throw data away by using listwise? First of all, some researchers are uncomfortable about using a "different sample" for each entry in the pairwise matrix. If, for example, 20% of the values are missing, it may not be difficult to find two correlations computed from substantially different subsets of the cases. Second, if you use the pairwise option in a multivariate procedure like multiple regression, the resulting matrix can cause computational difficulties because it is singular or has eigenvalues less than 0.

It is also very important to assess the pattern of how data values are missing. See the comments in "Correlations" on p. 183.

The examples in this chapter are organized as follows:

Example 1: Pearson correlations with pairwise and listwise methods for incomplete data. Some data values in the file *world95* are missing, so this example illustrates both the listwise and pairwise methods for selecting the values used in the computations (these methods are also available for Spearman and partial correlation computations). Correlations are requested for four demographic variables and an economic measure, gross domestic product per capita (*gdp_cap*). Because the distribution of the last variable is very skewed, you log transform its values to form a more symmetric distribution.

Example 2: Spearman rank correlations. The rank order of each data value is used to compute correlations for the variables in Example 1. The Spearman correlations agree more closely with Pearson correlations for the logged version of the economic measure than the untransformed values.

Example 3: Partial correlations. Continuing with the same variables, the linear effect of *log_gdp* is removed from the correlations among the other variables. The Pearson correlations, called zero-order correlations, are also displayed.

Example 1
Pearson Correlations with Pairwise and Listwise Methods for Incomplete Data

For this example, you request Pearson correlations among variables recording the percentage of population living in cities, percentage of females who read, birth rate, death rate, and gross domestic product per capita. The distribution of gross domestic product is highly skewed, so you also include a copy of the variable after log transforming its values (that is, the distribution of the transformed values is more symmetric than that of the raw data).

First use the default pairwise method for incomplete data and then request listwise deletion.

To produce this output, from the menus choose:

Analyze
  Correlate
    Bivariate...

Click *Reset* to restore the dialog box defaults, and then select:

▸ Variables: urban, lit_fema, birth_rt, death_rt, gdp_cap, log_gdp

Run these instructions two times: first, using the default *Exclude cases pairwise* method for handling missing data, and second, in the Bivariate Correlations dialog box, select:

Options...
  Missing Values
  ⊙ Exclude cases listwise

Correlations

		URBAN	LIT_FEMA	BIRTH_RT	DEATH_RT	GDP_CAP	LOG_GDP
Pearson Correlation	URBAN	1.000	.612**	-.629**	-.483**	.605**	.754**
	LIT_FEMA	.612**	1.000	-.835**	-.510**	.429**	.632**
	BIRTH_RT	-.629**	-.835**	1.000	.367**	-.651**	-.769**
	DEATH_RT	-.483**	-.510**	.367**	1.000	-.166	-.402**
	GDP_CAP	.605**	.429**	-.651**	-.166	1.000	.867**
	LOG_GDP	.754**	.632**	-.769**	-.402**	.867**	1.000
Significance(2-tailed)	URBAN		.000	.000	.000	.000	.000
	LIT_FEMA	.000		.000	.000	.000	.000
	BIRTH_RT	.000	.000		.000	.000	.000
	DEATH_RT	.000	.000	.000		.086	.000
	GDP_CAP	.000	.000	.000	.086		.000
	LOG_GDP	.000	.000	.000	.000	.000	
N	URBAN	108	85	108	107	108	108
	LIT_FEMA	85	85	85	85	85	85
	BIRTH_RT	108	85	109	108	109	109
	DEATH_RT	107	85	108	108	108	108
	GDP_CAP	108	85	109	108	109	109
	LOG_GDP	108	85	109	108	109	109

**. Correlation is significant at the 0.01 level (2-tailed).

Correlations (pairwise option). Among the six variables selected, there are 15 pairs—thus, 15 correlation coefficients. In the top panel, each correlation coefficient is displayed twice. See the 1's on the diagonal (for each variable with itself). The correlations below the diagonal are the same as those above it. For example, in the first column, the correlation of *urban* (percentage living in cities) with *lit_fema* (percentage of females who read) is 0.612. This correlation is repeated at the top of the second column.

The correlation between *urban* and *lit_fema* is positive indicating that as female literacy increases so does the percentage of urban dwellers. The correlation between *urban* and *birth_rt* is negative (–0.629) indicating that as the birth rate increases, the proportion of city dwellers in a country decreases.

The correlations 0.612 and –0.629 are estimates of the population parameter for each pair of variables. Can you reject the hypothesis that the population value for each is 0 (that is, no relation)? Probabilities associated with these correlations are displayed in the second panel in the same format as the statistics. The probability associated with both 0.612 and –0.629 is printed as 0.000 (or less than 0.0005) indicating that the two correlations do differ significantly from 0.

However, if you scan results for more than one pair of variables, these probabilities are *pseudo probabilities* because they are designed to test one and only one correlation for significance and do not reflect the number of correlations tested. As a result some correlations appear significant when they are not. Even if you want to scan these *p* values to get a sense of the size of one correlation relative to another, be cautious—especially with the pairwise option where the sample size varies from pair to pair.

If you are concerned about identifying too many correlations as significant, you can make your own Bonferroni adjustment to the probabilities. The Bonferroni method adjusts your stated significance level (for example, 0.05) by the *m*, number of correlations. That is, for a correlation to be reported in your paper as significant at the 0.05 level, the probability in the second panel must be less than 0.05 / *m*. In this example, *m* is 15, so the probability must be less than 0.05 / 15 = 0.0033. Thus 14 of the correlations do differ significantly from 0. Even without the adjustment the correlation between *gdp_cap* and *death_rt* is not significant. Notice that the correlation of death rate (*death_rt*) with gross domestic product in log units (*log_gdp*) is highly significant.

The sample size for each variable is reported along the diagonal of the third panel (108 for *urban*, 85 for *lit_fema*, 109 for *birth_rt*, and so on). The sample sizes for complete pairs of cases are reported off the diagonal. There are 109 countries in this sample. When a variable is paired with *lit_fema*, the sample size for the pair drops to 85.

Correlations

		URBAN	LIT_FEMA	BIRTH_RT	DEATH_RT	GDP_CAP	LOG_GDP
Pearson Correlation	URBAN	1.000	.612**	-.593**	-.588**	.591**	.777**
	LIT_FEMA	.612**	1.000	-.835**	-.510**	.429**	.632**
	BIRTH_RT	-.593**	-.835**	1.000	.469**	-.584**	-.721**
	DEATH_RT	-.588**	-.510**	.469**	1.000	-.263*	-.499**
	GDP_CAP	.591**	.429**	-.584**	-.263*	1.000	.836**
	LOG_GDP	.777**	.632**	-.721**	-.499**	.836**	1.000
Significance(2-tailed)	URBAN	.	.000	.000	.000	.000	.000
	LIT_FEMA	.000	.	.000	.000	.000	.000
	BIRTH_RT	.000	.000	.	.000	.000	.000
	DEATH_RT	.000	.000	.000	.	.015	.000
	GDP_CAP	.000	.000	.000	.015	.	.000
	LOG_GDP	.000	.000	.000	.000	.000	.

**. Correlation is significant at the 0.01 level (2-tailed).
*. Correlation is significant at the 0.05 level (2-tailed).

Correlations (listwise option). The sample size for each Pearson correlation computed with the listwise option is 85. Look at the following table to compare the pairwise and listwise correlations of variables with *death_rt* (107 or 108 cases are used in each pairwise correlation):

Table 11.1 **Comparison of pairwise and listwise correlations**

	Pairwise	**Listwise**
urban	–0.483	–0.588
birth_rt	0.367	0.469
log_gdp	–0.402	–0.499

It is hard to believe that the data are missing randomly, since the loss of 22 or 23 cases appears to strengthen the correlations. One way to identify a possible pattern is:

- Separate the cases into two groups by generating a new grouping variable with code 1 for cases where the value of *lit_fema* is present and code 0 for cases where the value is missing.

- Request a two-sample separate variances *t* for the other quantitative variables using the new grouping variable.

Doing this, you will find highly significant differences in the means of *urban*, *birth_rt*, and *log_gdp*. The 23 or 24 countries for which *lit_fema* is missing are more urban (68% versus 53% for the 85 countries reporting *lit_fema*), have a lower birth rate (15.15 versus 28.97), and *log_gdp* is higher. Surprisingly, it is the more developed countries that are not reporting rates for female literacy.

Care needs to be exercised when reporting correlations. The greatest abuse is to use data that have not been screened and have values that are not missing randomly, to use the pairwise option, and then to report results using unadjusted probabilities. Also be careful about implying that a significant correlation implies causation. The comments in "Residuals Statistics" on p. 200 describe the difference between association and causation.

Example 2
Spearman Rank Correlations

In this example, you continue with the variables used in Example 1, but this time you will request Spearman correlations. For these statistics, the rank order of each observation is used instead of the value as recorded. Thus, the computations for this coefficient are not sensitive to asymmetrical distributions or to the presence of outliers. The usual transformations, such as square root and log, do not reorder the data values, so ranks remain the same before and after transformation.

Because the listwise option for incomplete data is used, these results should be compared with those in the table on p. 183.

To produce this output, in the Bivariate Correlations dialog box, click *Reset* to restore the dialog box defaults, and then select:

▶ Variables: urban, lit_fema, birth_rt, death_rt, gdp_cap, log_gdp

Correlation Coefficients
☐ Pearson (deselect)
☑ Spearman

Options...
Missing Values
◉ Exclude cases listwise

Correlations

			URBAN	LIT_FEMA	BIRTH_RT	DEATH_RT	GDP_CAP	LOG_GDP
Spearman's rho	Correlation Coefficient	URBAN	1.000	.565**	-.586**	-.505**	.769**	.769**
		LIT_FEMA	.565**	1.000	-.832**	-.335**	.622**	.622**
		BIRTH_RT	-.586**	-.832**	1.000	.268*	-.716**	-.716**
		DEATH_RT	-.505**	-.335**	.268*	1.000	-.391**	-.391**
		GDP_CAP	.769**	.622**	-.716**	-.391**	1.000	1.000**
		LOG_GDP	.769**	.622**	-.716**	-.391**	1.000**	1.000
	Significance (2-tailed)	URBAN	.	.000	.000	.000	.000	.000
		LIT_FEMA	.000	.	.000	.002	.000	.000
		BIRTH_RT	.000	.000	.	.013	.000	.000
		DEATH_RT	.000	.002	.013	.	.000	.000
		GDP_CAP	.000	.000	.000	.000	.	.000
		LOG_GDP	.000	.000	.000	.000	.000	.

**. Correlation is significant at the .01 level (2-tailed).
*. Correlation is significant at the .05 level (2-tailed).

Correlations (Spearman). These rank-order coefficients are similar in magnitude to those in the Correlations table on p. 183. However, the correlation here of *death_rt* with *birth_rt* is 0.268 (it is marked as significant at the 0.05 level), while the Pearson correlation is 0.469 (significant at the 0.01 level). A quick look at a scatterplot of the two variables shows that the relationship is not linear.

Notice that the log-transformed values of GDP in the table of Pearson correlations agree more closely with the Spearman rank-order correlations than do those for the untransformed data. Nonlinear relationships exist in scatterplots of *gdp_cap* against the other variables. After transforming the economic measure to log units, the relation is considerably more linear.

Example 3
Partial Correlations

When you study the correlation between two variables, you need to consider the effects other variables exert on the relationship. Partial correlations provide a measure of correlation between two variables by removing or adjusting for the linear effects of one or more *control variables*.

The correlations among the five variables in the previous examples were significant. Does the economic strength of the countries enhance or diminish any of these relations? Here you remove the effects of *log_gdp* and request zero-order partial correlations.

To produce this output, from the menus choose:

Analyze
  Correlate
    Partial...

Click *Reset* to restore the dialog box defaults, and then select:

▶ Variables: urban, lit_fema, birth_rt, death_rt
▶ Controlling for: log_gdp

Options...
  Statistics
  ☑ Zero-order correlations

```
- - -  P A R T I A L    C O R R E L A T I O N    C O E F F I C I E N T S  - - -

Zero Order Partials

                URBAN     LIT_FEMA    BIRTH_RT    DEATH_RT    LOG_GDP

URBAN          1.0000       .6116      -.5932      -.5877       .7772
              (     0)     (    83)    (    83)    (    83)    (    83)
               P= .        P= .000     P= .000     P= .000     P= .000

LIT_FEMA        .6116      1.0000      -.8349      -.5096       .6323
              (    83)     (     0)    (    83)    (    83)    (    83)
               P= .000     P= .        P= .000     P= .000     P= .000

BIRTH_RT       -.5932      -.8349      1.0000       .4688      -.7214
              (    83)     (    83)    (     0)    (    83)    (    83)
               P= .000     P= .000     P= .         P= .000     P= .000

DEATH_RT       -.5877      -.5096       .4688      1.0000      -.4990
              (    83)     (    83)    (    83)    (     0)    (    83)
               P= .000     P= .000     P= .000     P= .         P= .000

LOG_GDP         .7772       .6323      -.7214      -.4990      1.0000
              (    83)     (    83)    (    83)    (    83)    (     0)
               P= .000     P= .000     P= .000     P= .000     P= .

(Coefficient / (D.F.) / 2-tailed Significance)

" . " is printed if a coefficient cannot be computed
```

Partial Correlation Coefficients (Zero Order Partials). Compare these correlations with those in the table on p. 183, because **zero-order partial correlations** are the usual Pearson correlations. The number under each correlation is its degrees of freedom, not the sample size. The degrees of freedom for a zero-order partial equals $n - 2$.

The order of the partial correlation coefficient is determined by the number of control variables. If there is one control variable, the coefficient is a **first-order partial**. If there are four control variables, it is a fourth-order partial. The degrees of freedom for each ordered partial are the sample size minus the order minus 2 (that is, for a sample of size 100, the degrees of freedom for a fourth-order partial are $100 - 4 - 2$, or 94).

```
- - - P A R T I A L   C O R R E L A T I O N   C O E F F I C I E N T S - - -

Controlling for..    LOG_GDP

                URBAN     LIT_FEMA   BIRTH_RT    DEATH_RT

URBAN          1.0000       .2465      -.0746      -.3666
              (    0)      (   82)     (   82)     (   82)
              P= .         P= .024     P= .500     P= .001

LIT_FEMA        .2465      1.0000      -.7061      -.2891
              (   82)      (    0)     (   82)     (   82)
              P= .024      P= .        P= .000     P= .008

BIRTH_RT       -.0746      -.7061      1.0000       .1813
              (   82)      (   82)     (    0)     (   82)
              P= .500      P= .000     P= .        P= .099

DEATH_RT       -.3666      -.2891       .1813      1.0000
              (   82)      (   82)     (   82)     (    0)
              P= .001      P= .008     P= .099     P= .

(Coefficient / (D.F.) / 2-tailed Significance)

" . " is printed if a coefficient cannot be computed
```

Partial Correlation Coefficients (Controlling for log_gdp). Removing the linear effect of economics from *urban* and *birth_rt* erases the correlation between the variables. Their simple correlation is –0.5932, their partial correlation, –0.0746. The partial correlations for the other variables are also less strong than the simple correlations.

12 Simple and Multiple Linear Regression

In many statistical studies, the goal is to establish a relationship, expressed via an equation, for predicting typical values of one variable given the value of another variable. The simplest equation is that of a straight line:

y = *a* + *b*x

Scatterplots can help you to determine if a straight line is appropriate to summarize the relationship. In Figure 12.1, values of female life expectancy are plotted on the *y* (vertical) axis and literacy on the *x* (horizontal) axis. Each plot point displays data for one country. For example, Hong Kong is at the top center—its life expectancy is 80 years and 64% of its females are literate. The line is the *line of best fit* that is estimated in Example 1.

Figure 12.1   Line of best fit for female life expectancy versus literacy

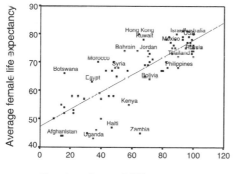

Females who read (%)

From scanning the line in the plot, you can see that when literacy is high, so is life expectancy; and when literacy is low, life expectancy tends to be short. The relationship is *linear* because the points scatter fairly evenly around the line.

A linear relationship can also occur when the line tilts from the upper left corner down to the lower right. For example, life expectancy tends to go down as infant mortality rate goes up (Example 2). If the line is flat, extending horizontally across the plot, there is no linear relation. If you see that a straight line summarizes the relationship poorly, you should seek a transformation to achieve linearity or consider other methods of analysis such as nonlinear regression (in SPSS Regression Models).

The regression model. To write the equation of the straight line as a statistical model, add a term for random error (ε) because the points do not all fall on the line:

$$y = \beta_0 + \beta_1 x + \varepsilon$$
female life expectancy $= \beta_0 + \beta_1$female literacy $+ \varepsilon$

The **slope** (β_1) is the ratio between the vertical change and the horizontal change along the line. For example, when literacy increases from 40% to 80%, life expectancy increases 12 or 13 years.

$$\beta_1 = \frac{\text{vertical change}}{\text{horizontal change}} = \frac{72 - 12.5}{80 - 40} = 0.31$$

Thus, if literacy increases 1%, the corresponding increase in life expectancy is roughly one-third (0.31) of a year.

The **intercept** (β_0 or **constant** as it is often called) is where the line intercepts the vertical axis at $x = 0$ (that is, when literacy equals 0, the intercept is the height from 0 on the life expectancy scale to the line). Guessing from Figure 12.1, the intercept is around 47 years.

To represent the **errors** (ε) in the model, draw a short vertical line from each point to the line. The lengths of these line segments between the line and the plot points are called **residuals** and are estimates for the true errors. SPSS uses the method of *least squares* to estimate the slope and intercept. This method minimizes the sum of the squared residuals (that is, the sum of the squares of the vertical line segments).

In the first equation, y is the **dependent** or **outcome** variable, the one you are trying to predict; x is the **independent** or **predictor** variable; and the intercept (β_0) and slope (β_1) are **coefficients**. If the model is a good descriptor of the relation between the variables, you can use the estimates of the coefficients to *predict* the value of the dependent variable for new cases.

Models with two or more predictors. Adding a second independent variable results in the equation:

$$z = a + bx + cy$$

This equation is the basis of the statistical model used in Example 2:

$$y = \beta_0 + \beta_1 x_1 + \beta_2 x_2 + \varepsilon$$
female life expectancy $= \beta_0 + \beta_1$infant mortality $+ \beta_2$fertility $+ \varepsilon$

where infant mortality (for every 1000 live births, the number of babies who die during the first year of life) and fertility (average number of children per family) are the independent variables and female life expectancy is the dependent variable.

The equation with one independent variable is the model for **simple linear regression**; the equation with two variables is a model for **multiple regression**. SPSS allows you to include more than two independent variables in a multiple regression:

$$y = \beta_0 + \beta_1 x_1 + \ldots + \beta_p x_p + \varepsilon$$

In applications, a researcher may not know which set of p variables to include in a multiple regression model. The strategies for finding a good model are many and varied, and are discussed in Example 3 and Example 4.

Why fit a regression model? In addition to predicting the outcome variable for a new sample of data, regression analysis serves other purposes:

- To assess how well the dependent variable can be explained by knowing the value of the independent variable (or a set of independent variables). See multiple R^2 in Example 2.

- To identify which subset from many measures is most effective for estimating the dependent variable. See Example 3 and Example 4.

Assumptions. First explore your variables graphically in scatterplots to ascertain if a linear model is appropriate for describing the relationship and to identify any possible rogue values (outliers) that might distort results. Ideally, in an observational study, the configuration of plot points should form the shape of an American football, for there are fewer points at the low and high ends of the independent variable than in the middle. In an experimental study, the values of x are fixed or set at specified levels, so the configuration may not exhibit such a clear pattern.

In assessing the suitability of your data for a regression, it helps to think of the *fixed x* situation. Visually scan the distribution of y values for each x (or each small range of x's)—that is, look at vertical strips or bands of points extending up from the x axis. Do the y values within each strip look like a sample from a normal distribution? Is the spread (variance) within each strip roughly the same across the strips? Or is it considerably greater at one side of the plot than at the other? If you guess an average value of y for each strip, do these averages fall along a straight line?

More formally, normality is not required for the estimates of the coefficients. To make tests and estimate confidence intervals, however, these assumptions are required:

- The errors are normally distributed with mean 0.
- The errors have constant variance.
- The errors are independent of each other.

These assumptions are checked by studying the residuals from the model. In the examples that follow, graphical displays are used to investigate possible departures from normality and nonconstant variance. The **Durbin-Watson** statistic (available on the Linear Regression Statistics subdialog box) can be used to test for the serial correlation of adjacent error terms.

Screening. To help identify problems, always look at plots of y versus x before the regression and plots of residuals and diagnostics after the analysis. For simple regression, study a scatterplot like that in Figure 12.1; for multiple regression, try a scatterplot matrix. In each plot, look for problems like these:

Figure 12.2   Data screening

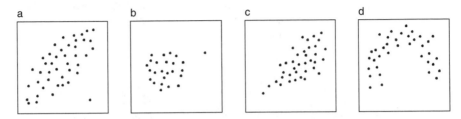

- A *bivariate outlier* is identified in plot a. If you look at the values of each variable separately, the point in the lower right corner is not unusual.
- In plot b, moving the one point at the right up or down changes the slope of the line. This point is a called a *leverage point*.
- If, in plot c, you were to take vertical slices and study the distribution of points within each strip, you would find that the spread or variance is much smaller for small values of x than for large values. This violates the assumption that the error variance is constant across the range of the independent variable.
- In plot d, there is a strong relation between x and y, but it is not linear.

The following example emphasizes the importance of using graphics. The four data sets from Frank Anscombe all have the same regression line:

$$y = 3 + 0.5x$$

and the same correlation (0.816).

Figure 12.3   Anscombe's quartet

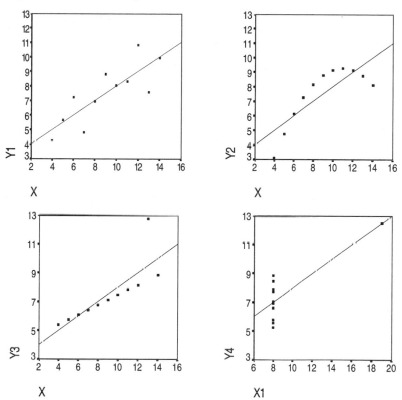

For which data are the regression line and correlation coefficient useful descriptors? Only for the plot at the top left. The variable $Y2$ has a nonlinear relation with X; there is an outlier in the plot of $Y3$ versus X; and $X1$ is constant except for one outlier in the plot with $Y4$.

The actual data will help you verify the results:

X	Y1	Y2	Y3	Y4	X1
4	4.26	3.10	5.39	6.58	8
5	5.68	4.74	5.73	5.76	8
6	7.24	6.13	6.08	7.71	8
7	4.82	7.26	6.42	8.84	8
8	6.95	8.14	6.77	8.47	8
9	8.81	8.77	7.11	7.04	8
10	8.04	9.14	7.46	5.25	8
11	8.33	9.26	7.81	5.56	8
12	10.84	9.13	8.15	7.91	8
13	7.58	8.74	12.74	6.89	8
14	9.96	8.10	8.84	12.50	19

The results of a regression analysis can be distorted by:

- **Nonlinearity.** To make relationships more linear, try transforming the dependent variable, one or more of the independent variables, or both types of variables.

- **Outliers.** Use SPSS regression diagnostics to identify outliers among your independent variables and in the dependent variable. These are discussed in the examples.

- **The presence of subpopulations.** Relationships among the dependent and independent variables may be *masked* or *falsely enhanced* if your sample contains subpopulations (that is, the sample is not homogeneous).

In summary, to help identify problems, always look at plots of *y* versus *x* before the regression and plots of residuals and diagnostics after the analysis.

The data. The data for the examples in this chapter are stored in the file *world95*. There is one case for each of 109 countries. The data file is organized like this:

COUNTRY	...	LIFEEXPF	...	LIT_FEMA	BABYMORT	FERTILITY
Afghanistan	...	44	...	14	168.0	6.9
Austria	...	79	...		6.7	1.5
⋮	⋮	⋮	⋮	⋮	⋮	⋮
Zambia	...	45	...	65	85	6.7

Names of the countries are stored in the variable *country* and are used to illustrate SPSS's option for labeling plot points and casewise results.

Example 1: Simple linear regression. This model predicts female life expectancy from literacy. Several plots are used to evaluate the fit of the model: a normal probability plot of the standardized residuals, and scatterplots of the Studentized residuals against predicted values and predicted values against the observed values of the dependent variable.

Example 2: Multiple linear regression. Infant mortality and fertility rates are the independent variables in this model. Partial residual plots show how each independent variable relates to the dependent variable after the effect of the other independent variable is removed. SPSS provides a wealth of diagnostics for assessing a possible failure to meet model assumptions. Several diagnostics are saved, and Scatter and Sequence on the Graphs menu are used to display them.

Example 3: Variable selection—the backward elimination method. SPSS's methods for selecting a useful subset of the independent variables are introduced. This example begins with a model that includes eight candidate predictors and illustrates backward stepping to remove variables step-by-step until four variables remain. Measures of collinearity and criteria for removing (or adding) variables into the model are discussed.

Example 4: Variable selection—the stepwise method. Model building here begins by adding one variable at a time to the model. Already entered variables are tested for removal at each step, and the second variable to enter the model is removed at step 5.

You should read this section sequentially because the models are presented in order of increasing complexity. Information on interpreting a given part of the output is presented with the first example that generates it.

Example 1
Simple Linear Regression

Is a measure of education useful for predicting life expectancy? More specifically, is the literacy rate for females in a country useful for predicting their life expectancy? In this first example, the linear relation between female life expectancy and literacy is explored using the model introduced at the beginning of this chapter:

female life expectancy $= \beta_0 + \beta_1$ female literacy $+ \varepsilon$

where *female life expectancy* is the *dependent* or *outcome* variable, *female literacy* is the *independent* or *predictor* variable, β_0 is the *intercept* of the line of best fit, β_1 is its *slope*, and ε is the *error* term. Both *lifeexpf* and *lit_fema* are quantitative variables, which should have symmetric distributions (the residuals from the model fit should follow a normal distribution).

To produce this output, from the menus choose:

Analyze
  Regression
    Linear...

Click *Reset* to restore dialog box defaults, and then select:

▸ Dependent: lifeexpf
▸ Independent: lit_fema
▸ Case Labels: country

Statistics...
   ☑ Descriptives

   Residuals
   ☑ Casewise diagnostics
   ⊙ Outliers outside 1.0 standard deviations

Plots...
   ▸ Y: SDRESID
   ▸ X: ZPRED

Click *Next*
   ▸ Y: ZPRED
   ▸ X: DEPENDNT

   Standardized Residual Plots
   ☑ Normal probability plot

 To hide footnotes, select them and then choose *Hide* from the View menu.

Descriptive Statistics

	Mean	Std. Deviation	N
Average female life expectancy	67.81	10.72	85
Females who read (%)	67.26	28.61	85

Descriptive statistics. On average, in this sample of 85 countries, females live 67.81 years, and 67.26% of the females are literate. The *world95* data file contains information about 109 countries, so for 24 countries, data are missing for one or both variables. (To find this, open Notes in the Viewer and read *N of Rows in Working Data.*)

Correlations

		Average female life expectancy	Females who read (%)
Pearson Correlation	Average female life expectancy	1.000	.819
	Females who read (%)	.819	1.000
Significance (1-tailed)	Average female life expectancy	.	.000
	Females who read (%)	.000	.
N	Average female life expectancy	85	85
	Females who read (%)	85	85

Correlations. The Pearson correlation between the two variables is 0.819. It is highly significant with a p value less than 0.0005, indicating the hypothesis that the correlation is 0 (no linear relation between the variables) is rejected. When your model includes more than one independent variable, SPSS displays correlations for all pairs of variables. In the last panel, labeled N, sample sizes are reported for each variable individually and for each pair of variables.

By default, SPSS uses only the cases that have complete data for *lifeexpf* and *lit_fema*; so here the sample sizes are all 85 (if either value is missing, SPSS omits the case from the computations). When there are two or more predictor variables, however, SPSS can compute correlations separately for each pair of variables using all cases that have both values. See Exclude cases pairwise under Missing Values on the Linear Regression Options subdialog box. Here, if you select this option and rerun the regression, you will discover that life expectancy has 109 values and female literacy has 85 values.

Model Summary

Model	R	R Square	Adjusted R Square	Std. Error of the Estimate
1	.819	.670	.666	6.20

Model Summary. The value of R (also called multiple R) is 0.819. When there is only one independent variable, R is the simple correlation between life expectancy and literacy (see the same correlation in the Correlations table above). R^2 (0.670) is the square of this value and often is interpreted as the proportion of the total variation in life expectancy accounted for by literacy (literacy "explains" 67% of the variability of life expectancy). R^2 ranges from 0 to 1. If there is no *linear* relation between the dependent and independent variable, R^2 is 0 or very small. If all the observations fall on the regression line, R^2 is 1. This measure of the goodness of fit of a linear model is also called the **coefficient of determination.**

The sample estimate of R^2 tends to be an optimistic estimate of the population value. *Adjusted R Square* is designed to more closely reflect how well the model fits the population and is usually of interest for models with more than one predictor, so it is discussed in Example 2.

Std. Error of the Estimate (6.20) is the square root of the residual mean square (RMS) in the ANOVA table below and measures the spread of the residuals (or errors) about the fitted line. Its units are years—those of the dependent variable. You can compare its size loosely with the standard deviation of life expectancy. If it is not less than the standard deviation, then the regression model is no better than the mean as a predictor of the dependent variable. (The comparison is not exact—the RMS has $(n - 2)$ in the denominator; the standard deviation, $(n - 1)$.) In this example, 6.20 compares favorably to 10.72 years.

ANOVA

			Sum of Squares	df	Mean Square	F	Sig.
Model	1	Regression	6475.18	1	6475.18	168.698	.000
		Residual	3185.81	83	38.38		
		Total	9660.99	84			

ANOVA. This is an analysis of variance or ANOVA table. Most introductory statistics text books define the columns of this table. The F statistic (168.698) is used to test the hypothesis that the slope (β_1) is 0 (or, for multiple linear regression, that $\beta_1, \ldots \beta_p = 0$). F is large when the independent variable(s) helps to explain the variation in the dependent variable. Here, the linear relation is highly significant (the p value for the F is less than 0.0005).

Coefficients

			Unstandardized Coefficients		Standardized Coefficients		
			B	Std. Error	Beta	t	Sig.
Model	1	(Constant)	47.170	1.726		27.337	.000
		Females who read (%)	.307	.024	.819	12.988	.000

Coefficients. The estimates of the model coefficients β_0 (intercept) and β_1 (slope) are, respectively, 47.17 and 0.307. So the estimated model is:

female life expectancy $= 47.17 + 0.307 \times$ female literacy

You could use this model to compute predicted values for a new sample. For example, a country named Candyland is not in your sample and you know its female literacy rate is 90%. Simply multiply 90 by the estimate of the slope (0.307) and add the intercept (47.17) to find the *predicted value* of life expectancy (74.8 years). SPSS computes predicted values for the cases in your sample (see the Residuals Statistics table below).

The standard errors of the estimated coefficients, *Std. Error*, are in the next column. Their formulas are

$$\sigma_{B_0} = \sigma\sqrt{\frac{1}{n} + \frac{\bar{x}^2}{(n-1)s_x^2}} \qquad \sigma_{B_1} = \frac{\sigma}{\sqrt{(n-1)s_x^2}}$$

where s_x^2 is the sample variance of the independent variable and σ is estimated as:

$$s^2 = \frac{\sum_{i=1}^{N}(y_i - \beta_0 - \beta_1 x_i)^2}{n-2}$$

Standardized coefficients follow. Some social scientists call these last coefficients **betas**. If you transformed each variable to z scores, these betas would be the unstandardized coefficients. For simple regression, the standardized coefficient for *lit_fema* is the correlation between life expectancy and literacy.

Next are *t* **statistics** (each coefficient divided by its standard error). The second *t* statistic (12.988) tests the significance of the slope, which is equivalent to testing the significance of the correlation between life expectancy and literacy. For simple linear regression, the square of this *t* is the *F* in the ANOVA table. The first *t* tests the significance of the difference of the constant from 0 and rarely is of interest. In the last column are *p* values or probabilities associated with the *t* statistics. See "Coefficients" on p. 209 for more about these statistics.

Residuals Statistics

	Minimum	Maximum	Mean	Std. Deviation	N
Predicted Value	49.93	77.86	67.81	8.78	85
Standardized Predicted Value	-2.036	1.144	.000	1.000	85
Standard Error of Predicted Value	.67	1.53	.93	.21	85
Residual	-22.12	13.92	-9.20E-16	6.16	85
Standardized Residual	-3.570	2.247	.000	.994	85
Studentized Residual	-3.591	2.305	.000	1.005	85
Studentized Deleted Residual	-3.884	2.368	-.005	1.028	85

Residuals Statistics. To calculate a **predicted value** for each case (country), SPSS multiplies its value of literacy by 0.307 (the estimated slope) and adds 47.17 (the intercept). The average predicted life expectancy for this sample is 67.81 years.

For each case (country), the **residual** is the difference between the observed value of the dependent variable (life expectancy) and the value predicted by the model. Residuals are estimates of the true errors (ε) in the model; if the model is appropriate for the data, the residuals should follow a normal distribution. Often, plots are used to assess this assumption. See the normal probability plot at the end of this example.

Notice that SPSS uses ($n - 1$) in the denominator to calculate the standard deviation of these residuals, and ($n - 2$) to calculate the Residual Mean Square, so 6.16 is slightly smaller than the standard error of the estimate in the ANOVA table.

The **standardized predicted values** are predicted values standardized to have mean 0 and a standard deviation 1; **standardized residuals** are ordinary residuals divided by the sample standard deviation of the residuals and have mean 0 and standard deviation 1. (SPSS also provides Studentized residuals—see the subsection at the end of this example.) The minimum standardized residual is –3.570, so at least one country has a residual more than three standard deviations below the mean of all residuals. In the Casewise Diagnostics table on p. 202, this country is identified as Zambia. Its value of life expectancy is considerably lower than those for countries with similar literacy rates (Zambia's plot point falls way below the point on the line of best fit for its literacy rate).

A caution. Be careful about concluding, "If literacy is increased, the population will live longer." There is a strong *association* between literacy and life expectancy. However, these data come from an observational study, not a controlled experiment, so any statements about cause-and-effect relationships can be misleading. Association is not the same as causation. Before the Salk vaccine was developed against polio, a study showed that there were more new cases of polio during weeks when soft drink sales were high than when they were low. Do soft drinks transmit polio? No, a third variable (sometimes called a *lurking* variable), season, is related to both polio and soft drinks. Polio epidemics were the worst in the summer when soft drink sales are high.

If an investigator observes the values of the independent and dependent variables for a set of subjects (cases), association does not establish causation. If an investigator does an experiment where he or she sets the values of the independent variable (for example, six specific doses of a drug) and watches the effect on the dependent variable, there may be little question that the results were *caused* by the independent variable.

Optional Plots and a First Look at Diagnostics

Numbers alone may not provide a complete or accurate description of your regression analysis. For example, for the four data sets displayed in Figure 12.3, the correlations, coefficients, F statistics, and so on are all the same.

One or two countries (cases) with unusual values (or errors) can distort results. Before reporting results, it is a good idea to find out whether your data contain observations that violate important assumptions. SPSS provides diagnostics to help with this task. They fall roughly into three groups:

- **Residuals** to identify potential outliers in the dependent variable.
- **Leverage** statistics to identify potential outliers among the values of the independent or predictor variables.
- **Influence** measures to identify cases that exert influence on the calculation of one or more coefficients.

Measures of leverage and influence are most commonly used in multiple linear regression and are discussed in later examples. The graphical displays of residuals discussed in the following sections are very useful for assessing how well the model fits the data: standardized residuals for each case; a normal probability plot of the residuals; and a scatterplot of Studentized deleted residuals against standardized predicted values. Finally, it is often useful to plot the predicted values against the observed values.

Some common patterns of residuals are displayed in Figure 12.4.

Figure 12.4 Residual plots

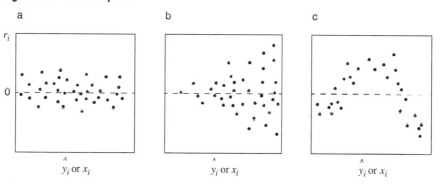

The configuration of points in plot a is what the data analyst wants. The points fall in a horizontal band with no apparent systematic features. In plot b, the residual variance is an increasing function of the quantity on the x-axis (an independent variable or predicted values). A transformation (such as the log of y or one or more of the x's or both) can remedy this problem. Consider power transforms as explained in Chapter 4, Example 4. The configuration in plot c indicates a nonlinear relationship that might not be helped by a simple transformation.

Casewise diagnostics are shown below; later examples show how to save residuals and other diagnostics and use Sequence plots to create the graphical display.

Casewise Diagnostics

		COUNTRY	Standardized Residual	LIFEEXPF	Predicted Value	Residual
Case Number	1	Afghanis	-1.205	44	51.47	-7.47
	7	Bahrain	1.606	74	64.05	9.95
	14	Botswana	2.247	66	52.08	13.92
	18	Burundi	-1.525	50	59.45	-9.45
	22	Cent. Af	-1.255	44	51.77	-7.77
	45	Haiti	-2.356	47	61.59	-14.59
	47	Hong Kon	2.129	80	66.81	13.19
	52	Iran	1.071	67	60.37	6.63
	59	Kenya	-1.609	55	64.97	-9.97
	60	Kuwait	1.657	78	67.73	10.27
	68	Morocco	1.803	70	58.83	11.17
	80	Philippi	-1.096	68	74.79	-6.79
	85	Rwanda	-2.022	46	58.53	-12.53
	87	Saudi Ar	1.307	70	61.90	8.10
	97	Tanzania	-1.886	45	56.68	-11.68
	100	U.Arab E	1.210	74	66.50	7.50
	103	Uganda	-2.407	43	57.91	-14.91
	109	Zambia	-3.570	45	67.12	-22.12

Casewise diagnostics. Standardized residuals are defined in "Residual Statistics" on p. 200, where it is noted that one country has a residual more than three standard deviations below the mean. Here you see that it is Zambia. The value of its unstandardized residual is –22.12. Find Zambia in the scatterplot in the introduction; female literacy for its population is 65%. Notice that other countries with similar values of literacy tend to have much longer average life expectancies.

SPSS can display diagnostics for *all* cases in the file. In this example, you chose to view diagnostics for countries with standardized residuals more than one standard deviation away from the mean.

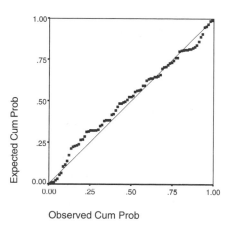

Observed Cum Prob

Normal probability plot. Normal probability plots are defined in Chapter 4, Example 3. If the residuals are from a normal distribution, the plotted values should fall roughly along the line. Here, this is true for most of the values, except around 0.25, where there are fewer negative residuals than expected under normality.

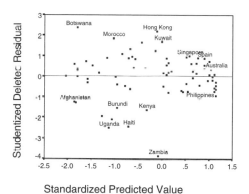

Standardized Predicted Value

Scatterplot of Studentized deleted residuals versus standardized predicted values. In assessing whether regression assumptions are satisfied, it is important to plot residuals against predicted values and also against the independent variable (or each independent variable in multiple regression). Many researchers prefer using Studentized residuals in the plots because, when the model used to compute the residuals is valid, they have mean 0 and variance 1. If the errors are normally distributed and the form of the model is correct, then about 95% of the residuals should fall between −2 and +2 (only 1 in 1000 should fall outside ±3).

For each case, a deleted residual is calculated by excluding the case from the calculation of the regression coefficients (this procedure is repeated for each case in turn). A **Studentized deleted residual** for a case is the deleted residual standardized by an estimate of its standard error. (Cases with values close to the mean(s) of the independent variable(s) have smaller standard errors than those at a greater distance.) These residuals follow a t distribution with $(n - p - 1)$ degrees of freedom. This is helpful for defining what a *large* value is.

For each case, the **standardized predicted value** is the predicted value standardized by subtracting the mean of the dependent variable and dividing by the standard deviation of the predicted values.

Plots of the Studentized residuals against the predicted value of the dependent variable are useful for identifying problems of nonconstant variance. For example, see the middle plot in Figure 12.4. Ideally, the points should fall in a horizontal band across the plot, you should see no systematic trends, and you should be concerned if gross outliers are identified.

Plotting residuals against independent variables. To obtain plots of these residuals against each independent variable, save them (using the Save dialog box) and then use Scatter on the Graphs menu to request your plot.

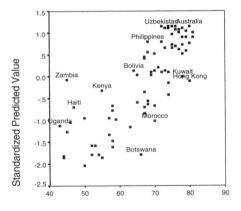

Average female life expectancy

Standardized predicted values versus observed values. If the model fits each data value exactly, the observed and predicted values would coincide on a straight line extending from the lower left corner to the upper right. Look at Zambia—life expectancy for its females is among the lowest in this sample, yet its predicted value is close to the mean of all predicted values (0.0). The opposite is true for Botswana—the predicted value of its life expectancy is lower than its observed value.

Example 2
Multiple Linear Regression

A linear regression model may have more than one independent variable. The following is a model with two independent variables:

$$y = \beta_0 + \beta_1 x_1 + \beta_2 x_2 + \varepsilon$$

This is an equation of a plane in three dimensional space that you can visualize geometrically. For example, say that female life expectancy is the dependent variable, and infant mortality (for every 1000 live births, the number of babies who die during their first year of life) and fertility (average number of children per family) are the independent variables:

$$\text{female life expectancy} = \beta_0 + \beta_1 \text{ infant mortality} + \beta_2 \text{ fertility} + \varepsilon$$

The parameter β_0 is still the intercept (or constant), and β_1 and β_2 are both slopes. One gives the slope along the x_1 dimension and the other along the x_2 dimension. Imagine placing a ruler for infant mortality (with values from 4 babies extending to 170 babies) along the length of a wall of a room and a second ruler for fertility (with values from 1 to 9 children along the wall next to it). Then, for each country, you could walk to a point in the center of the floor where the country's values for infant mortality and fertility intersect. At this point, hold a ruler marked in years of life expectancy parallel to yourself and float a ball at the height of the country's life expectancy. Then, in a similar manner, float a ball for each of the other countries. Finally, tilt a huge cookie sheet among the balls minimizing the vertical distance between the balls and the cookie sheet. The multiple linear regression equation positions and tilts the cookie sheet.

In Example 1, you found that literacy explained 67% of the variability of life expectancy. Here, you examine a model using infant mortality (*babymort*) and fertility (*fertilty*) to predict life expectancy.

Partial residual plots are requested to assess the contribution of each independent variable to the model. Several diagnostics useful for identifying influential cases and problems with the model fit are saved. Scatter and Sequence on the Graphs menu are used to plot them. These diagnostics and plots are described in a subsection at the end of this example.

To produce this output, in the Linear Regression dialog box, click *Reset* to restore the dialog box defaults, and then select:

▶ Dependent: lifeexpf
▶ Independent: fertility, babymort
▶ Case Labels: country

Statistics...
    ☑ Descriptives

Plots...
    ☑ Produce all partial plots

Save...

Predicted Values
☑ Standardized

Distances
☑ Cook's   ☑ Leverage values

Residuals
☑ Studentized deleted

Influence Statistics
☑ Standardized DfBeta(s)   ☑ DfFit

 On the Correlations table select and hide the *Sig. (1-tailed)* and *N* rows.

To hide footnotes, select them and then choose *Hide* from the View menu.

Descriptive Statistics

	Mean	Std. Deviation	N
Average female life expectancy	70.01	10.62	107
Fertility: average number of kids	3.563	1.902	107
Infant mortality (deaths per 1000 live births)	42.937	38.153	107

Descriptive Statistics. Of the 109 countries (cases) in this sample, 107 have values for the three variables in the model. The average female life expectancy for these countries is 70 years; the average fertility, 3.563 children; and the average infant mortality rate, roughly 43 deaths for each 1000 live births.

Correlations

		Average female life expectancy	Fertility: average number of kids	Infant mortality (deaths per 1000 live births)
Pearson Correlation	Average female life expectancy	1.000	-.838	-.962
	Fertility: average number of kids	-.838	1.000	.833
	Infant mortality (deaths per 1000 live births)	-.962	.833	1.000

Correlations. The independent variables have strong correlations with life expectancy (−0.838 for fertility and −0.962 for infant mortality). Notice that the correlation between the two independent variables is also strong (0.833). The default output includes probabilities (*Sig.*) associated with these statistics, but these probabilities are appropriate for testing a single correlation and not for searching a matrix of correlations for significant statistics; they are hidden here.

Infant mortality appears to have the strongest linear relation with life expectancy. The negative sign, not surprisingly, indicates that as infant mortality increases, life expectancy tends to decrease. The same relationship holds for fertility with life expectancy.

Model Summary

Model	Variables Entered	Removed	R	R Square	Adjusted R Square	Std. Error of the Estimate
1	Infant mortality (deaths per 1000 live births), Fertility: average number of kids	.	.964	.929	.928	2.85

Model Summary. For multiple regression models, R is the correlation between the observed and predicted values of the dependent variable. (For this example, the correlation between life expectancy and the values of life expectancy predicted by the model.) R^2 is the square of this correlation.

For this model with two variables, R^2 is 0.929, an increase of more than 25% over the model using literacy. Knowing infant mortality and fertility explains almost 93% of the variability of life expectancy.

The sample estimate of R^2 tends to be an overestimate of the population parameter. Adjusted R^2 is designed to compensate for the optimistic bias of R^2. It is a function of R^2 adjusted by the number of variables in the model and the sample size

$$R_a^2 \; = \; R^2 - \frac{p(1 - R^2)}{N - p - 1}$$

where p is the number of independent variables in the equation (2 in this example).

R^2 and adjusted R^2 are also defined as:

$$R^2 \; = \; 1 - \frac{\text{residual sum of squares}}{\text{total sum of squares}}$$

$$R_a^2 \; = \; 1 - \frac{\text{residual sum of squares}/(N - p - 1)}{\text{total sum of squares}/(N - 1)}$$

For this two-variable model, the *Std. Error of the Estimate* (or square root of the residual mean square) is 2.85, less than half that for the simple regression model in Example 1.

ANOVA

Model		Sum of Squares	df	Mean Square	F	Sig.
1	Regression	11101.959	2	5550.980	684.793	.000
	Residual	843.031	104	8.106		
	Total	11944.991	106			

ANOVA. The F statistic is highly significant, indicating that the simultaneous test that each coefficient is 0 is rejected. The fact that the associated probability (*Sig.*) is so small (< 0.0005) does not imply that each of the independent variables makes a meaningful contribution to the fit of the model.

Coefficients

Model		Unstandardized Coefficients		Standardized Coefficients	t	Sig.
		B	Std. Error	Beta		
1	(Constant)	82.677	.626		132.176	.000
	Fertility: average number of kids	-.662	.263	-.119	-2.518	.013
	Infant mortality (deaths per 1000 live births)	-.240	.013	-.863	-18.326	.000

Coefficients. The estimated model is:

female life expectancy $= 82.677 - 0.662$ fertility $- 0.240$ infant mortality

In order to assess the usefulness of each predictor in the model, you cannot simply compare the coefficients. Even if the independent variables are all measured in the same units, a comparison of their size may not be revealing. When they are correlated, it is hard to quantify the unique contribution of each variable. *Beta* coefficients are an attempt to make the regression coefficients more comparable. You would get the same coefficients if you transformed the data to *z* scores prior to your regression run.

The *t* statistics in the next column provide some clue regarding the relative importance of each variable in the model. SPSS obtains them by dividing each coefficient by its standard error (*Std. Error*). The same *t* statistic can be computed using a formula that involves the sum of squares of the residuals from the current model and the sum of squares of residuals from the model formed by removing the independent variable in question.

The probabilities (percentiles of the *t* distribution reported in the column labeled *Sig.*) should **not** be used for a formal test regarding the importance of each variable. These probabilities are appropriate if you want to do one preselected test and not if you are looking, say, for the *strongest* (or *weakest*) variable. For such a test, you would need the distribution of the largest (or smallest) *t,* and that is affected by the number of variables scanned, their correlation structure, and the sample size. When the independent variables are correlated, the critical value for the largest *t* can be much larger than that for testing one preselected variable.

As a guide regarding useful predictors, look for *t* values well below -2 or above $+2$. In this example, the *t*'s are -2.5 and -18.3, so both independent variables meet the guideline. However, infant mortality is clearly the stronger predictor; fertility is more marginal. It is better to study the partial residual plots as shown below. (In the plots shown here, only selected countries are labeled. The default output shows all countries labeled.)

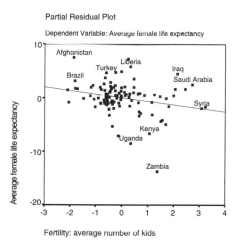

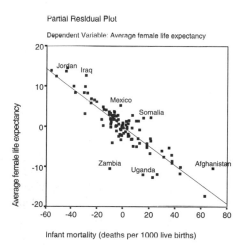

Partial Residual Plots. These plots, often called *added variable plots*, provide a graphical version of the *t* statistic for each predictor or its partial correlation with the dependent variable after removing the linear effect of the other variables in the model. The plots, introduced by Mosteller and Tukey, are useful for identifying cases that mask (or falsely enhance) the predictive power of a particular independent variable; and if the target model holds, linearity must be evident in the display. (In order to get these plots, your model needs at least two predictors.)

In a partial residual plot, two sets of residuals are displayed. For example, for the plot of infant mortality, the residuals are from:

- Regressing the dependent variable life expectancy on fertility.
- Regressing infant mortality on fertility.

When your model has three or more independent variables, each regression is computed using all independent variables. (Replace the word *fertility* above with *all independent variables except the predictor of interest.*)

The residuals from the life expectancy regression are plotted on the vertical axis, those from infant mortality on the horizontal axis. The correlation between the two sets of residuals is the partial correlation that measures the relation between life expectancy and infant mortality after adjusting for fertility.

The partial residual plot has interesting properties. In the plot of infant mortality, for example:

- Observations with influence on the infant mortality coefficient stand out on the *x* axis. Notice that Afghanistan is furthest from 0.
- The slope for the regression line through the origin is the same as that for the full model (–0.24).
- The residuals (vertical deviations from this regression) are the same as those from the full model.

The simple correlation between fertility and life expectancy is –0.838. In the plot here, after the effect of infant mortality has been removed, this relation is considerably diminished. Zambia is well separated from the other plot points vertically, but not extreme in the *x* direction. Thus, it may not exert undue influence on the coefficient for fertility.

Optional Plots and Diagnostics

In Example 1, you saw that numbers in the regression output do not provide a complete picture of how well the estimated model fits, and you plotted two types of residuals useful for identifying such problems as unusual values in the dependent variable, nonlinearity, and a need for transformation. Here, you will look at diagnostics for identifying outliers among the independent variables and also for identifying cases that exert influence on the calculation of the coefficients, and thus, the predicted values. These are the statistics requested on the Save dialog box at the beginning of this example. After the regression results appear in the Viewer, the diagnostics are available in the Data Editor and can be displayed in scatter and sequence plots.

SPSS provides two measures for identifying potential outliers among the independent variables: the Mahalanobis distance and leverage. The computations for both ignore the dependent variable and use the values of the independent variables to compute the distance of each case to the mean of all cases. Their formulas differ by a sample size factor.

The computational formulas for both (and for some other diagnostics, too) can be written using elements on the diagonal of the *hat matrix*. If you use matrix algebra to express the model for multiple linear regression, it looks like this:

$$\mathbf{Y} \ = \ \mathbf{XB} + \mathbf{E}$$

The fitted values and estimates of the coefficients for a sample of n cases are

$$\hat{\mathbf{Y}} \ = \ \mathbf{X'}\hat{\mathbf{B}}$$

$$\mathbf{B} \ = \ (\mathbf{X'X})^{-1}\mathbf{X'Y} \ \ \text{or} \ \ \mathbf{B} = \mathbf{HY}$$

where $\mathbf{X}$ is the centered matrix of independent variables and $\mathbf{H}$ is an $(n \times n)$ matrix that is called the **hat matrix** because it maps $\mathbf{Y}$ into $\mathbf{Y}$ (incidentally, the $\wedge$ on top of Y that denotes estimated values is called a "hat").

The diagonal elements of this matrix (there is one for each case) play a key role in many of the diagnostics. The centered **Leverage** value for each case is its element on the diagonal:

$$h_i - \frac{1}{n}$$

The **Mahalanobis distance** is $(n - 1)$ times leverage. (And as a digression, the Studentized deleted residuals introduced on p. 203 can be expressed as the usual residual divided by the square root of the model RMS (residual mean square) times $(1 - h_i)$. Thus, cases with high leverage have a smaller quantity in the denominator than those with small leverage.)

Values of leverage range from 0 to $(n - 1) / n$. What is a high value of leverage? In practice, it is useful to examine leverage values in a stem-and-leaf display to identify those that stand apart from the rest of the sample. However, various rules of thumb have been suggested. For example, values less than 0.2 appear safe, values between 0.2 and 0.5 are risky, and values above 0.5 are to be avoided. Another rule says if $p > 6$ and $(n - p) > 12$, use $3p / n$ as a cutoff, where p is the number of variables.

SPSS provides several measures of influence; three are summarized below.

Cook's distance measures the change in the estimates of the regression coefficients if the ith case is deleted. That is, if you were to remove the case with the largest Cook value, the estimates of the coefficients would change more than for any other single case. For each case, Cook can be viewed as a scaled Euclidean distance measure between two vectors of fitted values: in the first, the case is included; in the second, the case is excluded. Algebraically, this measure can be written as a function of both residuals and leverage. For each case,

$$\text{Cook} = \frac{h_i \times \text{the deleted residual squared}}{p \times \text{RMS}}$$

where RMS is the model residual mean square and p is the number of variables.

DfFits measures the influence of the ith case on the estimates of the regression coefficients and the variance of the coefficients. It is also viewed as a statistic that measures the impact on the predicted values. Unlike the Cook measure, the sign of the residual is preserved.

$$\text{DfFits} = \sqrt{\frac{h_i}{1 - h_1}} \times \text{the Studentized deleted residual}$$

DfBeta(s) measures the influence of the ith case on the estimate of *each* regression coefficient separately. That is, how does each coefficient change if the case were excluded? You could compute this statistic for a case by running two regressions, one with the case and one without it. Then, for each coefficient, find the difference in value between the two estimates.

Instead of using cutoffs or points based on distributional assumptions, many researchers plot the diagnostics, looking for points that stand apart from the others. The following plots were constructed using Scatter and Sequence on the Graphs menu. The diagnostics are those requested on the Save dialog box. The name assigned by SPSS to each diagnostic is displayed in the Notes at the beginning of the output. When you move to the Scatter or Sequence dialog box, the names of the diagnostics you have saved are available on the selection list.

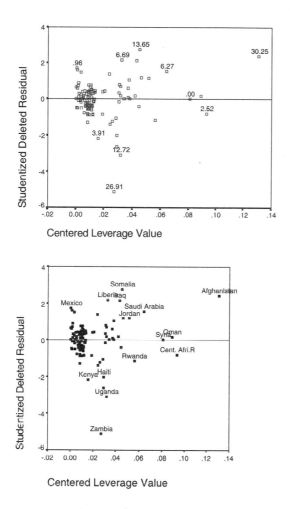

Studentized deleted residuals versus leverage. These two scatterplots, made using Scatter on the Graphs menu, are the same, except that points in the left plot are labeled by values of Cook's distance, while country names are used in the right plot. (Cook's distance is multiplied by 100.) Countries, ordered by Cook's measure, exerting the most influence on the estimates of the coefficients are Afghanistan (30.25), Zambia (26.91), Somalia (13.65), and Uganda (12.72). In the plot, notice that Afghanistan's leverage is large (indicating this country has extreme values among the independent variables) and Zambia's residual is very negative (it has a low value of life expectancy).

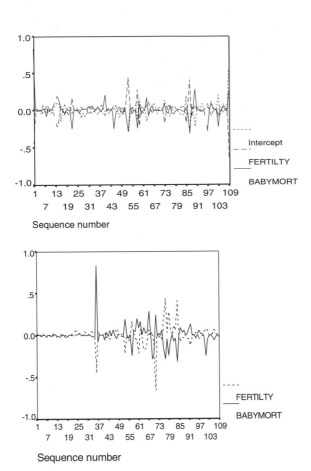

DfBetas. Sequence on the Graphs menu is used to make these **caseplots** of the standard-ized DfBetas against the case number (sequence number) of each country. The top plot with statistics for the intercept and for both coefficients is too confusing to see much. In the bottom plot, the DfBeta for the intercept is omitted and the countries are sorted by *region* (This variable, introduced in Chapter 2, Example 1, has six categories.)

The values of the DfBetas are relatively small for the first 21 cases that are OECD countries. Cases 36 through 52 are countries in the Pacific/Asia group. The DfBeta value for Afghanistan is the tall spike at the beginning of this group. The descending spike of dashes for *fertilty* is Zambia. You suspect that the sample may not be homogeneous; the model seems to fit less well for one or more subsets of observations.

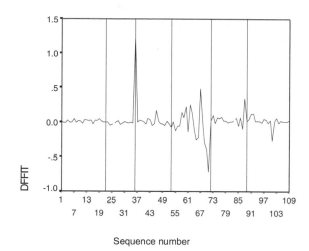

Sequence number

DfFit sorted by region. After sorting the countries by *region*, Sequence on the Graphs menu is used to construct this caseplot of the DfFit measure. The Time Axis Reference Line option on the Sequence dialog box is used to request the vertical reference lines separating the six regions. Except for Afghanistan (the tall spike at the beginning of the third interval for countries in the Pacific/Asia region), the estimates of the coefficients and their variances are most sensitive to countries in the fourth interval (Africa). These plots are a handy way to identify subpopulations for which the model fits poorly.

Example 3
Variable Selection: The Backward Elimination Method

SPSS can estimate coefficients for multiple linear regression models with more than two independent variables. When fitting such a model, you may know just which variables you want to include as predictors. If so, proceed as shown in Example 2 on p. 205, using SPSS's default equation-building method, Enter. All variables you select as independent variables are included in the model.

Selection methods. Often, however, a researcher may not know just which subset of variables constitutes a good model. For those instances, SPSS provides several methods for controlling the entry or removal of independent variables from the regression model.

- **Forward selection** enters variables into the model one by one (or *step* by *step*). The first variable entered at step 1 is the one with the strongest positive (or negative) simple correlation with the dependent variable. At step 2 (and at each subsequent step), the variable with the strongest partial correlation enters. At each step, the hypothesis that the coefficient of the entered variable is 0 is tested using its t statistic (actually an F statistic that is the square of the t). Stepping stops when an established criterion for the F no longer holds.

- **Backward elimination** begins with all candidate variables in the model, and at each step, removes the least useful predictor (lowest F-to-remove). Variables are removed until an established criterion for the F no longer holds. This method is illustrated in this example.

- **Stepwise selection** begins like forward stepping, but at each step, tests variables already in the model for removal. This is the most commonly used method, especially when there are correlations among the independent variables. For example, the entry of, say, a fourth variable can diminish the importance of an already entered variable, so the already entered variable is removed from the model (with the Forward method, it remains in the model). The stepwise method is illustrated in Example 4 on p. 225.

The models that result from these methods may differ, especially when the independent variables are highly intercorrelated. Also, be aware that none of these procedures is guaranteed to provide the *best* subset in an absolute sense.

More is not better: overfitting and a selection strategy. Variable selection and/or model building is seldom a simple process and usually involves many steps. Two aspects to variable selection are

- Selecting the dimensionality of the submodel (how many variables to include).

- Evaluating each model selected.

There is no one test to determine the dimensionality of the best submodel. Some researchers include too many variables in the model. This is called **overfitting**. Such a model will perform poorly when applied to a new sample drawn from the same population. That is, the size of the correlation between the predicted and observed values of the dependent variable (multiple R) is much smaller for the new sample than for the original sample. More is not better, and it may be worse.

Many data analysts use cross-validation techniques that involve 60%, 70%, or 80% random subsamples. To do this, they

- Randomly select 70% of the cases.

- Fit a model.

- Use the resulting coefficients to obtain predicted values for the remaining 30% of the cases.

- Compute R^2 (the square of the correlation between the predicted and observed values of the dependent variable) for the smaller sample.

In overfitting situations, the discrepancy between R^2 for the 70% sample used to estimate the coefficients and the 30% sample can be dramatic.

Automatic stepwise procedures cannot do all the work for you. Use them as a tool to determine roughly the number of predictors needed (for example, you might find three to five variables). If you try several methods of selection, you may identify candidate predictors that are not included by any method. Ignore them, and fit models, say, with three to five variables, selecting alternative subsets from among the better candidates.

You may find several subsets that perform equally as well. In this case knowledge of the subject matter, how accurately individual variables are measured, and what a variable "communicates" may guide selection of the model to report.

When data are missing, it may be particularly beneficial to ignore candidate variables with poor predictive power: there may be many more cases with complete data for the smaller set of candidate variables that remain.

What variables are most useful for predicting female life expectancy? Example 1 explored the relationship between life expectancy and female literacy. Example 2 examined infant mortality and fertility as the independent variables. This example includes five additional candidate variables and uses backward stepping to identify a useful subset of predictors. The new variables are the percentage of the population living in cities (*urban*), the literacy rate for males (*lit_male*), the ratio of each country's birth to death rate (*b_to_d*), the percentage that each country's population increased during the previous year (*pop_incr*), and economic information (gross domestic product per capita). The distribution of gross domestic product is very right-skewed, so each value is log transformed and stored as a variable named *log_gdp*.

To make the output that follows more compact, short variable names are used instead of their longer, more informative labels. To do this, from the menus choose:

Edit
 Options...

Click the *Output Labels* tab.

 Pivot Table Labeling
  ▼ Variables in labels shown as: Names

To produce this output, in the Linear Regression dialog box, click *Reset* to restore the dialog box defaults, and then select:

▸ Dependent: lifeexpf

▸ Independent: babymort, fertility, lit_male, lit_fema, urban, log_gdp, b_to_d, pop_incr

▾ Method: Backward

▸ Case Labels: country

Statistics...
    ☑ Descriptives   ☑ Collinearity diagnostics

 On the Correlations table, select and hide the *Sig (1-tailed)* and *N* rows.

To hide footnotes, select them and then choose *Hide* from the View menu.

The Coefficients table has been separated into two tables so that it is easier to read.

Correlations

		LIFEEXPF	BABYMORT	FERTILTY	LIT_MALE	LIT_FEMA	URBAN	LOG_GDP	B_TO_D	POP_INCR
Pearson Correlation	LIFEEXPF	1.000	-.955	-.816	.777	.819	.748	.797	.112	-.475
	BABYMORT	-.955	1.000	.809	-.809	-.843	-.724	-.786	-.080	.494
	FERTILTY	-.816	.809	1.000	-.796	-.839	-.563	-.642	.303	.795
	LIT_MALE	.777	-.809	-.796	1.000	.964	.587	.611	-.153	-.619
	LIT_FEMA	.819	-.843	-.839	.964	1.000	.612	.632	-.148	-.638
	URBAN	.748	-.724	-.563	.587	.612	1.000	.777	.172	-.254
	LOG_GDP	.797	-.786	-.642	.611	.632	.777	1.000	-.005	-.427
	B_TO_D	.112	-.080	.303	-.153	-.148	.172	-.005	1.000	.746
	POP_INCR	-.475	.494	.795	-.619	-.638	-.254	-.427	.746	1.000

Correlations. The simple correlations of each candidate predictor with the dependent variable life expectancy are displayed in the top row of this matrix. Infant mortality has the highest correlation (–0.955); female literacy, the next largest (0.819); and the birth-to-death ratio, the lowest (0.112). The correlations not in the first row or first column are the correlations among the independent variables. There are strong interrelations among the candidate predictors.

Variables Entered/Removed. This table provides an overview of the stepwise results.

Variables Entered/Removed

Model	Variables Entered	Variables Removed	Method
1	POP_INCR, URBAN, LIT_MALE, LOG_GDP, B_TO_D, FERTILTY, BABYMORT, LIT_FEMA	.	Enter
2	.	POP_INCR	Backward (criterion: Probability of F-to-remove >= .100).
3	.	LIT_MALE	Backward (criterion: Probability of F-to-remove >= .100).
4	.	LIT_FEMA	Backward (criterion: Probability of F-to-remove >= .100).
5	.	URBAN	Backward (criterion: Probability of F-to-remove >= .100).

First, SPSS fits a model with all eight candidate predictors; then, at each step (model), it removes the variable that contributes least to the fit.

In the *Removed* column, *pop_incr* is the first variable removed from the model. Next is *lit_male*, followed by *lit_fema*, *urban*, the last variable removed. Four variables remain in the model when stepping stops.

Model Summary

Model	R	R Square	Adjusted R Square	Std. Error of the Estimate
1	.968	.938	.931	2.81
2	.968	.938	.932	2.80
3	.968	.937	.933	2.79
4	.968	.937	.933	2.77
5	.968	.936	.933	2.77

Model Summary. The value of R^2 for the model with all eight predictors in step 1 is 0.938 and adjusted R^2 is 0.931. (See the discussion in "Coefficients (part 2)" on p. 222 regarding worrisome problems about this fit.) R^2 for the last model with four variables is 0.936, a negligible drop from 0.938 for the full model. Adjusted R^2 for this smaller model (0.933) is larger than that for the full model (0.931).

R^2 and adjusted R^2 are defined in Example 2. As you include more and more variables in a model, R^2 will continue to increase—even if the variables are columns of random numbers unrelated to your outcome variable. Including irrelevant variables also increases the standard errors of the estimates.

If you experiment by including more and more variables in your model, adjusted R^2 will eventually decrease in size (it is smaller here for the eight-variable model than for the four-variable model). This provides a clue that overfitting has occurred. However, some researchers feel that the adjustment to R^2 is not strong enough—that is, a model that predicts well for a new sample from the same population will be slightly smaller than that indicated *best* by adjusted R^2. Users new to regression may be surprised to learn that a model with more variables (and a higher R^2) can perform worse than a smaller one on a new sample. A model with many variables also is hard to interpret.

Coefficients[1]

Model		Unstandardized Coefficients		Standardized Coefficients	t	Sig.	Collinearity Statistics	
		B	Std. Error	Beta			Tolerance	VIF
1	(Constant)	72.109	5.084		14.184	.000		
	BABYMORT	-.163	.023	-.581	-6.973	.000	.117	8.511
	FERTILTY	-1.339	.473	-.235	-2.831	.006	.118	8.460
	LIT_MALE	-3.90E-02	.057	-.074	-.681	.498	.069	14.589
	LIT_FEMA	3.215E-02	.047	.086	.683	.497	.052	19.330
	URBAN	2.250E-02	.022	.051	1.008	.317	.321	3.119
	LOG_GDP	2.163	1.051	.115	2.058	.043	.261	3.835
	B_TO_D	.887	.360	.175	2.468	.016	.162	6.166
	POP_INCR	-.589	.972	-.061	-.606	.546	.080	12.491

1. Dependent Variable: LIFEEXPF

Coefficients (part 1). This is the first section of a large table that displays results for each step in the model selection process. It contains the coefficients and statistics for the equation at step 1, which includes all eight candidate predictors. (This is the same as the table produced using the default selection method, Enter.) Results for steps 2 through 5 are displayed in the table on p. 222.

While R^2 for this eight-variable model is almost 94%, many data analysts would consider it to be a poor model because it has four small *t* statistics and several low values of tolerance.

The values in the first five columns were introduced in previous examples, along with a guideline for identifying useful predictors: look for *t* statistics well below –2 or above +2. Thus, *pop_incr, lit_male, lit_fema,* and *urban* are candidates for removal. The backward method removes *pop_incr* first because it has the smallest *t* and then, for the model that now has seven variables instead of eight, checks the results for the next variable to remove.

The collinearity statistics tolerance and VIF are reported here because Collinearity diagnostics is selected on the Linear Regression dialog box. **Collinearity** refers to the troublesome situation where the correlations among the independent variables are strong. When you suspect that collinearity may be a problem, study the **tolerance** statistic. Only the values of the independent variables are used to calculate it; the dependent variable is ignored. For each variable,

$$tolerance = 1 - R_i^2$$

where R_i^2 is the squared multiple correlation of that variable with the other independent variables. For example, if the names of the independent variables are A, B, and C, SPSS essentially calculates R^2 for three models:

- R_A^2 for variable A regressed on variables B and C.
- R_B^2 for B regressed on A and C.
- R_C^2 for C regressed on A and B.

and uses these quantities to compute tolerance for each variable. Values of tolerance range from 0 to 1. When its value is small (close to 0), the variable is almost a linear combination of the other independent variables. Consequently, the estimate of the variable's regression coefficient is unstable, and the computations can lose numerical accuracy.

The tolerance for *lit_fema* is 0.052—thus, its R^2 with the other seven independent variables is 0.948 (94.8% of the variability of *lit_fema* is explained by the other predictors). The variables *lit_male* and *pop_incr* also have low tolerances.

In SPSS, the default value for tolerance is 0.0001. All variables must pass this criterion to be included in an equation, regardless of the selection method used. In some situations, the default value allows more variables to remain than are needed for a stable fit. (With syntax, you can specify a larger value.)

The **variance inflation factor (VIF)** is the reciprocal of tolerance. So, by definition, the variables here with low tolerances have large variance inflation factors. The calculations of the variance for the ith regression coefficient use VIF_i, thus, its name. As the variance inflation factor increases, so does the variance of the regression coefficient.

Coefficients[1]

Model	Variables	Unstandardized Coefficients		Standardized Coefficients	Statistics		Collinearity Statistics	
		B	Std. Error	Beta	t	Significance	Tolerance	VIF
2	(Constant)	72.171	5.062		14.258	.000		
	BABYMORT	-.165	.023	-.588	-7.151	.000	.120	8.354
	FERTILTY	-1.508	.380	-.265	-3.970	.000	.182	5.506
	LIT_MALE	-3.73E-02	.057	-.071	-.656	.514	.069	14.557
	LIT_FEMA	3.268E-02	.047	.087	.697	.488	.052	19.323
	URBAN	2.061E-02	.022	.047	.936	.352	.327	3.059
	LOG_GDP	2.200	1.045	.117	2.105	.039	.262	3.823
	B_TO_D	.706	.199	.139	3.553	.001	.527	1.899
3	(Constant)	71.116	4.782		14.873	.000		
	BABYMORT	-.164	.023	-.586	-7.159	.000	.120	8.344
	FERTILTY	-1.540	.376	-.270	-4.100	.000	.185	5.419
	LIT_FEMA	6.104E-03	.023	.016	.260	.796	.205	4.888
	URBAN	2.059E-02	.022	.047	.939	.351	.327	3.059
	LOG_GDP	2.187	1.041	.116	2.101	.039	.262	3.821
	B_TO_D	.718	.197	.142	3.639	.000	.531	1.884
4	(Constant)	71.958	3.496		20.585	.000		
	BABYMORT	-.167	.020	-.596	-8.349	.000	.156	6.426
	FERTILTY	-1.571	.353	-.276	-4.447	.000	.206	4.854
	URBAN	2.147E-02	.022	.049	.997	.322	.335	2.985
	LOG_GDP	2.134	1.015	.114	2.103	.039	.272	3.672
	B_TO_D	.708	.193	.140	3.677	.000	.550	1.817
5	(Constant)	71.451	3.458		20.660	.000		
	BABYMORT	-.169	.020	-.603	-8.473	.000	.157	6.374
	FERTILTY	-1.612	.351	-.283	-4.592	.000	.209	4.790
	LOG_GDP	2.663	.865	.142	3.080	.003	.375	2.667
	B_TO_D	.759	.186	.150	4.093	.000	.593	1.687

Coefficients (part 2). In the first section of this table (above), *pop_incr* was found to be the least useful predictor among the set of eight variables. The statistics listed for Model 2 are for the seven-variable model formed after *pop_incr* is removed. The variable *lit_male* has the smallest *t*, so is removed next. Its tolerance is very low and as is the tolerance for *lit_fema*. (The simple correlation between these two variables is very high—see the Correlations table on p. 218.)

Both *pop_incr* and *lit_male* are omitted from Model 3. The variable *lit_fema* has the smallest *t,* so it is not used in Model 4. The variable *urban* is the least useful predictor among the five variables in Model 4, so it is removed when Model 5 is estimated.

The smallest t in Model 5 is larger than 3, so its size satisfies the rough absolute-value-of-2 rule. Stepping stops and no more variables are removed. The model identified via the backward method is:

life expectancy $= 71.45 - 0.169$ babymort $+ 2.663$ log_gdp
$+ 0.759$ b_to_d $- 1.612$ fertility

Its R^2 and adjusted R^2 are reported in the last row of the Model Summary table on p. 219.

This may not be the *best* model of all time. You should now try other methods of variable selection and also try fitting models with other subsets of four independent variables. And, after studying the Collincarity Diagnostics table on p. 229, you might consider models with three variables.

Criteria for moving variables. More formally, SPSS provides two criteria for moving variables. They are based on an F statistic that is the square of the t statistics used above in the rough absolute-value-of-2 rule. The first criterion for removing variables is the minimum F value that a variable must have to remain in the model. Variables with F statistics less than the value specified for removal in the Linear Regression Options subdialog box are eligible for removal. Some texts and software packages call this statistic **F-to-remove**. The second criterion is the **maximum probability of F-to-remove**. The default F-to-remove is 2.71, and the default probability is 0.10. Some feel that when the predictors are highly correlated, the F-to-remove should be set to a higher value, and the probability to a lower value.

Notice that the two criteria are not necessarily equivalent. If you specify a minimum F value, its significance level changes as the models contain fewer and fewer variables. This does not mean that the probability criterion is better, however. There is no one test to tell you when to stop removing variables (or entering variables when you use the Forward method). Remember from the "Coefficients" discussion on p. 209 that the true significance level is difficult to compute because it depends on the number of variables in the model, their correlation structure, and the sample size. Within a single step, either the size of the F (t in the output) or its probability is useful for ordering the importance or contribution of the predictors.

The problem of when to stop removing variables (or adding variables) has no easy answer, and many researchers rely on the cross-validation technique described in the introduction to this example. If you are in the process of trying several exploratory models, include partial residual plots, for they provide a graphical view of the F or t statistic. You may find that one or two points mask or falsely inflate the significance of the t.

Excluded Variables

Model		Beta In	t	Sig.	Partial Correlation	Collinearity Statistics		
						Tolerance	VIF	Minimum Tolerance
2	POP_INCR	-.061	-.606	.546	-.069	.006E-02	12.491	.173E-02
3	POP_INCR	-.058	-.577	.566	-.066	.023E-02	12.464	.023E-02
	LIT_MALE	-.071	-.656	.514	-.075	.870E-02	14.557	.175E-02
4	POP_INCR	-.060	-.607	.546	-.069	.134E-02	12.294	.134E-02
	LIT_MALE	-.006	-.106	.916	-.012	.272	3.682	.125
	LIT_FEMA	.016	.260	.796	.029	.205	4.888	.120
5	POP_INCR	-.047	-.480	.632	-.054	.257E-02	12.110	.257E-02
	LIT_MALE	.002	.028	.977	.003	.277	3.615	.125
	LIT_FEMA	.025	.411	.682	.046	.210	4.770	.120
	URBAN	.049	.997	.322	.111	.335	2.985	.156

Excluded Variables. In the Coefficients tables, SPSS reported results at each step for the variables included in the model. The Excluded Variables table above presents information about the variables not in those equations. Use it to track what variables are removed and if there are any closely contending variables that you might prefer to use instead because they are measured (or recorded) more accurately or they communicate better.

At step 2 (Model 2), *pop_incr* is removed from the model. *Beta In* is the standardized regression coefficient that would result if *pop_incr* were put back in the model. Look for this value in the Coefficients (part 1) table, Model 1. Notice that the same is true for *t*, significance, tolerance, and VIF—they are the values that would result if *pop_incr* were added back into the model.

At step 3, *lit_male* is removed. Its values in Model 3 above are the same as those for Model 2 in the Coefficients (part 2) table. The variable *lit_fema* is removed at step 4 and *urban* at step 5. Look for the same values in the step previous to each in the Coefficients (part 2) table.

For each variable, beta in, *t*, significance, tolerance, and VIF are the values that would result if that variable were included in the model. For example, look at *pop_incr* in Model 5. If you were to fit a model with *babymort*, *log_gdp*, *b_to_d*, and *fertilty* (the variables *in* the model at step 5) and also include *pop_incr*, beta for *pop_incr* in this model with five variables would be –.047; *t* would be –0.48, . . . ,VIF would be 12.11.

The **Partial Correlation** is the correlation of each independent variable with the dependent variable after removing the linear effect of variables already in the equation. For *pop_incr* in Model 2:

• Regress the dependent variable on the other seven variables in the model.
• Regress *pop_incr* on the other seven variables in the model.
• Compute the correlation between the two sets of residuals.

These are the same residuals used to construct the partial residual plots on p. 209. The *F* (or *t*) statistics used for moving variables in and out of the model can be written as functions of partial correlations. Thus, it is convenient, especially in forward-stepping procedures, to choose the variable with the largest partial correlation in absolute value when selecting the variable for entry (it will have the largest *F* or *t*).

Example 4
Variable Selection: The Stepwise Method

When correlations among the independent variables are strong, try more than one method of variable selection. The stepwise method is the one most frequently used. It works like the forward method, except, with stepwise, an already entered variable can be removed from the equation. Both methods begin by entering into the model the variable that has the strongest positive or negative correlation with the dependent variable; and at each subsequent step, both add the variable with the strongest partial correlation. With stepwise, at each step, variables are tested for removal.

This example continues to use female life expectancy as the dependent variable. In the last example illustrating variable selection via backward stepping, female literacy had the second largest simple correlation with the dependent variable (0.819) but was not included in the final model. Male literacy was also excluded. For both of these variables, 24 of the 109 countries in the sample have values missing; by omitting them as candidate predictors here, you increase the sample size to 106. The other independent variables are infant mortality (*babymort*), average number of children per family (*fertilty*), percentage of the population living in cities (*urban*), the logarithm of gross domestic product per capita (*log_gdp*), the ratio of birth rate to death rate (*b_to_d*), and the percentage a country's population increased during the previous year (*pop_incr*).

Again, because of the strong intercorrelations among the independent variables, you request collinearity diagnostics. Assuming that you still have selected *Names* for variable labeling in pivot tables (as in Example 3), in the Linear Regression dialog box, click *Reset* to restore the defaults, and then select:

▶ Dependent: lifeexpf

▶ Independent: babymort, fertility, urban, log_gdp, b_to_d, pop_incr

▼ Method: Stepwise

▶ Case Labels: country

Statistics...
 ☑ Descriptives ☑ Collinearity diagnostics

 To hide footnotes, select them and then choose *Hide* from the View menu.

Variables Entered/Removed

Model	Variables Entered	Variables Removed	Method
1	BABYMORT	.	Stepwise (Criteria: Probability-of-F-to-enter <= .050, Probability-of-F-to-remove >= .100).
2	URBAN	.	Stepwise (Criteria: Probability-of-F-to-enter <= .050, Probability-of-F-to-remove >= .100).
3	FERTILTY	.	Stepwise (Criteria: Probability-of-F-to-enter <= .050, Probability-of-F-to-remove >= .100).
4	B_TO_D	.	Stepwise (Criteria: Probability-of-F-to-enter <= .050, Probability-of-F-to-remove >= .100).
5	LOG_GDP	.	Stepwise (Criteria: Probability-of-F-to-enter <= .050, Probability-of-F-to-remove >= .100).
6	.	URBAN	Stepwise (Criteria: Probability-of-F-to-enter <= .050, Probability-of-F-to-remove >= .100).

Variables Entered/Removed. This overview of the stepping process indicates that four of the six candidate predictors are included in the final model. They are entered into the equation in this order: *babymort, urban, fertility, b_to_d, log_gdp*. The second variable to enter, *urban*, is removed at step 6 (if using the Forward method, *urban* would not be removed).

The final model includes the same four variables found via backward stepping in Example 3. Because the independent variables are correlated, you would not be surprised if the models had differed. Also, another difference is that the sample size here is about 25% larger. (Sample size information is reported in the bottom panel of the Correlations table, but it is not shown here.)

Model Summary

Model	R	R Square	Adjusted R Square	Std. Error of the Estimate
1	.962	.925	.924	2.93
2	.965	.931	.930	2.82
3	.967	.935	.933	2.75
4	.971	.942	.940	2.62
5	.973	.947	.944	2.51
6	.973	.946	.944	2.52

Model Summary. Here, R^2 for the final model is 0.946 and adjusted R^2 is 0.944. Notice that these values did not drop when *urban* was removed. The standard error of the estimate decreases from 2.93 years when infant mortality is the only predictor to 2.52 years when the model includes four variables.

Excluded Variables

Model		Beta In	t	Sig.	Partial Correlation	Collinearity Statistics		Minimum Tolerance
						Tolerance	VIF	
1	FERTILTY	-.119	-2.536	.013	-.242	.308	3.246	.308
	URBAN	.112	2.980	.004	.282	.470	2.127	.470
	LOG_GDP	.121	2.630	.010	.251	.322	3.106	.322
	B_TO_D	.025	.942	.348	.092	.988	1.012	.988
	POP INCR	-.002	-.058	.954	-.006	.647	1.546	.647
2	FERTILTY	-.115	-2.526	.013	-.243	.308	3.250	.234
	LOG_GDP	.079	1.595	.114	.156	.269	3.714	.269
	B_TO_D	.021	.793	.429	.078	.985	1.016	.463
	POP_INCR	-.011	-.334	.739	-.033	.642	1.559	.353
3	LOG_GDP	.078	1.619	.109	.159	.269	3.714	.182
	B_TO_D	.109	3.421	.001	.322	.565	1.771	.177
	POP_INCR	.129	2.654	.009	.255	.253	3.947	.122
4	LOG_GDP	.144	3.075	.003	.294	.241	4.148	.131
	POP_INCR	-.043	-.457	.648	-.046	6.571E-02	15.218	6.571E-02
5	POP_INCR	-.030	-.335	.738	-.034	6.557E-02	15.250	6.557E-02
6	URBAN	.044	1.152	.252	.114	.370	2.700	.131
	POP_INCR	-.011	-.121	.904	-.012	6.781E-02	14.748	6.781E-02

Excluded Variables. At each step (Model), the candidate predictors are listed with statistics that you can use to track how SPSS selects a variable for entry at the next step (and possibly identify variables that barely miss selection—you might include them in other smaller models to explore later). See earlier examples for definitions of the statistics.

At step 1, SPSS enters *babymort* as the first variable because it has the highest correlation with the dependent variable life expectancy. Then you can use either of these statistics in this table to see how variables are entered (or removed):

- The *t* statistic for each candidate variable. At step 1, *urban* has the largest *t* (2.980), so it is entered into the step 2 model. Then at step 2, *fertilty* has the largest *t* in absolute value (–2.526); at step 3, *b_to_d* has the largest (3.421); and at step 4, *log_gdp* has the largest (3.075); so each of these variables is entered at the next step.

At step 5, the *t* for *pop_incr* (–0.335) fails the default entrance criterion that an *F* statistic must be greater than 3.84 (see the Linear Regression Options subdialog box). The square root of the *F* statistic is the *t* reported in the output. The square root of 3.84 is 1.96, so no variable enters if its *t* is less than 1.96. Meanwhile, among the values reported in the Excluded Variables table, SPSS checks the *t* values for already entered variables to see if any have values less than 1.65 (the square root of the default *F* removal criterion (2.71)). In step 5 of the Coefficients table, the *t* for *urban* is 1.152, so it is removed from the model.

- The partial correlation of each candidate variable with the dependent variable after removing the linear effect of the variables already entered. Notice that at each step, the candidate variable with the largest *t* also has the strongest partial correlation.

Coefficients[1]

Model		Unstandardized Coefficients		Standardized Coefficients	t	Sig.	Collinearity Statistics	
		B	Std. Error	Beta			Tolerance	VIF
1	(Constant)	81.538	.431		189.401	.000		
	BABYMORT	-.268	.007	-.962	-35.855	.000	1.000	1.000
2	(Constant)	77.767	1.332		58.384	.000		
	BABYMORT	-.245	.011	-.880	-23.328	.000	.470	2.127
	URBAN	4.92E-02	.017	.112	2.980	.004	.470	2.127
3	(Constant)	79.021	1.390		56.843	.000		
	BABYMORT	-.219	.015	-.787	-15.107	.000	.234	4.267
	URBAN	4.78E-02	.016	.109	2.967	.004	.470	2.130
	FERTILTY	-.642	.254	-.115	-2.526	.013	.308	3.250
4	(Constant)	79.123	1.323		59.813	.000		
	BABYMORT	-.196	.015	-.702	-12.681	.000	.188	5.330
	URBAN	4.20E-02	.015	.096	2.721	.008	.464	2.156
	FERTILTY	-1.355	.319	-.242	-4.245	.000	.177	5.666
	B_TO_D	.545	.159	.109	3.421	.001	.565	1.771
5	(Constant)	70.955	2.944		24.098	.000		
	BABYMORT	-.166	.018	-.594	-9.329	.000	.131	7.646
	URBAN	1.91E-02	.017	.044	1.152	.252	.370	2.700
	FERTILTY	-1.560	.314	-.279	-4.971	.000	.169	5.934
	B_TO_D	.706	.162	.141	4.365	.000	.506	1.978
	LOG_GDP	2.454	.798	.144	3.075	.003	.241	4.148
6	(Constant)	70.754	2.944		24.033	.000		
	BABYMORT	-.166	.018	-.597	-9.369	.000	.131	7.634
	FERTILTY	-1.625	.309	-.291	-5.259	.000	.174	5.739
	B_TO_D	.750	.157	.150	4.770	.000	.536	1.865
	LOG_GDP	2.867	.714	.169	4.013	.000	.302	3.313

[1]. Dependent Variable: LIFEEXPF

Coefficients. The coefficients for the final model are reported at step 6:

$$\text{life expectancy} = 70.754 - 0.166 \text{ babymort} + 2.867 \text{ log\_gdp} + 0.750 \text{ b\_to\_d} - 1.625 \text{ fertility}$$

Notice that the standard errors for the coefficients of *fertility*, *b_to_d*, and *log_gdp* are smaller for the model without *urban* than for the model with the variable.

Collinearity Diagnostics[1]

Model	Dimension	Eigenvalue	Condition Index	(Constant)	BABYMORT	URBAN	FERTILTY	B_TO_D	LOG_GDP
1	1	1.751	1.000	.12	.12				
	2	.249	2.653	.88	.88				
2	1	2.461	1.000	.01	.02	.01			
	2	.514	2.189	.00	.26	.05			
	3	2.505E-02	9.913	.99	.72	.94			
3	1	3.349	1.000	.00	.01	.00	.01		
	2	.581	2.400	.00	.07	.06	.01		
	3	4.544E-02	8.585	.01	.79	.05	.91		
	4	2.411E-02	11.786	.99	.14	.89	.08		
4	1	4.130	1.000	.00	.00	.00	.00	.01	
	2	.589	2.647	.00	.06	.05	.01	.00	
	3	.229	4.243	.02	.03	.03	.00	.53	
	4	2.787E-02	12.173	.11	.91	.22	.64	.35	
	5	2.333E-02	13.305	.87	.00	.69	.35	.11	
5	1	5.014	1.000	.00	.00	.00	.00	.00	.00
	2	.672	2.732	.00	.04	.02	.01	.00	.00
	3	.249	4.485	.00	.02	.01	.00	.47	.00
	4	3.548E-02	11.888	.03	.23	.77	.05	.02	.04
	5	2.556E-02	14.006	.03	.31	.13	.90	.39	.00
	6	3.706E-03	36.783	.95	.39	.07	.04	.12	.95
6	1	4.269	1.000	.00	.00		.00	.01	.00
	2	.464	3.033	.00	.07		.01	.02	.01
	3	.237	4.244	.00	.01		.00	.47	.01
	4	2.663E-02	12.661	.01	.49		.97	.41	.00
	5	3.944E-03	32.897	.99	.43		.02	.09	.99

[1]. Dependent Variable: LIFEEXPF

Collinearity Diagnostics. Eigenvalues are obtained by factoring the scaled (so that diagonal elements are 1's), uncentered cross-products matrix of the independent variables. Eigenvalues provide an indication of how many distinct dimensions there are among the independent variables. When several eigenvalues are close to 0, the variables are highly intercorrelated and the matrix is said to be *ill-conditioned*; small changes in the data values may lead to large changes in the estimates of the coefficients.

Condition indices are the square roots of the ratios of the largest eigenvalue to each successive eigenvalue. A condition index greater than 15 indicates a possible problem and an index greater than 30 suggests a serious problem with collinearity (see *Regression Diagnostics* by Belsley, Kuh, and Welsch, John Wiley & Sons, 1980).

The **Variance Proportions** are the proportions of the variance of the estimate accounted for by each principal component associated with each of the eigenvalues. Collinearity is a problem when a component associated with a high condition index contributes substantially to the variance of two or more variables.

Here, for the final set of four variables (Model 6), the last condition index is 32.897! The last component accounts for 99% of the variance of the constant, 99% of the variance of *log_gdp*, and 43% of the variance of *babymort*. Thus, for a more stable model, it might be wise to explore models with three variables.

13 Nonparametric Tests

Most classical statistics assume that the data being analyzed come from a specific distribution, usually the normal distribution. These statistics are calculated based on **parameters** of the distribution, such as the mean and variance. Many statistics, such as the *t* test or analysis of variance, also assume that the groups being analyzed have equal variances. Although most statistics are robust enough to withstand minor violations of these assumptions, what happens if you screen your data and realize that the data violate these assumptions so substantially that the results from your analyses may not be reliable? A class of statistics known as **nonparametric tests** exists for analyzing data under these circumstances. Nonparametric tests are known as **distribution-free tests** because they make no assumptions about the underlying distribution of the data. SPSS offers nonparametric versions of some commonly used tests such as *t* test, analysis of variance, one-sample tests (to see if a sample comes from a particular distribution), and other tests. The fact that some tests exist in both parametric and nonparametric versions raises the question of when to use which version. In general, the parametric versions of tests are more sensitive than the nonparametric versions and should be used when you reasonably believe that the necessary assumptions are met. However, nonparametric tests, while being *distribution* free, are not *assumption* free. These tests do require that certain assumptions be met, but in general they are met more easily than the assumptions required by parametric tests.

The nonparametric tests are organized by the number of samples being tested. One-sample tests include the chi-square test, runs test, binomial test, and one-sample Kolmogorov-Smirnov test. Menu items exist for tests for two independent and two related samples and several independent and several related samples.

Example 1: One-sample chi-square test. The one-sample chi-square test is used to test whether each color in a bag of jelly beans occurs equally often.

Example 2: Binomial test. Data collected by flipping a coin are analyzed to test whether the coin is fair.

Example 3: Runs test. The coin data are tested with the runs test to provide another measure of whether the coin is fair.

Example 4: Mann-Whitney test. The Mann-Whitney test is used as an example of tests for two or more independent samples. Treadmill times for healthy men and men with coronary heart disease are compared. The relationship between the Mann-Whitney test statistic and the Wilcoxon test statistic is discussed.

Example 5: Friedman test. This test is used as an example of tests for two or more related samples. Ratings of people's preferences for different types of music are compared.

One-Sample Tests

One-sample tests examine whether a set of observed values conform to the values that you might expect, given a certain distribution. The difference between the different tests arise from how the expected values are derived. The chi-square test makes no assumptions about the underlying distribution of the data, while the binomial test assumes a binomial distribution. The one-sample Kolmogorov-Smirnov test can test whether observed values come from a normal, Poisson, or uniform distribution.

Example 1
One-Sample Chi-Square Test

The one-sample chi-square test compares the observed frequencies of categories to frequencies that would be expected if the null hypothesis were true. The one-sample chi-square makes no assumptions about the underlying distribution of the data. Its only requirement is that the data be a random sample.

The chi-square statistic is calculated by collecting observed values for each of the categories and examining the differences between the observed and expected values. The formula for the chi-square statistic is

$$\chi^2 = \sum_{i=1}^{k} \frac{(o_i - e_i)^2}{e_i}$$

where o_i is the observed value for the ith category, e_i is the expected value for the ith category, and k is the total number of categories. In other words, the chi-square is the sum of the squared differences between the observed and expected values, divided by the expected values.

For example, if a bag of jelly beans contains jelly beans in six colors (blue, pink, green, yellow, orange, and red), you might assume that each color occurs equally often, so that a bag containing 56 jelly beans would contain about 9.3 beans of each color.

Table 13.1 Number of jelly beans

Color	Number of beans
blue	3
pink	17
green	6
yellow	10
orange	6
red	14

Table 13.1 shows the number of observed jelly beans. To test the null hypothesis that each color occurs equally often in a bag of jelly beans, run the chi-square test. In this example, *color* is the color of each jelly bean, weighted by its observed frequency. For more information on weight variables, see the *SPSS Base User's Guide*.

To produce this output, create the variable *color* (with a value label for each color) and assign a case number for each color. Create a second variable, *number*, and enter the number of beans for each color (see Table 13.1). Use Weight Cases from the Data menu to weight cases by *number*. Then, from the menus choose:

Analyze
  Nonparametric Tests
    Chi-Square...

▶ Test Variable List: color

 To hide the footnote on the Test Statistics table, select it and choose *Hide* from the View menu.

color of jelly bean

	Observed N	Expected N	Residual
blue	3	9.3	-6.3
pink	17	9.3	7.7
green	6	9.3	-3.3
yellow	10	9.3	.7
orange	6	9.3	-3.3
red	14	9.3	4.7
Total	56		

Observed and expected frequencies. The frequency table shows the actual observed number of jelly beans in the bag and the expected number of jelly beans, based on the assumption that the different colors occur equally often. SPSS does allow you to specify unequal expected values, if you have reason to hypothesize that some values occur more often than others. The *Residual* column shows the differences between the expected and observed values. Large absolute values for the residuals indicate that the observed values are very different from the expected values.

Test Statistics

	color of jelly bean
Chi-Square	15.357
df	5
Asymptotic Significance	.009

Test Statistics (Chi-Square test). The chi-square statistic has a value of 15.357, with an asymptotic significance of 0.009. You can therefore reject the null hypothesis that all colors of jelly beans occur equally frequently.

Example 2
Binomial Test

Like the chi-square test, the binomial test is a one-sample test that compares observed with expected values. The difference is that, in the case of the binomial test, the expected values are derived from the binomial distribution rather than from expected frequencies. A **binomial distribution** has only two possible outcomes. For example, you might want to find out if a coin is fair. You would expect that if you tossed a fair coin, it would come up heads about half of the time and tails about half of the time. Imagine that you tossed a quarter 30 times and came up with the following result, in which 1 represents a head and 0 represents a tail:

011010011011100001000011011100

In this example, the quarter came up heads 14 times and tails 16 times, which seems close to what you might expect from a fair coin. To be certain that the coin is fair, you could test the null hypothesis that the probability of heads is 0.50 by performing the binomial test. (It is possible to test a different probability for the null hypothesis.) In this example, *quarter* is the test variable. It has two values in the data: 1 represents heads and 0 represents tails.

To produce this output, from the menus choose:

Analyze
  Nonparametric Tests
    Binomial...

▶ Test Variable List: quarter

Define Dichotomy
⊙Cut point: 0

 To hide the footnote, select it and choose *Hide* from the View menu

Binomial Test

		Category	N	Observed Proportion	Test Proportion	Asymptotic Significance (2-tailed)
QUARTER	Group 1	tails	16	.53	.50	.855
	Group 2	heads	14	.47		
	Total		30	1.00		

Binomial Test. The results show that the observed probability of the coin coming up heads is 0.53, which is very close to the expected value of 0.50. The p value of this result is 0.86, indicating that you cannot reject the null hypothesis and should accept that this is a fair coin.

Example 3
Runs Test

The runs test provides another means of determining whether a sequence of observations conforms to expectations. The runs test examines a series of observations for runs, or repetitions, of the same outcome. For example, in the coin-tossing data above, the data show a run of one 0, followed by a run of two 1's, and another run of one 0, and so on. The longest runs in the data are a run of four 0's, consisting of observations 14–17, and another run of four 0's, consisting of observations 19–22. The question, then, is whether these runs fall within the bounds of expected behavior for a series of observations with two possible outcomes. In a random process, would you expect more or fewer runs? Too many or two few runs are indications of bias or non-randomness. One use of the runs test is to examine residuals. As discussed at the end of Chapter 12, Example 1, residuals should be randomly scattered around 0. You can use the runs test to check that residuals are indeed random.

To again test the null hypothesis from Example 2 that the coin is fair (and therefore that the number of runs falls within the boundaries that you might expect if the results are random), you can perform the runs test.

To produce this output, from the menus choose:

Analyze
  Nonparametric Tests
    Runs

▶ Test Variable List: quarter

Cut Point
  ☐ Median (deselect)
  ☑ Custom: 1

 To hide the footnote, select it and choose *Hide* from the View menu.

Runs Test

	QUARTER
Test Value	1
Total Cases	30
Number of Runs	15
Z	-.162
Asymptotic Significance (2-tailed)	.871

Runs Test. The results show that there were 15 runs among the 30 observations, and that the *p* value is 0.871, leading to the conclusion that the coin is indeed fair.

Tests for Two or More Independent Samples

Just as the *t* test compares the means of two independent samples, the nonparametric test for two independent samples compares the center of location for two samples. The difference is that the *t* test assumes that the populations are normally distributed, while the nonparametric tests are distribution free and do not make this assumption. If you do meet the assumptions for a *t* test or if you can meet them by performing a transformation, a *t* test can detect true differences between groups with a smaller sample size than their nonparametric counterparts. Therefore, it is preferable to use a *t* test when possible. However, if you have reason to believe that your samples do not come from normal populations, nonparametric tests for two independent samples offer an alternative. The nonparametric tests do assume, however, that the two distributions have the same shape, although this shape does not have to be normal.

Example 4
Mann-Whitney Test

The **Mann-Whitney test** and the related **Wilcoxon test** are nonparametric alternatives to the independent-samples t test. Like the t test, Mann-Whitney tests the null hypothesis that two independent samples come from the same population. Rather than being based on parameters of a normal distribution like mean and variance, the Wilcoxon and Mann-Whitney statistics are based on ranks. The Wilcoxon statistic, W, is calculated by ranking the pooled observations of the two samples and obtaining the sum of the ranks of the population with the smaller sample size. The Mann-Whitney statistic, U, which is equivalent to the Wilcoxon statistic, is obtained by counting the number of times an observation from the group with the smaller sample size precedes an observation from the larger group. The equation for the Mann-Whitney U is

$$U = N_1 N_2 + \frac{N_1(N_1 + 1)}{2} - T_1$$

where N_1 and N_2 are the sample sizes of the two groups, and T_1 is the sum of ranks of one of the samples. The Mann-Whitney U and the Wilcoxon W are related by the equation

$$U + W = \frac{m(m + 2n + 1)}{2}$$

where m is the number of observations in the smaller group, and n is the number of observations in the larger group. Because U and W sum to a constant, using one of them is equivalent to using the other. Another way of looking at the equivalency between U and W is that they have the same z score.

This example uses the *coronary artery data* file, a subset of data from the Coronary Artery Surgery Study [CASS, 1981] discussed in *Biostatistics: A methodology for the health sciences* (Fisher and Van Belle, 1993). These data compare treadmill times for healthy men with times for men with diagnosed coronary artery disease. The variable *time* contains the treadmill times, and *group* indicates whether the subject was healthy or had coronary artery disease. The variable *group* is numeric, with 1 specifying *healthy* and 2 specifying *disease*.

Figure 13.1   Data from Coronary Artery Surgery Study

	time	group
1	1014	healthy
2	684	healthy
3	810	healthy
4	990	healthy
5	840	healthy
6	978	healthy
7	1002	healthy
8	1110	healthy
9	864	disease
10	636	disease
11	638	disease
12	708	disease
13	786	disease
14	600	disease
15	1320	disease
16	750	disease
17	594	disease
18	750	disease

Figure 13.1 shows the data in the Data Editor, with variable labels displayed. You would expect that coronary disease would interfere with the ability to exercise vigorously and, therefore, that the coronary disease group would tire more quickly and spend less time on the treadmill than the normal group. Thus, the null hypothesis is that treadmill times are equal for the two groups.

To produce this output, from the menus choose:

Analyze
  Nonparametric Tests
    2 Independent Samples...

▶ Test Variable List: time

▶ Grouping Variable: group

Define Groups...
    Group 1: 1
    Group 2: 2

To hide the footnotes on the Test Statistics table, select them and choose *Hide* from the View menu.

Ranks

			N	Mean Rank	Sum of Ranks
Treadmill time (in seconds)	GROUP	healthy	8	12.63	101.00
		disease	10	7.00	70.00
		Total	18		

Ranks. The Mann-Whitney test and the Wilcoxon test are computed by ranking the combined sample of both populations, from smallest to largest. The Wilcoxon statistic is simply the value of the sum of ranks of the group with the smaller N.

Test Statistics

	Treadmill time (in seconds)
Mann-Whitney U	15.000
Wilcoxon W	70.000
Z	-2.222
Asymptotic Significance (2-tailed)	.026
Exact Significance [2*(1-tailed Sig.)]	.027

Test Statistics (Mann-Whitney test). The value of the Mann-Whitney U statistic is 15, and the value of the Wilcoxon W statistic is 70. Recall that these statistics are equivalent because they sum to a constant and have the same z score. The results are significant at the 0.026 level, leading you to reject the null hypothesis that treadmill times are equal for the coronary disease and normal groups.

Just as the t test can be generalized to more than two groups by the one-way analysis of variance, the Mann-Whitney test can be generalized to apply to more than two groups by the Kruskal-Wallis test. The **Kruskal-Wallis test** is a nonparametric version of the one-way analysis of variance for independent samples, calculated based on the sums of the ranks of the combined groups. The dialog box used to obtain tests for several related samples is very similar to the dialog box for two samples, and the layout of the output is also similar.

Tests for Two or More Related Samples

The Mann-Whitney and the Kruskall-Wallis tests represent nonparametric versions of the independent-samples *t* test and one-way analysis of variance. The related-samples *t* test is used when the two samples are not independent. The most common situation is when the same subjects are measured twice—for example, a person's weight before and after a weight loss program. When a related-samples test compares more than two means, it is a one-way repeated measures analysis of variance. In the case of the weight loss example, the same person's weight might be compared before the program, just after completion of the weight loss program, and six months after the completion of the program. There are nonparametric equivalents of both the two-related samples *t* test, and the one-way repeated measures analysis of variance.

Example 5
Friedman Test

This example uses 25 randomly selected cases from the first 500 cases in the *gss 93 subset* file, using a random number seed of 2,000,000. See the *SPSS Base User's Guide* for more information on randomly selecting cases and setting the random number seed.

One topic examined by the General Social Survey is music preference. People were asked to rate how they felt about different types of music, including classical music, jazz, and opera. Respondents rated each type of music on a five-point scale, from *like it very much* to *dislike it very much*. You can compare responses for each type of music to see whether there are any differences in people's preferences for different types. Because the same respondents rated each type of music, the samples are not independent, and you need to use a related-samples test. Further, because responses are ratings, rather than a continuous measure, these data are not suitable for analysis of variance. The nonparametric alternative to a repeated measures analysis of variance is the **Friedman test**. Like the Mann-Whitney and Kruskal-Wallis tests, the calculation of the Friedman test is based on ranks within each case. The scores for each variable are ranked and the mean ranks for the variables are compared. In this example, each subject's responses for the three types of music are ranked. A subject who likes classical music the most, then jazz, and likes opera the least would have ranks of 1, 2, and 3 for *classical*, *jazz*, and *opera*, respectively, for each variable. The mean ranks are then calculated and compared for the three music types.

Table 13.2 Calculating mean ranks for Friedman test

	classicl	jazz	opera
	1	2	3
	2	1	3
	,	,	,
	,	,	,
	,	,	,
	3	1	2
Mean Rank	**1.93**	**1.66**	**2.41**

Table 13.2 shows that ranks are assigned across each row, and the mean ranks are then calculated for each column.

The Friedman test is used to test the null hypothesis that there is no difference in preference between classical music, jazz, and opera. The Friedman test statistic is approximately distributed as a chi-square distribution. The idea behind this statistic is that if there is no difference between groups, each subject's rankings would be random, and there would be no difference in the mean ranks across the variables. The equation for the Friedman test is

$$\chi^2 = \frac{12}{Kj(j+1)}\left[\sum_i T_j^2\right] - 3K(j+1)$$

where K is the number of sets of matched observations, j is number of groups, and T_j is the sum of ranks for each group. In this example, $K = 25$, for the 25 subjects, and $j = 3$, for the 3 types of music.

To produce this output, from the menus choose:

Analyze
  Nonparametric Tests
    K Related Samples...

▶ Test Variables List: classicl, jazz, opera

Ranks

	Mean Rank
Classical Music	1.93
Jazz Music	1.66
Opera	2.41

Ranks. This table displays the mean ranks for each of the three types of music. Opera has the highest rank 2.41, indicating that it is the least popular type of music. Jazz is the most popular, with a mean rank of 1.66, and classical is in the middle, with a rank of 1.93. The Friedman test is used to determine whether the differences between these ranks are statistically significant.

Test Statistics

N	22
Chi-Square	9.458
df	2
Asymptotic Significance	.009

Test Statistics (Friedman test). The value of the chi-square statistic is 9.458, with a significance of 0.009. Therefore, you can reject the null hypothesis that there is no difference in preferences among classical music, jazz, and opera.

14 Discriminant Analysis

Discriminant analysis is related to both multivariate analysis of variance and multiple regression. You begin with cases or subjects in two or more known groups, like a one-way multivariate analysis of variance; then, you use the discriminant procedure to identify a linear combination of quantitative predictor variables that best characterizes the differences among the groups. The linear combination of variables (or **discriminant function**) looks like the right side of a multiple regression equation because it sums the products of variables multiplied by coefficients. The procedure estimates the coefficients, and the resulting function can be used to classify new cases.

Combining information from two or more variables can greatly enhance the separation of groups. Consider this simple example using two quantitative variables to separate two groups. Subsequent examples use more groups, include more variables, and define terms in more detail.

Figure 14.1 Scatterplots bordered by normal curves for each group

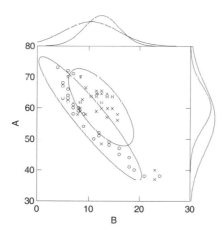

In the scatterplot of variable A against variable B, x is the plot symbol for cases in one group and o for the other group. The ellipses of concentration are constructed using the sample mean, standard deviation, and covariance within each group (if the observations in a group follow a bivariate normal distribution, the ellipse should include roughly 80% of the sample). Visually you see that while the groups overlap, the x's tend to fall above the o's. However, if you examine the distributions of each variable individually, there appears to be no separation.

The two curves along the top of the plot are for variable B alone, those on the right side for variable A by itself. The curves for the two variable B groups are drawn by moving or projecting the plot points straight up (the values of variable A are ignored) to form a histogram, and then replacing the histogram with normal curves constructed using the within-group sample means and standard deviations. Likewise, for the variable A curves, imagine sliding the points horizontally to the plot frame on the right. Not surprisingly, results of two-sample t tests for these data fail to show significant differences between the group means for variable A or for variable B.

Discriminant analysis determines a direction in which to project the plot points that maximizes the difference between the groups. The line in Figure 14.2 with the downward slope starting near 80 at the top left is the best straight line for separating the two groups (the plot height and width are adjusted so the perpendicular lines are not distorted).

Figure 14.2   Line perpendicular to the best line for group separation

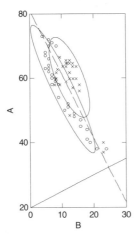

If you project or slide the plot points in the direction of this line to the line perpendicular to it at the bottom of the plot and construct normal curves like those bordering the plot frame in Figure 14.1, the result is shown in Figure 14.3. The separation between the groups is better than that for either variable alone. The following equation is used to compute the projected values or scores:

$$z = 0.3525\,A + 0.6991\,B - 28.585$$

That is, for each new case or subject, use the function to compute a score that is similar to a predicted value from a regression model. This equation is often called the **Fisher discriminant function** and was suggested by R. A. Fisher in 1936.

Figure 14.3 Normal curves superimposed over the discriminant scores

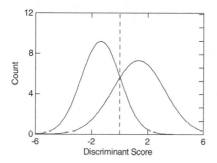

For two variables, the Fisher discriminant function is an equation of a plane. Setting z to 0 results in the equation of the line in Figure 14.2. The equation of the line that separates the groups is

$$A = 81.095 - 1.983B$$

and the line perpendicular to it is

$$A = 20 + 0.504B$$

How well does the discriminant function work? If you classify scores to the left of the dashed line in Figure 14.3 as members of group 1 and those to the right as members of group 2, how many cases are classified correctly? Overall 81.8% (54 out of 66) of the cases are assigned to their correct group. If, for two groups, you flip a coin for each case, assigning those with *heads* to group 1 and *tails* to group 2, you might expect to be correct about half the time (a 50% misclassification rate). So the discriminant function is probably doing better than chance alone. You can also examine the success of the classification within each group: 84.4% of the cases in group 1 are classified correctly, 79.4% in group 2.

Table 14.1   Classification by number and row percentage

		Predicted Group				Predicted Group	
		1	2			1	2
Actual Group	1	27	5	Actual Group	1	84.4	15.6
	2	7	27		2	20.6	79.4

ROC curves can be used to help determine how well the discriminant function performs for binary classification problems. Save the *Probabilities of group membership* from a discriminant analysis, use them as the *Test Variable* in the ROC procedure, and use the actual group membership as the *State Variable* in the ROC procedure.

Testing differences among groups. How well separated are the means or centroids of the two groups? **Wilks' lambda**, also called the *U* statistic, is available for testing the equality of group centroids. It is a multivariate analysis of variance test statistic that varies between 0 and 1. Small values indicate that the group means differ. For this example, Wilks' lambda is 0.589 with an associated probability less than 0.0005. There is a highly significant difference between the centroids of the two groups.

Models with more than two groups. For the two group model above, discriminant analysis found the best projection of the plot points (cases) for separating the groups and introduced the Fisher linear discriminant function. When there are more than two groups, canonical variables become the focus of the analysis.

The first **canonical variable** is the linear combination of the variables that maximizes the differences between the means of the *k* groups in one dimension. The second canonical variable represents the maximum dispersion of the means in a direction orthogonal (perpendicular) to the first direction, and the third represents the dispersion in a dimension independent of the first two dimensions, and so on. Another way to describe canonical variables is as *factors* that discriminate optimally among the group centroids relative to the dispersion within the groups.

When the first two canonical variables account for a large proportion of the variability within the original data, a scatterplot of the second canonical variable against the first canonical variable provides an excellent display of group differences. For example, look at the canonical variable plot of age-sex differences in Figure 14.4. The original data are blood chemistries recorded for 382 people separated into six age-sex groups and include blood urea nitrogen, uric acid, cholesterol, albumin, alkaline phosphatase, and so on. The group means of the first and second canonical variable are displayed in Table 14.2 and plotted in Figure 14.4.

Table 14.2   Group means for first two canonical variables

Gender	Age	First Canonical Variable	Second Canonical Variable	Label
Men	21 to 40	1.72	–0.37	a
Men	41 to 55	1.49	0.06	b
Men	56 and older	1.01	0.94	c
Women	21 to 40	–1.04	–1.07	d
Women	41 to 55	–1.03	0.20	e
Women	56 and older	–1.02	1.37	f

Figure 14.4   Canonical variable plot of age-sex differences

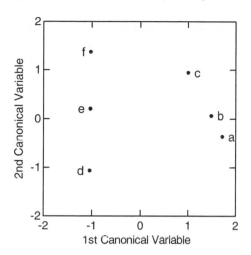

The plot is defined so that the greatest differences among the groups are displayed along the horizontal axis (the first canonical variable). The only information about groups input to the discriminant procedure is that there are six groups (not that the subjects in three groups are males and the other three are females and not that the groups are ordered by age within each sex). Notice that as a result of the analysis, the means for the three female groups fall on the left side and those for the three male groups fall on the right. Thus, the first canonical variable identifies sex differences. The second canonical variable, plotted on the vertical axis, shows an age separation, but it is not as distinct as that for sex. Also, the greatest difference occurs between the young males and females (groups *a* and *d*). Finally, the females exhibit a greater change (spread) in their blood chemistries as they age than do the males.

SPSS also provides Wilks' lambda for the multigroup problem to test if differences exist among the group centroids, and an F statistic computed from a Mahalanobis D^2 is available for testing the equality of centroids for each pair of groups. The Discriminant procedure provides a wealth of supporting statistics to describe group differences. Definitions of these, as well as estimates of the coefficients of classification functions and the canonical variables, are found in the examples that follow. Across textbooks and statistical packages, there is often a problem with names of terms and statistics. The term **discriminant function** can be found labeling classification functions, the one function that separates groups in the two-group problem, or the canonical variables (standardized or unstandardized). This chapter describes the use or interpretation of each.

How is discriminant analysis used? Consider constructing a discriminant function to classify or screen:

- **Applicants for a loan.** Begin with a group of people who repaid loans and another group who defaulted. As variables, use the time in their current (or previous) job, age, income, homeownership, outstanding debt, and marital status. Then, use the data for each new applicant in the discriminant function to determine in which group he or she belongs.

- **Applicants to college.** Start with a group of people who did graduate from college and another group who left school during their first year. As variables, consider math and verbal SAT scores, high school grade point average, a score representing the strength of their letters of recommendation, and another score measuring the extent of their extracurricular activities (music, sports, and others) in high school. Use the resulting function to classify each new prospective student.

- **Pot shards from an archaeological dig.** Start with ceramic pots known to come from specific tribes (the groups). As variables, use measurements of design elements, mineral content of the clay, and so on. Use the resulting function based on shards with certain characteristics to classify new shards.

- **Burn victims.** Start with data for patients known to survive or die after a fire. As variables, use values of blood gases, total area burned, degree of burn, age, and so on. If high risk patients can be identified early, special treatment and care may be administered to them.

As an example involving more than two groups, C. R. Rao published an article in 1948 titled "The Utilization of Multiple Measurements in Problems of Biological Classification" in the *Journal of the Royal Statistical Society.* He used sitting height, stature, nasal height, and nasal depth to classify Indians as being members of the Brahmin caste, the Artisan caste, or the Korwa caste (that is, he used four variables to classify individuals into one of three groups). He reported that he was able, for example, to classify 79% of the Brahmins correctly.

Overlooked reasons for using discriminant analysis. The Discriminant Analysis procedure can be used not only to build functions for classifying new cases or to test multivariate differences among groups, but also to explore or describe:

- Which variables among many are most useful for discriminating among groups.
- If one set of variables performs equally as well as another.
- Which groups are most alike.
- Which cases are outliers (differ markedly from others in their group).

Data and assumptions. In a formal discussion about discriminant analysis in a textbook, you will read that each of k populations with p variables should have a multivariate normal distribution with the same covariance matrix. Thus, the predictor variables are quantitative and should follow a normal distribution. Research has shown, however, as in regression analysis, that dummy variables (for example, codes 0 and 1 for the variable *sex*) can add to the success of a classification function.

Before requesting discriminant analysis, screen or study the data graphically as you would before regression and analysis of variance. Begin by studying boxplots of the within-group distributions of each variable individually using the Explore procedure. Identify your grouping variable as the factor. When the distribution within a group is asymmetric, sample means and standard deviations can be poor estimates of location and spread (this extends to covariances). Also check that the spreads or variances are about equal across groups. Look for transformations that symmetrize distributions, stabilize variances, and linearize relations among variables.

For each group, use scatterplots or a scatterplot matrix to study relations among pairs of variables. This provides an indication of how the variables covary. In the Figure 14.1 scatterplot, an ellipses of concentration was added. Imagine sketching these on your bivariate plots. If the assumption of equal covariances holds, the ellipses for each pair of variables should have almost the same shape and tilt across groups. If the plot scales vary from group to group, you cannot do this with great precision. If you find that the majority of points for one group tilts in the opposite direction from that of another, a failure of the equal covariance assumption is clearly identified. For the data in Figure 14.1, the ellipses have the same tilt, yet the configuration of points for one group is shorter and fatter than that of the other, indicating a slight departure from the assumption of equal variances and covariances.

Print a separate covariance matrix for each group to compare the covariance between variables *x* and *y* across the groups. Do the signs differ? Is the *xy* covariance for the first group 10 times that for the third group? If so, the assumption of equal covariance matrices fails to hold. Milder departures should still allow a useful analysis. SPSS also provides Box's *M* test for testing the equality of the group covariance matrices. However, as with several multivariate measures that combine information across variables and groups, the test may not provide a conclusive answer regarding the failure to meet assumptions because it is sensitive to departures from normality and sample size.

The data. The examples in this chapter use the *world95* data file. The file has one case for each country with the percentage of the population living in cities (*urban*), average daily calorie intake (*calories*), the logarithm of population (*log_pop*), the logarithm of gross domestic product per capita (*log_gdp*), average female life expectancy (*lifeexpf*), the percentage that each country's population increased during the previous year (*pop_incr*), the number of births and deaths per 1000 people in a year (*birth_rt* and *death_rt*), and a numeric code to identify climate (*climate*). The log transformation for population and GDP make their distributions more symmetric. The codes for *climate* range from 1 (desert) through 10 (arctic). The climate for countries located between the Tropic of Cancer and the Tropic of Capricorn is classified as *tropical* (code 5) and that for countries located between the Tropic of Cancer and the Arctic Circle or between the Tropic of Capricorn and the Antarctic Circle as *temperate* (code 8).

Example 1: Two groups: Describing differences and classifying cases. This example describes how to obtain the Fisher linear discriminant function from classification functions. Canonical variables, casewise descriptors including posterior probabilities and Mahalanobis distances, classification matrices to measure the success of the group separation, and leave-one-out classification are discussed.

Example 2: Revisiting the two-group model. The two-group model from Example 1 is revisted, but the variable *log_pop* is eliminated from the model. Data are screened to verify assumptions. For the two-group model, the relationship between discriminant analysis and regression is reviewed.

Example 3: A four-group model with variable selection. A four-group model is built using stepwise variable selection. Other methods of variable selection are discussed. A pairwise *F* matrix is useful for describing the distance between groups. Scatterplots and a territorial map aid in viewing group membership.

Example 4: Selecting variables that separate the closest groups. This example uses the Mahalanobis distance method of variable selection. Cross-validation is compared to the usual classification.

Example 1
Two Groups: Describing Differences and Classifying Cases

On average, people in temperate zone countries consume more calories per day than those in the tropics, and a greater proportion of the people in the temperate zone are city dwellers. Two-sample *t* tests for the variables *calories* and *urban* support this conclusion (see Chapter 8, Example 1). Assume that a researcher wants to combine information from these variables in a function to see how well she can discriminate between the two groups of countries. She thinks that population size and economic information may also be important.

This example uses discriminant analysis to determine how well a function that includes *calories*, *log_gdp*, *urban*, and *log_pop* distinguishes between temperate and tropical zone countries. The distribution of gross domestic product per capita and population are both very right-skewed, so they are log transformed (*log_gdp* and *log_pop*). To start, all four variables are included, ignoring whether they do or do not aid the discrimination.

To produce this output, use Select Cases from the Data menu to select cases with *climate* equal to 5 or *climate* equal to 8 (climate = 5 | climate = 8). Then, from the menus choose:

Analyze
  Classify
    Discriminant...

▶ Grouping Variable: climate

Define Range...
  Minimum: 5
  Maximum: 8

▶ Independents: calories, log_gdp, urban, log_pop

Statistics...

  Descriptives
  ☑ Means
  ☑ Univariate ANOVAs

  Function Coefficients
  ☑ Fisher's
  ☑ Unstandardized

Classify...

  Display
  ☑ Casewise results
  ☑ Summary table

Group Statistics

Climate		CALORIES	LOG_GDP	URBAN	LOG_POP
tropical	Mean	2374.9286	2.9299	42.9286	4.1704
	Std. Deviation	308.8087	.4733	22.8602	.6117
	Valid N (listwise)	28	28	28	28
temperate	Mean	3197.7727	3.7839	65.8636	4.2729
	Std. Deviation	533.8921	.6300	24.8927	.6584
	Valid N (listwise)	22	22	22	22
Total	Mean	2736.9800	3.3057	53.0200	4.2155
	Std. Deviation	587.3181	.6906	26.1873	.6282
	Valid N (listwise)	50	50	50	50

Group Statistics. Fifty cases are used in this analysis. If data are missing for one or more of the four variables (or *climate*), SPSS excludes the case from the analysis.

As you examine the sample means, it is easy to describe differences between temperate and tropical zone countries, one variable at a time. On average, people in temperate zone countries consume more calories per day (3,198 versus 2,375) and more of them live in cities (65.9% versus 42.9%). The gross domestic product also appears much higher in temperate countries, while population may be slightly greater. Tests for these differences are given in the discussion on "Tests of Equality of Group Means" below.

If the standard deviations vary greatly across the groups, the assumption of equal variances is not met. Here, *calories* has the largest difference in standard deviations (309 versus 534). In Chapter 8, the Levene test results for *calories* indicate that the hypothesis of equal variances is rejected at the 5% level but not at the 2% level, while no difference in variances was identified for *urban*. Differences for the other variables are inconsequential.

Tests of Equality of Group Means

	Wilks' Lambda	F	df1	df2	Sig.
CALORIES	.506	46.771	1	48	.000
LOG_GDP	.615	29.991	1	48	.000
URBAN	.807	11.469	1	48	.001
LOG_POP	.993	.323	1	48	.572

Tests of Equality of Group Means. This panel contains the first of many statistics that the Discriminant Analysis procedure borrows from analysis of variance (ANOVA). The *F* statistics and significance values in the third and sixth columns are from a one-way ANOVA computed for each variable individually. Because there are only two groups in this example, the *F* statistic is equivalent to the square of a *t* statistic for a two-sample pooled variances *t* test. Selecting *Univariate ANOVAs* on the Statistics subdialog box produces these tests.

Wilks' lambda also provides information regarding differences among groups. While the *F* statistic is a ratio of between-groups variability to the within-groups variability, **Wilks' lambda** is the ratio of the within-groups sum of squares to the total sum of squares. Its values range from 0 to 1.0. Small values indicate strong group differences; values close to 1.0, no differences.

Significant differences are identified for each variable except *log_pop*. However, (if you remember variables *A* and *B* in the overview of this chapter), the lack of significance for *log_pop* is not a strong enough reason to remove it from the model. Also, the fact that the tests are highly significant for the three other variables is not a clear indicator that all three should be included. The strength of the intercorrelations among the variables is important. As an extreme example, think of a study where the investigators inadvertently record body weight in pounds and again in kilograms. The two variables have a correlation of 1.0, and including both provides no more information than including one.

It is important to emphasize that relationships among variables are incorporated in multivariate procedures like discriminant analysis: variables are considered simultaneously, not individually.

Classification Function Coefficients

	CLIMATE	
	tropical	temperate
CALORIES	-1.8E-03	2.931E-03
LOG_GDP	21.458	21.864
URBAN	-.223	-.239
LOG_POP	12.871	13.187
(Constant)	-52.047	-67.050

Fisher's linear discriminant functions

Classification Function Coefficients. Each column contains estimates of the coefficients for a classification function for one group. The functions are used to assign or classify cases into groups; a case is predicted as being a member of the group in which the value of its classification function is largest. When there are more than two groups, SPSS also provides classification functions (that is, for k groups, k functions are computed and each case is predicted as a member of the group where its score is largest). The coefficients are computed to maximize the distance between the two groups. Cases with missing values are not used to estimate these coefficients. Selecting *Fisher's* on the Statistics subdialog box produces these functions.

The estimate of the classification function for countries in the tropical zone is

$$-0.0018\, calories + 21.458\, log\_gdp - 0.223\, urban + 12.871\, log\_pop - 52.047$$

and that for countries in the temperate zone is

$$0.0029\, calories + 21.8644\, log\_gdp - 0.239\, urban + 13.187\, log\_pop - 67.050$$

Thus, for each case in each group, the procedure multiplies each coefficient by the value of the corresponding variable, sums the products, and adds the constant to get a score.

Fisher's linear discriminant function. When there are only two groups, as in this example, you can use the classification functions to obtain the linear discriminant function. The line in Figure 14.2 that separates the two groups is derived from it. To compute estimates of the coefficients of Fisher's linear discriminant function for the data in this example, take the difference between the coefficients of the tropical and temperate classification functions:

$$z = (0.0029 - (-0.0018))calories + (21.8644 - 21.458)log\_gdp - (0.239 - 0.223)urban + (13.187 - 12.871)log\_pop - (67.050 - 52.047)$$

or

$$z = 0.0047calories + 0.4064log\_gdp - 0.016urban + 0.316log\_pop - 15.003$$

These coefficients, for the two-group problem, are proportional to the unstandardized canonical variable coefficients you request on the Statistics subdialog box (see "Canonical Discriminate Function Coefficients" on p. 255).

An analysis of variance framework is useful for defining the statistics in these tables. Here is a one-way ANOVA for the tropical and temperate zone groups using the scores from the Fisher linear discriminant function:

Table 14.3   One-way ANOVA

Source	Sum of Squares	df	Mean Square	F	Significance
Between Groups	185.922	1	185.922	48.103	0.000
Within Groups	185.525	48	3.865		
Total	371.447	49			

Eigenvalues

Function	Eigenvalue	% of Variance	Cumulative %	Canonical Correlation
1	1.002	100.0	100.0	.707

Eigenvalues. The **eigenvalue** is a ratio of the between-groups sum of squares to the within-in-groups or error sum of squares:

$$eigenvalue = \frac{185.922}{185.525} = 1.002$$

When more than two groups are analyzed, the size of each eigenvalue is helpful for measuring the spread of the group centroids in the corresponding dimension of the multivariate space. The percentage of variance and cumulative percentage of variance are always 100 for the two group model and are explained further in Example 3.

The **canonical correlation** measures the association between the discriminant scores and the groups. For this example with only two groups, it is the usual Pearson correlation between the scores and the groups coded as 0 and 1. When there are more groups, it is equivalent to eta from a one-way analysis of variance (the square root of the ratio of the between-groups sum of squares to the total sum of squares). For these data, the canonical correlation is the square root of 185.922 / 371.447.

Wilks' Lambda

Test of Function(s)	Wilks' Lambda	Chi-square	df	Sig.
1	.499	31.934	4	.000

Wilks' Lambda. Wilks' lambda is the proportion of the total variance in the discriminant scores not explained by differences among the groups. In this example, almost 50% (0.499) of the variance is not explained by group differences. Notice that lambda ı eta^2 = 1. Lambda is used to test the null hypothesis that the means of all the variables across groups are equal and provides little information regarding the success of the model for classifying cases. As a test of its size, lambda is transformed to a variable with an approximate chi-square distribution. Here, the chi-square is 31.934, indicating a highly significant difference between the two group centroids (the means of the four variables simultaneously).

Canonical Discriminant Function Coefficients

	Function
	I
CALORIES	.002
LOG_GDP	.206
URBAN	-.008
LOG_POP	.160
(Constant)	-7.475

Canonical Discriminant Function Coefficients. These are the coefficients of a canonical variable. Use them to compute a canonical variable score for each case:

$$score = 0.00239 calories + 0.2058 log\_gdp - 0.008 urban + 0.16 log\_pop - 7.4746$$

For case 18 (Burundi), the score is

$$\text{score} = (0.00239 \times 1932) + (0.2058 \times 2.318) - (0.008 \times 5) + (0.16 \times 3.778) - 7.4746 = -1.8156$$

The signs of the coefficients are arbitrary—the separation among the groups would be the same if you multiplied each coefficient by -1.

When the number of groups is two, there is only one canonical variable, and its coefficients are proportional to the values of the Fisher discriminant function coefficients. That is, for these data, multiply each of the coefficients by 1.97 to get the coefficients derived in the "Classification Function Coefficients" section on p. 253 (for example, $1.97*0.00239 = 0.0047$). When there are more than two groups, the number of canonical variables is $k-1$ (where k is the number of groups) or p (the number of variables), whichever is smaller.

Standardized Canonical Discriminant Function Coefficients

	Function
	1
CALORIES	1.010
LOG_GDP	.113
URBAN	-.190
LOG_POP	.101

Standardized Canonical Discriminant Function Coefficients. When variables are measured in different units (for example, a value of *calories* could be 3000, while a value of *gdp_cap* might be 2.91), the magnitude of an unstandardized coefficient provides little indication of the relative contribution of the variable to the overall discrimination. Researchers often prefer to examine the coefficients after they are standardized. In this example, *calories* appears to have the greatest impact.

You can use the unstandardized coefficients on p. 255 to compute the standardized coefficients. First, for each variable, find the pooled estimate of its standard deviation by taking the square root of its diagonal term in the within-groups covariance matrix (available on the Statistics subdialog box). Then, multiply the unstandardized coefficient by the estimate. The within-groups variance of *calories* is 178346.91, so the estimate of the pooled standard deviation is 422.31139. Multiplying this by the canonical variable coefficient for *calories* (0.002) gives 1.010 as the standardized coefficient.

Structure Matrix

	Function
	1
CALORIES	.986
LOG_GDP	.790
URBAN	.488
LOG_POP	.082

Structure Matrix. This panel of within-groups correlations of each predictor variable with the canonical variable provides another way to study the usefulness of each variable in the discriminant function. Here, *calories* has the largest correlation with the canonical variable scores.

When there are more than two groups (and more than two variables), within-group correlations are printed for each canonical variable, and variables with large correlations for a particular canonical variable are grouped together and marked with an asterisk.

Functions at Group Centroids

CLIMATE	Function
	1
tropical	-.869
temperate	1.107

Functions at Group Centroids. Within-group means are computed for each canonical variable. Here, there is one canonical variable and the average discriminant or canonical variable score for the tropical countries (code 5) is –0.869 and that for the temperate countries 1.107. The score for each country (case) is displayed on p. 258.

Casewise Statistics

	Case Number	Actual Group	Highest Group Pred. Group	Highest Group P(G=g | D=d)	Highest Group Squared Mahalanobis Distance to Centroid	Second Highest Group Group	Second Highest Group P(G=g | D=d)	Second Highest Group Squared Mahalanobis Distance to Centroid	Discrim. Scores Function 1
	2	8	8	.771	.140	5	.229	2.565	.732
	5	8	8	.972	.662	5	.028	7.781	1.920
	8	5	5	.959	.373	8	.041	6.692	-1.480
	15	5	5	.545	.805	8	.455	1.164	.028
	17	5	5	.894	.008	8	.106	4.265	-.959
Burundi	18	8	5**	.978	.891	8	.022	8.526	-1.813
	19	5	5	.938	.148	8	.062	5.575	-1.255
	22	5	5	.981	1.006	8	.019	8.874	-1.872
Chile	23	8	5**	.811	.063	8	.189	2.974	-.618
China	24	8	8	.506	.953	5	.494	1.000	.131
	25	5	5	.751	.185	8	.249	2.389	-.439
	****cases 26 through 49 are omitted***								
Indonesia	51	5	8**	.589	.651	5	.411	5.124	.300
	54	8	8	.991	1.976	5	.009	11.435	2.512
	63	5	5	.909	.032	8	.091	4.642	-1.048
Malaysia	66	5	8**	.548	.793	5	.452	1.178	.216
	****cases 70 through 83 are omitted***								
Rwanda	85	8	5**	.972	.648	8	.028	7.734	-1.675
	88	5	5	.884	.002	8	.116	4.063	-.909
Singapore	89	5	8**	.789	.104	5	.211	2.736	.785
	92	8	8	.977	.841	5	.023	8.370	2.024
	94	8	8	.979	.902	5	.021	8.560	2.056
	98	5	5	.829	.036	8	.171	3.189	-.679
	99	8	8	.908	.029	5	.092	4.604	1.276
	101	8	8	.843	.019	5	.157	3.383	.970
	102	8	8	.990	1.855	5	.010	11.142	2.469
	103	5	5	.932	.116	8	.068	5.367	-1.210
Uruguay	105	8	5**	.794	.094	8	.206	2.789	-.563
	107	5	5	.814	.058	8	.186	3.012	-.629
	108	5	5	.907	.026	8	.093	4.570	-1.031
	109	5	5	.970	.599	8	.030	7.563	-1.644

**. Misclassified case

Casewise Statistics. For each case in this panel, you can compare information about its actual group membership to its membership predicted by the discriminant analysis. To see in which group SPSS classifies each case, you could use the estimates of the classification function coefficients on p. 253 to compute a score for each group and then say that the case belongs to the group with the maximum score. However, these scores are not measured in units that are easy to interpret; so it is difficult to ascertain if case I is clearly a member of its correct group, almost as likely to be a member of another group, or extremely likely to be a member of another group. SPSS prints posterior probabilities that indicate how likely each case is of being a member of each group. One way to compute these probabilities for each case is to first compute the Mahalanobis distance (D^2) to each group mean from the case, and then compute the ratio of $\exp(-D^2)$ for the group over the sum of $\exp(-D^2)$ for all the groups. If prior probabilities are assigned, they affect these computations.

Under the heading *Highest Group*, SPSS lists the group in which each case is most likely a member (*Pred. Group*) and the posterior probability for belonging to this group $(P(G=g|D=d))$. Results for the next most likely group are displayed in the next set of columns. When there are only two groups, as in this example, the posterior probabilities sum to 1.0. Case 2 (Argentina) is a temperate zone country (code 8). Its probability of belonging to group 8 is 0.771 and its probability of belonging to the group of tropical countries is 0.229. The classification for China (case 24) is unclear; its posterior probability of belonging to the correct group is 0.506 and to the wrong group is 0.494.

The probability labeled $P(G=g|D=d)$ in the *Highest Group* panel, often called the **conditional probability**, is the probability of the observed score given membership in the most likely group.

Cases with large values of the **Mahalanobis distance** from their group mean can be identified as outliers. For large samples from a multivariate normal distribution, the square of the Mahalanobis distance from a case to its group mean is approximately distributed as a chi-square with degrees of freedom equal to the number of variables in the function.

The canonical variable or discriminant scores for each case are displayed at the right side of this panel (in this example, because there is one canonical variable, there is only one score). On p. 255 in the "Canonical Discriminant Function Coefficients" section, the score for case 18 (Burundi) is computed.

Classification Results[1]

		Predominant climate	Predicted Group Membership		Total
			tropical	temperate	
Original	Count	tropical	25	3	28
		temperate	4	18	22
	%	tropical	89.3	10.7	100.0
		temperate	18.2	81.8	100.0

[1] 86.0% of original grouped cases correctly classified.

Classification Results. For these results, select *Summary table* on the Classify subdialog box. To measure the degree of success of the classification for this sample, SPSS counts how many countries within each group are correctly classified and how many are misclassified. Among the 28 tropical countries (code 5), 25 (or 89.3%) of the countries are correctly classified into group 5; 3 (10.7%) of the countries are misclassified. For the temperate group, 18 (81.8%) are correct; 4 (18.2%) are wrong. Overall, 86% of the cases are classified correctly.

Cross-validation. In the tally of correctly classified and misclassified cases in "Classification Results" above, the classified cases are the same ones used to estimate the coefficients. This produces an overly optimistic estimate of the success of the classification. It is better to use one sample to compute the classification functions and another sample drawn from the same population to estimate the proportion misclassified. This procedure is called cross-validation and produces unbiased estimates.

SPSS provides a leave-one-out cross-validation method to help diminish the optimistic bias. Each case is classified into a group according to the classification functions computed from all the data *except* the case being classified. For a data set with n cases, you do not have to wait for the computer to do the complete analysis n times because only the Mahalanobis distances in the posterior probability computations ("Casewise Statistics" on p. 258) require an adjustment. The proportion of misclassified cases after removing the effect of each case one at a time is the leave-one-out estimate of misclassification.

The usual percentage of correct classification is 86%. The leave-one-out classification is 80%.

Example 2
Revisiting the Two-Group Model

Often a model with fewer variables is more useful for classifying new cases than one with more variables. In the last example with four predictors, the discrepancy between the percentage of correct classification and the leave-one-out classification was 86% versus 80%. Beware that leave-one-out estimates of the percentage of correct classification can still be overly optimistic.

To produce this output, use Select Cases from the Data menu to select cases with *climate* equal to 5 or *climate* equal to 8 (climate = 5 | climate = 8). Then, in the Discriminant Analysis dialog box, click *Reset* to restore the dialog box defaults and select:

▶ Grouping Variable: climate

Define Range...
   Minimum: 5
   Maximum: 8

▶ Independents: calories, log_gdp, urban

Statistics...

   Descriptives
   ☑ Box's M

   Function Coefficients
   ☑ Fisher's

   Matrices
   ☑ Separate-groups covariance

Classify...

   Display
   ☑ Summary table
   ☑ Leave-one-out classification

Note: Only selected portions of the output from the above setup are displayed.

Eigenvalues

Function	Eigenvalue	% of Variance	Cumulative %	Canonical Correlation
1	.993	100.0	100.0	.706

Wilks' Lambda

Test of Function(s)	Wilks' Lambda	Chi-square	df	Sig.
1	.502	32.070	3	.000

Eigenvalues and Wilks' Lambda. Compare these values for the three-variable model with those for the four-variable model in Example 1 on p. 254 and p. 255. The eigenvalues are close to the same size (0.993 versus 1.002), and the probability associated with the chi-square statistic transformation of Wilks' lambda is less than 0.0005, indicating a highly significant difference in group means.

Structure Matrix

	Function
	1
CALORIES	.991
LOG_GDP	.793
URBAN	.491

Structure Matrix. In the four-variable model, these correlations with the canonical variables are, respectively, 0.986, 0.790, and 0.488. The removal of *log_pop* has done little to alter the results.

Functions at Group Centroids

CLIMATE	Function
	1
tropical	-.865
temperate	1.102

Functions at Group Centroids. The means for the four-variable model are –0.865 and 1.102.

Classification Results[1,2]

		Predominant climate	Predicted Group Membership		Total
			tropical	temperate	
Original	Count	tropical	24	4	28
		temperate	5	17	22
	%	tropical	85.7	14.3	100.0
		temperate	22.7	77.3	100.0
Cross-validated	Count	tropical	24	4	28
		temperate	5	17	22
	%	tropical	85.7	14.3	100.0
		temperate	22.7	77.3	100.0

[1.] 82.0% of original grouped cases correctly classified.
[2.] 82.0% of cross-validated grouped cases correctly classified.

Classification Results. After removing *log_pop* from the classification functions, the percentage of correct classification drops from 86% to 82%. However, the leave-one-out estimate increases from 80% to 82%—the smaller model has a better rate of successful classification! Compare the following classification rates:

Table 14.4   Comparison of classification rates

	Usual classification	Cross-validation
Four variables from Example 1	86	80
Three variables this example	82	82
One variable (*calories*)	86	86

When the predictor variables are highly intercorrelated, you might try other subsets of similar sizes (of course, study the success and failure of individual cases too—remember China in Example 1). For example, here are some results:

Table 14.5   Comparison of other subsets

Variables in the model			Usual classification	Cross-validation
calories	*fertilty*	*pop_incr*	88	86
lifeexpf	*death_rt*	*log_pop*	90	88
calories	*log_gdp*	*pop_incr*	88	86

Remember, if your goal is building a model for classifying new cases in the future, the leave-one-out estimates may still be overly optimistic.

Checking Assumptions

One of the necessary assumptions for discriminant analysis is equality of group covariance matrices. For example, the population variances of *calories* should be equal for the two groups of countries (or all groups in a multigroup problem), and the population covariances between *calories* and *urban* should be equal for the groups.

SPSS provides Box's multivariate *M* statistic to test the null hypothesis that the covariance matrices are equal (use the Statistics subdialog box to request this test). Many data analysts have little confidence regarding results of Box's *M* test because it is sensitive to mild departures from multivariate normality and large sample sizes.

Log Determinants

CLIMATE	Rank	Log Determinant
tropical	3	14.276
temperate	3	15.722
Pooled within-groups	3	15.147

Log Determinants. In the multigroup model, log-determinant values provide an indication of which groups' covariance matrices differ most. See Example 4, p. 290, for a discussion of log-determinant values.

Test Results

Box's M		11.433
F	Approx.	1.773
	df1	6
	df2	14244.369
	Sig.	.100

Test Results (Box's M). The value of Box's M statistic is 11.4, and its significance probability, based on an F transformation, is 0.100. The null hypothesis of equal group covariance matrices is not rejected. Note, however, that in some situations where the group covariance matrices are not too dissimilar, the test can be significant. This can occur when within-group sample sizes are large or when the assumption of multivariate normality is violated.

For each variable in Example 1 (see the Group Statistics table on p. 251), you compared the sample standard deviations across groups. This provides numerical information about how the spreads of each variable differ across groups. Because outliers and skewed distributions may distort these estimates, it is a good idea to study the within-group distributions graphically.

While you can use the Explore procedure to study the distributions of each variable individually, you can also use Boxplot on the Graphs menu to include all predictors in a single display. Because the scales for the variables in this example differ markedly, use the Descriptives procedure on the Statistics menu to transform the variables to z scores before plotting the values (using the sample that includes all code 5 and code 8 values of *climate*, compute z scores for *calories*, *log_gdp*, and *urban*). Then request a Cluster Boxplot and select *Summaries of separate variables* on the Boxplot dialog box.

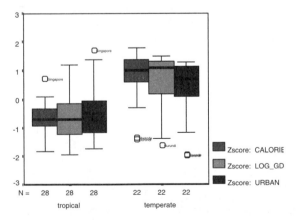

Boxplot. The goal in studying the boxplot is not to compare the three distributions within the tropical group or the three within the temperate group, but to compare the distribution of *calories* in the tropical group with *calories* in the temperate group, the tropical distribution of *log_gdp* with its temperate counterpart, and so on. Notice that while the horizontal line within each box marks the median, the basis of discriminant analysis is means. Still, from this display, you can assess the symmetry of each within-group distribution and see if there are any unusual outliers. The distribution of *log_gdp* for the temperate group is more skewed than what you would like to see.

Rwanda (case 85) and Burundi (case 18) are the temperate group outliers with low values; Singapore (case 89), in the tropical group, has high values for *calories* and *urban*. These outliers were misclassified in Example 1.

Covariances. Use within-group scatterplots or scatterplot matrices to screen for equal covariances. To view covariances in discriminant analysis, select *Separate-groups covariance* under Matrices on the Statistics subdialog box.

Covariance Matrices

Climate		CALORIES	LOG_GDP	URBAN
tropical	CALORIES	95362.810	118.644	4815.180
	LOG_GDP	118.644	.224	8.165
	URBAN	4815.180	8.165	522.587
temperate	CALORIES	285040.76	288.820	7670.634
	LOG_GDP	288.820	.397	12.185
	URBAN	7670.634	12.185	619.647

Covariance Matrices (separate-groups). The standard deviations (the square root of the variances on the diagonal of the matrices) are displayed in the Group Statistics table in Example 1. Visually, the variances for *calories* appear to differ most (95,362 versus 285,040). If you request a two-sample *t* test as shown in Chapter 8, the Levene test of equal variances is reported.

Table 14.6   Levene test of equal variances

Variable	Significance	*t* statistic
calories	0.027	−6.4
log_gdp	0.187	−5.5
urban	0.727	−3.4

Thus, you are not able to identify a difference in variances for *log_gdp* or *urban*, and because the significance value is 0.027 for *calories*, a difference is found at the 5% level but not the 1% level.

There is no quick and easy Levene test for covariances. None of the differences here, however, are as great as the difference in variances for *calories*. It is still recommended that you study within-group scatterplots (setting all the plot scales the same).

Regression

For two groups, there is a relationship between discriminant analysis and multiple regression that does not extend to more than two groups. However, with k groups, there is a correspondence between discriminant analysis and canonical correlation.

To request a regression using the same predictor variables as above, from the Statistics menu choose *Regression*, then *Linear*. In the Linear Regression dialog box, select *climate* as a dummy Dependent variable with two codes for the groups and select *calories*, *log_gdp*, and *urban* as Independent variables. In this example, *5* is the code for tropical countries and *8* is the code for temperate countries (any two codes will do).

Table 14.7   Classification function coefficients with their differences

Variable	Tropical	Temperate	Difference
calories	0.0076929	0.0126505	0.004960
log_gdp	12.0440269	12.2194554	0.175430
urban	–0.2181129	–0.2338126	–0.015703
constant	–22.7903225	–36.3389364	

Table 14.8   Canonical discriminant function coefficients

Variable	Coefficient
calories	0.00252
log_gdp	0.08919
urban	–0.00798
constant	–6.76991

The estimates of the regression coefficients that result are proportional to those of the Fisher discriminant function (the differences of the estimates of the tropical and temperate zone classification functions) or the unstandardized canonical variable.

Table 14.9   Estimates of coefficients from both procedures

	CALORIES	LOG_GDP	URBAN
Discriminant	0.004960	0.175430	–0.015703
Regression	0.001915	0.067775	–0.006065
Ratio	2.59	2.59	2.59

The constant of proportionality (ratio) is approximately 2.6. The same relation does not hold for the constants.

Model Summary

	Model
	1
R	.706
R Square	.498
Adjusted R Square	.466
Std. Error of the Estimate	1.10

Coefficients

Model		Unstandardized Coefficients		Standardized Coefficients	t	Sig.
		B	Std. Error	Beta		
1	(Constant)	1.175	.916		1.283	.206
	CALORIES	1.92E-03	.001	.748	3.060	.004
	LOG_GDP	6.78E-02	.653	.031	.104	.918
	URBAN	-6.1E-03	.010	-.106	-.587	.560

Model Summary and Coefficients. The value of R^2 (0.498) from the Regression output indicates that almost 50% of the variance of the dummy dependent variable is explained by the variables *calories*, *log_gdp*, and *urban*. More interesting, however, are the *t* statistics associated with each predictor—*calories* is the only useful variable. Indeed, if you repeat the discriminant analysis using the variable selection procedure described in Example 3, only *calories* is selected. A model with too many variables may not perform as well for future classifications as a model with fewer variables.

Example 3
A Four-Group Model with Variable Selection

Even if your goal is not variable selection or stepwise model building, you may want to read about features for models with more than two groups described in this example. These include:

- An *F* statistic for each pair of groups that is useful for describing the distance between the groups or for testing differences between group centroids.
- A scatterplot of the first two canonical variables (canonical discriminant functions), either for all groups combined or for each group individually.
- A territorial map with boundaries that define group membership (the boundaries are laid upon a bivariate plot of the second canonical variable against the first).
- A pooled within-groups correlation matrix for studying the correlation structure within the predictor variables.
- The canonical variable scores (canonical discriminant function scores) which can be saved, allowing you to construct displays that identify outliers.

Variable selection for two or more groups. The model in Example 1 included four variables because the researcher wanted those four specific variables. For many applications, a key goal may be to identify a useful subset of predictor variables. Strategies for identifying a good model are many and varied. There is no one exact procedure for selecting the best set of predictors, nor one ideal test to tell you that you have found it. The use of variable selection methods in discriminant analysis is like that for multiple regression. (If you have not already done so, please read the introduction to Example 3 on p. 215 in Chapter 12 before continuing with this chapter.)

SPSS provides several methods for building a model in a stepwise manner—entering or removing one predictor variable from the model at each step. Stepwise selection begins by identifying the variable for which the means are most different and continues by adding the next best variable step by step. The methods for controlling the entry or removal of predictor variables from the discriminant function are:

- **Wilks' lambda.** For each candidate predictor variable, an *F* statistic is computed that measures the change in Wilks' lambda when the variable is added to the model. The variable with the largest *F* (or smallest value of Wilks' lambda) enters the model. SPSS also checks variables already included and removes a variable if its *F*-to-remove value is too small. The *F* value for the change in Wilks' lambda when a variable is added to a model that contains *p* independent variables is

$$F_{\text{change}} = \left(\frac{n-g-p}{g-1}\right)\left(\frac{(1-\lambda_{p+1}/\lambda_p)}{\lambda_{p+1}/\lambda_p}\right)$$

where *n* is the total number of cases, *g* is the number of groups, λ_p is Wilks' lambda before adding the variable, and λ_{p+1} is Wilks' lambda after inclusion.

- **Mahalanobis distance.** At each step, the variable that maximizes the Mahalanobis distance between the two closest groups enters. The distance between groups *a* and *b* is defined as

$$D_{ab}^2 = (n-g)\sum_{i=1}^{p}\sum_{j=1}^{p} w_{ij}*(\overline{X}_{ia} - \overline{X}_{ib})(\overline{X}_{ja} - \overline{X}_{jb})$$

- **Smallest F ratio.** At each step, the variable that maximizes the smallest *F* ratio for pairs of groups enters. The *F* statistic is

$$F = \frac{(n-1-p)n_1 n_2}{p(n-2)(n_1+n_2)}D_{ab}^2$$

Notice that this method weights the Mahalanobis distance by sample size, so the two methods may differ.

- **Rao's V.** Also known as the Lawley-Hotelling trace, Rao's V is defined as

$$V = (n_k - g)\sum_{i=1}^{p}\sum_{j=1}^{p} w_{ij}*\sum_{k=1}^{g}(\overline{X}_{ik} - \overline{X}_i)(\overline{X}_{jk} - \overline{X}_j)$$

where *p* is the number of variables in the model, *g* is the number of groups, n_k is the sample size in the *k*th group, $\overline{X}_{ik}$ is the mean of the *i*th variable for the *k*th group, $\overline{X}_i$ is the mean of the *i*th variable for all groups combined, and $w_{ij}*$ is an element of the inverse of the within-groups covariance matrix. The larger the differences between group means, the larger the Rao's V.

- **Sum of unexplained variance.** The sum of the unexplained variation for all pairs of groups can also be used as a criterion for variable selection. The variable chosen for inclusion is the one that minimizes the sum of the unexplained variation. Mahalanobis distance and R^2 are proportional. Thus,

$$R^2 = cD^2 \text{ where } c \text{ is a constant.}$$

For each pair of groups, a and $b,$ the unexplained variation from the regression is $223 \, 1 - R_{ab}^2$, where R_{ab}^2 is the square of the multiple correlation coefficient when a variable coded as 0 or 1 (depending on whether the case is a member of a or b) is considered the dependent variable.

Instead of using *climate* to form two groups of countries, this example groups countries into four regions of the world: Europe (code 1), Pacific/Asia (code 3), Middle East (code 5), and Latin America (code 6). The codes are stored in the variable *region2*. In order to make the output shorter, countries with codes 2 and 4 are not shown.

You begin building a model to separate the four groups of countries using a set of 11 candidate predictor variables (because *calories* has so many missing values, it is not included).

Table 14.10 Default run in which five variables enter the model

Step	Variable entered	Wilks' lambda	Variable description
1	*pop_incr*	0.448	Population increase (% per year)
2	*log_gdp*	0.279	Log (base 10) of *gdp_cap*
3	*death_rt*	0.214	Death rate per 1000 people
4	*lifeexpf*	0.169	Average female life expectancy
5	*urban*	0.142	People living in cities (%)

To produce this output, use Select Cases from the Data menu to omit cases with *region2* equal to 2 or *region2* equal to 4 (region2 ~= 2 & region2 ~= 4). Then, in the Discriminant Analysis dialog box, click *Reset* to restore the dialog box defaults and select:

▶ Grouping Variable: region2

Define Range...
   Minimum: 1
   Maximum: 6

▶ Independents: urban, lifeexpf, literacy, pop_incr, babymort, birth_rt, death_rt, log_gdp, b_to_d, fertility, log_pop

☑ Use stepwise method

Statistics...

   Descriptives
   ☑ Means

   Function Coefficients
   ☑ Fisher's

   Matrices
   ☑ Within-groups correlation

Method...

   Display
   ☑ F for pairwise distances

Classify...

   Display
   ☑ Summary table
   ☑ Leave-one-out classification

   Plots
   ☑ Combined-groups
   ☑ Separate-groups
   ☑ Territorial map

Save...
   ☑ Discriminant scores

Group Statistics

		REGION2				
		Europe	Pacific/Asia	Middle East	Latn America	Total
URBAN	Mean	73.4118	47.7222	69.3750	61.3810	62.5833
	Std. Deviation	16.2175	30.0584	16.8676	17.9596	22.8354
	Valid N (listwise)	17	18	16	21	72
LIFEEXPF	Mean	80.1176	68.2222	71.6875	71.7619	72.8333
	Std. Deviation	1.2690	11.0855	4.6292	7.3885	8.2718
	Valid N (listwise)	17	18	16	21	72
LITERACY	Mean	97.5294	74.8889	74.7500	82.6667	82.4722
	Std. Deviation	3.6932	25.6122	15.8724	13.4846	18.6253
	Valid N (listwise)	17	18	16	21	72
POP_INCR	Mean	.4171	1.6161	2.9138	1.8767	1.6974
	Std. Deviation	.2636	.8554	1.1506	.6762	1.1560
	Valid N (listwise)	17	18	16	21	72
BABYMORT	Mean	6.7059	51.5056	41.6875	39.1143	35.1319
	Std. Deviation	1.1513	46.1588	19.7684	24.5244	32.2219
	Valid N (listwise)	17	18	16	21	72
BIRTH_RT	Mean	12.4706	25.6667	32.2500	26.9048	24.3750
	Std. Deviation	1.4194	11.7373	8.3227	6.8037	10.5516
	Valid N (listwise)	17	18	16	21	72
DEATH_RT	Mean	9.9588	8.7500	6.1250	7.3286	8.0375
	Std. Deviation	1.1848	4.2157	1.8574	3.1460	3.1739
	Valid N (listwise)	17	18	16	21	72
LOG_GDP	Mean	4.1047	3.1870	3.5260	3.2000	3.5040
	Std. Deviation	.1160	.7667	.3903	.3061	.6077
	Valid N (listwise)	17	18	16	21	72
B_TO_D	Mean	1.2809	3.0377	5.9393	4.0988	3.5772
	Std. Deviation	.3052	1.0226	2.8474	1.5675	2.3131
	Valid N (listwise)	17	18	16	21	72
FERTILITY	Mean	1.6988	3.2256	4.6113	3.3357	3.2051
	Std. Deviation	.2483	1.7485	1.5107	1.0562	1.5926
	Valid N (listwise)	17	18	16	21	72
LOG_POP	Mean	4.0443	4.6538	3.9386	3.9738	4.1526
	Std. Deviation	.6107	.7363	.5891	.5894	.6865
	Valid N (listwise)	17	18	16	21	72

Group Statistics. The total sample size in this analysis is 72. Of note here is the fact that the standard deviations for the European countries are considerably smaller than those for the Pacific/Asia group (see *lifeexpf, literacy, babymort, birth_rt,* and so on).

Pooled Within-Groups Matrices

		URBAN	LIFEEXPF	LITERACY	POP_INCR	BABYMORT	BIRTH_RT	DEATH_RT	LOG_GDP	B_TO_D	FERTILITY	LOG_POP
Correlation	URBAN	1.000										
	LIFEEXPF	.644	1.000									
	LITERACY	.493	.838	1.000								
	POP_INCR	-.247	-.413	-.563	1.000							
	BABYMORT	-.633	-.967	-.816	.385	1.000						
	BIRTH_RT	-.542	-.807	-.804	.704	.801	1.000					
	DEATH_RT	-.389	-.782	-.577	.015	.786	.526	1.000				
	LOG_GDP	.760	.784	.614	-.366	-.771	-.664	-.471	1.000			
	B_TO_D	-.001	.077	-.141	.758	-.118	.288	-.464	-.019	1.000		
	FERTILITY	-.467	-.775	-.812	.696	.756	.963	.527	-.568	.279	1.000	
	LOG_POP	-.228	-.237	-.174	-.008	.297	.081	.103	-.363	-.165	.077	1.000

Pooled Within-Groups Matrices. These correlations can be very different from the usual correlations where all cases are treated as a single sample. The computations for these correlations begin by computing variances and covariances separately for each group (if your groups are males and females, for each variable, deviations are computed from the mean of the males and the mean of the females, respectively). The variances and covariances are then pooled across groups to form a pooled covariance matrix. Correlations are computed from the covariances and variances.

Within the set of variables that includes *lifeexpf, literacy, babymort, birth_rt,* and *fertilty,* there are a number of correlations greater than 0.75 (or less than –0.75). Because these correlations are strong, there may be several alternative subsets of variables that perform equally well.

Variables Not in the Analysis

Step		Tolerance	Min. Tolerance	F to Enter	Wilks' Lambda
0	URBAN	1.000	1.000	5.042	.818
	LIFEEXPF	1.000	1.000	8.544	.726
	LITERACY	1.000	1.000	7.052	.763
	POP_INCR	1.000	1.000	27.876	.448
	BABYMORT	1.000	1.000	8.200	.734
	BIRTH_RT	1.000	1.000	18.627	.549
	DEATH_RT	1.000	1.000	5.564	.803
	LOG_GDP	1.000	1.000	18.705	.548
	B_TO_D	1.000	1.000	22.647	.500
	FERTILITY	1.000	1.000	14.608	.608
	LOG_POP	1.000	1.000	5.078	.817
1	URBAN	.939	.939	5.631	.358
	LIFEEXPF	.829	.829	5.547	.359
	LITERACY	.683	.683	3.293	.391
	BABYMORT	.852	.852	4.454	.374
	BIRTH_RT	.504	.504	2.192	.408
	DEATH_RT	1.000	1.000	2.840	.398
	LOG_GDP	.866	.866	13.532	.279
	B_TO_D	.425	.425	1.546	.419
	FERTILITY	.516	.516	.163	.445
	LOG_POP	1.000	1.000	4.901	.368
2	URBAN	.421	.389	5.239	.226
	LIFEEXPF	.367	.367	3.260	.243
	LITERACY	.491	.491	3.332	.243
	BABYMORT	.393	.393	2.772	.248
	BIRTH_RT	.313	.313	.771	.270
	DEATH_RT	.750	.650	6.761	.214
	B_TO_D	.348	.302	2.765	.248
	FERTILITY	.402	.402	2.222	.254
	LOG_POP	.845	.732	3.806	.238
3	URBAN	.420	.345	3.873	.181
	LIFEEXPF	.113	.113	5.745	.169
	LITERACY	.328	.328	1.594	.199
	BABYMORT	.133	.133	5.516	.170
	BIRTH_RT	.196	.196	2.797	.189
	B_TO_D	.197	.197	.663	.207
	FERTILITY	.241	.241	2.623	.191
	LOG_POP	.834	.547	4.102	.180
4	URBAN	.407	.110	4.066	.142
	LITERACY	.232	.080	.659	.164
	BABYMORT	.061	.052	1.310	.159
	BIRTH_RT	.177	.103	2.336	.152
	B_TO_D	.197	.113	.413	.166
	FERTILITY	.213	.100	2.486	.151
	LOG_POP	.827	.112	3.628	.144
5	LITERACY	.232	.078	.619	.138
	BABYMORT	.061	.052	1.303	.134
	BIRTH_RT	.175	.101	2.556	.126
	B_TO_D	.195	.110	.466	.139
	FERTILITY	.212	.099	2.573	.126
	LOG_POP	.818	.109	3.773	.120

Variables Not in the Analysis. In order to understand the stepwise selection of variables, you need to scan back and forth between the Variables Not in the Analysis and the Variables in the Analysis tables. From the statistics in the table on p. 273, you can determine which variable SPSS selects for entry at the next step. The statistics in the table on p. 275 provide information about variables after they are included in the model.

At step 0 in this table, *pop_incr*, the percentage a country's population increased during the last year, has the largest *F*-to-enter and, likewise, the smallest value of Wilks' lambda (27.876 and 0.448); so, SPSS enters this variable into the model first. At step 1 in the Variables in the Analysis table, *pop_incr* is listed as the only variable in the model. Now, look at the step 1 list in the Variables Not in the Analysis table to see which variable will enter at step 2—*log_gdp* has the largest *F*-to-enter (and the smallest Wilks' lambda), so at step 2 in Variables in the Analysis, both *pop_incr* and *log_gdp* are included in the model. At later steps, *death_rt*, *lifeexpf*, and *urban* are selected in a similar manner.

The *F*-to-enter statistics for variables not in the analysis at step 0 are the same as those reported if you select *Univariate ANOVAs* on the Statistics subdialog box (see the Test of Equality of Group Means table on p. 252). The value of *F* is the same as that computed from a one-way analysis of variance for the groups used in the discriminant analysis.

At later steps, the *F*-to-enter corresponds to the *F* computed from a one-way analysis of covariance where the covariates are the previously entered variables. It is not easy to associate probabilities with these *F*'s because the distribution of the largest *F* is needed (you are not looking at the *F* for a variable independently of the other variables in the model). The distribution of the largest *F* is affected by the number of variables scanned, their correlation structure, the number of groups, and the sample sizes of the groups. When the predictor variables are highly correlated, the critical value of the largest *F* can be much larger than that for testing one preselected variable. When looking for useful predictors, look for *F* values larger than 4.0.

At step 4, the *F*-to-enter for *urban* is small (4.066)—this variable may not add much to the success of the classification. At step 5, the *F*-to-enter for all candidates is less than SPSS's default value of 3.84, so the stepping stops.

For each variable, Wilks' lambda is used to test equality among the group centroids using the set of variables including that variable and those already in the model. The values of lambda for the variables that do enter the model are listed in on p. 273.

A variable with very low tolerance is nearly a linear function of the other variables; its inclusion in the model could make the calculations very unstable. The default value of tolerance is 0.001. No variable is entered into the classification function whose squared multiple correlation (R^2) exceeds 1 minus tolerance, or whose entry will cause the tolerance of an already entered variable to exceed the same limit. At step 4, the tolerance for *babymort* is rather low (its multiple R^2 with the model variables is $1 - 0.061$ or 0.939).

Variables in the Analysis

Step		Tolerance	F to Remove	Wilks' Lambda
1	POP_INCR	1.000	27.876	
2	POP_INCR	.866	21.482	.548
	LOG_GDP	.866	13.532	.448
3	POP_INCR	.835	14.057	.350
	LOG_GDP	.650	18.977	.398
	DEATH_RT	.750	6.761	.279
4	POP_INCR	.569	6.557	.220
	LOG_GDP	.325	4.930	.207
	DEATH_RT	.231	9.545	.243
	LIFEEXPF	.113	5.745	.214
5	POP_INCR	.559	5.678	.180
	LOG_GDP	.250	6.911	.188
	DEATH_RT	.228	9.848	.207
	LIFEEXPF	.110	5.928	.181
	URBAN	.407	4.066	.169

Variables in the Analysis. For each variable in the model, the F-to-remove and Wilks' lambda statistics are useful for describing what happens if the variable is removed from the current model (given that the other variables remain). Thus, Wilks' lambda for the entering variable is the same as Wilks' lambda for the full model at the previous step. The F-to-remove statistic for the entering variable is the same as its F-to-enter at the previous step.

For each other variable in turn, consider the remaining variables in the current set to be the previous model. Read step 3. For a model without *pop_incr* (but including *log gdp* and *death rt*), Wilks' lambda would be 0.350 and the F-to-enter for adding *pop_incr* would be 14.057.

Classification Function Coefficients

	REGION2			
	Europe	Pacific/Asia	Middle East	Latn America
URBAN	-.754	-.686	-.643	-.628
LIFEEXPF	12.297	11.500	11.532	11.782
POP_INCR	37.009	35.768	38.531	36.739
DEATH_RT	21.422	19.684	19.644	19.914
LOG_GDP	-17.764	-21.065	-19.739	-25.211
(Constant)	-543.425	-458.743	-473.925	-471.955

Classification Function Coefficients. In the multigroup model, there is one classification function for each group. These coefficients form functions as described in the "Classification Function Coefficients" section on p. 253.

Eigenvalues

Function	Eigenvalue	% of Variance	Cumulative %	Canonical Correlation
1	2.597	75.8	75.8	.850
2	.621	18.1	93.9	.619
3	.209	6.1	100.0	.416

Eigenvalues. The largest eigenvalue (2.597) corresponds to the eigenvector (canonical variable or canonical discriminant function) in the direction of the maximum spread of the group means, the second eigenvalue (0.621) corresponds to the eigenvector in the direction that has the next largest spread, and so on. The square root of each eigenvalue provides an indication of the length of the corresponding eigenvector (or spread of canonical variable means for that dimension). Tiny eigenvalues result in eigenvectors of essentially no length and account for very little of the total dispersion.

Here, the first two canonical variables (or canonical discriminant functions) account for 93.9% of the total dispersion—most of the spread is attributable to the first canonical variable (75.8%). This last value is displayed for function 1 (the first canonical variable) in the column labeled *% of Variance* and 93.9% is in the column labeled *Cumulative %*. The correlation between each canonical variable and the dummy set of variables defining the structure of the groups is displayed in the last column.

Wilks' Lambda

Test of Function(s)	Wilks' Lambda	Chi-square	df	Sig.
1 through 3	.142	129.890	15	.000
2 through 3	.510	44.767	8	.000
3	.827	12.641	3	.005

Wilks' Lambda. In the Wilks' lambda table, the test of functions labeled *1 through 3* tests the hypothesis that the means (centroids) of all three functions (the three canonical variables) are equal in the four groups. A chi-square transformation of Wilks' lambda is used to determine significance. Here, the *p* value or observed significance level (*Sig.*) is less than 0.0005, so the hypothesis of equality is rejected. The tests labeled *2 through 3* and *3* are successive tests useful for identifying whether or not the additional functions reflect population differences or only random variation. Here, after removing the first canonical variable (function 1), Wilks' lambda is 0.510 and the associated significance level is still less than 0.0005, indicating that the centroids of functions 2 and 3 do differ significantly across the four groups. When both functions 1 and 2 are removed, Wilks' lambda is 0.827 with a p value of 0.005. Thus, it is worth keeping all three functions.

Standardized Canonical Variables

	Function		
	1	2	3
URBAN	-.613	-.031	.838
LIFEEXPF	1.294	.211	2.083
POP_INCR	-.084	.947	.399
DEATH_RT	1.289	.314	.923
LOG_GDP	.517	.026	1.628

Standardized canonical variables. The number of canonical variables is $k–1$ (where k is the number of groups) or p (the number of variables), whichever is smaller. Thus, for our four groups, there are three canonical variables.

Structure Matrix

	Function		
	1	2	3
POP_INCR	-.637*	.533	-.060
BIRTH_RT[1]	-.436*	.063	-.287
LITERACY	.403*	.016	.402
FERTILITY	-.390*	.149	-.316
DEATH_RT	.270*	-.201	-.259
LOG_GDP	.489	.574*	.060
B_TO_D[1]	-.571	.571*	.067
LOG_POP	-.221	-.355*	-.002
URBAN	.133	.453	.483*
LIFEEXPF	.331	.280	.459*
BABYMORT[1]	-.281	-.288	-.409*

*. Largest absolute correlation between each variable and any discriminant function.
[1]. This variable not used in the analysis.

Structure Matrix. For each variable, an asterisk marks its largest absolute correlation with one of the three canonical variables (functions). With each function, these marked variables are then ordered by the size of the correlation.

Notice that all candidate predictors are included, not just the five variables in the final model (a footnote marker ([1]) follows the name of variables that are not used).

The strongest correlations for *pop_incr* and *death_rt* occur with function 1. The variable *log_gdp* has its strongest correlation with function 2 and *urban* and *lifeexpf* with function 3.

Functions at Group Centroids

REGION2	Function		
	1	2	3
Europe	2.758	.264	5.48E-02
Pacific/Asia	-.429	-.773	-.614
Middle East	-1.356	1.250	-.132
Latn America	-.832	-.503	.582

Function of Group Centroids. This is the canonical variable means by group. The difference among these means (centroids) is tested for each pair of groups is shown below and the means are plotted on p. 279 and p. 280.

Pairwise Group Comparisons

Step	REGION2		Europe	Pacific/Asia	Middle East	Latn America
5	Europe	F				
	Pacific/Asia	F	19.221			
	Middle East	F	27.822	8.264		
	Latn America	F	24.323	3.041	6.591	

Pairwise Group Comparisons. These F statistics can be used to describe which groups are most alike (or different) and to test the equality of means (centroids) for each pair of groups. The data are canonical variable scores and the group means are displayed in the Functions at Group Centroids table above. The F statistic for each pair of groups is proportional to Hotelling's T^2 statistic and the Mahalanobis D^2. Thus, you can view each F as a measure of the distance between each pair.

Europe and the Middle East have the largest F (27.822), indicating that these two groups are furthest apart or differ the most; while the Latin American and Pacific/Asia groups are closest ($F=3.041$). Look at the canonical variable plot on p. 279 to see how the F's in this panel reflect the distances among the means. Remember from the test results on p. 264 that the first two canonical variables account for almost 94% of the variability among the groups.

The Latin American and Pacific/Asia groups appear to differ the least. However, are the centroids of these two groups significantly different? At first glance, you see the *p* value (observed significance) is 0.016 and might conclude that the groups do differ. However, results for six tests are displayed and the problem of multiple testing arises (see Chapter 9, Example 2). A caution flag should appear: the *p* value (significance) is appropriate for one and only one comparison. You can make your own quick adjustment to the probability by multiplying the probability by the number of pairs tested (in this example, six). Thus, no difference is identified between the centroids of the Latin American and Pacific/Asia countries (6*0.016 = 0.096).

Canonical Discriminant Functions

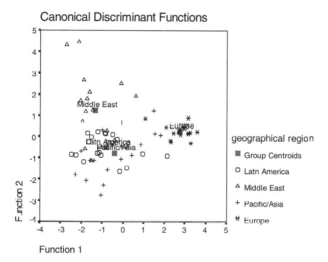

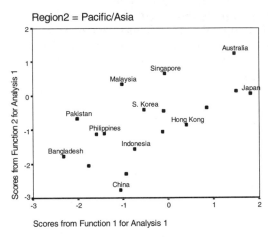

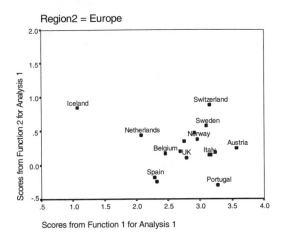

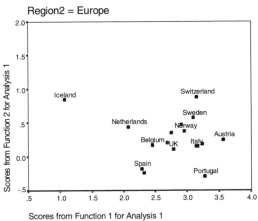

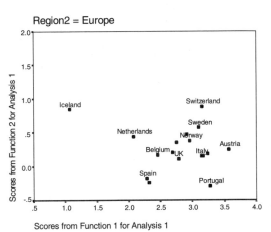

Territorial Map
                    (Assuming all functions but the first two are zero)

Canonical Discriminant
Function 2
          -6.0   -4.0   -2.0   .0   2.0   4.0   6.0
         +---------+---------+---------+---------+---------+---------+
     6.0 +   31   +
         | 31 |
         | 31 |
         | 31 |
         | 31 |
         | 31 |
     4.0 +   +   +   +   31+   +   +
         | 31 |
         | 31 |
         | 31 |
         | 31 |
         | 31 |
     2.0 +   +   +   +   31   +   +   +
         | 31 |
         | *   31 |
         | 31 |
         | 3333321 |
         | 333334442221   * |
      .0 +   +   333333344444 42   21 +   +   +
         | 333333444444   42   21 |
         | 33333444444   *4*2   21 |
         | 33333344444   422   21 |
         |3444444   42   21 |
         |4   42   21 |
    -2.0 +   +   + 42   +   21+   +   +
         | 42   21 |
         | 42   21 |
         | 42   21 |
         | 442   21 |
         | 422   21 |
    -4.0 +   +   42 +   +   +21   +   +
         | 42   21 |
         | 42   21 |
         | 42   21 |
         | 42   21 |
         | 42   21 |
    -6.0 +   42   21   +
         +---------+---------+---------+---------+---------+---------+
          -6.0   -4.0   -2.0   .0   2.0   4.0   6.0
                    Canonical Discriminant Function 1

Symbols used in territorial map

Symbol Group Label
------ ----- -----

   1   1   Europe
   2   3   Pacific/Asia
   3   5   Middle East
   4   6   Latn America
   *   Indicates a group centroid

Territorial Map. This is a cruder version of the canonical variable plot displayed on p. 279, but, now, numbered boundaries mark the regions into which each group is classified. For example, all points for countries falling to the right of the 1's are classified into the first region Europe; those bordered by 2's, Pacific/Asia, and so on. So if, for a country, the value of its first canonical variable (horizontal axis) is negative and the value of the second canonical variable (vertical axis) is positive, the country is classified into group 3, the Middle East.

A little below the coordinates (0,0), notice *4*2. The asterisks mark the means of the Pacific/Asia and Latin American groups. They are very close together, as the earlier pairwise *F* values indicated.

Classification Results[1,2]

			Europe	Pacific/Asia	Middle East	Latn America	Total
		REGION2					
Original	Count	Europe	17	0	0	0	17
		Pacific/Asia	3	12	1	2	18
		Middle East	0	4	10	3	17
		Latn America	1	4	0	16	21
	%	Europe	100.0	.0	.0	.0	100.0
		Pacific/Asia	16.7	66.7	5.6	11.1	100.0
		Middle East	.0	23.5	58.8	17.6	100.0
		Latn America	4.8	19.0	.0	76.2	100.0
Cross-validated[1]	Count	Europe	17	0	0	0	17
		Pacific/Asia	2	9	1	6	18
		Middle East	12	0	0	5	17
		Latn America	17	0	0	4	21
	%	Europe	100.0	.0	.0	.0	100.0
		Pacific/Asia	11.1	50.0	5.6	33.3	100.0
		Middle East	70.6	.0	.0	29.4	100.0
		Latn America	81.0	.0	.0	19.0	100.0

[1.] Cross validation is done only for those cases in the analysis. In cross validation, each case is classified by the functions derived from all cases other than that case.
[2.] 75.3% of original grouped cases correctly classified.
[3.] 41.1% of cross-validated grouped cases correctly classified.

Classification Results. The overall success of this five variable model for classifying cases into one of four groups is 75.3%. If you randomly assigned cases into groups, you might expect to classify 25% correctly. Notice that the classification works best for the European countries (all 17 of them are classified correctly). The Middle East has the highest misclassification rate: 41.2% (100% − 58.8%). In the Pairwise Group Comparisons table on p. 278, the centroids for the Latin American and Pacific/Asian countries were not found to differ. Here, two Pacific/Asia countries are classified as Latin American; and four Latin American countries, as Pacific/Asian. That is, 6 out of 18 misclassified cases involve one pair of groups.

Stepwise variable selection does not always produce the best model. The overall rate of correct classification for the five-variable model containing *urban*, *lifeexpf*, *death_rt*, *log_gdp*, and *fertilty* is 76%.

Example 4
Selecting Variables to Separate the Closest Groups

In the Pairwise Group Comparison table from Example 3 on p. 278, the *F* statistic for testing the equality of the centroids of the Latin American and Pacific/Asian groups was not significant when the problem of multiple testing was considered. The final model in Example 3 included 5 of the 11 candidate predictor variables. Given the strong intercorrelations among these variables, a different subset might do better at separating the Latin American and Pacific/Asian groups.

This example requests the **Mahalanobis distance method** of variable selection—at each step, the variable is entered that maximizes the Mahalanobis distance between the two closest groups. The final subset of variables selected by this method includes the five variables identified in Example 3 via the default method plus *log_pop*, the logarithm of a country's population. However, the variables enter the model in a different order with the ratio of birth rate to death rate (*b_to_d*) entering first—but after four other variables enter, *b_to_d* is removed from the model.

Table 14.11 Order in which variables enter for the two methods

Step	Wilks' lambda	Mahalanobis distance
1	*pop_incr*	*b_to_d*
2	*log_gdp*	*log_pop*
3	*death_rt*	*log_gdp*
4	*lifeexpf*	*urban*
5	*urban*	*pop_incr*
6		*b_to_d (out)*
7		*death_rt*
8		*lifeexpf*

To produce this output, use Select Cases from the Data menu to omit cases with *region2* equal to 2 or *region2* equal to 4 (region2 ~= 2 & region2 ~= 4). Then, in the Discriminant Analysis dialog box, click *Reset* to restore the dialog box defaults and select:

▶ Grouping Variable: region2

Define Range...
   Minimum: 1
   Maximum: 6

▶ Independents: urban, lifeexpf, literacy, pop_incr, babymort, birth_rt, death_rt, log_gdp, b_to_d, fertility, log_pop

☑ Use stepwise method

Statistics...

   Descriptives
   ☑ Box's M

Method...

   Method
   ☑ Mahalanobis distance

   Display
   ☑ F for pairwise distances

Classify...

   Display
   ☑ Summary table
   ☑ Leave-one-out classification

   Plots
   ☑ Territorial map

Variables Not in the Analysis

Step		Tolerance	Min. Tolerance	F to Enter	Min. D Squared	Between Groups
0	URBAN	1.000	1.000	5.042	.037	1 and 5
	LIFEEXPF	1.000	1.000	8.544	.000	5 and 6
	LITERACY	1.000	1.000	7.052	.000	3 and 5
	POP_INCR	1.000	1.000	27.876	.108	3 and 6
	BABYMORT	1.000	1.000	8.200	.008	5 and 6
	BIRTH_RT	1.000	1.000	18.627	.024	3 and 6
	DEATH_RT	1.000	1.000	5.564	.172	5 and 6
	LOG_GDP	1.000	1.000	18.705	.001	3 and 6
	B_TO_D	1.000	1.000	22.047	.403	3 and 6
	FERTILITY	1.000	1.000	14.608	.008	3 and 6
	LOG_POP	1.000	1.000	5.078	.003	5 and 6
1	URBAN	1.000	1.000	4.965	.822	3 and 6
	LIFEEXPF	.994	.994	7.706	.600	3 and 6
	LITERACY	.980	.980	3.882	.720	3 and 6
	POP_INCR	.425	.425	4.302	.457	3 and 6
	BABYMORT	.986	.986	7.683	.538	3 and 6
	BIRTH_RT	.917	.917	6.085	.404	3 and 6
	DEATH_RT	.785	.785	.149	.451	3 and 6
	LOG_GDP	1.000	1.000	15.375	.405	3 and 6
	FERTILITY	.922	.922	3.793	.412	3 and 6
	LOG_POP	.973	.973	4.641	1.228	5 and 6

Variables Not in the Analysis. The variable *b_to_d* has the largest value of the Mahalanobis distance squared between groups 3 (Pacific/Asia) and 6 (Latin America): the value is 0.403. Thus, it will be the first variable to enter at step 1. Notice that *pop_incr* has the largest F-to-enter (27.876). (When the default selection method was used in Example 3, *pop_incr* entered the model first.) At step 1, *log_pop* has the largest D^2, so it enters the model at step 2. Five other variables have higher F-to-enter values.

Variables in the Analysis

Step		Tolerance	F to Remove	Min. D Squared	Between Groups
1	B_TO_D	1.000	22.647		
2	B_TO_D	.973	21.722	.003	5 and 6
	LOG_POP	.973	4.641	.403	3 and 6
8	LOG_POP	.818	3.773	1.667	3 and 6
	LOG_GDP	.234	8.428	1.559	3 and 6
	URBAN	.403	4.207	2.224	3 and 6
	POP_INCR	.534	4.706	2.799	5 and 6
	DEATH_RT	.223	9.871	3.028	3 and 6
	LIFEEXPF	.109	5.554	2.753	3 and 6

Variables in the Analysis. At step 8, *lifeexpf* was included in the analysis. Notice that the *F*-to-remove for *log_pop* is rather low (3.773).

Pairwise Group Comparisons

	Step	REGION2	Europe	Pacific/Asia	Middle East	Latn America
F	8	Europe		15.788	23.648	22.407
		Pacific/Asia	15.788		7.383	4.561
		Middle East	23.648	7.383		5.751
		Latn America	22.407	4.561	5.751	
Sig.	8	Europe		.000	.000	.000
		Pacific/Asia	.000		.000	.001
		Middle East	.000	.000		.000
		Latn America	.000	.001	.000	

Pairwise Group Comparisons. Compare these *F* statistics with those for the five-variable model in Example 3 on p. 278. The *F*'s (think of them as distances) for all pairs are smaller here except the *F* for the Latin America and Pacific/Asia pair is larger. Here, even when an adjustment is made for multiple testing, the centroids of the Latin American and Pacific/Asian groups now differ significantly. Notice, however, that the smaller *F*'s for the other pairs do not result in a loss of significance.

Eigenvalues

Function	Eigenvalue	% of Variance	Cumulative %	Canonical Correlation
1	2.748	73.5	73.5	.856
2	.621	16.6	90.1	.619
3	.369	9.9	100.0	.519

Wilks' Lambda

Test of Function(s)	Wilks' Lambda	Chi-square	df	Sig.
1 through 3	.120	139.820	18	.000
2 through 3	.451	52.617	10	.000
3	.731	20.725	4	.000

Eigenvalues and Wilks' Lambda. Interestingly, the first two canonical variables (canonical discriminant functions) in the model with five variables in Example 3 account for 93.8% of the total dispersion. Here, with six variables, the first two variables account for 90.1%. See Example 3 for a discussion of the Wilks' lambda table.

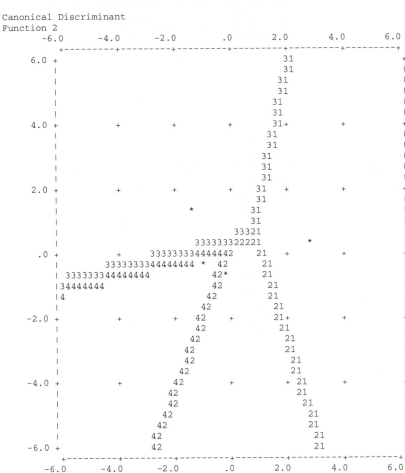

```
Territorial Map
               (Assuming all functions but the first two are zero)

Canonical Discriminant
Function 2
       -6.0      -4.0      -2.0       .0       2.0       4.0       6.0
        +---------+---------+---------+---------+---------+---------+
   6.0 +                                        31                    +
       |                                        31
       |                                        31
       |                                        31
       |                                        31
       |                                        31
   4.0 +         +         +         +          31+        +          +
       |                                        31
       |                                        31
       |                                        31
       |                                        31
       |                                        31
   2.0 +         +         +         +         31   +         +       +
       |                                        31
       |                          *            31
       |                                        31
       |                                     33321
       |                            333333322221
    .0 +         +        333333334444442   21    +         +        +
       |             3333333344444444  *  42     21
       | 3333333344444444              42*      21
       |34444444                       42       21
       |4                              42       21
       |                               42      21
  -2.0 +         +         +    42     +    21+        +          +
       |                              42      21
       |                              42     21
       |                             42      21
       |                             42     21
       |                            42      21
  -4.0 +         +         +    42   +      + 21     +         +      +
       |                           42        21
       |                           42          21
       |                          42           21
       |                          42           21
       |                         42             21
  -6.0 +                         42             21                    +
        +---------+---------+---------+---------+---------+---------+
       -6.0      -4.0      -2.0       .0       2.0       4.0       6.0
              Canonical Discriminant Function 1
```

Symbols used in territorial map

Symbol Group Label
------ ----- -----

   1   1   Europe
   2   3   Pacific/Asia
   3   5   Middle East
   4   6   Latn America

   *   Indicates a group centroid

Territorial Map. Compare this map with Example 3 on p. 281. Groups 2 and 4 now appear further apart than they did in Example 3 (the asterisks for their centroids are plotted near the coordinates (0,0). However, the group boundaries appear fairly similar.

Classification Results[1,2]

			Predicted Group Membership				
		REGION2	Europe	Pacific/Asia	Middle East	Latn America	Total
Count	Original	Europe	16	0	0	1	17
		Pacific/Asia	3	12	0	3	18
		Middle East	0	3	10	4	17
		Latn America	1	4	0	16	21
	Cross-validated[1]	Europe	17	0	0	0	17
		Pacific/Asia	17	1	0	0	18
		Middle East	17	0	0	0	17
		Latn America	0	0	0	21	21
%	Original	Europe	94.1	.0	.0	5.9	100.0
		Pacific/Asia	16.7	66.7	.0	16.7	100.0
		Middle East	.0	17.6	58.8	23.5	100.0
		Latn America	4.8	19.0	.0	76.2	100.0
	Cross-validated[1]	Europe	100.0	.0	.0	.0	100.0
		Pacific/Asia	94.4	5.6	.0	.0	100.0
		Middle East	100.0	.0	.0	.0	100.0
		Latn America	.0	.0	.0	100.0	100.0

[1.] Cross validation is done only for those cases in the analysis. In cross validation, each case is classified by the functions derived from all cases other than that case.
[2.] 74.0% of original grouped cases correctly classified.
[3.] 53.4% of cross-validated grouped cases correctly classified.

Classification Results. Even though the model in this example contains one more variable than that in Example 3, the overall rate of successfully classified cases is lower here (74% versus 75.3% in Example 3 on p. 283). And surprisingly, the number of misclassification between the Latin American and Pacific/Asian countries has increased from six to seven (four Latin American countries are classified as Pacific/Asian and three, the other way around). A total of 53.4% of the cross-validated grouped cases are correctly classified.

Log Determinants

REGION2	Rank	Log Determinant
Europe	6	-4.040
Pacific/Asia	6	5.684
Middle East	6	3.450
Latn America	6	3.051
Pooled within-groups	6	5.540

Test Results

Box's M		231.979
F	Approx.	3.078
	df1	63
	df2	10082.422
	Sig.	.000

Log Determinants and Test Results (Box's M). The Example 2 two-group discriminant analysis results for Box's *M* test are displayed on p. 264. There, the hypothesis of equal covariance matrices was not rejected. Here, the hypothesis is rejected with a significance level less than 0.0005!

In the introduction to this chapter, you used an ellipse for each group to characterize the distribution of the points (cases) in two dimensions. The model in this example includes six variables, instead of two. Can you visualize a six-dimensional ellipsoid? Each group has one and, if the assumption of equal covariance matrices is satisfied, they should have the same volume. The values in the Log Determinant table are proportional to the volume of the ellipsoid for each group.

Remember in the Group Statistics table in Example 3, you observed that the spread (standard deviation) of the European country's data was very small relative to that of Pacific/Asia. The values of the log determinant are telling you the same thing: the volume of the Europe group is very small relative to that of the others, especially to that of Pacific/Asia. Possibly, if Europe were omitted from the analysis, the equal covariance assumption would be met.

Cross-Validation

You can ask SPSS to compute classification functions for a subset of each group and then see how the procedure classifies the unused cases. This means that new data may be classified using functions derived from the original groups. More importantly, for model building, this means it is easy to design your own cross-validation. You can randomly assign the cases in each group to a training (learning) set and to a test set. Then ask SPSS to estimate the functions using the training set and to apply the function to the remaining cases (test set). The proportion of correct classification for the test set is a good empirical measure of the success of the discrimination.

Some researchers feel that when sample sizes are small, one cross-validation may not provide a reliable measure of the classification; so they suggest dividing your data into roughly 10 equal groups and computing 10 estimates. For the first measure of the classification, use the first 9 groups as the training sample and the 10th as the test sample. Repeat the analysis, each time holding out a different 1/10 as the test sample. This is called *10-fold cross-validation*.

This example shows how to use SPSS to get one estimate via cross-validation. First, select the percentage you want to hold back for the test sample. We selected 31%. Construct a new variable containing all 1's and then randomly insert 0's in the desired proportion. The name of the new variable with 0's and 1's is *use7* (we generated uniform random numbers seven times before the sample sizes in the test sample were fairly equal).

The variable *use7* is defined as a case selection variable on the Discriminant Analysis dialog box. Only the cases with the value 1 are used in the discriminant function computations. The cases with code 0, the test sample, are classified, however.

Our SPSS instructions request a cross-validation for the Example 3 model with four variables (*pop_incr*, *log_gdp*, *death_rt*, *lifeexpf*). You also repeat the procedure for each model in the Example 3 stepwise results, plus some extra variables.

Table 14.12 Comparison of usual classification with cross-validation

No. of Variables in Model	Variable Added	Usual Classification	Cross-Validation
1	*pop_incr*	66	30
2	*log_gdp*	72	39
3	*death_rt*	72	48
4	*lifeexpf*	74	65
5	*urban*	76	65
6	*log_pop*	78	61
7	*fertilty*	82	57
8	*birth_rt*	82	57
9	*babymort*	82	56

For the cross-validation, the proportion of successful classification reaches its maximum (65%) for a model with four variables.

To obtain the results for the model with four variables, use Select Cases from the Data menu to omit cases with *region2* equal to 2 or *region2* equal to 4 (region2 ~= 2 & region2 ~= 4).

Then, in the Discriminant Analysis dialog box, click *Reset* to restore the dialog box defaults and select:

▶ Grouping Variable: region2

Define Range...
    Minimum: 1
    Maximum: 6

▶ Independents: pop_incr, log_gdp, death_rt, lifeexpf

Select▷▷

▶ Selection Variable: use7
    Set Value...
        Value for Selection Variable: 1

Classify...

Display
    ☑ Summary table

Classification Results[1,2]

		geographical region	Predicted Group Membership				Total
			Europe	Pacific/Asia	Middle East	Latn America	
Cases Selected	Count	Europe	12	0	0	0	12
		Pacific/Asia	2	6	0	3	11
		Middle East	1	2	8	1	12
		Latn America	2	2	0	11	15
	%	Europe	100.0	.0	.0	.0	100.0
		Pacific/Asia	18.2	54.5	.0	27.3	100.0
		Middle East	8.3	16.7	66.7	8.3	100.0
		Latn America	13.3	13.3	.0	73.3	100.0
Cases Not Selected	Count	Europe	5	0	0	0	5
		Pacific/Asia	1	5	0	1	7
		Middle East	0	1	1	3	5
		Latn America	0	2	0	4	6
	%	Europe	100.0	.0	.0	.0	100.0
		Pacific/Asia	14.3	71.4	.0	14.3	100.0
		Middle East	.0	20.0	20.0	60.0	100.0
		Latn America	.0	33.3	.0	66.7	100.0

[1] 74.0% of selected original grouped cases correctly classified.
[2] 65.2% of unselected original grouped cases correctly classified.

Classification Results. Overall, 65.2% of the cases not selected are classified correctly. All of the European countries are classified correctly, but only one out of five Middle East countries are correctly classified.

15 Cluster Analysis

Cluster analysis is a multivariate procedure for detecting groupings in the data. The objects in these groups may be cases or variables. A cluster analysis of cases resembles discriminant analysis in one respect—the researcher seeks to classify a set of objects into groups or categories, but, in cluster analysis, neither the number nor the members of the groups are known. That is, in cluster analysis, you begin with no knowledge of group membership and often do not know just how many clusters there are. A cluster analysis of variables resembles factor analysis because both procedures identify related groups of variables. However, factor analysis has an underlying theoretical model, while cluster analysis is more ad hoc. Clustering is a good technique to use in exploratory data analysis when you suspect the sample is not homogeneous.

SPSS provides two methods for clustering objects into categories: **Hierarchical Cluster Analysis** and **K-Means Cluster Analysis**. The former clusters either cases or variables; the latter, cases only. Each procedure has useful features.

Hierarchical clustering. In the hierarchical method, clustering begins by finding the closest pair of objects (cases or variables) according to a distance measure and combines them to form a cluster. The algorithm continues one step at a time, joining pairs of objects, pairs of clusters, or an object with a cluster, until all the data are in one cluster. The clustering steps are displayed in an icicle plot or tree (dendrogram)—see p. 302 and p. 303 in Example 1. The method is *hierarchical* because once two objects or clusters are joined, they remain together until the final step. That is, a cluster formed in a later stage of the analysis contains clusters from an earlier stage that contain clusters from a still earlier stage.

K-means clustering. The K-Means Cluster Analysis procedure begins by using the values of the first k cases in the data file as temporary estimates of the k cluster means, where k is the number of clusters specified by the user. Initial cluster centers are formed by assigning each case in turn to the cluster with the closest center and then updating the center. Then, an iterative process is used to find the final cluster centers. At each step, cases are grouped into the cluster with the closest center, and the cluster centers are recomputed. This process continues until no further changes occur in the centers or until a maximum number of iterations is reached. You can specify cluster centers, and SPSS will allocate cases to your centers. This allows you to cluster new cases based on earlier results. The K-Means Cluster Analysis procedure is useful when you have a large number of cases.

Decisions to Make Before Starting

In requesting your cluster analysis, you may want to consider the following points:

Standardization method. Variables with large values contribute more to the calculations of distance measures than those with small values. For example, a value of infant mortality could be 168 babies, while an increase in the population of a country might be 0.1%. One way to avoid this problem is to transform or re-express all variables on the same scale. For example, if you transform each variable to z scores, each new variable has a mean of 0 and a standard deviation of 1 (see the squared Euclidean distance measure discussion below, where distances are computed in original units and standardized units). Or you could put each variable on a range of 0 to 1, where the smallest value is 0 and the largest becomes 1.

Hierarchical Cluster Analysis provides several ways to standardize or transform the data in order to avoid problems caused by scale differences. With K-Means Cluster Analysis, you need to standardize the data before using the K-Means Cluster Analysis dialog box (for example, compute z scores in Descriptives).

Distance measure. The Hierarchical Cluster Analysis procedure provides approximately 37 distance or similarity measures for defining how different or alike two objects are. When two cases are very similar, the value of a distance measure is small and the value of a similarity measure is large. That is, *distances* measure how far apart two objects are and *similarities* measure how close they are. The squared Euclidean distance is used frequently as a distance measure for clustering cases, and the usual Pearson correlation is used often for clustering variables. The **squared Euclidean distance** is the sum of the squared distances over all variables. For example, if your data have values of *age* and monthly *income* (in thousands of dollars) for Joan and David (and there are other subjects in the sample),

	Original Units		**Standardized Units**	
	Age	Income	Zage	Zincome
Joan	45	7	1.1	1.9
David	30	2	0.1	0.1

the squared Euclidean distance in original units is

$$15^2 + 5^2 = 225 + 25 = 250$$

and, in standardized units, is

$$1^2 + 1.8^2 = 1 + 3.24 = 4.24$$

So, in the original units, *age*, with its larger values, comprises 90% of the distance measure; while in standardized units, it accounts for 23.6% of the measure.

Among the many distance and similarity measures available in the Hierarchical Cluster Analysis procedure, some are appropriate for interval data, some for data that are counts, and others for binary data (for example, the value of each variable is *present* or *absent*).

Linking method. The hierarchical clustering method offers seven methods for combining or linking clusters. At each step, two objects (cases or variables) are joined, two clusters are joined, or an object and a cluster are joined. There are many criteria for deciding which objects or clusters to join. See "Methods for Combining Clusters" at the end of Example 1.

You probably should try different linking methods. If the clustering results differ greatly, your data are unlikely to have highly separated and distinct clusters.

Uses of Cluster Analysis

As examples, consider using cluster analysis to group:

- Makes of automobiles, using miles per gallon, frequency of repair, head room, cylinders, braking distance, and cost as variables. Each case is a different brand of car.
- Mammals, using the percentages of water, protein, fat, and lactose in their milk as variables. Each case is a mammal.
- Countries, using health indicators such as the relative number of doctors, dentists, pharmacists, nurses, and hospital beds, the percentages of animal fat and starch in the diet, and life expectancy.

Sometimes, in a single study, it may be interesting to cluster cases and to cluster variables. Consider answers to five questions each about the quality, agreeability, and price of breakfast cereals. The cases are 40 brands of cereal. You could use cluster analysis to see how the 40 brands of cereal cluster into groups, or you could cluster the 15 variables to see whether questions designed to assess *quality*, for example, do indeed group together.

The Data

Cluster analysis can be used to analyze interval data, count data (frequencies), or binary data. It is important that variables are measured on comparable scales. As shown above, variables measured on larger scales contribute more than those measured on smaller scales, even if they empirically are less useful for classification. If your variables are measured on different scales, you can convert them to similar scales by standardizing them. The Hierarchical Cluster Analysis procedure provides a means to automatically standardize the variables in your analysis. When using the K-Means Cluster Analysis procedure, any standardization should be done prior to the cluster analysis. (The

Descriptives procedure provides a convenient method for computing standardized scores for variables. See Chapter 3 and the *SPSS Base User's Guide* for more information on the Descriptives procedure.)

Differences between K-Means and Hierarchical Cluster Analysis

The *k*-means clustering method handles large problems (200 or more cases) more easily. Hierarchical clustering computes a distance matrix with entries for every pair of cases (or variables), so large problems become unwieldy. More importantly, when the sample size is large, icicle plots and dendrograms are hard to read and interpret because they spread across many pages. For small data sets, icicle plots and dendrograms provide an excellent picture of just when each case (or variable) is joined with another, and distance matrices can also be informative.

By providing the distance from each case to its cluster center, *k*-means clustering characterizes whether or not a case is close to the others within its cluster or is an outlier. The size of *F* statistics in *k*-means' one-way ANOVA is useful for identifying variables that drive the clustering and also those that differ little across the clusters. In the *k*-means clustering method, by inputting cluster centers, you can classify new cases.

The K-Means Cluster Analysis procedure requires that you specify the number of clusters, so you may need to try several analyses (for example, requesting three, four, and five clusters). Alternatively, you might consider running a subset of the cases in the Hierarchical Cluster Analysis procedure, as shown in Example 1, to determine a reasonable number of clusters. Of course, with hierarchical clustering, you still have to make a judgment about the number of clusters (by studying the graphical displays); there is no magical test that tells the number.

The Hierarchical Cluster Analysis procedure has many options for standardizing your data, computing distances, and linking clusters. With the K-Means Cluster Analysis procedure, you need to standardize your data before requesting the cluster analysis. The Euclidean distance metric is used automatically.

Hierarchical clustering excludes all cases with values missing for variables used in the analysis. K-means clustering has an option that assigns cases to clusters based on distances computed from all variables with nonmissing values.

Example 1: Clustering cases via the hierarchical method. A random subset of countries (cases) from the *world95m* data set is clustered. Data are transformed to a 0 to 1 scale for the analysis, and dendrograms and icicle plots are used to assess the steps in cluster formation.

Example 2: Clustering variables. Values of absolute correlations among 11 variables from the *world95m* data set are used to cluster the variables.

Example 3: Clustering cases via the k-means method. Data are transformed to standardized values (z scores), and a four-factor solution is generated. Variables are evaluated for their contribution to cluster identification. Cluster membership and distance from cluster center for each case are saved as new variables, which are used in tables and plots to assess characteristics of the cluster solution.

Example 1
Clustering Cases via the Hierarchical Method

In this example, you study the same data set used in Discriminant Analysis, Chapter 14. You use 11 variables from the data set to cluster countries (cases). The values of each variable are standardized to a range of 0 to 1 (that is, the smallest value for each variable becomes 0 and the largest becomes 1). The default distance measure and linking method are used: squared Euclidean distance and between-groups linkage.

Because results for large data sets are hard to interpret, the example also illustrates how to use a random sample of the data in the clustering. For the example of cross-validation in the Discriminant Analysis chapter, you constructed a variable named *use7* with 0's and 1's, where 0 was randomly assigned to roughly 30% of the cases. You use Select Cases on the Data menu to select this random subset of cases; also, in order to make the output shorter, Eastern European and African countries (codes 2 and 4 for the variable *region2*) are eliminated.

From the output that follows, it appears that there are three or four clusters in the data. Since the distances between each pair of cases are the basis of the clustering, let's take a close look at them in the figure on p. 298 before proceeding to the output. The cases are sorted by the cluster membership found in this example. The shaded area indicates distances between items from *different* clusters, whereas the unshaded area indicates distances between items within the *same* cluster.

Squared Euclidean Distances

	Argentina	Brazil	Chile	Domin R.	Indon	Austria	Denmk	Italy	Japan	Norway	Switz	Bangl	India	Bolivia	
Brazil	.44														
Chile	.42	.92													
Domincan R.	.94	.79	.45												Cluster 1
Indonesia	1.35	.55	1.72	.91											
Austria	1.01	1.89	1.90	2.67	2.75										
Denmark	1.02	2.11	2.08	3.12	3.49	.18									
Italy	.88	1.61	1.77	2.77	2.66	.19	.36								Cluster 2
Japan	.84	1.45	1.22	2.29	2.64	.74	.99	.31							
Norway	.69	1.72	1.34	2.23	2.87	.14	.15	.31	.63						
Switzerland	.84	1.84	1.44	2.31	2.76	.13	.34	.24	.56	.11					
Bangladesh	4.88	3.03	5.11	3.02	1.73	7.67	8.50	7.89	7.87	7.66	7.83				Cluster 3
India	3.16	1.66	3.54	2.16	.74	5.65	6.44	5.48	5.27	5.68	5.76	.48			
Bolivia	2.23	1.59	1.88	.79	1.26	4.81	5.28	5.16	4.82	4.32	4.60	1.40	1.37		Cluster 4
Paraguay	2.29	2.57	1.31	.92	2.32	4.66	5.24	4.88	4.24	4.01	3.95	4.09	3.34	1.37	

For these 15 cases, distances are computed between every pair (105 distances). The distance (0.11) between Switzerland and Norway in cluster 2 is the shortest. Notice that the distances between these countries and Austria, Denmark, and Italy are also rather small (those with Japan, the other member of cluster 2, are slightly larger). These distances are small especially when contrasted with the distances between the same countries and Bangladesh and India (7.67, 8.50, 7.89, 7.87, and so on).

A similar pattern exists for the Latin American countries in cluster 1. Indonesia is the most distant member of this cluster.

To produce the output, use Select Cases from the Data menu to keep cases where *region2* equals neither 2 nor 4, and *use7* is not 1 (region2 ~= 2 & region2 ~= 4 & use7 ~= 1). Then, from the menus choose:

Analyze
  Classify
    Hierarchical Cluster...

Click *Reset* to restore dialog box defaults, and then select:

▶Variables: urban, lifeexpf, literacy, pop_incr, babymort, birth_rt, calories, death_rt, log_gdp, b_to_d, fertilty, log_pop

▶Label Cases by: country

Statistics...
 ☑ Proximity matrix
 Cluster Membership
 ⊙ Range of solutions: From 2 through 4 clusters

Plots...
 ☑ Dendrogram

Method...
 Transform Values
 Standardize: Range 0 to 1

Proximity Matrix

								Squared Euclidean Distance							
		1:Argentina	2:Austria	3:Bangladesh	4:Bolivia	5:Brazil	6:Chile	7:Denmark	8:Domincan R.	9:India	10:Indonesia	11:Italy	12:Japan	13:Norway	14:Paraguay	15:Switzerland
Case	1:Argentina		1.01	4.88	2.23	.44	.42	1.02	.94	3.16	1.35	.88	.84	.69	2.29	.84
	2:Austria	1.01		7.07	4.81	1.89	1.90	.18	2.67	5.65	2.75	.19	.74	.14	4.66	.13
	3:Bangladesh	4.88	7.67		1.40	3.03	5.11	8.50	3.02	.48	1.73	7.89	7.87	7.66	4.09	7.83
	4:Bolivia	2.23	4.81	1.40		1.59	1.88	5.28	.79	1.37	1.26	5.16	4.82	4.32	1.37	4.60
	5:Brazil	.44	1.89	3.03	1.59		.92	2.11	.79	1.66	.55	1.61	1.45	1.72	2.57	1.84
	6:Chile	.42	1.90	5.11	1.88	.92		2.08	.45	3.54	1.72	1.77	1.22	1.34	1.31	1.44
	7:Denmark	1.02	.18	8.50	5.28	2.11	2.08		3.12	6.44	3.49	.36	.99	.15	5.24	.34
	8:Domincan R.	.94	2.67	3.02	.79	.79	.45	3.12		2.16	.91	2.77	2.29	2.23	.92	2.31
	9:India	3.16	5.65	.48	1.37	1.66	3.54	6.44	2.16		.74	5.48	5.27	5.68	3.34	5.76
	10:Indonesia	1.35	2.75	1.73	1.26	.55	1.72	3.49	.91	.74		2.66	2.64	2.87	2.32	2.76
	11:Italy	.88	.19	7.89	5.16	1.61	1.77	.36	2.77	5.48	2.66		.31	.31	4.88	.24
	12:Japan	.84	.74	7.87	4.82	1.45	1.22	.99	2.29	5.27	2.64	.31		.63	4.24	.56
	13:Norway	.69	.14	7.66	4.32	1.72	1.34	.15	2.23	5.68	2.87	.31	.63		4.01	.11
	14:Paraguay	2.29	4.66	4.09	1.37	2.57	1.31	5.24	.92	3.34	2.32	4.88	4.24	4.01		3.95
	15:Switzerland	.84	.13	7.83	4.60	1.84	1.44	.34	2.31	5.76	2.76	.24	.56	.11	3.95	

Proximity Matrix. This figure shows how the distances appear in the output. At the top, the distance between Argentina and Austria is 1.01. Notice that the distance matrix is symmetric, so that entries above the diagonal equal corresponding entries below the diagonal. For example, the distance is the same whether you read Argentina in the row and Austria in the column or vice versa.

Note: This output was edited to rotate the column headings and reformat the values to show only two decimal places.

Agglomeration Schedule

		Cluster Combined			Stage Cluster First Appears		
		Cluster 1	Cluster 2	Coefficients	Cluster 1	Cluster 2	Next Stage
Stage	1	13	15	.112	0	0	2
	2	2	13	.132	0	1	3
	3	2	7	.227	2	0	4
	4	2	11	.273	3	0	8
	5	1	6	.423	0	0	9
	6	3	9	.484	0	0	14
	7	5	10	.547	0	0	10
	8	2	12	.649	4	0	13
	9	1	8	.691	5	0	10
	10	1	5	1.023	9	7	12
	11	4	14	1.370	0	0	12
	12	1	4	1.716	10	11	13
	13	1	2	2.718	12	8	14
	14	1	3	4.651	13	6	0

Agglomeration Schedule. From the agglomeration schedule, you can identify which cases or clusters are combined at each step. First, case 13 (Norway) is joined with case 15 (Switzerland). Remember that the distance between this pair is smaller than that for any other pair. The distance (in this case, the squared Euclidean distance) is displayed in the column labeled *Coefficients*. (The actual value of these coefficients depends on the distance measure and linkage method used.) Next, case 2 (Austria) is joined with the first two. The value printed under *Coefficients* at stage 2 is the joining measure for combining a case with a cluster when the default between-groups linkage (average linkage) is used. Austria's distances with the first two countries are 0.128 and 0.135, with an average of about 0.132. Case 7 is added at stage 3 and case 11 at stage 4.

SPSS uses the number of the first case in a cluster to assign a number to the cluster, so the first cluster is cluster 13 and the second with three cases is cluster 2. In reading the two columns labeled *Cluster 2* on the *Stage 2* line, *13* is listed as the *Cluster Combined* and *1* is listed as the stage where cluster 13 first appears. The *Next Stage* column indicates the next stage (3) where a case or cluster is joined with what is now cluster 2. The *Next Stage* column indicates that cluster 2 is not increased in size until stage 8.

At stage 5, case 1 (Argentina) and case 6 (Chile) are joined and not seen again until stage 9.

It is often much easier to follow the joining of clusters in a tree diagram, or **dendrogram**, as shown in the dendrogram on p. 303. However, the graphical display does not print this joining distance, which gives you an indication of whether homogeneous or nonhomogeneous clusters are joined. Smaller coefficients indicate that fairly homogeneous clusters are joined, while larger coefficients are an indication that the members of the clusters are more dissimilar. Look at the difference in the coefficients between two adjacent steps. If there is a sudden jump in the size of the difference, you might consider that a solution is reached. At stage 10, the coefficient is 1.023; and at stage 11, it jumps to 1.370. At this point, the clusters labeled in the introduction to this example as 1 (Latin American countries, plus Indonesia), 2 (European countries plus Japan), and 3 (Bangladesh and India) have been formed. At stage 11, Bolivia and Paraguay are joined and all countries are now members of a cluster.

Cluster Membership

		Label	4 Clusters	3 Clusters	2 Clusters
Case	1	Argentina	1	1	1
	2	Austria	2	2	1
	3	Bangladesh	3	3	2
	4	Bolivia	4	1	1
	5	Brazil	1	1	1
	6	Chile	1	1	1
	7	Denmark	2	2	1
	8	Domincan R.	1	1	1
	9	India	3	3	2
	10	Indonesia	1	1	1
	11	Italy	2	2	1
	12	Japan	2	2	1
	13	Norway	2	2	1
	14	Paraguay	4	1	1
	15	Switzerland	2	2	1

Cluster Membership. The preceding table shows output for cluster membership. Use *Range of solutions* (from 2 to 4 clusters) on the Statistics subdialog box to request this table. The cluster membership for the four-cluster solution is listed in the first column following the country names. If you draw a vertical line on the dendrogram on p. 303 at a distance between 7 and 8, four clusters are formed—Bangladesh and India at the bottom of the dendrogram are identified as cluster 3 in this panel. Above them in the dendrogram, Bolivia and Paraguay are listed as cluster 4 here; next higher in the dendrogram, the four Latin American countries plus Indonesia are identified as cluster 1; and at the top, the European countries plus Japan as cluster 2.

To see the three-cluster solution, draw a vertical line between distances 10 and 15. The only difference between the results for three and four clusters is that Bolivia and Paraguay, the only countries in cluster 4, become members of cluster 1 in the three-cluster solution. For the two-cluster solution, draw a line between distances 15 and 25. Now Bangladesh and India form one cluster, and all the other countries are members of the other cluster.

Vertical Icicle

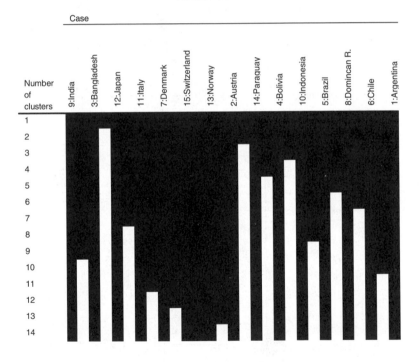

Vertical Icicle. This figure shows an **icicle plot** (some people think it resembles a row of icicles hanging from eaves; hence, its name), which summarizes the steps in forming clusters. To produce this output, you must enable the icicle plot autoscript. From the Edit menu choose *Options*. Click the *Scripts* tab, select *Enable Autoscripting*, and select *Cluster_Table_Icicle_Create*. This will automatically reformat all subsequent icicle plots. Each country (case) is represented by a black bar hanging from the top, with columns between variables representing linkages. In row 1, all cases are joined into one cluster so all are black. To understand how clusters are formed start at the bottom of the display.

At the first step (row 14), Switzerland and Norway are combined into a cluster because they have the shortest distance (0.11 in the Agglomeration Schedule on p. 300). Notice that the black bar in the column between them extends to the bottom of the display. At step 13, Austria is added, followed by Denmark in step 12, and Italy in step 11. To see where each bar ends, it helps to lay a straight edge horizontally below the number at each step. Doing this slightly below 10, you see that Chile and Argentina form a cluster at this step.

Step 4 corresponds to a solution with four clusters: 1) India and Bangladesh, 2) Japan, Italy, Denmark, Switzerland, Norway, and Austria, 3) Paraguay and Bolivia, 4) Indonesia, Brazil, Dominican Republic, Chile, and Argentina.

```
* * * * * H I E R A R C H I C A L   C L U S T E R   A N A L Y S I S * * * * * *
  Dendrogram using Average Linkage (Between Groups)
                            Rescaled Distance Cluster Combine
       C A S E          0         5        10        15        20        25
     Label      Num    +---------+---------+---------+---------+---------+
     Norway      13     -+
     Switzerland 15     -+
     Austria      2     -+
     Denmark      7     -+---+
     Italy       11     -| |---------        ---------+
     Japan       13      |                           I
     Brazil       5     -----+-----+          +------------------+
     Indonesia   10     -----+     +-----+    |                  |
     Argentina    1     ---+---+   |     |    |                  |
     Chile        6     ---+   +---+     +-----------+           |
     Dominican R. 8     -------+         |                       |
     Bolivia      4     ------------+---+                        |
     Paraguay    14     ------------+                            |
     Bangladesh   3     -----+--------------------------------------+
     India        9     -----+
```

Dendrogram. This **dendrogram** (or cluster tree) gives a good picture of the cluster agglomeration tabulated on p. 300, but notice that the distances along the top of this display are scaled differently from the coefficients in the cluster agglomeration—here, they are rescaled to numbers between 0 and 25.

From the distances in the figure on p. 300, you learned that Norway and Switzerland are the countries that are most alike, so in the cluster agglomeration, they were joined first, followed by cases 2, 7, and 11. The vertical line (indicated by a vertical string of pluses) close to zero indicates that these cases were joined first (the distances are similar in magnitude, so it is hard to recover the exact joining order from the display). The vertical line a little further away from zero connects Argentina (case 1) and Chile (case 6)— this joining is displayed at stage 5 on p. 300. Cases 3 and 9 are joined at stage 6.

Thus, the dendrogram indicates how the clusters are formed and provides some measure of the linkage distance for clustering. Clearly, Bangladesh and India differ from all the other countries. Less clear is whether the joining should stop between 5 and 10 (four clusters) or between 10 and 15 (three clusters).

Methods for combining clusters. There are several methods available for combining cluster. Use the following guidelines to select a method:

- For spherical clusters with equal variances and sample sizes, use Between-groups linkage or Ward's method.

- For elongated clusters with unequal variances and unequal sample sizes, use Nearest neighbor (single linkage).

- For globular clusters with unequal variances and unequal sample sizes, use Furthest neighbor (complete linkage).

The best cluster structure for k-means is globular clusters with equal variances and sample sizes.

Example 2
Clustering Variables

In this example, you join columns (variables) instead of rows (cases) to see which variables cluster together. When the Euclidean distance was used to cluster cases in Example 1, you standardized the variables to remove the influence of different measurement scales. A similar remedy, when clustering variables, is to use the Pearson correlation. Because you want to measure the strength of the relationships among the variables, however, you use the absolute value of each correlation. If you want clusters to reflect the positive correlations only, retain the sign of the correlations.

Factor analysis and cluster analysis both identify related groups of variables, although factor analysis has an underlying theoretical model and cluster analysis is more ad hoc.

To produce the output, use Select Cases from the Data menu to omit cases with *region2* equal 2 or *region2* equal 4 (region2 ~= 2 & region2 ~= 4). Then, in the Hierarchical Cluster dialog box, click *Reset* to restore dialog box defaults and select:

▶ Variables: urban, lifeexpf, literacy, pop_incr, babymort, birth_rt, death_rt, log_gdp, b_to_d, fertilty, log_pop

Cluster
⊙ Variables

Statistics...
   Cluster Membership
   ⊙ Range of solutions: From 2 through 4 clusters

Plots...
   ☑ Dendrogram

Method...
   Measure
   Pearson correlation
   Transform Measures
   ☑ Absolute values

Proximity Matrix

		Matrix file input									
		URBAN	LIFEEXPF	LITERACY	POP_INCR	BABYMORT	BIRTH_RT	DEATH_RT	LOG_GDP	B_TO_D	FERTILTY	LOG_POP
Case	URBAN		.681	.521	.196	.663	.466	.320	.734	.010	.381	.342
	LIFEEXPF	.681		.864	.498	.975	.797	.474	.826	.170	.747	.300
	LITERACY	.521	.864		.634	.853	.820	.302	.666	.350	.820	.215
	POP_INCR	.196	.498	.634		.500	.834	.309	.488	.879	.827	.062
	BABYMORT	.663	.975	.853	.500		.806	.469	.813	.163	.750	.334
	BIRTH_RT	.466	.797	.820	.834	.806		.075	.717	.600	.966	.049
	DEATH_RT	.320	.474	.302	.309	.469	.075		.149	.605	.106	.162
	LOG_GDP	.734	.826	.666	.488	.813	.717	.149		.274	.592	.347
	B_TO_D	.010	.170	.350	.879	.163	.600	.605	.274		.586	.200
	FERTILTY	.381	.747	.820	.827	.750	.966	.106	.592	.586		.024
	LOG_POP	.342	.300	.215	.062	.334	.049	.162	.347	.200	.024	

Proximity Matrix. This figure shows the proximities between variables. In this case, you use the usual Pearson correlations except the sign is removed because you requested that absolute values be used. For example, the strongest correlation is the one between *lifeexpf* and *babymort* (–0.97)—as female life expectancy increases, infant mortality tends to decrease.

Agglomeration Schedule

		Cluster Combined			Stage Cluster First Appears		
		Cluster 1	Cluster 2	Coefficients	Cluster 1	Cluster 2	Next Stage
Stage	1	2	5	.975	0	0	4
	2	6	10	.966	0	0	5
	3	4	9	.879	0	0	8
	4	2	3	.859	1	0	5
	5	2	6	.790	4	2	7
	6	1	8	.734	0	0	7
	7	1	2	.632	6	5	9
	8	4	7	.457	3	0	9
	9	1	4	.382	7	8	10
	10	1	11	.203	9	0	0

Agglomeration Schedule. The steps in the clustering procedure are the same whether cases or variables are clustered. In the beginning, each variable is in a cluster by itself; then, at each step, two variables are joined, a variable is joined with a cluster, or two clusters are joined.

The headings for this table are explained in Example 1. Here, when two variables are joined, the value in the column labeled *Coefficients* is the usual Pearson correlation (without its sign). That is, at stage 1, the correlation between *lifeexpf* (variable 2) and *babymort* (variable 5) is 0.975. This is the strongest correlation among all pairs of variables, so variables 2 and 5 are joined first. Next, variables 6 and 10 are joined, followed by 4 and 9. At stage 4, variable 3 (*literacy*) is joined to the first cluster.

Between stages 7 and 8, there is a large decrease in the correlations, and a smaller, but sizable decrease, between stages 6 and 7. At stage 6, *urban* and *log_gdp* are joined; and at stage 7, this new cluster is joined with *lifeexpf*, *babymort*, *literacy*, *birth_rt*, and *fertilty*. The variable *log_pop* appears to be independent of the other variables (look at the correlation matrix again to see how small the correlations are with this variable).

Cluster Membership

		4 Clusters	3 Clusters	2 Clusters
Case	URBAN	1	1	1
	LIFEEXPF	1	1	1
	LITERACY	1	1	1
	POP_INCR	2	2	1
	BABYMORT	1	1	1
	RIRTH_RT	1	1	1
	DEATH_RT	3	2	1
	LOG_GDP	1	1	1
	B_TO_D	2	2	1
	FERTILTY	1	1	1
	LOG_POP	4	3	2

Cluster Membership. As you can see in this figure, for the four-cluster solution, *log_pop* is in a cluster by itself. This is also true for the two- and three-cluster solutions. Ignoring *log_pop*, there appear to be two or three clusters.

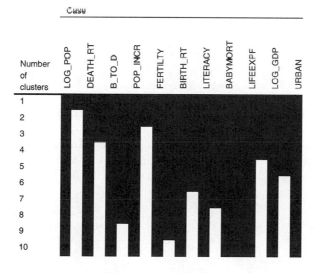

Vertical Icicle

```
* * * * * * H I E R A R C H I C A L   C L U S T E R    A N A L Y S I S * * * * * *


Dendrogram using Average Linkage (Between Groups)


                    Rescaled Distance Cluster Combine


    C A S E       0        5       10       15       20       25
    Label    Num  +--------+--------+--------+--------+--------+

    LIFEEXPF   2
    BABYMORT   5
    LITERACY   3
    BIRTH_RT   6
    FERTILTY  10
    URBAN      1
    LOG_GDP    8
    POP_INCR   4
    B_TO_D     9
    DEATH_RT   7
    LOG_POP   11
```

Vertical Icicle and Dendrogram. The icicle plot and dendrogram are interpreted similarly to those shown in Example 1. From the dendrogram, it seems that, aside from *log_pop* (which appears to be unlike any of the other variables), there are two groups of variables: the upper group in the plot, including *lifeexpf*, *babymort*, *literacy*, *birth_rt*, *fertility*, *urban*, and *log_gdp*; and the lower group, including *pop_incr*, *b_to_d*, and *death_rt*.

Example 3
Clustering Cases via the K-Means Method

Since the scales for the variables in this example differ markedly (a value of infant mortality could be 168 babies, while an increase in population might be 0.1%), you use the Descriptives procedure on the Statistics menu to transform the variable to *z* scores (the result being that the values of each variable are rescaled to have a mean of 0 and a standard deviation of 1). See Chapter 3 for more information on the Descriptives procedure.

To produce the output, use Select Cases from the Data menu to omit cases with *region2* equal 2 or *region2* equal 4 (region2 ~= 2 & region2 ~= 4). Then, from the menus choose:

Analyze
  Descriptive Statistics
    Descriptives...

▶ Variables: urban, lifeexpf, literacy, pop_incr, babymort, birth_rt, death_rt, log_gdp, b_to_d, fertilty, log_pop

☑ Save standardized values as variables

This creates the standardized variables with z added to the beginning of the variable names. Next, from the menus choose:

Analyze
  Classify
    K-Means Cluster...

Click *Reset* to restore dialog box defaults, and then select:

▶ Variables: zurban, zlifeexp, zliterac, zpop_inc, zbabymor, zbirth_r, zdeath_r, zlog_gdp, zb_to_d, zfertilt, zlog_pop

▶ Label Cases by: country

Number of clusters: 4

Save...
    ☑ Cluster membership
    ☑ Distance from cluster center

Options...
    Statistics
    ☑ ANOVA table
    ☑ Cluster information for each case

Cluster Membership

		COUNTRY	Cluster	Distance
Case Number	1	Afghanistan	1	3.489
	2	Argentina	4	1.814
	3	Armenia	2	1.919
	4	Australia	4	.971
	5	Austria	4	1.195
	6	Azerbaijan	2	1.389
	7	Bahrain	3	2.535
	8	Bangladesh	1	1.603
	9	Barbados	4	2.779
	10	Belgium	4	1.190
	11	Bolivia	2	2.248
	12	Brazil	2	2.206
	13	Cambodia	1	1.372
	14	Chile	2	1.936

Cluster Membership (excerpt). Select *Cluster information for each case* under *Statistics* on the Options subdialog box to request the listing shown above. (In order to save space, this figure shows an excerpt from the complete output.) This table gives specific information for each case. Among the cases shown, Afghanistan is furthest from its cluster center (cluster 1)—its distance is 3.489.

Final Cluster Centers

	Cluster			
	1	2	3	4
ZURBAN	-1.71	-.31	.17	.63
ZLIFEEXP	-2.53	-.16	-.28	.81
ZLITERAC	-2.31	.14	-.82	.73
ZPOP_INC	.60	.13	1.45	-.95
ZBABYMOR	2.43	.22	.26	-.81
ZBIRTH_R	1.53	.13	1.14	-.99
ZDEATH_R	2.10	-.45	-.71	.31
ZLOG_GDP	-1.78	-.59	-.17	.94
ZB_TO_D	-.30	.19	1.45	-.85
ZFERTILT	1.51	-.12	1.27	-.88
ZLOG_POP	.83	.35	-.49	-.22

Final Cluster Centers. This output reports the means of the standardized variables for each cluster. The means for each cluster define the **cluster center**. In the next figure, you learn that the means of *birth_rt* across the four clusters are more different from those for the other variables, and *lifeexpf* also has sizeable differences. In this panel, you can read that the average birth rate (*birth_rt*) for cluster 1 countries is 1.53 standard deviation units above the mean for all countries; while the average for cluster 4 is almost one standard deviation (–0.99) below the overall mean. For *lifeexpf*, the mean of cluster 1 is two and a half standard deviations (–2.53) below the overall mean, while the average female life expectancy for countries in cluster 4 is above the overall mean (0.81).

Later, you will see that most of the European countries are members of cluster 4. In comparison with the other three clusters, the members of cluster 4 tend to have a larger proportion of their population living in cities (*zurban*=0.63), a higher rate of literacy (*zliterac*=0.73), a smaller increase in population (*zpop_inc*=–0.95), a lower infant mortality rate (*zbabymor*=–0.81), and so on.

Distances between Final Cluster Centers

		1	2	3	4
Cluster	1		5.627	5.640	7.924
	2	5.627		2.897	3.249
	3	5.640	2.897		5.246
	4	7.924	3.249	5.246	

Distances between Final Cluster Centers. The means of cluster 1 (mainly Pacific Rim/Asia) and cluster 4 (Europe) are furthest apart (7.924). Clusters 2 (mainly Latin America) and 3 (mainly Middle East) are closest together (2.897).

ANOVA

	Cluster		Error			
	Mean Square	df	Mean Square	df	F	Sig.
ZURBAN	10.409	3	.541	68	19.234	.000
ZLIFEEXP	19.410	3	.210	68	92.614	.000
ZLITERAC	18.731	3	.229	68	81.655	.000
ZPOP_INC	18.464	3	.219	68	84.428	.000
ZBABYMOR	18.621	3	.239	68	77.859	.000
ZBIRTH_R	19.599	3	.167	68	117.339	.000
ZDEATH_R	12.622	3	.111	68	30.676	.000
ZLOG_GDP	17.599	3	.287	68	61.313	.000
ZB_TO_D	16.316	3	.288	68	56.682	.000
ZFERTILT	18.829	3	.168	68	112.273	.000
ZLOG_POP	3.907	3	.877	68	4.457	.006

ANOVA (Analysis of Variance). For each variable individually, SPSS computes a one-way analysis of variance using the final clusters as groups, as shown in the figure. The between-cluster mean square is displayed in the column labeled *Cluster,* and the within-cluster mean square is displayed in the column labeled *Error.* The ratio of these two mean squares is the usual ANOVA F statistic. Ignore the significance levels in the last column, for you should **not** use these F ratios to test significance! The clusters are formed to characterize differences.

The means of *birth_rt* across the four clusters differ the most ($F=117.339$). In comparison with the other variables, the means of *log_pop* differ little across the four clusters ($F=4.457$).

Number of Cases in each Cluster

Cluster	1	6.000
	2	25.000
	3	13.000
	4	28.000
Valid		72.000
Missing		2.000

Number of Cases in each Cluster. From the output, it is apparent that cases are not equally distributed across clusters in this case. There are relatively few cases in cluster 1, but many cases in cluster 4. If you assume that each cluster represents a *type* of country, you might say that there are more countries of the type represented by cluster 4 than there are of the type found in cluster 1.

Evaluating Clusters

In order to interpret or understand the meaning of the cluster, it is helpful to save the cluster membership and distance from cluster center for each case. The value of the cluster membership variable can be tabulated against other categorical variables in the data set, or it can be plotted against the distance measure or other continuous variables.

Here, the Crosstabs procedure is used to display a breakdown of *region2* by cluster membership (*qcl_1*, a variable saved during your previous analysis).

Count

		QCL_1				
		1	2	3	4	Total
	Europe				17	17
	Pacific/Asia	5	7		6	18
	Middle East		6	9	1	16
	Latn America	1	12	4	4	21
Total		6	25	13	28	72

% within REGION2

		QCL_1				
		1	2	3	4	Total
	Europe				100.0%	100.0%
	Pacific/Asia	27.8%	38.9%		33.3%	100.0%
	Middle East		37.5%	56.3%	6.3%	100.0%
	Latn America	4.8%	57.1%	19.0%	19.0%	100.0%
Total		8.3%	34.7%	18.1%	38.9%	100.0%

Distribution of regions by cluster. The upper panel gives the number of countries in each category for each cluster, and the lower panel gives the percentage within the given region for each cluster. This allows you to spot patterns in the way countries from different regions are classified. It appears that there are some patterns here. For example, cluster 4 is dominated by European countries, while cluster 1 consists mainly of Pacific/Asian countries (although this accounts for only about 28% of the Pacific/Asian countries in the sample).

It is also useful to plot cases based on cluster membership and distance from cluster center. This lets you identify cases that are far from their cluster centers, indicating that they are unrepresentative of the cluster to which they have been assigned.

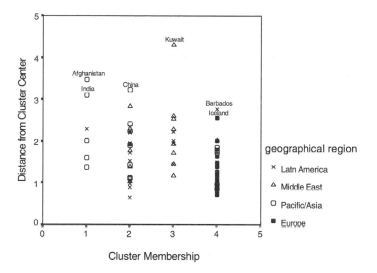

Scatterplot of cluster membership by distance from cluster center. From the figure, you can see that there are a few cases which are quite different from the rest of the cases in their clusters. For example, there are clearly dissimilarities between Kuwait and the rest of the countries in cluster 3. Additionally, you can see that cluster 4 seems to be more homogeneous (that is, cases are generally similar) than cluster 2, which is spread out over a higher range of values.

If you restrict your plot to the cases that are more or less representative of their clusters, you can get a better sense of the cases in each cluster and can start to hypothesize about what makes each cluster unique from the others. In the next figure, you plot cases where the distance from the cluster center is no greater than 2.

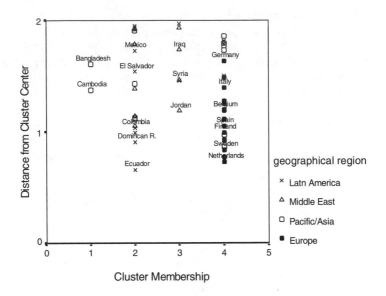

Representative cases for each cluster. From this figure, you can see again that European countries dominate cluster 4, while Latin American countries are prominent in cluster 2. In particular, Ecuador is closest to the center of cluster 2, indicating that, in some sense, it might be considered a *prototypical* country for that cluster.

It is also instructive to plot values for the variables that drive the clustering, using different markers to indicate cluster membership.

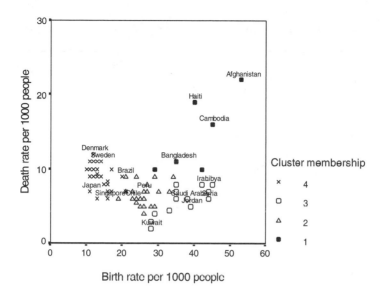

Scatterplot of cases by representative variables from variable clusters. This figure shows a plot of birth rate versus death rate for your example. These two variables were chosen because they represent the two variable clusters discovered in Example 2 and because they have sizable F values among the variables in their cluster.

You can see how countries in the same cluster tend to fall in the same region of the plot. This plot also helps to visualize homogeneity of clusters. For example, the countries from cluster 4 are in a fairly tight group in the lower left quadrant of the plot, whereas the countries from cluster 1 are spread over a relatively wide area in the upper right portion of the plot. It is also clear that Afghanistan, isolated in the upper right corner, has a rather unique profile with respect to the other countries in the sample.

16 Factor Analysis

Principal components and common factor analyses are often placed under the heading *Factor Analysis*. Although they are based on different mathematical models, they can be used on the same data, and both produce similar results. These procedures are often used in exploratory data analysis to:

- Study the correlations among a large number of interrelated quantitative variables by grouping the variables into a few factors; after grouping, the variables within each factor are more highly correlated with variables in that factor than with variables in other factors.

- Interpret each factor according to the meaning of the variables. For example, the answers to a set of six or seven questions that cluster together might measure the respondent's *satisfaction* with a product.

- Summarize many variables by a few factors. SPSS can compute a score for each factor that you can use as input variable(s) for *t* tests, regression, analysis of variance, discriminant analysis, and so on.

Thus, factor analysis helps you unravel and understand the structure of a correlation (or covariance) matrix. For example, here are 12 items from a 43-item questionnaire developed by Murray Jarvik, M.D. and cited in the 1985 *BMDP Statistical Software Manual*. The questionnaire was administered to subjects during smoking cessation treatment. Several items are queries regarding the subject's desire to smoke—for example, "After a good meal, how much do you want to have a cigarette?" Each question is scored on a scale from 1 to 5, where a low score is *good* and a high one is *bad*. The other questions relate to the psychological and physical state of the subject.

The following is a correlation matrix for 12 of the items:

	Concentr	Annoy	Smoking1	Sleepy	Smoking2	Tense	Smoking3	Alert	Irritabl	Tired	Content	Smoking4
Concentr	1.000											
Annoy	0.562	1.000										
Smoking1	0.086	0.144	1.000									
Sleepy	0.200	0.360	0.140	1.000								
Smoking2	0.579	0.119	0.785	0.211	1.000							
Tense	0.041	0.705	0.222	0.273	0.301	1.000						
Smoking3	0.802	0.060	0.810	0.126	0.816	0.120	1.000					
Alert	0.592	0.578	0.101	0.606	0.223	0.594	0.039	1.000				
Irritabl	0.595	0.796	0.189	0.337	0.221	0.725	0.108	0.605	1.000			
Tired	0.512	0.413	0.199	0.798	0.274	0.364	0.139	0.698	0.428	1.000		
Content	0.492	0.739	0.239	0.240	0.235	0.711	0.100	0.605	0.697	0.394	1.000	
Smoking4	0.228	0.122	0.775	0.277	0.813	0.214	0.845	0.201	0.156	0.271	0.171	1.000

Imagine trying to study correlations for all 43 items! By using the loadings from one default run of Factor with an orthogonal rotation, you can reorder the questions to produce the following correlation matrix:

	Smoking3	Smoking4	Smoking1	Smoking2	Annoy	Irritabl	Content	Tense	Concentr	Sleepy	Tired	Alert
Smoking3	1.00											
Smoking4	0.85	1.00										
Smoking1	0.81	0.78	1.00									
Smoking2	0.82	0.81	0.79	1.00								
Annoy	0.06	0.12	0.14	0.12	1.00							
Irritabl	0.11	0.16	0.19	0.22	0.80	1.00						
Content	0.10	0.17	0.24	0.24	0.74	0.70	1.00					
Tense	0.12	0.21	0.22	0.30	0.71	0.73	0.71	1.00				
Concentr	0.04	0.23	0.09	0.20	0.56	0.60	0.49	0.58	1.00			
Sleepy	0.13	0.28	0.14	0.21	0.36	0.34	0.24	0.27	0.46	1.00		
Tired	0.14	0.27	0.20	0.27	0.41	0.43	0.34	0.36	0.51	0.80	1.00	
Alert	0.04	0.20	0.10	0.22	0.58	0.61	0.61	0.59	0.80	0.61	0.70	1.00

Now it is easy to see that the four smoking items are more related to one another than to the other questions; and that the remaining items fall into two groups—except that *alert* and *concentr* (concentration) overlap somewhat. For each subject, SPSS can compute a score for each of the three groups (factors) of variables that is a linear combination of the variables. The score for the first factor, for example, is a measure of the *desire to smoke*. That is, for each subject, using standardized values of the original variables, SPSS computes:

$$\text{Desire to smoke} = \; 0.274 \text{ Smoking1} + 0.267 \text{ Smoking2} + 0.290 \text{ Smoking3} + 0.267 \text{ Smoking4}$$
$$- 0.034 \text{ Annoy} - 0.014 \text{ Irritabl} + 0.001 \text{ Content} + 0.009 \text{ Tense}$$
$$- 0.040 \text{ Concentr} - 0.018 \text{ Sleepy} - 0.012 \text{ Tired} - 0.048 \text{ Alert}$$

For these data, the scores for the three factors explain almost as much of the total variance as the original 12 variables. The scores can be used in further analyses along with other data collected on the subjects.

Steps in a factor analysis. There are four main steps in factor analysis. They are introduced here, but the definition of new terms are found in the discussion and examples that follow.

1) The correlation or covariance matrix is computed. If a variable has very small correlations with all the others, you may consider eliminating it in the next run. Be sure, however, to check the size of its communality and loadings.

2) The factor loadings are estimated. Here, you decide whether the method of factor extraction is principal components or one of the factor analysis methods of extraction. We recommend beginning with principal components.

3) The loadings are rotated to make the loadings more interpretable. Rotation methods make the loadings for each factor either large or small, not in-between. After seeing these results, you may want to request fewer factors than chosen by default.

4) For each case, scores can be computed for each factor and saved for use as input variables in other procedures. You can also use saved scores to identify outliers and formulate a strategy for dealing with them.

Before you undertake these steps, be sure to screen each variable individually for outliers and skewed distributions. If you find problems, you may need to transform one or more variables. Also check how many values are missing. For the variables you are using, you may want to compare descriptive statistics (means and standard deviations) for the sample that has no missing data (complete cases only) with descriptive statistics computed for each variable individually. If the sample size for cases with no values missing is considerably smaller than that for the total sample, compare listwise results with pairwise results at each step.

Principal components analysis (PCA). In Chapter 14, Discriminant Analysis, you learned that linear combinations of the variables are useful for maximizing the distance between group means in a multivariate space. Linear combinations of variables are also useful for characterizing or accounting for the variation (spread) of *each* dimension in a multivariate space. Principal components analysis does this for you: the first linear combination of variables accounts for the largest amount of variation in the sample; the second for the next largest amount of variance in a dimension independent of the first, and so on. Successive components explain smaller and smaller portions of the total variance and are independent of one another.

In each solution, there are as many components as there are original variables. Ideally, for your data, the first few components should account for a large proportion of the variance of the original variables. With the PCA solution for the smoking data above, the three factors account for 82% of the variability of the original 12 variables.

The variances of the components are commonly known as **eigenvalues** (also called **characteristic roots** or **latent roots**). The sizes of the eigenvalues describe the dispersion or shape of the cloud of data points in a multivariate space that has one axis for each variable. As an example of a three-dimensional space, imagine an American football with a pointed end placed in the corner of a box and tilted upward along a 45-degree line. It is filled with tiny flies (the data points) frozen in space (the covering is clear so you can see inside). The flies fill the tilted ball and can be located in the 3-D space by using their length, width, and height coordinates measured from the corner of the box. This three-dimensional space has three principal components and each is a linear combination of the variables *length*, *width*, and *height*:

$a_1 \cdot$ length $+ b_1 \cdot$ width $+ c_1 \cdot$ height

$a_2 \cdot$ length $+ b_2 \cdot$ width $+ c_2 \cdot$ height

$a_3 \cdot$ length $+ b_3 \cdot$ width $+ c_3 \cdot$ height

where the coefficients a_i, b_i, and c_i are called **factor loadings**.

The eigenvalue or variance for the first component might be 1.86, measuring the length of the football, while the eigenvalues for the second and third components are shorter. These components fall along the dimensions perpendicular to the length of the ball and their eigenvalues are both 0.57 (because cross-sections of the ball are round). Thus, the components are a rotation of the original axes with the first component falling along the major axis or length of the football (the 45-degree line).

What if the flies are not spread through the three dimensional space evenly, but concentrate around an elliptical plate extending the length of the football? Then the third eigenvalue is considerably smaller than the second; and, if ignored, the first two components would account for most of the total variability of the three original variables—that is, two components summarize the variation measured for three variables.

For a useful factor analysis, there should be some strong correlations among the original variables. As an extreme, suppose, for the fly data, each coordinate is measured in both inches and centimeters, making a total of six variables. Theoretically, this multivariate space has six eigenvalues. However, due to the perfect correlation between the coordinates in inches and centimeters, the last three eigenvalues would be zero.

Normality is not a necessary assumption for principal components analysis. However, skewed distributions and outliers can distort results, just as they do in multiple regression (think about how such problems distort estimates of means and standard deviations, so certainly estimates of covariances and correlations are impacted.) It is wise to screen graphically and apply symmetrizing transformations where appropriate—see Chapter 2, Example 3.

Factor analysis. While components are linear combinations of the observed variables, factors are linear combinations of *unobserved* variables. The usual factor analysis model expresses each variable as a function of factors common to several variables and a factor unique to the variable:

$$z_j = a_{j1}F_1 + a_{j2}F_2 + \ldots + a_{jm}F_m + U_j$$

where:

z_j = the *j*th standardized variable
F_i = the common factors
m = the number of factors *common* to all the variables
U_j = the factor unique to variable z_j
a_{ji} = the factor loadings

Ideally, the number of factors, *m*, will be small, and the contribution of the unique factors will also be small. The individual factor loadings, a_{ji}, for each variable should be either very large or very small so each variable is associated with a minimal number of factors. Thus, you want to explain the observed correlations using as few factors as possible. The unique factors, U's, are assumed to be uncorrelated with each other and with the common factors.

For example, *smoking1*, the first smoking question, might be

$$smoking1 = 0.864 \cdot factor1 + 0.128 \cdot factor2 + 0.023 \cdot factor3 + \varepsilon$$

where *factor1* is called *desire to smoke*, *factor2*, *emotional stress*, *factor3*, *physical condition*, and ε represents measurement error. So, the factor loadings (0.864, 0.128, and 0.023) are like standardized regression coefficients in a multiple regression model with an original variable as the dependent variable and the factors as the independent variables.

Rotation. Usually the initial factor extraction does not give interpretable factors. One of the purposes of **rotation** is to obtain factors that can be named and interpreted. That is, if you can make the large loadings larger than before and the smaller loadings smaller, then each variable is associated with a minimal number of factors. Hopefully, the variables that load strongly together on a particular factor will indicate a clear meaning with respect to the subject area at hand.

It helps to study plots of loadings for one factor against those for another. Ideally, you want to see clusters of loadings at extreme values for each factor: like what *a* and *c* are for factor 1, and *b* and *d* are for factor 2 in the left plot, and not like *e* and *f* in the middle plot.

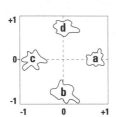 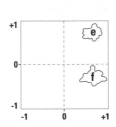 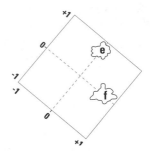

In the middle plot, the loadings in groups *e* and *f* are sizeable for *both* factors 1 and 2. However, if you lift the plot axes away from *e* and *f*, rotating them 45 degrees, and then set them down as on the right, you achieve the desired effect. Sounds easy for two factors. For three factors, imagine that the loadings are balls floating in a room and that you rotate the floor and walls so that each loading is as close to the floor or a wall as it can be. This concept generalizes to more than three dimensions as well.

If you request a rotation, SPSS will compute the rotated solution automatically. There are many criteria for achieving a *simple structure* among component loadings, although Thurstone's are most widely cited. For *p* variables and *m* components:

- Each component should have at least *m* near-zero loadings.
- Few components should have non-zero loadings on the same variable.

There are several rotation methods available in SPSS. **Varimax**, **Quartimax**, and **Equamax** are orthogonal rotations, meaning the resulting factors (or components) are uncorrelated. The **Direct Oblimin** and **Promax** rotations are oblique rotations, meaning the resulting factors are correlated with one another. For more details on the different rotation methods, see the online Help.

Practical applications. Factor analysis may be the procedure for you, if you:

- Need a few scores to stand in as parsimonious descriptors for many variables.
- Simply want to *get a handle on* relationships that otherwise might seem unmanageable in a data set with many variables.
- Want to construct a score for constructs that are not directly observable. How do you measure *love*? A patient's *attitude* about his doctor? A subject's *satisfaction* with coffee brands? How *depressed* a person is?

The last point relates to the design of instruments or questionnaires. Analysts often ask a set of questions directed at a hard-to-measure construct. To measure depression, for example, researchers might ask a dozen questions, such as: "How many days last week did you feel blue?" "Feel sad?" "Feel lonely?" "Cry?" "Talk less than usual?" "Not feel like eating?" A simplistic way of measuring depression might be the total number of days reported across all questions. Instead of a simple sum, factor analysis provides a score that weights the highly correlated responses.

Factor analysis can facilitate the design of questionnaires by helping you ferret out questions that do not work as planned. In a study about why some patients with long-term psychiatric illness stop taking their medication, researchers hypothesized that the patient's attitude about their doctor might be one aspect of compliance. They wrote seven questions asking patients to evaluate their doctor. In the pilot study of the instrument, a factor analysis showed that responses to six of the seven questions were highly correlated; but for the other question (*Do you view your doctor as an authority figure?*), many patients responded *definitely not*, regardless of their answers to the other questions. In other words, this question did not seem to be related to the other six. Thus, for each patient, the response to this question should not be included with the other items in a factor score. After some investigation, the researchers learned that the meaning of the word "authority" differed for the patients and the researchers. The patients tended to be poorly educated, many not having completed high school. In their state, a 15-year-old convicted of burglary is sent to the "Youth Authority" instead of a prison for adults.

The examples. In factor analysis, the gap between theory and practice can be large. Factor analysis, more than most statistical procedures, has its friends and foes, and these folks often argue intensely about aspects that seldom matter for a real study. In this chapter, we try to offer practical hints and encourage you to try both principal components and a common factor method—and then an orthogonal and an oblique rotation. It is important to realize that you may need to make several passes through the procedure, changing options each time, until the results give you the necessary information for your problem.

The smoking cessation example above illustrates the fine tuning of items during the process of constructing scores that measure *desire to smoke*. Different methods of extraction and rotation make little difference in the results for these highly correlated questions that fall into relatively distinct subsets.

The examples that follow do not illustrate perfect factor analyses. The problems encountered are not atypical among those found in real studies.

Example 1: Principal components with varimax rotation. When approaching a new data set, the methods of extraction and rotation described here are a good way to start. The results of this analysis can be compared with those in Cluster Analysis (Chapter 15) because the same set of variables from the *world95m* data set is used. Factor scores are saved and plotted. Countries with extreme scores are identified and their data values are listed.

Example 2: Maximum Likelihood with oblique rotation. You revisit the data from Example 1 but request different methods of extraction and rotation.

Example 3: Exploring survey responses when data are missing. The data for this example are responses to items from the 1993 General Social Survey and, in addition to quantitative variables, include binary variables and variables with ordered categories. While the total sample size is 1500 respondents, 752 people did not respond to one or more questions. Results are presented using the sample of 748 complete cases (listwise deletion of missing data) and using all available values to compute each correlation individually (pairwise deletion of missing data). The results of the two methods are compared. You also examine some graphical methods for examining factor solutions.

Example 1
Principal Components with a Varimax Rotation

Simple choices are made for this first example. You use the default method of factor extraction (principal components) and the default number of factors that equals the number of eigenvalues greater than one. Varimax rotation is requested. These options may not be optimal, but they generally are a good way to begin analysis of the data.

As the result of such a run, you may learn that the correlations among your variables are strong enough for a useful factor analysis and you may possibly want to try runs:

• Requesting fewer factors than the default number.

• Eliminating variables that do not load strongly on any factors.

• Eliminating cases identified as outliers.

The data in this example are the same subset of *world95* variables and cases used in Chapter 14 and Chapter 15. The order in which variables are selected is taken from the results of clustering variables (Example 2 in Chapter 15). Here, this determines only the order of variables in panels of variable statistics and the correlation matrix.

Table 16.1   Variables used in Factor Analysis

lifeexpf	Average female life expectancy in years
babymort	Infant mortality (deaths per 1000 live births during the first year)
literacy	Percentage of population who read
birth_rt	Birth rate per 1000 people
fertilty	Fertility: average number of children
urban	Percentage of population living in cities
log_gdp	Log (base 10) of *gdp_cap* (gross domestic product per capita)
pop_incr	Population increase (percentage for the previous year)
b_to_d	Ratio of birth rate to death rate
death_rt	Death rate per 1000 people
log_pop	Log (base 10) of population

To use the same cases as in the examples in Chapter 14 and Chapter 15, eliminate countries with codes 2 and 4 (East Europe and Africa, respectively) for the variable *region2*.

To produce the following output, use Select Cases from the Data menu to omit cases with *region2* equal 2 or equal 4 (region2 ~= 2 & region2 ~= 4). Then from the menus choose:

Analyze
  Data Reduction
    Factor...

Click *Reset* to restore dialog box defaults, and then select:

▶Variables: lifeexpf, babymort, literlty, birth_rt, fertilty, urban, log_gdp, pop_incr, b_to_d, death_rt, log_pop

Descriptives...
  Statistics
  ☑ Univariate descriptives
  Correlation Matrix
  ☑ Coefficients

Extraction...
  Display
  ☑ Scree plot

Rotation...
  Method
  ⊙ Varimax
  Display
  ☑ Loading plots

Scores...
  ☑ Save as variables

Options...
  Coefficient Display Format
  ☑Sorted by size
  ☑Suppress absolute values less than: 0.20

Descriptive Statistics

	Mean	Std. Deviation	Analysis N
Average female life expectancy	72.83	8.27	72
Infant mortality (deaths per 1000 live births)	35.13	32.22	72
People who read (%)	82.47	18.63	72
Birth rate per 1000 people	24.38	10.55	72
Fertility: average number of kids	3.21	1.59	72
People living in cities (%)	62.58	22.84	72
Log (base 10) of GDP_CAP	3.50	.61	72
Population increase (% per year)	1.70	1.16	72
Birth to death ratio	3.58	2.31	72
Death rate per 1000 people	8.04	3.17	72
Log (base 10) of Population	4.15	.69	72

Descriptive Statistics. For 72 countries, the average female life expectancy is 72.83 years; and for every 1000 babies born alive, on the average, about 35 will die during their first year of life.

Correlation Matrix

		LIFEEXPF	BABYMORT	LITERACY	BIRTH_RT	FERTILTY	URBAN	LOG_GDP	POP_INCR	B_TO_D	DEATH_RT	LOG_POP
Correlation	LIFEEXPF	1.00	-.97	.86	-.80	-.75	.68	.83	-.50	-.17	-.47	-.30
	BABYMORT	-.97	1.00	-.85	.81	.75	-.66	-.81	.50	.16	.47	.33
	LITERACY	.86	-.85	1.00	-.82	-.82	.52	.67	-.63	-.35	-.30	-.22
	BIRTH_RT	-.80	.81	-.82	1.00	.97	-.47	-.72	.83	.60	.08	.05
	FERTILTY	-.75	.75	-.82	.97	1.00	-.38	-.59	.83	.59	.11	.02
	URBAN	.68	-.66	.52	-.47	-.38	1.00	.73	-.20	-.01	-.32	-.34
	LOG_GDP	.83	-.81	.67	-.72	-.59	.73	1.00	-.49	-.27	-.15	-.35
	POP_INCR	-.50	.50	-.63	.83	.83	-.20	-.49	1.00	.88	-.31	-.06
	B_TO_D	-.17	.16	-.35	.60	.59	-.01	-.27	.88	1.00	-.60	-.20
	DEATH_RT	-.47	.47	-.30	.08	.11	-.32	-.15	-.31	-.60	1.00	.16
	LOG_POP	-.30	.33	-.22	.05	.02	-.34	-.35	-.06	-.20	.16	1.00

Correlation Matrix. These correlations are the usual Pearson correlations. In the cluster analysis of variables, SPSS joined *lifeexpf* and *babymort* first because their correlation is strongest (−0.97) among all the pairs of variables. This strong negative correlation indicates, not surprisingly, that high values of life expectancy are associated with low values of infant mortality and vice versa.

The results of this factor analysis (see the rotated component matrix on p. 331) include the first eight variables in this matrix in factor 1 and the last three variables in factor 2. Notice that, within each column, the correlations for the last three variables tend to be weaker than those displayed above them (that is, correlations among variables within factor 1 tend to be stronger than those of a factor 1 variable paired with a factor 2 variable).

The only discrepancies between these results and the results of clustering variables (Chapter 15) is that in the clustering, *pop_incr* (shown shaded) is included with *b_to_d* (their simple correlation is 0.88) and *log_pop* is not joined with any other variables until the last step. Notice that the correlations of *log_pop* with the other variables are among the weakest in this panel.

Such discrepancies between factor analysis and cluster analysis of variables can occur because of differences in how the two approaches handle relationships between items. Because cluster analysis is hierarchical, it is driven by the strength of individual correlations; in contrast, factor analysis considers the relationships between all variables simultaneously.

Communalities

	Initial	Extraction
LIFEEXPF	1.000	.953
BABYMORT	1.000	.949
LITERACY	1.000	.825
BIRTH_RT	1.000	.943
FERTILTY	1.000	.875
URBAN	1.000	.604
LOG_GDP	1.000	.738
POP_INCR	1.000	.945
B_TO_D	1.000	.925
DEATH_RT	1.000	.689
LOG_POP	1.000	.292

Communalities. For each variable, the **communality** is the proportion of the variance of that variable that can be explained by the common factors—in other words, the squared multiple correlation of the variable with the factors. Here, communalities are reported before and after the desired number of factors are extracted.

In the principal components solution, all **initial** communalities are 1. There can be as many factors (principal components) as there are variables. If so, there is no need for a unique factor in the model, and all the variance of each variable is accounted for (that is, the proportion of variance accounted for by the common factors is 1 for each variable). For the other methods of extraction, the estimate for each variable is the multiple R^2 from regressing all the other variables on that variable.

In this example, two components are extracted, so the estimates of communalities in the next column report the proportion of variance explained by these two factors. Communalities range from 0 to 1, with 0 indicating that the common factors explain none of the variance of the variable and 1 that they explain all the variance.

The communality for *log_pop* is low (0.292), so it has little relation to the two factors. In the cluster analysis of variables, *log_pop* was not joined with the other variables until the very last step.

Total Variance Explained

Initial Eigenvalues

		Total	% of Variance	Cumulative %
Component	1	6.24	56.75	56.75
	2	2.50	22.68	79.43
	3	.99	8.99	88.42
	4	.59	5.37	93.79
	5	.24	2.14	95.93
	6	.17	1.56	97.50
	7	.12	1.13	98.62
	8	.07	.63	99.25
	9	.04	.41	99.66
	10	.02	.22	99.88
	11	.01	.12	100.00

Extraction Sums of Squared Loadings

		Total	% of Variance	Cumulative %
Component	1	6.242	56.750	56.750
	2	2.495	22.685	79.435

Rotation Sums of Squared Loadings

		Total	% of Variance	Cumulative %
Component	1	6.108	55.525	55.525
	2	2.630	23.910	79.435

Total Variance Explained. These tables show statistics for each factor before and after the components are extracted. For principal components, the initial and extraction statistics are always the same. After rotation, the percentage of total variance accounted for by all factors (79.43%) does not change. However, the percentage accounted for by each factor does change.

In the column labeled *Total*, the eigenvalues for the multivariate space of the original variables are ordered by size. They are also plotted in the scree plot below. Each value is the total variance explained by a factor. (The **total variance** is the sum of the diagonal elements of the correlation matrix or, for principal components, the number of variables). The percentage of the total variance attributable to each factor is displayed in the column labeled *% of Variance*. The first factor accounts for 56.75% of the variance and the second accounts for 22.68%. Together, the first two factors account for 79.43% of the variability of the original 11 variables.

Be default, SPSS computes as many components as there are eigenvalues greater than 1. If our 11 variables were independent of one another, there would be 11 components, each with a variance of 1. One criterion for determining the number of useful factors for extraction is to exclude factors with variances less than 1 because they do no better than a single independent variable.

Often, for real data, there may be one or more eigenvalues close to 1, so you may need to request fewer factors than extracted by default. To select a cut point, look for a place where there is a relatively large interval between values. And, of course, examine the loadings for solutions with different numbers of factors to see which results provide the best interpretation of your data.

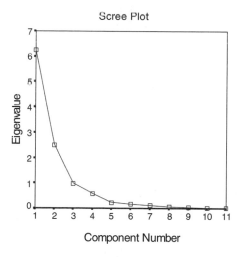

Scree Plot

Scree Plot. The eigenvalues listed in the tables on p. 328 are plotted against their order (or associated component). Use this display to identify a useful number of factors to retain by looking for large values that separate well from smaller eigenvalues. The name *scree plot* arises because *scree* is the rubble at the bottom of a cliff; so the large (retained) eigenvalues are the cliff, and the deleted ones the rubble.

Component Matrix

	Component	
	1	2
BIRTH_RT	.94	.24
LIFEEXPF	-.93	.30
BABYMORT	.93	-.30
LITERACY	-.91	
FERTILTY	.90	.27
LOG_GDP	-.84	
POP_INCR	.74	.63
URBAN	-.65	.42
B_TO_D	.46	.84
DEATH_RT	.23	-.80
LOG_POP	.24	-.48

Component Matrix. This table displays coefficients (or **loadings**) that relate the variables to the two unrotated factors (components). Unrotated loadings and orthogonally rotated loadings are the correlations of the variables with the factors. The correlation between birth rate and factor 1 is 0.94, while the correlation between birth rate and factor 2 is much smaller (0.24). Thus, you can say that birth rate is associated with factor 1. The results for *pop_incr* are not so clear, for it has relatively high loadings on both factors.

On the Options subdialog box, you requested that the loadings be sorted by size and that values less than 0.20 be replaced with blanks.

Often, the initial factor extraction does not give interpretable factors, and analysts usually do not attempt to name the factors until they are rotated. The first unrotated factor sometimes can be interpreted as a general factor. Here, it includes almost all the variables except the death rate and the ratio of the birth to death rate. The variable *log_pop* does not have a strong relation to either factor. Considering this and remembering its communality, you conclude that this variable might be a candidate for removal in later runs.

Rotated Component Matrix

	Component	
	1	2
BIRTH_RT	.97	
FERTILTY	.93	
LITERACY	-.88	.23
LIFEEXPF	-.86	.47
BABYMORT	.85	-.47
POP_INCR	.85	.48
LOG_GDP	-.79	.33
URBAN	-.56	.54
DEATH_RT		-.83
B_TO_D	.61	.74
LOG_POP		-.52

Rotated Component Matrix. The objective of rotation is to make larger loadings larger and smaller loadings smaller than their unrotated values. This is not an ideal example for illustrating this goal; we do not like the fact that the factor 2 loadings for the variables *lifeexpf, babymort, pop_incr,* and *urban* (these variables have high loadings on factor 1) are larger than 0.45 and that the factor 1 loading is 0.614 for the factor 2 variable *b_to_d*. See the plot of these loadings on p. 332.

For most studies, this panel of sorted rotated loadings is useful in naming the factors. Here, ignoring *log_pop,* all the variables except *death_rt* are strongly associated with factor 1. Thus, the economic strength of a country (*log_gdp*) is highly interrelated with literacy, birth rate, female life expectancy, and so on. Only the death rate stands apart (death rate is in the denominator of *b_to_d*).

Component Transformation Matrix

		1	2
Component	1	.982	-.190
	2	.190	.982

Component Transformation Matrix. This is the rotation matrix for transforming the loadings in the Component Matrix on p. 330 to those in the Rotated Component Matrix above.

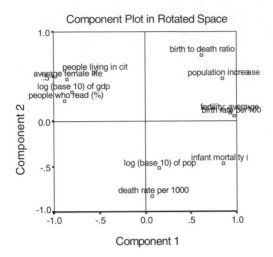

Component Plot in Rotated Space

Component Plot in Rotated Space. The points in this plot are the variables and the coordinates of each variable are its factor loadings (see the matrix on p. 331). You hope to see clusters of variables only at the ends of the lines through zero and at the intersection of these lines. Variables at the ends of the zero lines have high loadings on only that factor. Variables near the intersection (the point 0,0) are associated with neither factor.

At the left and right sides of this plot, the positive and negative loadings for factor 1 fall into two distinct clumps, and their values are close to −1 and +1, respectively. However, on the left, you would like to see the horizontal zero line pass through the center of the cluster floating above it. Notice that the correlations among the original variables within each clump are positive, but that the correlation of a variable in the left group with one on the right is negative—for example, the correlation between *literacy* and *birth_rt* is −0.82, while *literacy* with *lifeexpf* is 0.86.

Also, disappointingly, *b_to_d*, *pop_incr*, *babymort*, and *urban* do not identify clearly with a single factor.

When the solution for your data results in more than two factors, SPSS produces a 3-D plot of the first three factors. You can obtain a 2-D plot if you edit the 3-D plot in the Chart Editor, as shown in Example 3.

Using Plots of Factor Scores to Identify Outliers

For each case, SPSS can compute factor scores, one for each component or factor, and add them as variables to the right side of the Data Editor. The scores can be used in subsequent analyses as data. The scores are also useful for identifying outliers and unusual cases. For case k, the score for the jth factor is

$$\hat{F}_{jk} = \sum_{i=1}^{p} w_{ji} x_{ik}$$

where x_{ik} is the standardized value of the ith variable for case k, and w_{ji} is the factor score coefficient for the jth factor and the ith variable. The scores are linear combinations of the original variables, and the sizes of the coefficients correspond to the sizes of the loadings. Notice that the coefficients are multiplied by the *standardized* values (or z scores) of the original variables.

For principal components, exact factor scores are computed, but for the other methods of extraction, estimates are provided because no unique set of factor scores can be computed to fit the factor model.

Let's plot the factor scores for this example. First in the Data Editor, rename factor score variables *fac1_1* and *fac2_1* to *factor_1* and *factor_2*. Then from the menus choose:

Graphs
  Scatter...

Simple

Define...

▶ Y Axis: factor_2

▶ X Axis: factor_1

▶ Label Cases by: country

After the plot is first displayed, double-click it to open it for editing. From the Chart menu choose *Reference Lines* and place a reference line at 0 for both the x and y axes.

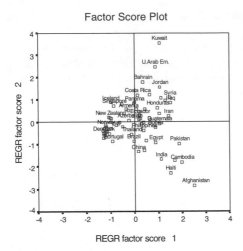

Factor Score Plot

Factor Score Plot (for countries). The axes in this plot are factor scores, and one point is plotted for each country. When the factor scores have a normal distribution, the configuration of points should look like a shotgun blast with a circular shape for factors after an orthogonal rotation and an elliptical shape for oblique factors. Here, for *factor_2*, the variability for the European countries with negative *factor_1* scores (left side) is much less than for the countries with positive *factor_1* scores.

Look for outliers near the borders of the plot. The scores are standardized with mean 0, standard deviation 1; so, depending on the size of your sample, scores outside ±2 or 2.5 or 3.0 may be considered extreme. For factor 1, Afghanistan has the most extreme score. It is around 2.5, so it is 2.5 standard deviations larger than the mean of the factor 1 scores. Kuwait, for factor 2, is even more extreme with a score close to 3.5. The score for the United Arab Emirates is also large (2.5).

You can ask SPSS to list the extreme countries (cases) with scores less than −2 and greater than +2. First, from the menus choose:

Data
  Select Cases...

⊙ If condition is satisfied: If... ABS(factor_1) >2 | ABS(factor_2) >2

Analyze
  Reports
    Case Summaries...

▸ Variables: country, factor_1, factor_2

SPSS finds four countries:

	COUNTRY	FACTOR_1	FACTOR_2
1	Afghanistan	2.51	-2.84
2	Haiti	1.51	-2.28
3	Kuwait	1.04	3.54
4	U.Arab Em.	.86	2.48

	COUNTRY	BIRTH_RT	FERTILTY	LITERACY	LIFEEXPF	BABYMORT	POP_INCR	LOG_GDP	URBAN
Mean		24.38	3.21	82.47	72.83	35.13	1.70	3.50	62.58
1	Afghanistan	53.00	6.90	29.00	44.00	168.00	2.80	2.31	18.00

To understand why a country is unusual, compare its data with the mean of the overall sample. For the variables that load strongly on factor 1, Afghanistan has higher fertility, infant mortality, and population increase than the average, while its literacy rate, female life expectancy, gross domestic product, and urban population are lower than average.

	COUNTRY	3_TO_D	DEATH_RT	LOG_POP
Mean		3.64	8.00	4.14
1	Afghanistan	2.41	22.0	4.31
29	Haiti	2.11	19.0	3.81
42	Kuwait	14.00	2.00	3.26
68	U.Arab Em.	9.33	3.00	3.45

For the factor 2 variables, Afghanistan and Haiti are at one extreme, and Kuwait and U.Arab Em. at the other. The former have high death rates and low birth-to-death ratios, while the opposite is true for the latter. You might attempt to account for this by further investigating differences between these countries in terms of other substantive variables, such as access to health care.

Example 2
Maximum-Likelihood Extraction with an Oblique Rotation

Even after rotation, some of the loadings for the Example 1 principal components solution remained sizable for more than one factor. In this example, you request the maximum-likelihood method of factor extraction, hoping to find more variables that load strongly on a single factor. You also request an oblique rotation.

You continue using the data from Example 1, eliminating countries with codes 2 and 4 for the variable *region2*.

To produce the following output, use Select Cases from the Data menu to omit cases with *region2* equal 2 or equal 4 (region2 ~= 2 & region2 ~= 4). Then, in the Factor Analysis dialog box, click *Reset* to restore the dialog box defaults and select:

▶ Variables: lifeexpf, babymort, literacy, birth_rt, fertilty, urban, log_gdp, pop_incr, b_to_d, death_rt, log_pop

Extraction...
    Method: Maximum likelihood
    Extract
    ⊙ Number of factors: 2

Rotation...
    Method
    ⊙ Direct Oblimin
    Display
    ☑ Loading plot(s)

Scores...
    ☑ Save as variables

Options...
    Coefficient Display Format
    ☑ Sorted by size
    ☑ Suppress absolute values less than 0.20

Communalities

	Initial	Extraction
LIFEEXPF	.966	.974
BABYMORT	.963	.974
LITERACY	.832	.809
BIRTH_RT	.977	.924
FERTILTY	.965	.864
URBAN	.608	.481
LOG_GDP	.868	.680
POP_INCR	.931	.963
B_TO_D	.908	.910
DEATH_RT	.804	.667
LOG_POP	.393	.173

Communalities. Communalities are reported before and after two factors are extracted. For every method of extraction except principal components, the *Initial* estimate for each variable is the multiple R^2 from regressing all the other variables on that variable. The initial communalities are used in the extraction computations.

By default, even though the method of extraction here is maximum likelihood, the principal components solution is used to determine the number of factors because of its computational simplicity. For comparison with Example 1, you request that two factors be retained.

The communality for *log_pop* is very low, so it has little to do with the two factors.

Total Variance Explained

Initial Eigenvalues

		Total	% of Variance	Cumulative %
Factor	1	6.24	56.75	56.75
	2	2.50	22.68	79.43
	3	.99	8.99	88.42
	4	.59	5.37	93.79
	5	.24	2.14	95.93
	6	.17	1.56	97.50
	7	.12	1.13	98.62
	8	.07	.63	99.25
	9	.04	.41	99.66
	10	.02	.22	99.88
	11	.01	.12	100.00

Extraction Sums of Squared Loadings

		Total	% of Variance	Cumulative %
Factor	1	6.09	55.40	55.40
	2	2.32	21.13	76.53

Rotation Sums of Squared Loadings

		Total
Factor	1	6.01
	2	2.41

Total Variance Explained. The initial and extraction percentage of variance explained by each factor differ (for principal components, they do not). Here, the first two factors account for 76.53% of the total variance, as compared to 79.43% for the first two principal components. Because the factors are correlated, the rotation sums-of-squared loadings cannot be interpreted in terms of proportion of variance.

Factor Matrix

	Factor	
	1	2
BABYMORT	.95	-.28
LIFEEXPF	-.95	.28
BIRTH_RT	.93	.26
LITERACY	-.90	
FERTILTY	.88	.29
LOG_GDP	-.81	
POP_INCR	.72	.66
URBAN	-.61	.34
B_TO_D	.42	.85
DEATH_RT	.27	.77
LOG_POP	.22	-.35

Factor Matrix. These coefficients or loadings appear similar to those from the principal components solution in the Component Matrix on p. 330. This can clearly be seen in the figures below, which show that the unrotated factor plots for the two solutions are nearly identical.

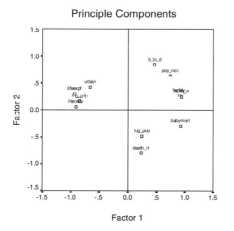

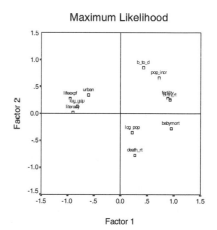

Goodness-of-fit Test

Chi-Square	df	Sig.
178.259	34	.000

Goodness-of-fit Test. This chi-square statistic is used to test the adequacy of a k-factor model and is reported when factors are extracted using generalized least squares or maximum likelihood estimation. The result here is highly significant ($p < 0.0005$), indicating that the two-factor model's predictions are not very good estimates of the observed correlations. In other words, your two factors are *not* enough to adequately represent the *world95m* data.

The goodness-of-fit statistic, especially for large sample sizes, may imply that more factors are needed than are really necessary. Some analysts feel that this statistic is too sensitive to mild departures from the assumption of multivariate normality and pay little attention to its results. Also, we caution you about trying a solution with, say, two factors and finding the results are significant; trying three factors and finding the results are still significant; and continuing to try more factors until the results are no longer significant. The true significance level for such an approach is not the same as the significance level at each step.

Pattern Matrix

	Factor	
	1	2
BABYMORT	.972	
LIFEEXPF	-.972	
LITERACY	-.896	
BIRTH_RT	.891	.360
FERTILTY	.846	.384
LOG_GDP	-.824	
URBAN	-.640	.268
B_TO_D	.325	.897
POP_INCR	.642	.742
DEATH_RT	.359	-.734
LOG_POP	.259	-.325

Pattern Matrix. Loadings after an oblique rotation are displayed in the Pattern Matrix. They may fall outside the range of –1 to +1. The correlations between the variables and factors are shown in the Structure Matrix on p. 341. This type of rotation allows some correlation among the factors (as does the promax rotation); the other methods of rotation produce factors that are independent or orthogonal of one another. See the Factor Correlation Matrix table on p. 342 for the correlation of factor 1 with factor 2.

The variable *pop_incr* loads strongly on both factors, while *log_pop* has a very weak association with both.

The **direct oblimin** rotation used here is one of the methods SPSS provides for obtaining oblique solutions. You can use a parameter called *delta* (δ) to control the extent of obliqueness. Harman (1967) recommends that δ be either 0 or negative. The factors become less oblique as δ becomes more negative. (The new **promax** rotation also gives oblique solutions and has the advantage that it can be computed more quickly for large data files.)

Structure Matrix

	Factor	
	1	2
BABYMORT	.972	
LIFEEXPF	-.972	
LITERACY	-.896	
BIRTH_RT	.891	.360
FERTILTY	.846	.384
LOG_GDP	-.824	
URBAN	-.640	.268
B_TO_D	.325	.897
POP_INCR	.642	.742
DEATH_RT	.359	-.734
LOG_POP	.250	.325

Structure Matrix. This table shows the correlations between the variables and the factors. These values are computed by multiplying the pattern matrix by the factor correlation matrix.

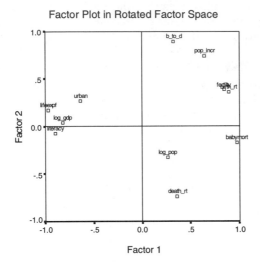

Factor Plot in Rotated Factor Space

Factor Plot in Rotated Factor Space. Compare the loadings in this plot with those for the principal components extraction with a varimax rotation in Example 1 on p. 332. The clump of four factor 1 variables on the left in this plot is closer to the horizontal line through zero than they are in the plot on p. 332. The variable *babymort*, on the right, is now closer to the line, but *fertilty* and *birth_rt* have moved further above the line. Neither solution appears ideal.

Factor Correlation Matrix

Factor		1	2
Factor	1	1.0000	.0001
	2	.0001	1.0000

Factor Correlation Matrix. The correlation between factor 1 and factor 2 is very small (0.0001), meaning that the factors are still nearly orthogonal. It appears that there is not much to be gained by allowing the factors to correlate in this example.

Example 3
Exploring Survey Responses When Data Are Missing

In this example, you explore the interrelations among many responses from a survey, having no preconceived constructs like those designed into the smoking study described in the introduction. The factor solutions for the *world95m* data in Example 1 and Example 2 are not textbook perfect (some variables do not load strongly on a single factor), but there are sizable simple correlations among the variables. Here there are considerably fewer sizable correlations, so a case could be made that the data are not well suited for a factor analysis. The spirit of this example is *exploration*—that is, you just want to see what relations exist in a new data set and plan to study them further later. This example also illustrates an approach to the problem of missing data.

Preliminaries. We began this example by selecting a set of 36 questions from the 1993 General Social Survey conducted by the National Opinion Research Center. After several preliminary screening runs, we now focus on these 21 variables:

age	Age of respondent
educ	Highest year of school completed
degree	Respondent's highest degree
padeg	Father's highest degree
madeg	Mother's highest degree
income91	Total family income
tvhours	Hours spent per day watching TV
bigband	Bigband music
blugrass	Bluegrass music
country	Country western music
blues	Blues or R & B music
musicals	Broadway musicals
classicl	Classical music
folk	Folk music
jazz	Jazz music
opera	Opera
attsprts	Did respondent attend a sports event during the last year
tvshows	How often respondent watches TV drama or sitcoms
tvnews	How often respondent watches TV news
tvpbs	How often respondent watches public TV shows
sexfreq	Frequency of sex during last year

The variables in Examples 1 and 2 are quantitative, while in this example, they include quantitative variables, ordered codes, and binary variables. The variable *age*, for example, is a quantitative variable. The values of the music variables (*country, classicl, opera*) are ordered categories. Each subject rated each of nine types of music on a 1 to 5 scale labeled *Like it very much, Like it, Mixed feelings, Dislike it, Dislike it very much*. Notice that high scores indicate disapproval. The variable *tvhours*, a quantitative variable, is the number of hours per day spent watching TV, while *tvshows*, *tvnews*, and *tvpbs* are coded on an ordered scale in the opposite direction (1 = *daily*, 2 = *several days per week*, 3 = *several days per month*, 4 = *rarely*, and 5 = *never*). The variable *attsprts* is a binary variable with 1 indicating the respondent attended a sports event during the last year and 2 that he or she did not.

Missing data. In the preliminary runs of the General Social Survey data, we found only 66 of the 1500 cases were complete for the original 36 variables; for the final set of 21 variables, there are 748 cases with no values missing.

In its Factor Analysis procedure, SPSS provides *Listwise* and *Pairwise* methods on the Options subdialog box for handling cases with values missing. **Listwise**, the default, omits any case if it has one or more values missing for the variables selected for the factor analysis. When the number of variables for a multivariate procedure is large, a relatively small percentage of missing values can diminish the sample size of complete cases markedly. With the Listwise method in this example, more than half the cases (752) are not used. With the **Pairwise** method, SPSS treats the calculation of each correlation as a separate problem, using all cases with complete data for the pair. In factor analysis, the Pairwise option can have computational problems because the resulting matrix may be singular or have eigenvalues less than 0.

Which method should you use? Formal hypothesis testing is not essential to factor analysis, so degrees of freedom are not a major concern (although a sample of 66 complete cases among 1500 is rather disconcerting). More important, however, is whether the values are missing randomly. By using the complete cases only, is a bias introduced? In other words, are the subjects who answer all the questions different from those who skip questions? Are some questions so sensitive that certain subjects avoid them ("Are you HIV positive?")?

Sadly, some of the more interesting questions are not included in this example because of the paucity of complete cases. For example, for three questions eliciting the respondent's opinion regarding 1) laws about guns, 2) marijuana, and 3) euthanasia, almost two-thirds of the 1500 subjects answered each question (sample sizes for *gunlaw*, *grass*, and *letdie* are, respectively, 984, 930, and 956); yet no subject answered all three questions. Here is a cross-tabulation of the number of values present and missing for each variable:

		gunlaw	
letdie	grass	absent	present
absent	absent	7	55
	present	34	448
present	absent	27	481
	present	448	0

The zero frequency on the bottom right corner of the table indicates that **no** cases had values present for all three variables.

In this example, we compare results from the Listwise and Pairwise methods. After several exploratory runs, we decided to request four factors. The simple correlations sorted by the results of the Listwise analysis are displayed in the following figure.

	EDUC	DEGREE	PADEG	MADEG	ATTSPRTS	AGE	INCOME91	SEXFREQ	OPERA	MUSICALS	BIGBAND	CLASSICL	FOLK	TVSHOWS	TVNEWS	TVPBS	TVHOURS	BLUES	BLUGRASS	JAZZ	
DEGREE	.88																				
PADEG	.37	.35																			
MADEG	.38	.35	.55																		Factor 1
ATTSPRTS	-.31	-.25	-.27	.22																	
AGE	-.23	-.16	-.31	-.30	.27																
INCOME91	.34	.33	.14	.10	-.26	.08															
SEXFREQ	.16	.12	.14	.12	-.14	-.45	.28														
OPERA	-.19	-.18	-.05	-.06	.04	.16	-.09	.05													
MUSICALS	-.26	-.23	-.10	-.12	.15	-.12	-.20	.09	.48												
BIGBAND	-.17	-.10	-.04	-.05	.06	.27	-.12	.14	.41	.50											Factor 2
CLASSICL	-.36	-.33	-.19	-.20	.14	-.03	-.18	.01	.58	.54	.39										
FOLK	-.15	-.13	.02	.04	.00	-.22	-.05	.06	.32	.34	.26	.36									
TVSHOWS	.13	.14	.06	.07	.05	.04	.06	.02	-.03	.04	.00	-.07	-.03								
TVNEWS	.05	.03	.09	.11	.01	-.24	-.10	.12	.14	.06	.12	.08	.10	.28							
TVPBS	-.10	-.05	.02	.06	.05	-.05	-.05	-.03	.15	.09	.10	.15	.15	.20	.32						Factor 3
TVHOURS	-.30	-.27	-.18	-.17	.17	.14	-.25	-.13	.11	.09	.05	.19	.05	-.39	-.20	-.19					
BLUES	-.16	-.13	-.09	-.14	.09	.08	-.08	-.07	.22	.23	.27	.21	.16	.06	.11	.06	.01				
BLUGRASS	.07	.09	.05	.03	-.01	-.08	.03	.00	.13	.10	.23	.08	.08	.08	.13	.13	-.03	.24			
JAZZ	-.21	-.15	-.22	-.20	.16	.14	-.14	-.12	.29	.30	.31	.29	.12	.03	.08	.04	.08	.56	.12		Factor 4
COUNTRY	-.20	-.22	-.03	-.20	-.09	-.08	.12	.00	-.03	-.05	.04	-.10	.15	.16	.12	.04	-.16	.01	.38	-.11	

Listwise correlations. There are 210 correlations among the 21 variables. They fall into four groups. The first includes *general* information about the respondents: age, education, income, attendance at sporting events, and frequency of sexual intercourse. Most of the correlations in this group appear rather small. For example, the largest correlation for *income91* is 0.34 with *educ* and the largest for *age* is –0.45 with *sexfreq*.

The correlations among the variables in the second factor (*opera* through *folk*) are all significant if you make a Bonferroni adjustment (for multiple testing) to the probabilities (see Chapter 11, Example 1). This is also true for the variables in the third factor (*tvshows*, *tvnews*, *tvpbs*, *tvhours*); three of the six correlations in the fourth group (*blues*, *blugrass*, *jazz*, *country*) would not be significant, however.

To produce output for the Listwise method, in the Factor Analysis dialog box, click *Reset* to restore dialog box defaults, and then select:

▶Variables: age, educ, degree, padeg, madeg, income91, tvhours, bigband, blugrass, country, blues, musicals, classicl, folk, jazz, opera, attsprts, tvshows, tvnews, tvpbs, sexfreq

Descriptives...
   Statistics
   ☑ Univariate descriptives

Extraction...
   Display
   ☑ Scree plot
   Extract
   ⊙ Number of factors: 4

Rotation...
   Method
   ☑ Varimax
   Display
   ☑ Loading plot(s)

Scores...
   ☑ Save as variables

Options...
   Coefficient Display Format
   ☑ Sorted by size
   ☑ Suppress absolute values less than 0.20

To produce output for the Pairwise method (using all cases complete for each pair of selected variables), use the instructions above and also choose:

Options...
   Missing Values
   ☑ Exclude cases pairwise

The output that follows includes both Listwise and Pairwise results.

Descriptive Statistics

Listwise					Pairwise				
	Mean	Std. Deviation	Analysis N			Mean	Std. Deviation	Analysis N	Missing N
AGE	45.32	15.97	748		AGE	46.23	17.42	1495	5
EDUC	13.66	2.88	748		EDUC	13.04	3.07	1496	4
DEGREE	1.65	1.19	748		DEGREE	1.41	1.18	1496	4
PADEG	1.02	1.22	748		PADEG	.93	1.19	1207	293
MADEG	.89	.94	748		MADEG	.84	.94	1352	148
INCOME91	15.33	4.97	748		INCOME91	14.68	5.46	1434	66
TVHOURS	2.53	1.77	748		TVHOURS	2.90	2.24	1489	11
BIGBAND	2.41	1.04	748		BIGBAND	2.45	1.09	1337	163
BLUGRASS	2.64	.98	748		BLUGRASS	2.66	1.02	1335	165
COUNTRY	2.32	1.08	748		COUNTRY	2.32	1.09	1468	32
BLUES	2.45	.99	748		BLUES	2.51	1.03	1434	66
MUSICALS	2.55	1.09	748		MUSICALS	2.60	1.09	1412	88
CLASSICL	2.53	1.17	748		CLASSICL	2.66	1.22	1425	75
FOLK	2.67	.98	748		FOLK	2.76	1.04	1414	86
JAZZ	2.57	1.08	748		JAZZ	2.62	1.11	1451	49
OPERA	3.44	1.12	748		OPERA	3.49	1.13	1410	90
ATTSPRTS	1.39	.49	748		ATTSPRTS	1.47	.50	1489	11
TVSHOWS	2.53	1.15	748		TVSHOWS	2.52	1.19	1490	10
TVNEWS	1.61	1.00	748		TVNEWS	1.60	1.00	1492	8
TVPBS	2.70	1.21	748		TVPBS	2.71	1.25	1486	14
SEXFREQ	2.97	1.89	748		SEXFREQ	2.88	1.98	1330	170

Descriptive Statistics (Listwise and Pairwise). The means and standard deviations in the left panel (using Listwise deletion) are computed using the same 748 cases, while all available values for each variable are used for the computations in the right panel (with Pairwise deletion). The variable *padeg* (father's highest degree) has 19.5% (293 cases out of 1500) of its values missing. Thirteen of the 21 variables have fewer than 5% of their values missing, and only four have between 10% and 20% of their values missing—yet less than half the sample has complete data for these 21 variables.

Since the cases used in the Listwise computations are a subset of those used in the Pairwise computations (and the sample sizes vary for the Pairwise computations), it is hard to identify differences between the results of the two methods. On the average, the respondents in the Listwise sample are almost a year younger (45.32 versus 46.23 years) than the larger set of cases for the Pairwise method. The subjects in the Listwise sample, on the average, have completed more years of school, their parents have more education, their income is higher, and they like various types of music more. Can the Listwise sample of 748 cases be considered to be a random subset of the 1500 cases?

Communalities

Listwise				Pairwise		
	Initial	Extraction			Initial	Extraction
AGE	1.000	.643		AGE	1.000	.680
EDUC	1.000	.714		EDUC	1.000	.713
DEGREE	1.000	.659		DEGREE	1.000	.645
PADEG	1.000	.427		PADEG	1.000	.428
MADEG	1.000	.411		MADEG	1.000	.396
INCOME91	1.000	.268		INCOME91	1.000	.322
TVHOURS	1.000	.467		TVHOURS	1.000	.502
BIGBAND	1.000	.514		BIGBAND	1.000	.511
BLUGRASS	1.000	.474		BLUGRASS	1.000	.506
COUNTRY	1.000	.366		COUNTRY	1.000	.440
BLUES	1.000	.513		BLUES	1.000	.475
MUSICALS	1.000	.549		MUSICALS	1.000	.532
CLASSICL	1.000	.598		CLASSICL	1.000	.584
FOLK	1.000	.382		FOLK	1.000	.479
JAZZ	1.000	.504		JAZZ	1.000	.448
OPERA	1.000	.535		OPERA	1.000	.496
ATTSPRTS	1.000	.308		ATTSPRTS	1.000	.292
TVSHOWS	1.000	.539		TVSHOWS	1.000	.522
TVNEWS	1.000	.517		TVNEWS	1.000	.399
TVPBS	1.000	.466		TVPBS	1.000	.421
SEXFREQ	1.000	.386		SEXFREQ	1.000	.445

Communalities (Listwise and Pairwise). Communalities were introduced on p. 327. The communalities for the variable *tvnews* differ the most between the two methods (0.517 for Listwise and 0.399 for Pairwise). For Listwise, *income91* has the lowest value (0.268); for Pairwise, *attsprts* has the smallest (0.292).

Total Variance Explained

Listwise

Initial Eigenvalues

		Total	% of Variance	Cumulative %
Component	1	4.128	19.658	19.658
	2	2.940	14.002	33.660
	3	1.742	8.297	41.957
	4	1.430	6.809	48.766
	5	1.298	6.183	54.949
	6	1.094	5.209	60.158
	7	.942	4.485	64.643
	8	.922	4.391	69.033
	9	.813	3.873	72.906
	10	.744	3.543	76.449
	11	.668	3.181	79.631
	12	.656	3.126	82.756
	13	.549	2.616	85.372
	14	.497	2.365	87.737
	15	.484	2.303	90.040
	16	.444	2.117	92.157
	17	.430	2.047	94.204
	18	.387	1.843	96.048
	19	.375	1.783	97.831
	20	.351	1.674	99.505
	21	.104	.495	100.000

Pairwise

Initial Eigenvalues

		Total	% of Variance	Cumulative %
Component	1	4.125	19.642	19.642
	2	3.024	14.402	34.043
	3	1.636	7.788	41.832
	4	1.451	6.907	48.739
	5	1.356	6.459	55.198
	6	1.068	5.087	60.285
	7	.957	4.556	64.841
	8	.860	4.094	68.935
	9	.803	3.825	72.760
	10	.726	3.458	76.217
	11	.691	3.292	79.509
	12	.598	2.847	82.356
	13	.594	2.829	85.185
	14	.515	2.454	87.639
	15	.505	2.407	90.046
	16	.454	2.164	92.210
	17	.419	1.993	94.203
	18	.393	1.871	96.074
	19	.368	1.752	97.827
	20	.337	1.605	99.432
	21	.119	.568	100.000

Extraction Sums of Squared Loadings (Listwise)

		Total	% of Variance	Cumulative %
Component	1	4.128	19.658	19.658
	2	2.940	14.002	33.660
	3	1.742	8.297	41.957
	4	1.430	6.809	48.766

Extraction Sums of Squared Loadings (Pairwise)

		Total	% of Variance	Cumulative %
Component	1	4.125	19.642	19.642
	2	3.024	14.402	34.043
	3	1.636	7.788	41.832
	4	1.451	6.907	48.739

Total Variance Explained (Listwise and Pairwise). Eigenvalues and variance explained are introduced on p. 329. Here, we request that four factors be extracted—by default, for either solution, SPSS would extract six factors. We examined the results for five factors (because a gap occurs between the size of the 5th and 6th eigenvalues in the scree plot), but prefer the results for the four-factor solution. The sixth eigenvalue is so close to 1.0 that we did not consider extracting six factors.

Since two of the final factors are music preference factors, we also checked a three-factor solution to see if all the music variables would combine together—they didn't. Instead, they spread across the three factors differently for the Listwise and Pairwise solutions.

For both methods of dealing with missing data, the four factors account for almost 49% of the variability of the original 21 variables. There is no great disparity in the eigenvalues of the individual factors between the two methods. Notice, however, that the third and fourth factors in the Listwise solution are reversed in the Pairwise solution; the *TV* factor has a smaller variance in the Pairwise solution than in that using the Listwise method.

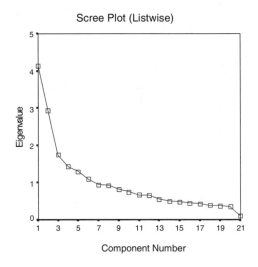

Scree Plot (Listwise)

Scree Plot (Listwise). Scree plots are introduced on p. 329. The two largest eigenvalues clearly stand apart from the others. Visually, there is no clear separation among the next three values.

Rotated Component Matrix (Listwise)

	Component			
	1	2	3	4
EDUC	.773	-.294		
DEGREE	.720	-.287		.236
PADEG	.636			
MADEG	.609			
AGE	-.557	-.463		.323
ATTSPRTS	-.538			
INCOME91	.483			
SEXFREQ	.428	.307		-.326
OPERA		.721		
MUSICALS		.712		
CLASSICL	-.310	.708		
BIGBAND		.692		
FOLK		.581		
TVSHOWS			.696	
TVNEWS		.201	.688	
TVPBS			.652	
TVHOURS	-.316		-.577	
BLUES		.291		.624
BLUGRASS		.239		.610
JAZZ	-.330	.322		.540
COUNTRY	.373			.442

Rotated Component Matrix (Listwise). See p. 330 and p. 331 for a discussion of factor loadings before and after rotation. Here, we do not display the loadings before rotation. At the end of this example, we describe how to produce scatterplots and a scatterplot matrix of the loadings.

These loadings (or coefficients) are sorted by size, and those less than 0.20 are replaced by blanks.

From this display, we decided to name factor 1 *general* because the variables with high loadings on this factor (*educ* through *sexfreq*) provide a general description of the respondents. The names for the other factors are *classical and bigband*, *TV*, and *blues and country*. The nine music preference items form two factors.

The signs of the loadings within components are arbitrary. If a component (or factor) has more negative than positive loadings, you may change minus signs to plus and plus to minus. Often, it helps to look at the simple correlations to think about the meaning of relationships. For example, *educ* and *income91* both load positively on factor 1. The simple correlation of these variables is 0.34—as education increases, income tends to increase.

The variable *attsprts*, the binary variable recording attendance at sports events, has a negative loading on the same factor and its correlation with *educ* is negative. A two-sample *t* test provides more information about the relation. In the full sample, the average number of school years completed for the group coded 1 (*yes, did attend*) is 13.96 years, and for the group coded 2 (*no, did not attend*) is 11.99 years. The difference in means of almost two years is highly significant ($t = 13.0$, *p* value < 0.0005).

The sign for *tvhours* is opposite those of the other *TV* factor variables because of how the data are coded—large values mean many hours for the former, but few hours for the latter.

Notice that *age* is associated with factors 1 and 2, and both loadings are negative. If you add a regression line to a plot of *educ* against *age*, its slope is negative—the subjects in their 20's and 30's tend to have completed more years of school than those in their 70's and 80's.

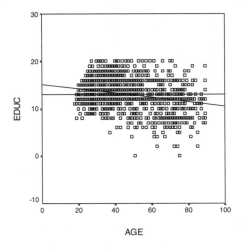

Scatterplot of education versus age. The correlation of *age* with the factor 1 variable *educ* is negative.

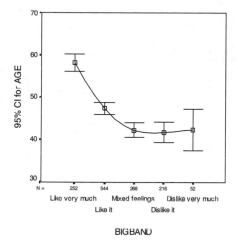

Error bar plot of age versus bigband. The correlation of *age* with the factor 2 variable *bigband* (it has ordered categories) is also negative. An error bar chart is one way to examine this relation.

Rotated Component Matrix (Pairwise)

	Component			
	1	2	3	4
EDUC	.788	-.281		
DEGREE	.715	-.306		
PADEG	.654			
MADEG	.629			
AGE	-.571	-.516	.293	
INCOME91	.520			
ATTSPRTS	-.509			
SEXFREQ	.449	.349	-.339	
MUSICALS		.700		
CLASSICL	-.320	.692		
OPERA		.691		
BIGBAND		.676	.225	
FOLK		.613	.302	
BLUES	-.200	.225	.598	
BLUGRASS	.237	.306	.596	
COUNTRY	.398		.522	
JAZZ	-.376	.227	.481	
TVSHOWS		-.221		.671
TVPBS				.606
TVHOURS	-.338			-.594
TVNEWS		.242		.576

Rotated Component Matrix (Pairwise). The pattern of loadings for the Pairwise solution agrees favorably with that on p. 351 for the Listwise solution. Notice that again *age* loads on both factors 1 and 2.

Factor 4 here compares with factor 3 on p. 351 and vice versa. The loadings for the *blues and country* factor are smaller here, and there is more spill over into factor 1 than in the Listwise solution. We tried an oblique rotation, but the improvement was marginal.

Graphical Displays for More Than Two Factors

When your principal components or factor analysis includes three or more factors, SPSS displays a 3-D plot of the loadings for the first three factors. Here is the graph of the loadings from the Listwise solution displayed in the figure on p. 351.

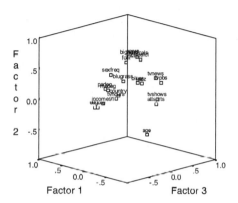

Three-dimensional loading plot (Listwise). Three-dimensional plots like this can be hard to decipher. If you like, you can edit it and request bivariate scatterplots or a matrix of scatterplots.

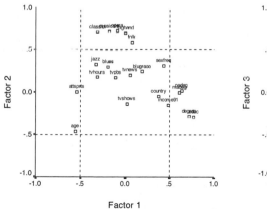
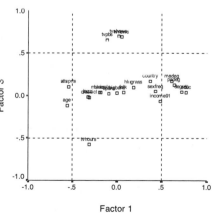

Scatterplots. Bivariate displays for each pair of factors may be easier to study than the 3-D plot. Two scatterplots of the loadings of factor 2 versus factor 1 and factor 3 versus factor 1 are shown above.

Identify the variables by scanning the table on p. 351. The grid lines placed at –0.5 and +0.5 on each axis make it easy to focus on the variables with larger loadings.

We made each plot by double-clicking the 3-D plot to enter Edit mode.

First, from the Gallery menu choose *Scatter*, then select *Simple* from the Scatterplots dialog box. Click *Replace* and select the factors you want. If you want, using the Chart menu in Edit mode, you can also rescale the axes to go from –1 to +1 and add reference lines, as we have done here.

Scatterplot matrix. Instead of constructing one scatterplot at a time, you can combine bivariate plots for all pairs of loadings into one display.

To construct a matrix of plots, start with the 3-D plot and enter Edit mode. From the Gallery menu choose *Scatter*, then select *Matrix*. Click *Replace* and select the factors you want. Set minimum and maximum limits for each axis as described for scatterplots.

How much does the choice of a method of extraction or rotation matter? One practical way of assessing possible differences is to plot scores from one method against those of another. You could plot scores comparing:

- Principal components versus maximum likelihood extraction.
- An orthogonal versus an oblique rotation.
- A Listwise versus a Pairwise solution.

We compare scores from the Listwise and Pairwise solutions in this example. For each case, at the right side of the Data Editor, the four scores from the Listwise method are followed by the four scores from the Pairwise method. We replaced the default label for each score (variable) as *F # list* or *F # pair*, where # indicates the number of the factor and *list* or *pair*, the method.

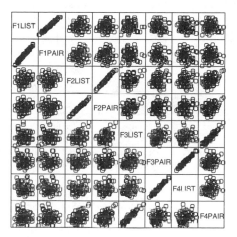

Scatterplot Matrix of Factor Scores (Listwise and Pairwise). A scatterplot matrix of all eight scores is displayed in the figure. (Because there are so many cases in this example, it may take some time to generate the scatterplot matrix.)

In this scatterplot matrix, we can compare factor scores for individual cases between the listwise and pairwise solutions. Factors are identified on the diagonal of the plot. Notice that the scatterplots above the diagonal are equivalent to the ones below, with the axes reversed.

We notice right away that certain pairs of factors correlate highly with each other; but outside these factor pairs, the correlations are very small. Upon closer examination, we see that each factor from the listwise solution correlates highly with the corresponding factor from the pairwise solution (keeping in mind that factor 3 from the listwise solution corresponds to factor 4 from the pairwise solution, and vice versa). As we would expect with an orthogonal solution, non-corresponding factors show little relationship with each other.

Visually, the agreement between the scores from the two methods appears very good. Factor 1 scores (*general*) from the listwise and pairwise solutions form the tight ellipse in the 2nd row, 1st column. Factor 2 scores from the two methods (*classical and big-band*) form the ellipse in the 4th row, 3rd column. Scores for the *TV* factor (factor 3 for listwise and 4 for pairwise) are in the 8th row, 5th column; and scores for the *blues and country music* factor in the 7th row, 6th column.

Pearson Correlation

	F1LIST	F1PAIR	F2LIST	F2PAIR	F3LIST	F3PAIR	F4LIST	F4PAIR
F1LIST	1.000	.993	.000	-.007	.000	.006	.000	-.027
F1PAIR	.993	1.000	-.050	-.050	.090	-.009	-.026	.037
F2LIST	.000	-.050	1.000	.996	.000	.036	.000	.059
F2PAIR	-.007	-.050	.996	1.000	.036	-.009	-.049	.078
F3LIST	.000	.090	.000	.036	1.000	.052	.000	.942
F3PAIR	.006	-.009	.036	-.009	.052	1.000	.984	.065
F4LIST	.000	-.026	.000	-.049	.000	.984	1.000	.061
F4PAIR	-.027	.037	.059	.078	.942	.065	.061	1.000

Pearson Correlation. To display the correlations among these factors, choose *Bivariate* under Correlate on the Statistics menu. The results are shown above. (Shading has been added to the figure for emphasis.)

For the *general* factor 1, the correlation between the scores for the listwise and pairwise methods is 0.993; for the *classical and bigband* music factor 2, the correlation is 0.996; for the *TV* factor, it is 0.942; and for the *blues and country* music factor, it is 0.984.

17 Measures of Reliability in Scale Problems

Reliability refers to the property of a measurement instrument that causes it to give similar results for similar inputs. For example, consider the produce scales at grocery stores. At a given store, each of these scales was probably manufactured at the same factory. We would hope that the factory is reliable—that every scale produced at that factory would register the same weight (within a small margin of error) for the same head of lettuce.

It is important to note that reliability is not just a property of an individual produce scale. When buying groceries, we would expect the particular scale we use to be reliable and to record approximately the same weight when the same item is weighed a second time. However, the reliability of that particular scale is only of immediate importance to the customers using it, while the grocery store is concerned about all of the scales in the store, and the manufacturer is concerned about every scale produced at the factory. The deeper issue here is the reliability of the underlying process of scale manufacture. If that process is reliable, then the manufacturer can be confident that the product is reliable. (Of course, chance error in the manufacturing process will cause a few individual scales to malfunction.)

Worries about reliability are not limited to manufacturers of produce scales but extend to makers of all types of measurement instruments—for example, instructors who write exams for their students, pollsters and marketers who create surveys to gauge public opinion, or trainers who instruct judges for diving meets, beauty contests, or gymnastics competitions. The exams, surveys, and judges' scores are all "scales" that their makers hope are reliable.

However, the produce scale manufacturer likely has a set of standard weights whose exact mass is known; therefore, precise error measurements can be made for the scales. Unfortunately, it is difficult or impossible to establish absolute standards for academic and athletic excellence or the meaning of human responses to a survey. We can only hope to establish scales that are reasonably consistent. The methods discussed in this chapter are useful for situations in which the true state of the measured objects is not known.

Consider the executives at a TV studio. They are concerned about the number of people who watch the shows they produce. Recently, they needed to decide whether to continue producing a popular show. It had run for several years, and some of the actors, directors, and screenwriters wanted more money or wanted to move on to other projects. The studio was willing to spend more money on the show but only if it would continue to be popular, so they conducted a survey of randomly selected television viewers. Realizing that there are many reasons why a person may or may not watch a particular show, seven items were constructed for this survey. The questions were of the form, *Would you watch this show next season if:?* Answers from 906 respondents can be found in the *tv-survey.sav* data file. *Yes* answers are coded with a 1; *No* answers, with a 0.

Figure 17.1   Survey items

```
1.    ANY            Any reason
2.    BORED          No other popular shows on at that time
3.    CRITICS        Critics still give the show good reviews
4.    PEERS          Other people still watch the show
5.    WRITERS        The original screenwriters stay
6.    DIRECTOR       The original directors stay
7.    CAST           The original cast stays
```

To what degree were the makers of the survey successful in constructing questions that measure a person's opinion? A reliability analysis can help answer that question.

Descriptive Statistics

To see the individual summary statistics, from the menus choose:

Analyze
  Scale
    Reliability Analysis...

▶ Items: any, bored, critics, peers, writers, director, cast

Statistics...
Descriptives for
  ☑ Item

Figure 17.2   Individual summary statistics

		Mean	Std Dev	Cases
1.	ANY	.4868	.5001	906.0
2.	BORED	.5022	.5003	906.0
3.	CRITICS	.5033	.5003	906.0
4.	PEERS	.5287	.4995	906.0
5.	WRITERS	.8146	.3889	906.0
6.	DIRECTOR	.8278	.3778	906.0
7.	CAST	.8885	.3149	906.0

The individual summary statistics seem to indicate that there are three general groups of respondents: those who will watch the show under a wide variety of circumstances, comprising about 50% of the respondents; those who will watch the show as long as it doesn't change too much, comprising about 30% of the respondents; and those who will watch the show under very strict conditions or not at all, comprising about 20% of the respondents. (For a more detailed summary, the Frequencies procedure may be appropriate.) However, this may be misleading. We cannot be sure from this simple summary that the people who will watch the show because the critics like it are the same people who will watch the show because it's what the people at the office will be talking about. We can gain insight into this situation by looking at the inter-item correlations.

To generate inter-item correlations, recall the Reliability Analysis dialog box and select:

Statistics...
Descriptives for
☐ Item (deselect)

Inter-Item
☑ Correlations

Figure 17.3   Inter-item correlations

```
                         Correlation Matrix

                 ANY        BORED       CRITICS     PEERS      WRITERS

ANY            1.0000
BORED           .8150      1.0000
CRITICS         .8128       .8256      1.0000
PEERS           .7823       .8068       .8045      1.0000
WRITERS         .4078       .4224       .4576       .4428     1.0000
DIRECTOR        .4207       .4230       .4533       .4596      .6324
CAST            .3029       .3067       .3355       .3400      .6251


                 DIRECTOR   CAST

DIRECTOR        1.0000
CAST             .6002      1.0000
```

The responses for the first four items are highly correlated, reaffirming our suspicion that people who will watch the show in one of these cases will tend to watch it in other cases. Moreover, there is a positive correlation between each of the first four and last three questions, which we expected. People who are willing to watch the show for more frivolous reasons, such as out of boredom, are likely to watch the show next year if the quality of acting, writing, and directing remains at the level that made the show popular in the first place. On the other hand, people who do not watch the show now are unlikely to watch next year just because they're bored.

Measuring Reliability

While there is a lot of information to be gleaned from looking at correlations, what we really want is a single summary statistic that tells us how reliable our survey is. There are several ways to do this, the most common of which is Cronbach's alpha.

Cronbach's Alpha

Cronbach's alpha (Cronbach, 1951) is a measure of reliability. More specifically, alpha is a lower bound for the true reliability of the survey. Mathematically, reliability is defined as the proportion of the variability in the responses to the survey that is the result of differences in the respondents. That is, answers to a reliable survey will differ because respondents have different opinions, not because the survey is confusing or has multiple interpretations. The computation of Cronbach's alpha is based on the number of items on the survey (k) and the ratio of the average inter-item covariance to the average item variance.

$$\alpha = \frac{k\overline{\text{cov}}/\overline{\text{var}}}{1 + (k-1)\overline{\text{cov}}/\overline{\text{var}}}$$

Under the assumption that the item variances are all equal, this ratio simplifies to the average inter-item correlation, and the result is known as the **Standardized item alpha** (or Spearman-Brown stepped-up reliability coefficient).

$$\alpha = \frac{k\,\overline{\text{r}}}{1 + (k-1)\,\overline{\text{r}}}$$

To compute Cronbach's alpha, recall the Reliability Analysis dialog box and select the default:

▶ Model: Alpha

Inter-Item
  ☐ Correlations (deselect)

Figure 17.4   Cronbach's and standardized item alphas

```
Reliability Coefficients     7 items

Alpha =    .8976         Standardized item alpha =    .8940
```

Notice that the *Standardized item alpha* is computed only if inter-item statistics are specified. And remember, the coefficient of 0.8976 reported for these items is an estimate of the true alpha, which in turn is a lower bound for the true reliability. For comparison, several other reliability measures are available.

Split-Half

Ideally, in order to obtain a good estimate of the reliability of a survey, we would like to administer the survey twice to the same group of people and then correlate the two sets of results. However, this is often impractical because bias may be introduced in the second set of answers or because respondents may be unwilling or unable to take the survey a second time. One solution is to compute Cronbach's alpha. Another is to split the items into two groups and then to compare these groups as if they were two separate administrations of the same survey.

To compute the split-half coefficients, recall the Reliability Analysis dialog box and select:

▶ Model: Split-half

Statistics...
Descriptives for
    ☑ Scale

Figure 17.5   Split-half coefficients

Statistics for	Mean	Variance	Std Dev	N of Variables
PART 1	2.0210	3.4239	1.8504	4
PART 2	2.5309	.8747	.9353	3
SCALE	4.5519	6.0398	2.4576	7

Reliability Coefficients

N of Cases =   906.0   N of Items = 7

Correlation between forms =   .5031   Equal-length Spearman-Brown =   .6694

Guttman Split-half =   .5766   Unequal-length Spearman-Brown =   .6728

  4 Items in part 1   3 Items in part 2

Alpha for part 1 =   .9439   Alpha for part 2 =   .8260

If the items are entered in order, the procedure splits them so that the first four are in one group and the last three are in the other. The *Correlation between forms* is simply the correlation between the sums of the items in each group. The *Equal-length Spearman-Brown* coefficient is then computed using the formula for the standardized item alpha for two items, inserting the *Correlation between forms* as the correlation. The *Guttman Split-half* coefficient is computed using the formula for Cronbach's alpha for two items, inserting the covariance between the item sums of two groups and the average of the variances of the group sums.

Notice that different splits of the items will produce different estimates of the reliability coefficient. When they are split so that each group contains items that are highly correlated within the group but not between groups (as has been done here), the split-half coefficients will be close to their lowest values. When highly correlated items are paired off and placed into separate groups, then the split-half coefficients will reach their highest values.

Guttman's Lower Bounds

To compute Guttman's lower bounds (Guttman, 1945), recall the Reliability Analysis dialog box and select:

▶ Model: Guttman

Statistics...
Descriptives for
  ☐ Scale (deselect)

Figure 17.6   Guttman's lower bounds

```
Lambda 1 =  .7693    Lambda 2 =  .9148    Lambda 3 =  .8976
Lambda 4 =  .5766    Lambda 5 =  .8943    Lambda 6 =  .9265
```

Guttman proposed six measures of reliability that all give lower bounds for the true reliability of the survey. The first is a simple estimate that is the basis for computing some of the other lower bounds. L_3 is a better estimate than L_1, in the sense that it is larger, and is equivalent to Cronbach's alpha. L_2 is better than both L_1 and L_3 but is more complex (although, because of today's computers, this is no longer a hindrance to its use). L_5 is better than L_2 when there is one item that has a high covariance with the other items, which in turn do not have high covariances with each other. Such a situation may occur on a test that has items that each pertain to one of several different fields of knowledge, plus one question that can be answered with knowledge of any of those fields. L_6 is better than L_2 when the inter-item correlations are low compared to the squared multiple correlation of each item when regressed on the remaining items. For example, consider a test that covers many different fields of knowledge and each item covers some small subset of those fields. Most item pairs will not have overlapping fields, but the fields of a single item should be well represented given all the remaining items on the test.

L_4 is, in fact, the Guttman split-half coefficient. Moreover, it is a lower bound for the true reliability for any split of the test. Therefore, Guttman suggests finding the split that maximizes L_4, comparing it to the other lower bounds, and choosing the largest.

Parallel and Strictly Parallel

Parallel and strictly parallel are models that allow us to statistically test for equal means and variances (Kristof, 1963, 1969). The strictly parallel model hypothesizes that the true item scores have the same mean and variance, while the parallel model hypothesizes that they have the same variance but not necessarily the same mean. Note that elsewhere the strictly parallel model is simply known as the parallel model, and the parallel model is not often discussed.

To compute the Parallel model, recall the Reliability Analysis dialog box and select:

▶ Model: Parallel

Figure 17.7   Parallel model

```
Chi-square =       1968.2809       Degrees of Freedom =        26
Log of determinant of unconstrained matrix =      -16.884948
Log of determinant of constrained matrix    =      -14.703707
Probability =    .0000


      Parameter Estimates

Estimated common variance =             .1990
           Error variance =             .0884
            True variance =             .1106
Estimated common inter-item correlation =       .5559

Estimated reliability of scale   =    .8976
Unbiased estimate of reliability =    .8978
```

Probability is a measure of how well the model's hypothesis is justified by the data (more specifically, it is a *p* **value**). A value greater than 0.05 indicates that there is no statistically evident reason to reject that hypothesis. The *Probability* for the parallel model is smaller than 0.0001, which is far less than the cutoff of 0.05; therefore, we must reject the hypothesis of the parallel model. Notice that the reliability estimate for the parallel model is equivalent to Cronbach's alpha (the estimate for the strictly parallel model is also based on Cronbach's alpha but is penalized for differences in the item means).

Because the parallel model has been rejected, we know that the strictly parallel model will be rejected because the models are nested; that is, the assumptions of the parallel model are a subset of the assumptions of the strictly parallel model. Few data sets will actually satisfy the requirements of the parallel and strictly parallel models, but these models are still worth considering because they provide variance estimates unavailable in the previous models.

Intraclass Correlation Coefficients

Another set of models for measuring reliability, developed in the context of inter-rater agreement, involves constructing ANOVA-type models for the observations. For example, consider the International Olympic Committee (IOC), which must train judges for gymnastics competitions. Let's say they've asked seven trained judges to score 300 performances. These data can be found in the *judges.sav* file.

To open the data file and display the item summaries, from the menus choose:

Analyze
  Scale
    Reliability Analysis...

▶ Items: judge1, judge2, judge3, judge4, judge5, judge6, judge7

☑ List item labels

Statistics...
Descriptives for
  ☑ Item

Figure 17.8   Judge origins

```
1.     JUDGE1          Italy
2.     JUDGE2          South Korea
3.     JUDGE3          Romania
4.     JUDGE4          France
5.     JUDGE5          China
6.     JUDGE6          United States
7.     JUDGE7          Russia
```

Figure 17.9   Individual summary statistics

		Mean	Std Dev	Cases
1.	JUDGE1	8.4960	.8674	300.0
2.	JUDGE2	8.9183	.8199	300.0
3.	JUDGE3	8.0853	.8173	300.0
4.	JUDGE4	8.9703	.6773	300.0
5.	JUDGE5	8.0380	.6736	300.0
6.	JUDGE6	8.8763	.9593	300.0
7.	JUDGE7	8.1813	.9789	300.0

Simply looking at summary statistics for the individual judges reveals interesting information about the judges. The low mean scores of the Romanian, Chinese, and Russian judges indicate that they tend to score more harshly than the others; the high mean scores of the South Korean, French, and American judges show that they are more generous; and the Italian judge's mean score shows her to be middle-of-the-road. Moreover, the low standard deviations for the French and Chinese judges' scores mean that they mark deviations in performance quality on a finer scale than the others, while the high standard deviations for the American and Russian show that they make free use of the range of scores. A blunder or exceptional leap that may cause a change of 0.2 or 0.3 points in the French judge's score will cause a change of 0.3 or 0.4 points in the American judge's score.

However, while the judges seem to be quite different in their methods of scoring, the individual summaries don't give the whole story. It is entirely possible that although judges 4 and 5 give quite different scores for the same performances, their pattern of scoring is quite similar. That is, good performances receive higher scores than average performances, and average performances receive higher scores than poor performances; however, the two judges differ on the precise score that should be assigned to a particular performance. We can test for this possibility using the **intraclass correlation coefficient or ICC** (McGraw and Wong, 1996). It is an ANOVA-type model in which the judges' scores are responses. Choosing an appropriate model may take some thought. First, we must consider the sources of variation. One source is the performances, which we can suppose are a random sample from a large pool of performances. Another source is the judges, who we can suppose are a random sample from a large pool of trained judges. Thus, we should use a two-way random effects model. If this set of judges is unique in some way and cannot be considered part of a larger pool of judges, then we should use a two-way mixed effects model. If we did not know which scores were given by which judge, then we would have to use a one-way random effects model.

The possibility we are considering simply supposes that the judges have similar patterns of scores, so we will check for consistency rather than absolute agreement. If IOC regulations are stricter and if identical (rather than similar) patterns of scores are necessary for successful training, then we would look at the two-way random model with absolute agreement.

To generate the intraclass correlation coefficient, recall the Reliability Analysis dialog box and select:

☐ List item labels (deselect)

Statistics...
Descriptives for
   ☐ Item (deselect)

☑ Intraclass correlation coefficient
   ▸ Model: Two-Way Random
   ▸ Type: Consistency
   ▸ Confidence interval: 95%
   ▸ Test value: 0

Figure 17.10   ICC for two-way random model

```
                    Intraclass Correlation Coefficient

Two-Way Random Effect Model (Consistency Definition):
People and Measure Effect Random
 Single Measure Intraclass Correlation =    .8816*
     95.00% C.I.:              Lower =    .8625        Upper =    .8993
 F = 53.1110    DF = (   299, 1794.0)   Sig. = .0000  (Test Value = .0000 )
Average Measure Intraclass Correlation =    .9812
     95.00% C.I.:              Lower =    .9777        Upper =    .9843
 F = 53.1110    DF = (   299, 1794.0)   Sig. = .0000  (Test Value = .0000 )
*: Notice that the same estimator is used whether the interaction effect
   is present or not.
```

Here, we see that the average (or sum) of the scores of the seven IOC-trained judges are highly reliable (interval of 0.9777 to 0.9843 with 95% confidence), suggesting that despite their apparent differences in scoring, the process was successful in training the judges to separate different levels of performance. The *Single Measure Intraclass Correlation* is the reliability we would get if we used just one judge. In general, it will be lower than the reliability we would expect from using the average or sum of several raters.

Notice that the reliability estimates produced under the mixed and random ICC models are numerically identical. The difference lies in the interpretation. The results of an analysis using the mixed effects model cannot be generalized to other raters. Also, under the mixed model for the *Average Measure Intraclass Correlation*, we must assume that no rater-performance interaction exists; that is, judges do not give comparatively higher scores to performances by their own countrymen, and they do not give comparatively lower scores to performances because the gymnast is short or tall or has dark hair or for any other reason that has nothing to do with the performance.

While reliability is defined in terms of proportions of variances, it is possible to get negative reliability estimates when the samples are very badly correlated. In such cases, the scale is probably unsuitable for its intended purpose. Negative estimates will also result from reversely coded items, as would happen if one judge scored so that 0.0 were the highest score and 10.0 were the lowest score. It happens more often than you might think!

For more information on all aspects of reliability analysis, see the bibliography.

18 OLAP Cubes

One of the most powerful tools in your data mining arsenal is the OLAP cube. An **OLAP (online analytical processing) cube** is simply a table of results summarized across several fields, or dimensions, which can be manipulated or rearranged interactively. For example, you may have sales figures summarized by geographic region, product type, customer type, month, and sales indicator (units ordered, revenue, profit, and so on). In an OLAP cube, each of these fields becomes a **dimension** for the table, defining how the numbers are broken down.

The power of OLAP cubes lies in the following characteristics:

Ease of use. You don't need specialized training to read a table of numbers. This makes OLAP cubes ideal for disseminating results to people who need information but are not statisticians or power users.

Insight. The right table can give penetrating insight into what's going on in your business process. The ability to "slice and dice" OLAP cubes allows you to gain different perspectives on the patterns you see, and the ability to "drill down" allows you to examine patterns in more detail.

Flexibility. The basic structure of the table is very general, and you can put whatever you want in the cells of the table. You can use counts or percentages, sums and averages, other summary statistics, or any combination of these to fill your table. This gives you the power to identify which aspects of the data are most important for the question at hand.

Active OLAP cubes make it easy to explore your data and to gain penetrating insights into that data. With SPSS pivot table technology and the SPSS Smart Viewer, you can distribute the tables you generate to a wide audience. You can embed interesting views into tables, using bookmarks to help others to quickly see what you've discovered. Formatting options allow you to customize your tables to achieve the desired look and to increase usability.

This chapter provides examples that explore the advantages of OLAP cubes over static tables or reports. These examples use the *sales.sav* data file.

To create and expand an OLAP cube, from the menus choose:

Analyze
　Reports
　　OLAP Cubes...

Summary Variable(s): revenue
Grouping Variable(s): customer, support, industry, region

Statistics...
　　Cell Statistics: Sum, Number of Cases, Mean, Standard Deviation, Percent of Total
　　N, Percent of Total Sum, Percent of N in (support), Range, Variance, Minimum,
　　Maximum

 When the output appears, double-click the OLAP cube. Then, from the menus choose:

Pivot
　Pivoting Trays

Click and drag *Statistics* from *Column* to *Layer*.
Click and drag *Variables* from *Row* to *Layer*.
Click and drag *Territory* (*region*) from *Layer* to *Column*.
Click and drag *Industry* (*industry*) from *Layer* to *Row*.
Click and drag *Customer Status* (*customer*) from *Layer* to *Row*.
Click and drag *Time on Hold* (*support*) from *Layer* to *Row*.

Select *Sum* from the *Statistics* drop-down list in the OLAP cube.

For more information on the manipulation of these tables, see "Interacting with OLAP Cubes" on p. 384.

Figure 18.1   An expanded OLAP cube

OLAP Cubes

Sum
Revenue

Industry	Customer Status	Time on Hold	Territory				
			North	South	East	West	Total
Government	Regular customer	< 1 Minute	$28,287	$43,863	$19,078	$35,652	$126,880
		1-2 Minutes	$27,510	$39,471	$45,000	$44,932	$156,913
		2-4 Minutes	$38,580	$17,616	$28,393	$36,642	$121,232
		> 4 Minutes	$52,147	$51,279	$37,311	$46,317	$187,054
		Total	$146,523	$152,229	$129,783	$163,543	$592,078
	Preferred customer	< 1 Minute	$47,003	$35,631	$22,316	$37,096	$142,046
		1-2 Minutes	$28,522	$28,947	$50,579	$21,205	$129,253
		2-4 Minutes	$24,266	$32,238	$29,126	$24,536	$110,166
		> 4 Minutes	$75,839	$44,334	$90,631	$68,294	$279,098
		Total	$175,629	$141,150	$192,652	$151,131	$660,563
	Total	< 1 Minute	$75,290	$79,494	$41,395	$72,748	$268,926
		1-2 Minutes	$56,031	$68,418	$95,579	$66,137	$286,166
		2-4 Minutes	$60,846	$49,854	$57,520	$61,178	$231,398
		> 4 Minutes	$127,985	$95,613	$127,942	$114,611	$466,151
		Total	$322,152	$293,379	$322,436	$314,674	$1252641
Commercial	Regular customer	< 1 Minute	$20,618	$17,477	$32,264	$36,299	$100,059
		1-2 Minutes	$42,268	$37,366	$40,308	$46,078	$166,019
		2-4 Minutes	$31,263	$21,667	$14,554	$40,640	$108,125
		> 4 Minutes	$18,978	$57,449	$44,659	$39,616	$160,701
		Total	$113,129	$133,958	$131,705	$162,633	$541,505
	Preferred customer	< 1 Minute	$40,923	$39,124	$52,016	$46,354	$178,317
		1-2 Minutes	$55,089	$63,434	$43,607	$47,896	$210,026
		2-4 Minutes	$38,779	$34,024	$50,000	$39,304	$162,108
		> 4 Minutes	$55,382	$36,953	$51,684	$44,330	$188,349
		Total	$190,074	$173,534	$197,307	$177,885	$738,800
	Total	< 1 Minute	$61,442	$56,600	$84,280	$82,653	$284,975
		1-2 Minutes	$97,357	$100,800	$83,915	$93,974	$376,046
		2-4 Minutes	$70,044	$55,691	$64,554	$79,944	$270,233
		> 4 Minutes	$74,360	$94,402	$96,343	$83,946	$349,051
		Total	$363,202	$307,493	$329,092	$340,518	$1280304
Academic	Regular customer	< 1 Minute	$20,671	$18,342	$26,414	$47,000	$112,427
		1-2 Minutes	$29,703	$25,897	$20,116	$15,396	$91,112
		2-4 Minutes	$18,834	$28,308	$28,731	$53,206	$129,185
		> 4 Minutes	$55,074	$38,438	$40,975	$39,832	$174,319
		Total	$124,282	$111,072	$116,236	$155,434	$507,024
	Preferred customer	< 1 Minute	$36,352	$32,860	$36,488	$56,776	$162,478
		1-2 Minutes	$55,582	$42,626	$35,705	$49,629	$183,542
		2-4 Minutes	$24,967	$24,497	$38,879	$34,605	$122,948
		> 4 Minutes	$61,654	$50,156	$61,887	$62,034	$235,732
		Total	$178,556	$150,140	$172,959	$203,045	$704,700
	Total	< 1 Minute	$57,023	$51,202	$62,902	$103,777	$274,905
		1-2 Minutes	$85,284	$68,523	$55,821	$65,026	$274,654
		2-4 Minutes	$43,802	$52,892	$67,609	$87,810	$252,113
		> 4 Minutes	$116,728	$88,594	$102,862	$101,867	$410,052
		Total	$302,837	$261,212	$289,195	$358,479	$1211724
Total	Regular customer	< 1 Minute	$69,576	$79,681	$77,757	$110,951	$345,965
		1-2 Minutes	$99,480	$102,734	$105,425	$106,406	$414,045
		2-4 Minutes	$88,679	$67,678	$71,678	$130,488	$358,523
		> 4 Minutes	$126,199	$147,166	$122,946	$125,765	$522,074
		Total	$383,933	$397,259	$377,804	$481,609	$1640607
	Preferred customer	< 1 Minute	$124,179	$107,616	$110,820	$140,226	$482,841
		1-2 Minutes	$139,192	$135,007	$129,891	$118,731	$522,821
		2-4 Minutes	$88,012	$90,759	$118,005	$98,445	$395,222
		> 4 Minutes	$192,875	$131,443	$204,202	$174,659	$703,179
		Total	$544,258	$464,825	$562,918	$532,061	$2104063
	Total	< 1 Minute	$190,755	$187,297	$188,577	$259,178	$828,806
		1-2 Minutes	$238,672	$237,741	$235,315	$225,137	$936,866
		2-4 Minutes	$176,691	$158,437	$189,683	$228,933	$753,744
		> 4 Minutes	$319,074	$278,609	$327,147	$300,423	$1225254
		Total	$928,192	$862,084	$940,723	$1013671	$3744608

Types of Measures in a Table

The body of a traditional static table (the values displayed in the cells of the table) has relatively standard types of measures: counts, percentages, sums, and averages. These numbers often reveal important and interesting information. Other summary measures can be added to expand the information in a static table, but this is done at the cost of making it large and unwieldy.

Using OLAP cubes, you will be able to quickly view various summary statistics to gain important insights that are not obvious in traditional tables.

Counts and Percentages

Tables based on counts and percentages show you how units defined for the specific situation (they may be customers, products, accounts, and so forth) are distributed across groups of interest. For example, you may want to look at the pattern of waiting times for different customer groups and industries. Counts give absolute numbers in each subgroup, while percentages describe the distribution of cases within certain subgroups. Counts are most useful when you want to compare actual sizes of groups. Percentages are better when you want to compare patterns of cases across groups.

To display an OLAP cube with counts and percentages, double-click the previously created OLAP cube.

Click and drag *Territory* from *Column* to *Layer*.
Click and drag *Time on Hold* from *Row* to *Column*.

Ctrl-Alt-click the *Total* column heading.
Right-click the *Total* column heading.
Choose *Hide Category.*

Alternatively, select *N* or *% of N in Time on Hold* from the *Statistics* drop-down list to view the tables shown in Figure 18.2.

Figure 18.2   OLAP cubes with counts and percentages

OLAP Cubes

Territory: Total

N

Revenue

Industry	Customer Status	Time on Hold			
		< 1 Minute	1-2 Minutes	2-4 Minutes	> 4 Minutes
Government	Regular customer	43	60	45	72
	Preferred customer	45	51	50	130
	Total	88	111	95	202
Commercial	Regular customer	39	62	47	70
	Preferred customer	59	77	66	96
	Total	98	139	113	166
Academic	Regular customer	40	36	48	73
	Preferred customer	53	65	49	112
	Total	93	101	97	185
Total	Regular customer	122	158	140	215
	Preferred customer	157	193	165	338
	Total	279	351	305	553

OLAP Cubes

Territory: Total

% of N in Time on Hold

Revenue

Industry	Customer Status	Time on Hold			
		< 1 Minute	1-2 Minutes	2-4 Minutes	> 4 Minutes
Government	Regular customer	19.5%	27.3%	20.5%	32.7%
	Preferred customer	16.3%	18.5%	18.1%	47.1%
	Total	17.7%	22.4%	19.2%	40.7%
Commercial	Regular customer	17.9%	28.4%	21.6%	32.1%
	Preferred customer	19.8%	25.8%	22.1%	32.2%
	Total	19.0%	26.9%	21.9%	32.2%
Academic	Regular customer	20.3%	18.3%	24.4%	37.1%
	Preferred customer	19.0%	23.3%	17.6%	40.1%
	Total	19.5%	21.2%	20.4%	38.9%
Total	Regular customer	19.2%	24.9%	22.0%	33.9%
	Preferred customer	18.4%	22.6%	19.3%	39.6%
	Total	18.8%	23.6%	20.5%	37.2%

Look at the tables in Figure 18.2. The first table shows counts, and the second table shows percentages. The first table shows that more preferred commercial customers were on hold for less than one minute (59 customers) than any other group. On the other hand, *patterns* within customer groups are easier to see in the second table because everything is rescaled to 0–100%. For example, within the government group, preferred customers were more likely to spend longer on hold than regular customers. This might indicate the need for a special "preferred customer hotline" to expedite support calls for preferred customers.

Sums and Averages

In many cases, you need to know more than just the number of items in a certain category. You need a summary of some quantitative variable. The most commonly used summaries are the sum and the average. The **sum** is simply the total value across all cases in a particular subgroup. The **average** (also known as the **mean**) is the sum divided by the number of cases in the subgroup. It is the value you would expect for a new case if the only thing you knew was that the case fell into the given subgroup. For example, if the average revenue for regular government customers is $2,691.26, then for any new regular government customer, in the absence of other information, your best guess about what their revenue will be is $2,691.26.

To display an OLAP cube with means and sums, double-click the previously created OLAP cube.

 From the menus choose:

View
  Show All

Click and drag *Time on Hold* from *Column* to *Layer*.
Click and drag *Statistics* from *Layer* to *Column*.

Ctrl-Alt-click the *N* column heading.
Right-click the *N* column heading.
Choose *Hide Category*.

Repeat for *Percent of N in Time on Hold, Range, Variance, Minimum, Maximum*.

Figure 18.3   Revenue statistics by industry and customer status

OLAP Cubes

Time on Hold: Total

Territory: Total

Revenue

Industry	Customer Status	Sum	Mean	Std Deviation	% of Total Sum	% of Total N
Government	Regular customer	$592,078	$2,691.26	$877.32	15.8%	14.8%
	Preferred customer	$660,563	$2,393.34	$1,030.45	17.6%	18.5%
	Total	$1252641	$2,525.49	$975.90	33.5%	33.3%
Commercial	Regular customer	$541,505	$2,483.97	$979.78	14.5%	14.7%
	Preferred customer	$738,800	$2,479.19	$977.16	19.7%	20.0%
	Total	$1280304	$2,481.21	$977.32	34.2%	34.7%
Academic	Regular customer	$507,024	$2,573.73	$978.55	13.5%	13.2%
	Preferred customer	$704,700	$2,525.81	$1,070.50	18.8%	18.8%
	Total	$1211724	$2,545.64	$1,032.65	32.4%	32.0%
Total	Regular customer	$1640607	$2,583.63	$947.59	43.8%	42.7%
	Preferred customer	$2104063	$2,400.00	$1,025.88	56.2%	57.3%
	Total	$3744669	$2,516.58	$994.59	100.0%	100.0%

Remember that sums and averages, although related, measure fundamentally different things. Sums are used when you want to know the actual value of the variable *across* cases; averages are used when you want to know the value for the *typical* case. Figure 18.3 shows the difference nicely. The group with the highest *overall* revenue (measured by the sum) is preferred commercial customers, with a total of $738,800. In contrast, the group with the highest *average* revenue is regular government customers, with a mean of $2,691.26. While each regular government customer tends to spend more than each preferred commercial customer, there are more preferred commercial customers than there are regular government customers, so as a group they generate more revenue.

Measures of Variability

Counts, percentages, sums, and averages all convey important information about your data; however, there are some important aspects of the data that are difficult or impossible to see with these statistics. One important characteristic of any field is the **variability** in the values. In other words, it's just as important to know how much values vary from record to record as it is to know the total sum or the average value. There are several ways to measure variability:

Range. This is simply the highest value minus the lowest value. It indicates how big the range of values that appear in your data is.

Variance. This is a statistic that summarizes the variability in the values. It is based on all of the values in the data rather than on just the most extreme values. The variance gives higher weight to values that are farther from the mean.

Standard deviation. This statistic is simply the square root of the variance. It is a similar index based on all of the values, but it is measured in the same units as the original field.

Minimum and maximum values. By examining the smallest and largest values explicitly, you can see what the most extreme values are. Often, extreme values represent interesting cases that warrant further study.

Sometimes these different approaches to measuring variability lead to different conclusions because they measure different aspects of variability.

To display an OLAP cube with different measures of variability, double-click the previously created OLAP cube.

 Click and drag *Time on Hold* from *Layer* to *Row*.
Click and drag *Industry* from *Row* to *Layer*.
Click and drag *Customer Status* from *Row* to *Layer*.

Ctrl-Alt-click the *N* column heading.
Right-click the *N* column heading.
Choose *Hide Category.*

Repeat for *Sum, Percent of N in Time on Hold, Percent of Total N, Percent of Total Sum.*

Figure 18.4   OLAP cube of sales to preferred government customers in the Northern region by time on hold

OLAP Cubes

Customer Status: Preferred customer

Territory: North

Industry: Government

Revenue

| Time on Hold | Statistics | | | | | |
	Mean	Std. Deviation	Range	Variance	Minimum	Maximum
< 1 Minute	$3,133.53	$862.79	$2,918	744398.9	$1,458	$4,376
1-2 Minutes	$2,193.98	$1,188.68	$4,183	1412957	$514	$4,697
2-4 Minutes	$2,022.16	$1,142.84	$3,994	1306079	$482	$4,476
> 4 Minutes	$2,049.70	$792.81	$3,116	628549.0	$282	$3,398
Total	$2,280.90	$1,014.08	$4,415	1028365	$282	$4,697

For example, Figure 18.4 shows variability statistics for the sales data for preferred government customers in the Northern sales territory broken down by time on hold. Notice that the group with the smallest range is the < *1 Minute* group, but the group with the smallest standard deviation is the > *4 Minutes* group. This apparent discrepancy results because the range considers only two values, the minimum and the maximum, whereas the standard deviation considers the distance of every value from the mean value.

Figure 18.5   Two hypothetical distributions with equal ranges but different standard deviations

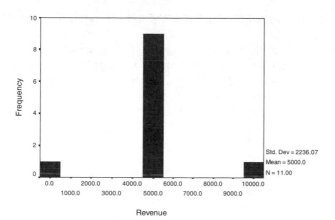

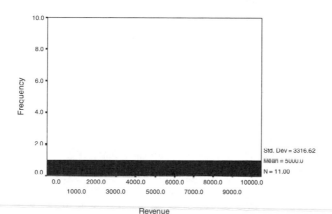

To help clarify what this means, look at Figure 18.5. Here, you see two hypothetical distributions of field values. Both distributions have the same minimum and maximum values, and hence the same range of values. However, the first distribution has all of the other points piled up in the center, whereas the second distribution has the other points evenly spread out between the extreme values. The standard deviation, by taking into account *all* values, reveals the difference in the two distributions.

Getting the Most from OLAP Cubes

Selecting summary statistics for an OLAP cube and generating the table are only the first steps to knowledge discovery. You must also be able to examine, manipulate, and distribute the table to make the best use of the data. The big advantage of OLAP cubes over traditional static reports is that you can interact with them to arrange the data so that you see the pattern you're interested in. The main factors that determine a table's usefulness are structure, contents, and format.

Structure

The **structure** of the table refers to how the dimensions "slice and dice" the data. OLAP cubes can slice data in rows, columns, and layers. Rows and columns should be familiar to anyone who has used a traditional table. **Layers** represent an additional way to slice data. Imagine that your table is a book—the rows represent lines on a page, the columns represent words, and the layers represent separate pages.

To generate the following tables:

 Double-click the previously created OLAP cube. Then, from the menus choose:

View
  Show All

Click and drag *Time on Hold* from *Row* to *Column*.
Click and drag *Statistics* from *Column* to *Layer*.
Click and drag *Territory* from *Layer* to *Row*.

Alternatively, select *Government, Commercial,* and *Academic* from the *Industry* drop-down list to display the tables shown in Figure 18.6.

Figure 18.6   An OLAP cube with layers shown separately

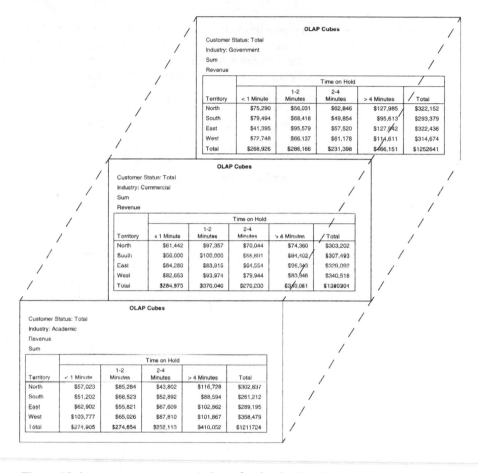

Figure 18.6 presents a conceptual view of a simple OLAP cube. In this table, rows represent *region*, columns represent *time on hold*, and layers represent *industry*. (Each value for the layer dimension is shown as a separate table in the figure; however, in the actual OLAP cube, the layers are all part of the same table.)

A dimension can define rows, columns, or layers in a table. Dimensions can also be nested, as shown in Figure 18.3. In that table, the *Customer Status* dimension is nested within the *Industry* dimension to define rows of the table. This kind of nesting allows you to examine data in three, four, or more dimensions without resorting to layers. Unfortunately, nesting multiple dimensions quickly leads to large, unwieldy tables. In such cases, an interactive table with layers is often clearer than a huge table without layers. With OLAP cubes, you can go back and forth between nested and layered dimensions very easily.

Contents

The **contents** of the table are at the heart of its value. You need to be sure that you've included all of the relevant fields as dimensions and that you've asked for the appropriate statistics to answer the question at hand. However, sometimes the ability to alter the contents after the table is constructed can be very useful as well.

To display the following OLAP cube, double-click the previously created OLAP cube.

Click and drag *Customer Status* from *Layer* to *Column*, above *Time on Hold*.
Click and drag *Territory* from *Layer* to *Row*.
Click and drag *Industry* from *Layer* to *Row*.

Figure 18.7   OLAP cube with extraneous information

OLAP Cubes

Sum

Revenue

Territory	Industry	Regular customer					Preferred customer					Total				
		Time on Hold					Time on Hold					Time on Hold				
		< 1 Minute	1-2 Minutes	2-4 Minutes	> 4 Minutes	Total	< 1 Minute	1-2 Minutes	2-4 Minutes	> 4 Minutes	Total	< 1 Minute	1-2 Minutes	2-4 Minutes	> 4 Minutes	Total
North	Government	$28,287	$27,510	$38,580	$52,147	$146,523	$47,003	$28,522	$24,266	$75,839	$175,629	$75,290	$56,031	$62,846	$127,985	$322,152
	Commercial	$20,618	$42,268	$31,265	$18,978	$113,129	$40,823	$55,089	$38,779	$55,382	$190,074	$61,442	$97,357	$70,044	$74,360	$303,202
	Academic	$20,671	$29,703	$18,834	$55,074	$124,282	$36,352	$55,582	$24,967	$61,654	$178,556	$57,023	$85,284	$43,802	$116,728	$302,837
	Total	$69,576	$99,480	$88,679	$126,199	$383,933	$124,179	$139,192	$88,012	$192,875	$544,258	$193,755	$238,672	$176,691	$319,074	$928,192
South	Government	$43,863	$39,471	$17,616	$51,279	$152,229	$35,631	$28,947	$32,238	$44,334	$141,150	$79,494	$68,418	$49,854	$95,613	$293,379
	Commercial	$17,477	$37,366	$21,667	$57,449	$133,958	$39,124	$63,434	$34,024	$36,953	$173,534	$56,600	$100,800	$55,691	$94,402	$307,493
	Academic	$18,342	$25,897	$28,396	$38,438	$111,072	$32,860	$42,626	$24,497	$50,156	$150,140	$51,202	$68,523	$52,892	$88,594	$261,212
	Total	$79,681	$102,734	$67,678	$147,166	$397,259	$107,616	$135,007	$90,759	$131,443	$464,825	$187,297	$237,741	$158,437	$278,609	$862,084
East	Government	$19,078	$45,000	$28,393	$37,311	$129,783	$22,316	$50,579	$29,126	$90,631	$192,652	$41,395	$95,579	$57,520	$127,942	$322,436
	Commercial	$32,264	$40,308	$14,554	$44,659	$131,785	$52,016	$43,607	$50,000	$51,684	$197,307	$84,280	$83,915	$64,554	$96,343	$329,092
	Academic	$26,414	$20,116	$28,731	$40,975	$116,236	$36,488	$35,705	$38,879	$61,887	$172,959	$62,902	$55,821	$67,609	$102,862	$289,195
	Total	$77,757	$105,425	$71,678	$122,946	$377,804	$110,820	$129,891	$118,005	$204,202	$562,918	$188,577	$235,315	$189,683	$327,147	$940,723
West	Government	$35,652	$44,932	$36,642	$46,317	$163,543	$37,096	$21,205	$24,536	$68,294	$151,131	$72,748	$66,137	$61,178	$114,611	$314,674
	Commercial	$36,299	$46,078	$40,640	$39,616	$162,633	$46,354	$47,896	$39,304	$44,330	$177,885	$82,653	$93,974	$79,944	$83,946	$340,518
	Academic	$47,000	$15,396	$53,205	$39,832	$155,434	$56,776	$49,629	$34,605	$62,034	$203,045	$103,777	$65,026	$87,810	$101,867	$358,479
	Total	$118,951	$106,406	$130,488	$125,765	$481,609	$140,226	$118,731	$118,445	$174,659	$532,061	$259,178	$225,137	$228,933	$300,423	$1013671
Total	Government	$126,880	$156,913	$121,232	$187,054	$592,078	$142,046	$129,253	$110,166	$279,098	$660,563	$268,926	$286,166	$231,398	$466,151	$1252641
	Commercial	$106,659	$166,019	$108,125	$160,701	$541,505	$178,317	$210,026	$162,108	$188,349	$738,800	$284,975	$376,046	$270,233	$349,051	$1280304
	Academic	$112,427	$91,112	$129,165	$174,319	$507,024	$162,478	$183,542	$122,948	$235,732	$704,700	$274,905	$274,654	$252,113	$410,052	$1211724
	Total	$345,965	$414,045	$358,523	$522,074	$1640607	$482,841	$522,821	$395,222	$703,179	$2104063	$828,806	$936,866	$753,744	$1,225,254	$3744669

For example, suppose you want to make comparisons between customers whose calls are answered within the first minute and those who wait on hold for a while (at least four minutes), broken down by territory, customer type, and industry. All of the information you need appears in the table shown in Figure 18.7. Unfortunately, there is also a good deal of extraneous data for those who were on hold between one and four minutes as well.

To display an OLAP cube with extraneous information removed, double-click the previously created OLAP cube.

Ctrl-Alt-click the *1-2 Minutes* column heading.
Right-click the *1-2 Minutes* column heading.
Choose *Hide Category*.

Repeat for *2-4 Minutes, Total*.

Figure 18.8   OLAP cube with relevant information only

OLAP Cubes

Sum

Revenue

Territory	Industry	Customer Status					
		Regular customer		Preferred customer		Total	
		Time on Hold		Time on Hold		Time on Hold	
		< 1 Minute	> 4 Minutes	< 1 Minute	> 4 Minutes	< 1 Minute	> 4 Minutes
North	Government	$28,287	$52,147	$47,003	$75,839	$75,290	$127,985
	Commercial	$20,618	$18,978	$40,823	$55,382	$61,442	$74,360
	Academic	$20,671	$55,074	$36,352	$61,654	$57,023	$116,728
	Total	$69,576	$126,199	$124,179	$192,875	$193,755	$319,074
South	Government	$43,863	$51,279	$35,631	$44,334	$79,494	$95,613
	Commercial	$17,477	$57,449	$39,124	$36,953	$56,600	$94,402
	Academic	$18,342	$38,438	$32,860	$50,156	$51,202	$88,594
	Total	$79,001	$147,100	$107,616	$131,443	$187,207	$279,609
East	Government	$19,078	$37,311	$22,316	$90,631	$41,395	$127,942
	Commercial	$32,264	$44,659	$52,016	$51,684	$84,280	$96,343
	Academic	$26,414	$40,975	$36,488	$61,887	$62,902	$102,862
	Total	$77,757	$122,946	$110,820	$204,202	$188,577	$327,147
West	Government	$35,652	$46,317	$37,096	$68,294	$72,748	$114,611
	Commercial	$36,299	$39,616	$46,354	$44,330	$82,653	$83,946
	Academic	$47,000	$39,832	$56,776	$62,034	$103,777	$101,867
	Total	$118,951	$125,765	$140,226	$174,659	$259,178	$300,423
Total	Government	$126,880	$187,054	$142,046	$279,098	$268,926	$466,151
	Commercial	$106,659	$160,701	$178,317	$188,349	$284,975	$349,051
	Academic	$112,427	$174,319	$162,478	$235,732	$274,905	$410,052
	Total	$345,965	$522,074	$482,841	$703,179	$828,806	$1,225,254

Wading through the extraneous data can be an arduous and error-prone chore. Notice how much easier it is to make direct comparisons between the lowest and highest hold-time groups in Figure 18.8 after the other categories have been removed.

Format

The **format** of the table refers to how it looks: what font, size, style, and color are used for the contents of the table, which cells are separated by lines in the table and which are not, how many decimal points are shown for numbers, what symbols are attached to values (that is, currency symbols or parentheses for negative values), and so on. While such elements may seem unimportant to a hard-core data analyst, such considerations can make the difference between a table that is easy to read and understand and one that is difficult.

To produce example output showing different formats:

 Double-click the previously created OLAP cube, and from the menus choose:

View
  Show All

Click and drag *Customer Status* from *Column* to *Layer*.
Click and drag *Industry* from *Row* to *Layer*.
Select *Commercial* for *Industry*.

Then, for the reformatted table, from the menus choose:

Format
  TableLooks...

Edit Look...
  Cell Formats
  Text: Impact Italic
  Area: Title, Layers, Corner Labels, Row Labels, Column Labels, Data

Figure 18.9   Different formatting choices for an OLAP cube.

OLAP Cubes

Customer Status: Total

Industry: Commercial

Sum

Revenue

Territory	Time on Hold				
	< 1 Minute	1-2 Minutes	2-4 Minutes	> 4 Minutes	Total
North	$61,442	$97,357	$70,044	$74,360	$303,202
South	$56,600	$100,800	$55,691	$94,402	$307,493
East	$84,280	$83,915	$64,554	$96,343	$329,092
West	$82,653	$93,974	$79,944	$83,946	$340,518
Total	$284,975	$376,046	$270,233	$349,051	$1280304

OLAP Cubes

Customer Status: Total

Industry: Commercial

Sum

Revenue

Territory	Time on Hold				
	< 1 Minute	1-2 Minutes	2-4 Minutes	> 4 Minutes	Total
North	$61,442	$97,357	$70,044	$74,360	$303,202
South	$56,800	$100,800	$55,691	$94,402	$307,493
East	$84,280	$83,915	$64,554	$96,343	$329,092
West	$82,653	$93,974	$79,944	$83,946	$340,518
Total	$284,975	$376,046	$270,233	$349,051	$1,280,304

Figure 18.9 shows two tables that differ only in formatting. Notice that the first table is very clear and easy to grasp, whereas the second table is almost painful to look at. Even though the two tables technically contain the same information, that information is much more accessible in the first table.

Interacting with OLAP Cubes

OLAP cubes use SPSS's pivot table technology to make interaction quick and easy. **Pivoting** refers to rearranging, transposing, or otherwise changing the way dimensions are displayed in the table.

When you generate an OLAP cube, all of the dimensions you specify are embedded in the table, even though you may not be able to see any of them at first. Some dimensions are put into layers. Pivoting allows you to move dimensions from layers to rows or columns, and vice versa.

Figure 18.10   Default structure of example pivot table

OLAP Cubes

Customer Status: Total

Time on Hold: Total

Territory: Total

Industry: Total

Variables	Statistics					
	Sum	N	Mean	Std. Deviation	% of Total Sum	% of Total N
Revenue	$3744669	1488	$2,516.58	$994.59	100.0%	100.0%

Figure 18.10 shows the default output for generating a pivot table summarizing revenue based on *Industry, Customer Status, Time on Hold*, and *Territory*. As you can see, most dimensions start in the layers, making for a very small (and relatively uninformative) presentation.

Suppose you are interested in breaking down the numbers by customer status and industry. You can bring those dimensions out of the layers and into columns and rows by pivoting the table. The first step is to activate the table by double-clicking it. The table will be outlined with a crosshatched line (see Figure 18.11). You should also see the **pivoting trays**, which provide controls for pivoting the table. (If you don't see pivoting trays when you activate a pivot table, choose *Pivoting Trays* from the Pivot menu.)

Figure 18.11   Activated default table

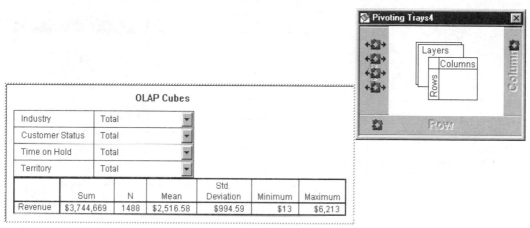

In the pivoting trays window, there are trays for rows, columns, and layers. Each dimension in the table is represented by an icon (⬡). By dragging the icon for a dimension from one tray to another, you can restructure the table. For example, by moving the icon for *Customer Status* from layers to rows, you see the revenue numbers broken down by status.

Figure 18.12   Revenue broken down by customer status

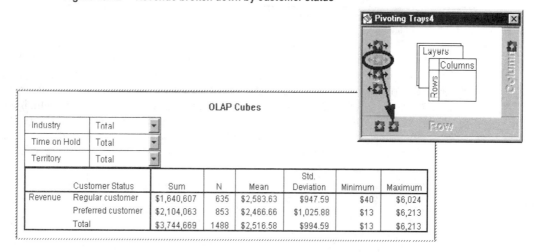

Similarly, you can move *Industry* into rows by dragging the appropriate icon from the layers tray to the row tray.

Figure 18.13   Revenue broken down by customer status and industry

OLAP Cubes

| Time on Hold | Total ▼ |
| Territory | Total ▼ |

	Customer Status	Industry	Sum	N	Mean	Std. Deviation	Minimum	Maximum
Revenue	Regular customer	Government	$592,078	220	$2,691.26	$877.32	$274	$5,246
		Commercial	$541,505	218	$2,483.97	$979.78	$40	$6,024
		Academic	$507,024	197	$2,573.73	$978.55	$307	$5,012
		Total	$1,640,607	635	$2,583.63	$947.59	$40	$6,024
	Preferred customer	Government	$660,563	276	$2,393.34	$1,030.45	$139	$5,262
		Commercial	$738,800	298	$2,479.19	$977.16	$13	$5,417
		Academic	$704,700	279	$2,525.81	$1,070.50	$34	$6,213
		Total	$2,104,063	853	$2,466.66	$1,025.88	$13	$6,213
	Total	Government	$1,252,641	496	$2,525.49	$975.90	$139	$5,262
		Commercial	$1,280,304	516	$2,481.21	$977.32	$13	$6,024
		Academic	$1,211,724	476	$2,545.64	$1,032.65	$34	$6,213
		Total	$3,744,669	1488	$2,516.58	$994.59	$13	$6,213

Notice that when you use more than one dimension to define rows, the dimensions are nested. This means that the table is broken down by one dimension *within* each level of the other dimension. For example, in the table shown in Figure 18.13, information is broken down by *Industry* within each level of *Customer Status*. The order in which the icons are arranged in the tray controls which dimensions are nested within which others. In the table, *Industry* is nested within *Customer Status*. If you want the nesting to be reversed so that *Customer Status* is nested within *Industry*, simply drag the icon for the *Industry* dimension to the left of the *Customer Status* icon, as shown in Figure 18.14.

Figure 18.14   Changing the order of nesting for rows

OLAP Cubes

| Time on Hold | Total |
| Territory | Total |

	Industry	Customer Status	Sum	N	Mean	Std. Deviation	Minimum	Maximum
Revenue	Government	Regular customer	$592,078	220	$2,691.26	$877.32	$274	$5,246
		Preferred customer	$660,563	276	$2,393.34	$1,030.45	$139	$5,262
		Total	$1,252,641	496	$2,525.49	$975.90	$139	$5,262
	Commercial	Regular customer	$541,505	218	$2,483.97	$979.78	$40	$6,024
		Preferred customer	$738,800	298	$2,479.19	$977.16	$13	$5,417
		Total	$1,280,304	516	$2,481.21	$977.32	$13	$6,024
	Academic	Regular customer	$507,024	197	$2,573.73	$978.55	$307	$5,012
		Preferred customer	$704,700	279	$2,525.81	$1,070.50	$34	$6,213
		Total	$1,211,724	476	$2,545.64	$1,032.65	$34	$6,213
	Total	Regular customer	$1,640,607	635	$2,583.63	$947.59	$40	$6,024
		Preferred customer	$2,104,063	853	$2,466.66	$1,025.88	$13	$6,213
		Total	$3,744,669	1488	$2,516.58	$994.59	$13	$6,213

In this table, you have *Time on Hold* and *Territory* in layers. For layer dimensions, only one value is shown at a time. By default, the value is total, which collapses records across all of the values of that dimension. For example, in the table shown above, values in the cells of the table represent statistics for cases collapsed across all values of *Time on Hold* and *Territory*. Suppose you are interested specifically in the East territory. You can select the layer representing this subset of records by selecting the appropriate value from the layers drop-down list, as shown in Figure 18.15.

Figure 18.15   Selecting a different layer for display

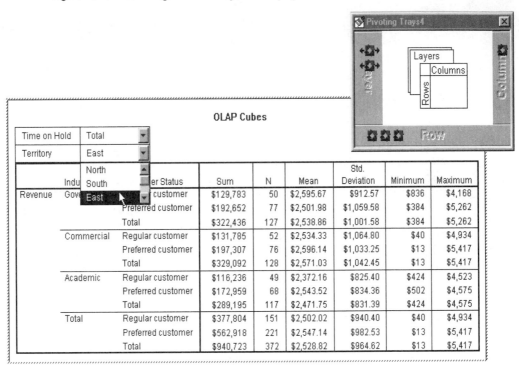

You can also select layers using the arrows on either side of the pivoting tray icon to cycle through the layers.

Drilling Down

The ability to switch dimensions to layers and select specific layers for viewing allows you to take detailed looks at specific subgroups. This process is often called **drilling down** because you start at a high level of aggregation and focus in on finer and finer levels of detail. Looking back at Figure 18.14, the difference in revenue due to customer status seems to be smaller for government accounts than for industry or academic accounts. If you want to get a more detailed look at these government accounts, you can move *Industry* to layers and select the layer corresponding to government accounts. You have now restricted the contents of the table (shown in Figure 18.16) to government accounts.

Figure 18.16   Table showing government accounts only

OLAP Cubes

Time on Hold	Total
Territory	Total
Industry	Government

	Customer Status	Sum	N	Mean	Std. Deviation	Minimum	Maximum
Revenue	Regular customer	$592,078	220	$2,691.26	$877.32	$274	$5,246
	Preferred customer	$660,563	276	$2,393.34	$1,030.45	$139	$5,262
	Total	$1,252,641	496	$2,525.49	$975.90	$139	$5,262

Notice that this table is basically just the first three rows of the table in Figure 18.14. Now you can take a closer look at these accounts by pivoting other dimensions of interest into rows and columns. If you want a breakdown of these government accounts by *Customer Status*, *Time on Hold*, and *Territory*, you can nest *Territory* within *Customer Status* in rows, and use *Time on Hold* to define columns. (In the original table, *Customer Status* is already used to define rows, so no change is necessary for this dimension.) Because you will usually consider only one summary statistic at a time, you can move the statistics dimension from columns to layers in order to simplify the table. To begin, select the *Sum* layer on the *Statistics* dimension. The resulting table is shown in Figure 18.17.

Figure 18.17   More detail for government accounts

OLAP Cubes

| Industry | Government ▼ |
| Statistics | Sum ▼ |

			Time on Hold				
	Customer Status	Territory	< 1 Minute	1-2 Minutes	2-4 Minutes	> 4 Minutes	Total
Revenue	Regular customer	North	$28,287	$27,510	$38,580	$52,147	$146,523
		South	$43,863	$39,471	$17,616	$51,279	$152,229
		East	$19,078	$45,000	$28,393	$37,311	$129,783
		West	$35,652	$44,932	$36,642	$46,317	$163,543
		Total	$126,880	$156,913	$121,232	$187,054	$592,078
	Preferred customer	North	$47,003	$28,522	$24,266	$75,839	$175,629
		South	$35,631	$28,947	$32,238	$44,334	$141,150
		East	$22,316	$50,579	$29,126	$90,631	$192,652
		West	$37,096	$21,205	$24,536	$68,294	$151,131
		Total	$142,046	$129,253	$110,166	$279,098	$660,563
	Total	North	$75,290	$56,031	$62,846	$127,985	$322,152
		South	$79,494	$68,418	$49,854	$95,613	$293,379
		East	$41,395	$95,579	$57,520	$127,942	$322,436
		West	$72,748	$66,137	$61,178	$114,611	$314,674
		Total	$268,926	$286,166	$231,398	$466,151	$1,252,641

This finer level of detail reveals that for preferred customers, accounts in the East region generate the highest revenues, but a great deal of that revenue (almost half) comes from customers who spent more than four minutes on hold. For regular accounts, the highest revenues come from the West region, and those revenues appear to be fairly evenly distributed across wait times. Also, for regular customers in the East region, the proportion of revenue from customers who wait more than four minutes is not as high as it is for the preferred status group. Such information can be very useful in evaluating your technical support organization and identifying opportunities for improvement.

Hiding Columns and Rows

In some situations, you may want to focus on only a few of the possible values for a dimension. In an earlier example, you wanted to compare revenue from customers with short wait times (< 1 minute) to that from customers with long wait times (> 4 minutes). To do this, you need to structure the table so that the appropriate dimensions are used to define rows and columns, as shown in Figure 18.7. Now you can select categories to hide in the table so that irrelevant information is not displayed. With the table still activated, Ctrl-Alt-click the column label for the category you want to hide. This will select the entire category. Then right-click the highlighted column label and choose *Hide Category* from the context menu, as shown in Figure 18.18. You need to do this for each category you want to hide. After doing this for the *1–2 minutes, 2–4 minutes,* and *Total* categories, the resulting table will be similar to Figure 18.8.

Figure 18.18   Hiding categories of a column dimension

Statistics	Sum
Variables	Revenue

Pivoting Trays2 — Layers / Columns / Rows / Row

Context menu:
- What's This?
- Cut   Ctrl+X
- Copy   Ctrl+C
- Paste   Ctrl+V
- Clear   del
- Select   ▸
- Hide Dimension Label
- Hide Category
- Ungroup
- Group
- Table Properties...
- Cell Properties...
- TableLooks...
- Insert Footnote
- Delete Footnotes
- Hide Footnotes
- ✓ Pivoting Trays
- Toolbar

		Customer Status								
		Regular customer					Preferred customer			
		Time on Hold					Time on Hold			
Territory	Industry	< 1 Minute	1-2 Minutes	2-4 Minutes	> 4 Minutes	Total	< 1 Minute	1-2 Minutes	2-4 Minutes	> 4 Minutes
North	Government	$28,287			...47	$146,523	$47,003	$28,522	$24,266	$75,839
	Commercial	$20,618			...78	$113,129	$40,823	$55,089	$38,779	$55,382
	Academic	$20,671			...74	$124,282	$36,352	$55,582	$24,967	$61,654
	Total	$69,576			...99	$383,933	$124,179	$139,192	$88,012	$192,875
South	Government	$43,863			...79	$152,229	$35,631	$28,947	$32,238	$44,334
	Commercial	$17,477			...49	$133,958	$39,124	$63,434	$34,024	$36,953
	Academic	$18,342			...38	$111,072	$32,860	$42,626	$24,497	$50,156
	Total	$79,681			...66	$397,259	$107,616	$135,007	$90,759	$131,443
East	Government	$19,078			...11	$129,783	$22,316	$50,579	$29,126	$90,631
	Commercial	$32,264			...59	$131,785	$52,016	$43,607	$50,000	$51,684
	Academic	$26,414			...75	$116,236	$36,488	$35,705	$38,879	$61,887
	Total	$77,757			...46	$377,804	$110,820	$129,891	$118,005	$204,202
West	Government	$35,652			...17	$163,543	$37,096	$21,205	$24,536	$68,294
	Commercial	$36,299			...16	$162,633	$46,354	$47,896	$39,304	$44,330
	Academic	$47,000			...32	$155,434	$56,776	$49,629	$34,605	$62,034
	Total	$118,951			...65	$481,609	$140,226	$118,731	$98,445	$174,659
Total	Government	$126,880			...54	$592,078	$142,046	$129,253	$110,166	$279,090
	Commercial	$106,659			...01	$541,505	$178,317	$210,026	$162,108	$188,349
	Academic	$112,427			...19	$507,024	$162,478	$183,542	$122,948	$235,732
	Total	$345,965	$414,045	$358,523	$522,074	$1,640,607	$482,841	$522,821	$395,222	$703,179

Bookmarks

Once you've discovered an interesting pattern, you need to be able to communicate this information to your colleagues and other decision makers at your company. If the information consumers in your company have copies of the SPSS Smart Viewer, you can send them the results of your analysis, and they can interact with the tables you generate just as if they were viewing the tables in the original application.

If you find several useful patterns, you can either distribute separate tables for each pattern you want to show, or you can distribute a single multidimensional table with bookmarks to show the relevant patterns. A **bookmark** is simply a way to embed certain table structures into a multidimensional table. This makes it easy for another user to quickly examine the patterns you've identified as particularly interesting without having to reproduce an elaborate series of pivoting steps each time.

To define a bookmark for a pivot table, set up the table as you want others to see it, and choose *Bookmarks* from the Pivot menu. Give the bookmark a name and click *Add*. Your list will now contain the named bookmark. For example, with the table shown in Figure 18.17, you can define a bookmark called *Gov't Detail*, as shown in Figure 18.19.

Figure 18.19   Defining a bookmark

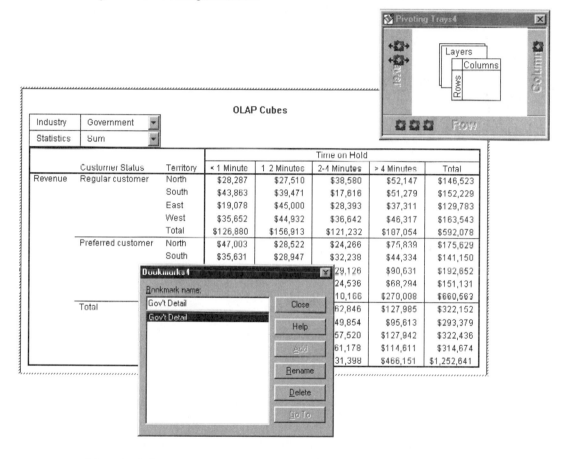

You can define multiple bookmarks for a single table. Once you've defined bookmarks for a pivot table, it is easy for other users to instantly see the different views you've defined. To see these views, you simply activate the pivot table, choose *Bookmarks* from the Pivot menu, select the bookmark of interest, and click *Go To*.

Formatting

You can also control various aspects of formatting in pivot tables. You can control the font, size, and style of text, cell border options, special formatting, such as currency or number of decimal places for numeric results, background colors, and so on. You can also define **TableLooks**, which specify a set of formatting options that can be applied to several tables or to all tables by default. This allows you to define a set of options to ensure that your tables have a consistent, high-quality appearance. See your SPSS, NewView, or Smart Viewer documentation for more details about formatting options for pivot tables.

Appendix A
Matrix Macros

You can use the matrix language with the macro facility (see the *SPSS Base Syntax Reference Guide*) to create fairly sophisticated statistical programs. Two SPSS command syntax files are included with the SPSS Base system as examples of the power and flexibility of the matrix language combined with the macro facility. Using these command syntax files, you can perform:

- Canonical correlation and redundancy analysis, with the CANCORR macro.
- Ridge regression and ridge trace plots, with the RIDGEREG macro.

With the CANCORR macro, you can estimate coefficients that maximize the correlation between two sets of variables. You can also calculate canonical scores for each of the cases. The RIDGEREG macro is useful when independent variables are nearly collinear and the usual least-squares estimators result in unstable coefficients with large variances.

Limitations of Macros

The macros described in this appendix define command syntax that you can enter and run in a syntax window, just like regular SPSS commands. However, macros in general are not as robust or stable as fully supported SPSS statistical procedures, and these macros have not been as extensively tested as regular SPSS commands. If you use these macros, keep the following in mind:

- The syntax must be entered exactly as documented. Enter subcommands in the order shown. Do not include a slash before the first subcommand, do not abbreviate keywords, and do not omit equals signs or add them if they are not displayed.
- The command names are, in fact, macro calls. Once the macro is defined in a session, SPSS attempts to call the macro whenever it encounters the name, even if it is not at the beginning of a command. For example, if you have run the CANCORR macro and you also have a variable named *cancorr*, any command specifications (or dialog box choices) that refer to the variable *cancorr* will cause SPSS to run the macro, resulting in numerous error messages. This remains in effect for the duration of the SPSS session.

- Because these macros utilize MATRIX routines that can require a good deal of memory, you may not be able to run the macros with a large number of variables.
- Error checking is not comprehensive, and a large number of uninformative error messages may be generated in some instances.
- The macros create new files in the current directory. If you do not have write permission to the current directory (this may happen if you are running SPSS on a network), you must change the current directory before you can run the macros. To change the current directory, open or save a data file in a directory for which you have write permission (for example, a directory on your own hard disk).

Using the Macros

All three macros should be located in the same directory as the SPSS executable program or with sample data. To use the macros:

1. From the menus choose:

   File
    New
     Syntax

   This opens a new syntax window that you can use to enter command syntax.

2. Use the INCLUDE command to access the macro. Specify the directory location and the filename of the macro in apostrophes or quotes, as in

   ```
   include file 'c:\Program Files\SPSS\Canonical correlation.sps'.
   ```

3. After the INCLUDE command, enter the syntax for the command, as in

   ```
   include file 'c:\Program Files\SPSS\Canonical correlation.sps'.
   cancorr set1=var1 var2 var3
    /set2=var4 var5 var6.
   ```

4. Highlight the commands, as shown in Figure A.1, and click on the Run Current syntax tool.

Figure A.1   Using a macro in a syntax window

INCLUDE command
with macro filename
and directory path

Command syntax
defined by macro

Commands
highlighted in
syntax window

Using the CANCORR Macro

The macro for canonical correlation is contained in the file *Canonical correlation.sps*. This command syntax file should be located in the same directory as the SPSS executable program. The syntax defined by the macro is

```
CANCORR SET1=variable list
 /SET2=variable list.
```

The variable lists specified for SET1 and SET2 must be numeric variables.

The canonical correlation macro creates two new data files in the current directory:

- The working data file is replaced with *cc__tmp1.sav*. This file contains the contents of the working data file immediately prior to running the macro.
- Canonical score variables, along with the contents of the original data file, are saved in a file named *cc__tmp2.sav*. The names of the canonical score variables are *s1__cv1*, *s2__cv1*, *s1__cv2*, *s2__cv2*, *s1__cv3*, *s2__cv3*, etc. The number of canonical score variables created is twice the smaller number of variables specified on SET1 or SET2. For example, if SET1 specifies four variables and SET2 specifies three variables, six canonical score variables will be created.

The filenames created by the macro use double underscores to minimize the risk of overwriting existing files. Each time you run the macro, the contents of these two data files are overwritten.

Using the RIDGEREG Macro

The macro for ridge regression is contained in the file *Ridge regression.sps*. This command syntax file should be located in the same directory as the SPSS executable program. The syntax defined by the macro is

```
RIDGEREG DEP=dependent variable
 /ENTER variable list
 /START=value
 /STOP=value
 /INC=value
 /K=value.
```

The ridge regression macro creates two new data files in the current directory:

- The working data file is replaced with *rr__tmp1.sav*. This file contains the contents of the working data file immediately prior to running the macro.
- The values of R^2 (variable *rsq*) and *Beta* values for each independent variable (using the original independent variable names) for each value of the bias parameter (variable *k*) are saved in a file named *rr__tmp2.sav*. The number of cases is determined by the number of bias parameter values defined by START, STOP, and INC. The

default values produce a file with 21 cases. If you use k to specify a bias parameter value, the file contains only one case.

The filenames created by the macro use double underscores to minimize the risk of overwriting existing files. Each time you run the macro, the contents of these two data files are overwritten.

Required Specifications

DEP and ENTER specifications are required. All variables specified must be numeric variables. If you do not use any of the optional specifications, the default START, STOP, and INC values are used to generate a ridge trace plot of standardized regression coefficients versus values of the bias parameter k, a plot of the model R^2 versus k, and a table listing the R^2 and *Beta* values for each k value.

Optional Specifications

The following optional specifications are also available:

- START specifies a starting bias parameter value for ridge trace mode. The value must be between 0 and 1. The default value is 0.
- STOP specifies an ending bias parameter value for ridge trace mode. The value must be greater than the START value but cannot exceed 1. The default value is 1.
- INC specifies the increment for the bias parameter value in ridge trace mode. The value must be less than the difference between the START and STOP values. The default is 0.05.
- K specifies a single value for the bias parameter and overrides any specifications on START, STOP, and INC. The value must be between 0 and 1. If you specify K, a full set of standard regression output is produced for the specified k value.

Appendix B
Data Files Used in This Book

Following is a brief description of the data files used in the examples that appear in this book:

cars.sav. Contains eight variables that describe characteristics of 406 cars. Variables include miles per gallon, number of cylinders, engine displacement, horsepower, weight, time to accelerate from 0–60 m.p.h., model year, and country of origin. In addition, the file contains a filter variable that filters out all cases except those with four or six cylinders. The Committee on Statistical Graphics of the American Statistical Association used this data set for its 1983 Exposition of Statistical Graphics. The data can be downloaded from the World Wide Web at http://lib.stat.cmu.edu/datasets/cars.data.

coronary artery data.sav. Compares treadmill times for normal men with suspected coronary artery disease to times for men with diagnosed coronary artery disease. This data set appears in *Biostatistics: A methodology for the health sciences* (Fisher and Van Belle, 1993) and is a subset of the data from the Coronary Artery Surgery Study [CASS, 1981]. The subset contains 8 cases for men with normal arteries and 10 cases for men with three-vessel disease.

gss 93 subset.sav. The General Social Survey has been administered yearly since 1972 by the National Opinion Research Center, University of Chicago. This data file contains a subset of the responses collected in 1993 for a sample of 1500 people, age 18 years or older. The examples in this book use the variables age, sex, marital status, religious preference, view about life (dull, routine, or exciting), voting history in 1992, dwelling (own or rent home), opinions about music (jazz, classical, rap, and others), and geographical region in the United States. Explanatory labels are stored with the code for each response.

judges.sav. Contains hypothetical data from 8 judges who scored the same 300 gymnastic performances.

sales.sav. Contains 6 variables that describe characteristics of 1500 customers. Variables include customer ID number, status, revenue, the amount of time spent on hold, territory the customer is from, and customer industry.

tv-survey.sav. Contains hypothetical data for 906 responses to a 7-item survey. The items are yes/no answers to the question of whether the respondent would watch a television show under the following conditions: the original cast remains for another season, the directors stay for another season, the screenwriters stay for another season, their peers continue to watch the show, critics continue to give it good reviews, there are no other shows on at that time, or for any reason at all.

world95.sav. For each of 109 countries, demographic and economic information was culled from several 1995 almanacs. The following variables were recorded: female and male life expectancy, birth rate, death rate, infant mortality, fertility, population, percentage of population living in cities, percentage of literate females and males, and gross domestic product per capita. The name of each country is also included. Interestingly, the values of some variables (for example, birth rate) did not always agree across the sources, so we cannot attest to their accuracy. Another version of this file, *world95m.sav*, is included for the Cluster and Factor examples.

Appendix C
Durbin-Watson Significance Tables

The Durbin-Watson test statistic tests the null hypothesis that the residuals from an ordinary least-squares regression are not autocorrelated against the alternative that the residuals follow an AR1 process. The Durbin-Watson statistic ranges in value from 0 to 4. A value near 2 indicates non-autocorrelation; a value toward 0 indicates positive autocorrelation; a value toward 4 indicates negative autocorrelation.

Because of the dependence of any computed Durbin-Watson value on the associated data matrix, exact critical values of the Durbin-Watson statistic are not tabulated for all possible cases. Instead, Durbin and Watson established upper and lower bounds for the critical values. Typically, tabulated bounds are used to test the hypothesis of zero autocorrelation against the alternative of *positive* first-order autocorrelation, since positive autocorrelation is seen much more frequently in practice than negative autocorrelation. To use the table, you must cross-reference the sample size against the number of regressors, excluding the constant from the count of the number of regressors.

The conventional Durbin-Watson tables are not applicable when you do not have a constant term in the regression. Instead, you must refer to an appropriate set of Durbin-Watson tables. The conventional Durbin-Watson tables are also not applicable when a lagged dependent variable appears among the regressors. Durbin has proposed alternative test procedures for this case.

Statisticians have compiled Durbin-Watson tables from some special cases, including:

- Regressions with a full set of quarterly seasonal dummies.
- Regressions with an intercept and a linear trend variable (CURVEFIT MODEL=LINEAR).
- Regressions with a full set of quarterly seasonal dummies and a linear trend variable.

In addition to obtaining the Durbin-Watson statistic for residuals from REGRESSION, you should also plot the ACF and PACF of the residuals series. The plots might suggest either that the residuals are random, or that they follow some ARMA process. If the residuals resemble an AR1 process, you can estimate an appropriate regression using the AREG procedure. If the residuals follow any ARMA process, you can estimate an appropriate regression using the ARIMA procedure.

In this appendix, we have reproduced two sets of tables. Savin and White (1977) present tables for sample sizes ranging from 6 to 200 and for 1 to 20 regressors for models in which an intercept is included. Farebrother (1980) presents tables for sample sizes ranging from 2 to 200 and for 0 to 21 regressors for models in which an intercept is not included.

Let's consider an example of how to use the tables. In *SPSS Trends*, we look at the classic Durbin and Watson data set concerning consumption of spirits. The sample size is 69, there are 2 regressors, and there is an intercept term in the model. The Durbin-Watson test statistic value is 0.24878. We want to test the null hypothesis of zero auto-correlation in the residuals against the alternative that the residuals are positively auto-correlated at the 1% level of significance. If you examine the Savin and White tables (Table C.2 and Table C.3), you will not find a row for sample size 69, so go to the next *lowest* sample size with a tabulated row, namely $N=65$. Since there are two regressors, find the column labeled $k=2$. Cross-referencing the indicated row and column, you will find that the printed bounds are dL = 1.377 and dU = 1.500. If the observed value of the test statistic is less than the tabulated lower bound, then you should reject the null hypothesis of non-autocorrelated errors in favor of the hypothesis of positive first-order autocorrelation. Since 0.24878 is less than 1.377, we reject the null hypothesis. If the test statistic value were greater than dU, we would not reject the null hypothesis.

A third outcome is also possible. If the test statistic value lies between dL and dU, the test is inconclusive. In this context, you might err on the side of conservatism and not reject the null hypothesis.

For models with an intercept, if the observed test statistic value is greater than 2, then you want to test the null hypothesis against the alternative hypothesis of negative first-order autocorrelation. To do this, compute the quantity 4-d and compare this value with the tabulated values of dL and dU as if you were testing for positive autocorrelation.

When the regression does not contain an intercept term, refer to Farebrother's tabu-lated values of the "minimal bound," denoted dM (Table C.4 and Table C.5), instead of Savin and White's lower bound dL. In this instance, the upper bound is the conventional bound dU found in the Savin and White tables. To test for negative first-order autocor-relation, use Table C.6 and Table C.7.

To continue with our example, had we run a regression with no intercept term, we would cross-reference N equals 65 and k equals 2 in Farebrother's table. The tabulated 1% minimal bound is 1.348.

We have reprinted the tables exactly as they originally appeared. There have been subsequent corrections to them, however, as published in Farebrother, *Econometrica* 48(6): 1554 and *Econometrica* 49(1): 277. The corrections are as follows:

Table C.1   Corrections for Table C.2—Table C.7

	k′	n	Bound	Incorrect	Correct
Table C.2	6	75	dU	1.646	1.649
	8	75	dU	1.716	1.714
	9	75	dU	1.746	1.748
	10	40	dL	0.789	0.749
	10	75	dU	1.785	1.783
	18	80	dU	2.057	2.059
Table C.3	10	40	dL	0.945	0.952

	k	n	Bound	Incorrect	Correct
Table C.4	0	7		0.389	0.398
Table C.5	8	15		9.185	0.185
	19	90		1.617	1.167
Table C.6	8	70		2.089	2.098
	10	200		1.116	2.116
	14	34		1.295	1.296
Table C.7	1	39		2.645	2.615
	3	15		2.432	2.423
	8	14		0.984	0.948

Table C.2 Models with an intercept (from Savin and White)

DURBIN–WATSON STATISTIC: 1 PER CENT SIGNIFICANCE POINTS OF *dL* AND *dU*[a]

	k'=1		k'=2		k'=3		k'=4		k'=5		k'=6		k'=7		k'=8		k'=9		k'=10	
n	dL	dU	dL	dU	dL	dU	dL	dU	dL	dU	dL	dU	dL	dU	dL	dU	dL	dU	dL	dU
6	0.390	1.142	-----	-----	-----	-----	-----	-----	-----	-----	-----	-----	-----	-----	-----	-----	-----	-----	-----	-----
7	0.435	1.036	0.294	1.676	-----	-----	-----	-----	-----	-----	-----	-----	-----	-----	-----	-----	-----	-----	-----	-----
8	0.497	1.003	0.345	1.489	0.229	2.102	-----	-----	-----	-----	-----	-----	-----	-----	-----	-----	-----	-----	-----	-----
9	0.554	0.998	0.408	1.389	0.279	1.875	0.183	2.433	-----	-----	-----	-----	-----	-----	-----	-----	-----	-----	-----	-----
10	0.604	1.001	0.466	1.333	0.340	1.733	0.230	2.193	0.150	2.690	-----	-----	-----	-----	-----	-----	-----	-----	-----	-----
11	0.653	1.010	0.519	1.297	0.396	1.640	0.286	2.030	0.193	2.453	0.124	2.892	-----	-----	-----	-----	-----	-----	-----	-----
12	0.697	1.023	0.569	1.274	0.449	1.575	0.339	1.913	0.244	2.280	0.164	2.665	0.105	3.053	-----	-----	-----	-----	-----	-----
13	0.738	1.038	0.616	1.261	0.499	1.526	0.391	1.826	0.294	2.150	0.211	2.490	0.140	2.838	0.090	3.182	-----	-----	-----	-----
14	0.776	1.054	0.660	1.254	0.547	1.490	0.441	1.757	0.343	2.049	0.257	2.354	0.183	2.667	0.122	2.981	0.078	3.287	-----	-----
15	0.811	1.070	0.700	1.252	0.591	1.464	0.488	1.704	0.391	1.967	0.303	2.244	0.226	2.530	0.161	2.817	0.107	3.101	0.068	3.374
16	0.844	1.086	0.737	1.252	0.633	1.446	0.532	1.663	0.437	1.900	0.349	2.153	0.269	2.416	0.200	2.681	0.142	2.944	0.094	3.201
17	0.874	1.102	0.772	1.255	0.672	1.432	0.574	1.630	0.480	1.847	0.393	2.078	0.313	2.319	0.241	2.566	0.179	2.811	0.127	3.053
18	0.902	1.118	0.805	1.259	0.708	1.422	0.613	1.604	0.522	1.803	0.435	2.015	0.355	2.238	0.282	2.467	0.216	2.697	0.160	2.925
19	0.928	1.132	0.835	1.265	0.742	1.415	0.650	1.584	0.561	1.767	0.476	1.963	0.396	2.169	0.322	2.381	0.255	2.597	0.196	2.813
20	0.952	1.147	0.863	1.271	0.773	1.411	0.685	1.567	0.598	1.737	0.515	1.918	0.436	2.110	0.362	2.308	0.294	2.510	0.232	2.714
21	0.975	1.161	0.890	1.277	0.803	1.408	0.718	1.554	0.633	1.712	0.552	1.881	0.474	2.059	0.400	2.244	0.331	2.434	0.268	2.625
22	0.997	1.174	0.914	1.284	0.831	1.407	0.748	1.543	0.667	1.691	0.587	1.849	0.510	2.015	0.437	2.188	0.368	2.367	0.304	2.548
23	1.018	1.187	0.938	1.291	0.858	1.407	0.777	1.534	0.699	1.673	0.620	1.821	0.545	1.977	0.473	2.140	0.404	2.308	0.340	2.479
24	1.037	1.199	0.960	1.298	0.882	1.407	0.805	1.528	0.728	1.658	0.652	1.797	0.578	1.944	0.507	2.097	0.439	2.255	0.375	2.417
25	1.055	1.211	0.981	1.305	0.906	1.409	0.831	1.523	0.756	1.645	0.682	1.776	0.610	1.915	0.540	2.059	0.473	2.209	0.409	2.362
26	1.072	1.222	1.001	1.312	0.928	1.411	0.855	1.518	0.783	1.635	0.711	1.759	0.640	1.889	0.572	2.026	0.505	2.168	0.441	2.313
27	1.089	1.233	1.019	1.319	0.949	1.413	0.878	1.515	0.808	1.626	0.738	1.743	0.669	1.867	0.602	1.997	0.536	2.131	0.473	2.269
28	1.104	1.244	1.037	1.325	0.969	1.415	0.900	1.513	0.832	1.618	0.764	1.729	0.696	1.847	0.630	1.970	0.566	2.098	0.504	2.229
29	1.119	1.254	1.054	1.332	0.988	1.418	0.921	1.512	0.855	1.611	0.788	1.718	0.723	1.830	0.658	1.947	0.595	2.068	0.533	2.193
30	1.133	1.263	1.070	1.339	1.006	1.421	0.941	1.511	0.877	1.606	0.812	1.707	0.748	1.814	0.684	1.925	0.622	2.041	0.562	2.160
31	1.147	1.273	1.085	1.345	1.023	1.425	0.960	1.510	0.897	1.601	0.834	1.698	0.772	1.800	0.710	1.906	0.649	2.017	0.589	2.131
32	1.160	1.282	1.100	1.352	1.040	1.428	0.979	1.510	0.917	1.597	0.856	1.690	0.794	1.788	0.734	1.889	0.674	1.995	0.615	2.104
33	1.172	1.291	1.114	1.358	1.055	1.432	0.996	1.510	0.936	1.594	0.876	1.683	0.816	1.776	0.757	1.874	0.698	1.975	0.641	2.080
34	1.184	1.299	1.128	1.364	1.070	1.435	1.012	1.511	0.954	1.591	0.896	1.677	0.837	1.766	0.779	1.860	0.722	1.957	0.665	2.057
35	1.195	1.307	1.140	1.370	1.085	1.439	1.028	1.512	0.971	1.589	0.914	1.671	0.857	1.757	0.800	1.847	0.744	1.940	0.689	2.037
36	1.206	1.315	1.153	1.376	1.098	1.442	1.043	1.513	0.988	1.588	0.932	1.666	0.877	1.749	0.821	1.836	0.766	1.925	0.711	2.018
37	1.217	1.323	1.165	1.382	1.112	1.446	1.058	1.514	1.004	1.586	0.950	1.662	0.895	1.742	0.841	1.825	0.787	1.911	0.733	2.001
38	1.227	1.330	1.176	1.388	1.124	1.449	1.072	1.515	1.019	1.585	0.966	1.658	0.913	1.735	0.860	1.816	0.807	1.899	0.754	1.985
39	1.237	1.337	1.187	1.393	1.137	1.453	1.085	1.517	1.034	1.584	0.982	1.655	0.930	1.729	0.878	1.807	0.826	1.887	0.774	1.970
40	1.246	1.344	1.198	1.398	1.148	1.457	1.098	1.518	1.048	1.584	0.997	1.652	0.946	1.724	0.895	1.799	0.844	1.876	0.789	1.956
45	1.288	1.376	1.245	1.423	1.201	1.474	1.156	1.528	1.111	1.584	1.065	1.643	1.019	1.704	0.974	1.768	0.927	1.834	0.881	1.902
50	1.324	1.403	1.285	1.446	1.245	1.491	1.205	1.538	1.164	1.587	1.123	1.639	1.081	1.692	1.039	1.748	0.997	1.805	0.955	1.864
55	1.356	1.427	1.320	1.466	1.284	1.506	1.247	1.548	1.209	1.592	1.172	1.638	1.134	1.685	1.095	1.734	1.057	1.785	1.018	1.837
60	1.383	1.449	1.350	1.484	1.317	1.520	1.283	1.558	1.249	1.598	1.214	1.639	1.179	1.682	1.144	1.726	1.108	1.771	1.072	1.817
65	1.407	1.468	1.377	1.500	1.346	1.534	1.315	1.568	1.283	1.604	1.251	1.642	1.218	1.680	1.186	1.720	1.153	1.761	1.120	1.802
70	1.429	1.485	1.400	1.515	1.372	1.546	1.343	1.578	1.313	1.611	1.283	1.645	1.253	1.680	1.223	1.716	1.192	1.754	1.162	1.792
75	1.448	1.501	1.422	1.529	1.395	1.557	1.368	1.587	1.340	1.617	1.313	1.646	1.284	1.682	1.256	1.716	1.227	1.746	1.199	1.785
80	1.466	1.515	1.441	1.541	1.416	1.568	1.390	1.595	1.364	1.624	1.338	1.653	1.312	1.683	1.285	1.714	1.259	1.745	1.232	1.777
85	1.482	1.528	1.458	1.553	1.435	1.578	1.411	1.603	1.386	1.630	1.362	1.657	1.337	1.685	1.312	1.714	1.287	1.743	1.262	1.773
90	1.496	1.540	1.474	1.563	1.452	1.587	1.429	1.611	1.406	1.636	1.383	1.661	1.360	1.687	1.336	1.714	1.312	1.741	1.288	1.769
95	1.510	1.552	1.489	1.573	1.468	1.596	1.446	1.618	1.425	1.642	1.403	1.666	1.381	1.690	1.358	1.715	1.336	1.741	1.313	1.767
100	1.522	1.562	1.503	1.583	1.482	1.604	1.462	1.625	1.441	1.647	1.421	1.670	1.400	1.693	1.378	1.717	1.357	1.741	1.335	1.765
150	1.611	1.637	1.598	1.651	1.584	1.665	1.571	1.679	1.557	1.693	1.543	1.708	1.530	1.722	1.515	1.737	1.501	1.752	1.486	1.767
200	1.664	1.684	1.653	1.693	1.643	1.704	1.633	1.715	1.623	1.725	1.613	1.735	1.603	1.746	1.592	1.757	1.582	1.768	1.571	1.779

	k'=11		k'=12		k'=13		k'=14		k'=15		k'=16		k'=17		k'=18		k'=19		k'=20	
n	dL	dU	dL	dU	dL	dU	dL	dU	dL	dU	dL	dU	dL	dU	dL	dU	dL	dU	dL	dU
16	0.060	3.446	-----	-----	-----	-----	-----	-----	-----	-----	-----	-----	-----	-----	-----	-----	-----	-----	-----	-----
17	0.084	3.286	0.053	3.506	-----	-----	-----	-----	-----	-----	-----	-----	-----	-----	-----	-----	-----	-----	-----	-----
18	0.113	3.146	0.075	3.358	0.047	3.557	-----	-----	-----	-----	-----	-----	-----	-----	-----	-----	-----	-----	-----	-----
19	0.145	3.023	0.102	3.227	0.067	3.420	0.043	3.601	-----	-----	-----	-----	-----	-----	-----	-----	-----	-----	-----	-----
20	0.178	2.914	0.131	3.109	0.092	3.297	0.061	3.474	0.038	3.639	-----	-----	-----	-----	-----	-----	-----	-----	-----	-----
21	0.212	2.817	0.162	3.004	0.119	3.185	0.084	3.358	0.055	3.521	0.035	3.671	-----	-----	-----	-----	-----	-----	-----	-----
22	0.246	2.729	0.194	2.909	0.148	3.084	0.109	3.252	0.077	3.412	0.050	3.562	0.032	3.700	-----	-----	-----	-----	-----	-----
23	0.281	2.651	0.227	2.822	0.178	2.991	0.136	3.155	0.100	3.311	0.070	3.459	0.046	3.597	0.029	3.725	-----	-----	-----	-----
24	0.315	2.580	0.260	2.744	0.209	2.906	0.165	3.065	0.125	3.218	0.092	3.363	0.065	3.501	0.043	3.629	0.027	3.747	-----	-----
25	0.348	2.517	0.292	2.674	0.240	2.829	0.194	2.982	0.152	3.131	0.116	3.274	0.085	3.410	0.060	3.538	0.039	3.657	0.025	3.766
26	0.381	2.460	0.324	2.610	0.272	2.758	0.224	2.906	0.180	3.050	0.141	3.191	0.107	3.325	0.079	3.452	0.055	3.572	0.036	3.682
27	0.413	2.409	0.356	2.552	0.303	2.694	0.253	2.836	0.208	2.976	0.167	3.113	0.131	3.245	0.100	3.371	0.073	3.490	0.051	3.602
28	0.444	2.363	0.387	2.499	0.333	2.635	0.283	2.772	0.237	2.907	0.194	3.040	0.156	3.169	0.122	3.294	0.093	3.412	0.068	3.524
29	0.474	2.321	0.417	2.451	0.363	2.582	0.313	2.713	0.266	2.843	0.222	2.972	0.182	3.098	0.146	3.220	0.114	3.338	0.087	3.450
30	0.503	2.283	0.447	2.407	0.393	2.533	0.342	2.659	0.294	2.785	0.249	2.909	0.208	3.032	0.171	3.152	0.137	3.267	0.107	3.379
31	0.531	2.248	0.475	2.367	0.422	2.487	0.371	2.609	0.322	2.730	0.277	2.851	0.234	2.970	0.193	3.087	0.160	3.201	0.128	3.311
32	0.558	2.216	0.503	2.330	0.450	2.446	0.399	2.563	0.350	2.680	0.304	2.797	0.261	2.912	0.221	3.026	0.184	3.137	0.151	3.246
33	0.585	2.187	0.530	2.296	0.477	2.408	0.426	2.520	0.377	2.633	0.331	2.746	0.287	2.858	0.246	2.969	0.209	3.078	0.174	3.184
34	0.610	2.160	0.556	2.266	0.503	2.373	0.452	2.481	0.404	2.590	0.357	2.699	0.313	2.808	0.272	2.915	0.233	3.022	0.197	3.126
35	0.634	2.136	0.581	2.237	0.529	2.340	0.478	2.444	0.430	2.550	0.383	2.655	0.339	2.761	0.297	2.865	0.257	2.969	0.221	3.071
36	0.658	2.113	0.605	2.210	0.554	2.310	0.504	2.410	0.455	2.512	0.409	2.614	0.364	2.717	0.322	2.818	0.282	2.919	0.244	3.019
37	0.680	2.092	0.628	2.186	0.578	2.282	0.528	2.379	0.480	2.477	0.434	2.576	0.389	2.675	0.347	2.774	0.306	2.872	0.268	2.969
38	0.702	2.073	0.651	2.164	0.601	2.256	0.552	2.350	0.504	2.445	0.458	2.540	0.414	2.637	0.371	2.733	0.330	2.828	0.291	2.923
39	0.723	2.055	0.673	2.143	0.623	2.232	0.575	2.323	0.528	2.414	0.482	2.507	0.438	2.600	0.395	2.694	0.354	2.787	0.315	2.879
40	0.744	2.039	0.694	2.123	0.645	2.210	0.597	2.297	0.551	2.386	0.505	2.476	0.461	2.566	0.418	2.657	0.377	2.748	0.338	2.838
45	0.835	1.972	0.790	2.044	0.744	2.118	0.700	2.193	0.655	2.269	0.612	2.346	0.570	2.424	0.528	2.503	0.488	2.582	0.448	2.661
50	0.913	1.925	0.871	1.987	0.829	2.051	0.787	2.116	0.746	2.182	0.705	2.250	0.665	2.318	0.625	2.387	0.586	2.456	0.548	2.526
55	0.979	1.891	0.940	1.945	0.902	2.002	0.863	2.059	0.825	2.117	0.786	2.176	0.748	2.237	0.711	2.298	0.674	2.359	0.637	2.421
60	1.037	1.865	1.001	1.914	0.965	1.964	0.929	2.015	0.893	2.067	0.857	2.120	0.822	2.173	0.786	2.227	0.751	2.283	0.716	2.338
65	1.087	1.845	1.053	1.889	1.020	1.934	0.986	1.980	0.953	2.027	0.919	2.075	0.886	2.123	0.852	2.172	0.819	2.221	0.786	2.272
70	1.131	1.831	1.099	1.870	1.068	1.911	1.037	1.953	1.005	1.995	0.974	2.038	0.943	2.082	0.911	2.127	0.880	2.172	0.849	2.217
75	1.170	1.819	1.141	1.856	1.111	1.893	1.082	1.931	1.052	1.970	1.023	2.009	0.993	2.049	0.964	2.090	0.934	2.131	0.905	2.172
80	1.205	1.810	1.177	1.844	1.150	1.878	1.122	1.913	1.094	1.949	1.066	1.984	1.039	2.022	1.011	2.057	0.983	2.097	0.955	2.135
85	1.236	1.803	1.210	1.834	1.184	1.866	1.158	1.898	1.132	1.931	1.106	1.965	1.080	1.999	1.053	2.033	1.027	2.068	1.000	2.104
90	1.264	1.798	1.240	1.827	1.215	1.856	1.191	1.886	1.166	1.917	1.141	1.948	1.116	1.979	1.091	2.012	1.066	2.044	1.041	2.077
95	1.290	1.793	1.267	1.821	1.244	1.848	1.221	1.876	1.197	1.905	1.174	1.934	1.150	1.963	1.126	1.993	1.102	2.023	1.079	2.054
100	1.314	1.790	1.292	1.816	1.270	1.841	1.248	1.868	1.225	1.895	1.203	1.922	1.181	1.949	1.158	1.977	1.136	2.006	1.113	2.034
150	1.473	1.783	1.458	1.799	1.444	1.814	1.429	1.830	1.414	1.847	1.400	1.863	1.385	1.880	1.370	1.897	1.355	1.913	1.340	1.931
200	1.561	1.791	1.550	1.801	1.539	1.813	1.528	1.824	1.518	1.836	1.507	1.847	1.495	1.860	1.484	1.871	1.474	1.883	1.462	1.896

[a] *k'* is the number of regressors excluding the intercept

Reprinted, with permission, from *Econometrica* 45(8): 1992-1995.

Table C.3   Models with an intercept (from Savin and White)

DURBIN–WATSON STATISTIC: 5 PER CENT SIGNIFICANCE POINTS OF dL AND dU[a]

n	k'=1 dL	dU	k'=2 dL	dU	k'=3 dL	dU	k'=4 dL	dU	k'=5 dL	dU	k'=6 dL	dU	k'=7 dL	dU	k'=8 dL	dU	k'=9 dL	dU	k'=10 dL	dU
6	0.610	1.400	-----	-----	-----	-----	-----	-----	-----	-----	-----	-----	-----	-----	-----	-----	-----	-----	-----	-----
7	0.700	1.356	0.467	1.896	-----	-----	-----	-----	-----	-----	-----	-----	-----	-----	-----	-----	-----	-----	-----	-----
8	0.763	1.332	0.559	1.777	0.368	2.287	-----	-----	-----	-----	-----	-----	-----	-----	-----	-----	-----	-----	-----	-----
9	0.824	1.320	0.629	1.699	0.455	2.128	0.296	2.588	-----	-----	-----	-----	-----	-----	-----	-----	-----	-----	-----	-----
10	0.879	1.320	0.697	1.641	0.525	2.016	0.376	2.414	0.243	2.822	-----	-----	-----	-----	-----	-----	-----	-----	-----	-----
11	0.927	1.324	0.758	1.604	0.595	1.928	0.444	2.283	0.316	2.645	0.203	3.005	-----	-----	-----	-----	-----	-----	-----	-----
12	0.971	1.331	0.812	1.579	0.658	1.864	0.512	2.177	0.379	2.506	0.268	2.832	0.171	3.149	-----	-----	-----	-----	-----	-----
13	1.010	1.340	0.861	1.562	0.715	1.816	0.574	2.094	0.445	2.390	0.328	2.692	0.230	2.985	0.147	3.266	-----	-----	-----	-----
14	1.045	1.350	0.905	1.551	0.767	1.779	0.632	2.030	0.505	2.296	0.389	2.572	0.286	2.848	0.200	3.111	0.127	3.360	-----	-----
15	1.077	1.361	0.946	1.543	0.814	1.750	0.685	1.977	0.562	2.220	0.447	2.472	0.343	2.727	0.251	2.979	0.175	3.216	0.111	3.438
16	1.106	1.371	0.982	1.539	0.857	1.728	0.734	1.935	0.615	2.157	0.502	2.388	0.398	2.624	0.304	2.860	0.222	3.090	0.155	3.304
17	1.133	1.381	1.015	1.536	0.897	1.710	0.779	1.900	0.664	2.104	0.554	2.318	0.451	2.537	0.356	2.757	0.272	2.975	0.198	3.184
18	1.158	1.391	1.046	1.535	0.933	1.696	0.820	1.872	0.710	2.060	0.603	2.257	0.502	2.461	0.407	2.667	0.321	2.873	0.244	3.073
19	1.180	1.401	1.074	1.536	0.967	1.685	0.859	1.848	0.752	2.023	0.649	2.206	0.549	2.396	0.456	2.589	0.369	2.783	0.290	2.974
20	1.201	1.411	1.100	1.537	0.998	1.676	0.894	1.828	0.792	1.991	0.692	2.162	0.595	2.339	0.502	2.521	0.416	2.704	0.336	2.885
21	1.221	1.420	1.125	1.538	1.026	1.669	0.927	1.812	0.829	1.964	0.732	2.124	0.637	2.290	0.547	2.460	0.461	2.633	0.380	2.806
22	1.239	1.429	1.147	1.541	1.053	1.664	0.958	1.797	0.863	1.940	0.769	2.090	0.677	2.246	0.588	2.407	0.504	2.571	0.424	2.734
23	1.257	1.437	1.168	1.543	1.078	1.660	0.986	1.785	0.895	1.920	0.804	2.061	0.715	2.208	0.628	2.360	0.545	2.514	0.465	2.670
24	1.273	1.446	1.188	1.546	1.101	1.656	1.013	1.775	0.925	1.902	0.837	2.035	0.751	2.174	0.666	2.318	0.584	2.464	0.506	2.613
25	1.288	1.454	1.206	1.550	1.123	1.654	1.038	1.767	0.953	1.886	0.868	2.012	0.784	2.144	0.702	2.280	0.621	2.419	0.544	2.560
26	1.302	1.461	1.224	1.553	1.143	1.652	1.062	1.759	0.979	1.873	0.897	1.992	0.816	2.117	0.735	2.246	0.657	2.379	0.581	2.513
27	1.316	1.469	1.240	1.556	1.162	1.651	1.084	1.753	1.004	1.861	0.925	1.974	0.845	2.093	0.767	2.216	0.691	2.342	0.616	2.470
28	1.328	1.476	1.255	1.560	1.181	1.650	1.104	1.747	1.028	1.850	0.951	1.958	0.874	2.071	0.798	2.188	0.723	2.309	0.650	2.431
29	1.341	1.483	1.270	1.563	1.198	1.650	1.124	1.743	1.050	1.841	0.975	1.944	0.900	2.052	0.826	2.164	0.753	2.278	0.682	2.396
30	1.352	1.489	1.284	1.567	1.214	1.650	1.143	1.739	1.071	1.833	0.998	1.931	0.926	2.034	0.854	2.141	0.782	2.251	0.712	2.363
31	1.363	1.496	1.297	1.570	1.229	1.650	1.160	1.735	1.090	1.825	1.020	1.920	0.950	2.018	0.879	2.120	0.810	2.226	0.741	2.333
32	1.373	1.502	1.309	1.574	1.244	1.650	1.177	1.732	1.109	1.819	1.041	1.909	0.972	2.004	0.904	2.102	0.836	2.203	0.769	2.306
33	1.383	1.508	1.321	1.577	1.258	1.651	1.193	1.730	1.127	1.813	1.061	1.900	0.994	1.991	0.927	2.085	0.861	2.181	0.795	2.281
34	1.393	1.514	1.333	1.580	1.271	1.652	1.208	1.728	1.144	1.808	1.080	1.891	1.015	1.979	0.950	2.069	0.885	2.162	0.821	2.257
35	1.402	1.519	1.343	1.584	1.283	1.653	1.222	1.726	1.160	1.803	1.097	1.884	1.034	1.967	0.971	2.054	0.908	2.144	0.845	2.236
36	1.411	1.525	1.354	1.587	1.295	1.654	1.236	1.724	1.175	1.799	1.114	1.877	1.053	1.957	0.991	2.041	0.930	2.127	0.868	2.216
37	1.419	1.530	1.364	1.590	1.307	1.655	1.249	1.723	1.190	1.795	1.131	1.870	1.071	1.948	1.011	2.029	0.951	2.112	0.891	2.198
38	1.427	1.535	1.373	1.594	1.318	1.656	1.261	1.722	1.204	1.792	1.146	1.864	1.088	1.939	1.029	2.017	0.970	2.098	0.912	2.180
39	1.435	1.540	1.382	1.597	1.328	1.658	1.273	1.722	1.218	1.789	1.161	1.859	1.104	1.932	1.047	2.007	0.990	2.085	0.932	2.164
40	1.442	1.544	1.391	1.600	1.338	1.659	1.285	1.721	1.230	1.786	1.175	1.854	1.120	1.924	1.064	1.997	1.008	2.072	0.945	2.149
45	1.475	1.566	1.430	1.615	1.383	1.666	1.336	1.720	1.287	1.776	1.238	1.835	1.189	1.895	1.139	1.958	1.089	2.022	1.038	2.088
50	1.503	1.585	1.462	1.628	1.421	1.674	1.378	1.721	1.335	1.771	1.291	1.822	1.246	1.875	1.201	1.930	1.156	1.986	1.110	2.044
55	1.528	1.601	1.490	1.641	1.452	1.681	1.414	1.724	1.374	1.768	1.334	1.814	1.294	1.861	1.253	1.909	1.212	1.959	1.170	2.010
60	1.549	1.616	1.514	1.652	1.480	1.689	1.444	1.727	1.408	1.767	1.372	1.808	1.335	1.850	1.298	1.894	1.260	1.939	1.222	1.984
65	1.567	1.629	1.536	1.662	1.503	1.696	1.471	1.731	1.438	1.767	1.404	1.805	1.370	1.843	1.336	1.882	1.301	1.923	1.266	1.964
70	1.583	1.641	1.554	1.672	1.525	1.703	1.494	1.735	1.464	1.768	1.433	1.802	1.401	1.837	1.369	1.873	1.337	1.910	1.305	1.948
75	1.598	1.652	1.571	1.680	1.543	1.709	1.515	1.739	1.487	1.770	1.458	1.801	1.428	1.834	1.399	1.867	1.369	1.901	1.339	1.935
80	1.611	1.662	1.586	1.688	1.560	1.715	1.534	1.743	1.507	1.772	1.480	1.801	1.453	1.831	1.425	1.861	1.397	1.893	1.369	1.925
85	1.624	1.671	1.600	1.696	1.575	1.721	1.550	1.747	1.525	1.774	1.500	1.801	1.474	1.829	1.448	1.857	1.422	1.886	1.396	1.916
90	1.635	1.679	1.612	1.703	1.589	1.726	1.566	1.751	1.542	1.776	1.518	1.801	1.494	1.827	1.469	1.854	1.445	1.881	1.420	1.909
95	1.645	1.687	1.623	1.709	1.602	1.732	1.579	1.755	1.557	1.778	1.535	1.802	1.512	1.827	1.489	1.852	1.465	1.877	1.442	1.903
100	1.654	1.694	1.634	1.715	1.613	1.736	1.592	1.758	1.571	1.780	1.550	1.803	1.528	1.826	1.506	1.850	1.484	1.874	1.462	1.898
150	1.720	1.746	1.706	1.760	1.693	1.774	1.679	1.788	1.665	1.802	1.651	1.817	1.637	1.832	1.622	1.847	1.608	1.862	1.594	1.877
200	1.758	1.778	1.748	1.789	1.738	1.799	1.728	1.810	1.718	1.820	1.707	1.831	1.697	1.841	1.686	1.852	1.675	1.863	1.665	1.874

n	k'=11 dL	dU	k'=12 dL	dU	k'=13 dL	dU	k'=14 dL	dU	k'=15 dL	dU	k'=16 dL	dU	k'=17 dL	dU	k'=18 dL	dU	k'=19 dL	dU	k'=20 dL	dU
16	0.098	3.503	-----	-----	-----	-----	-----	-----	-----	-----	-----	-----	-----	-----	-----	-----	-----	-----	-----	-----
17	0.138	3.378	0.087	3.557	-----	-----	-----	-----	-----	-----	-----	-----	-----	-----	-----	-----	-----	-----	-----	-----
18	0.177	3.265	0.123	3.441	0.078	3.603	-----	-----	-----	-----	-----	-----	-----	-----	-----	-----	-----	-----	-----	-----
19	0.220	3.159	0.160	3.335	0.111	3.496	0.070	3.642	-----	-----	-----	-----	-----	-----	-----	-----	-----	-----	-----	-----
20	0.263	3.063	0.200	3.234	0.145	3.395	0.100	3.542	0.063	3.676	-----	-----	-----	-----	-----	-----	-----	-----	-----	-----
21	0.307	2.976	0.240	3.141	0.182	3.300	0.132	3.448	0.091	3.583	0.058	3.705	-----	-----	-----	-----	-----	-----	-----	-----
22	0.349	2.897	0.281	3.057	0.220	3.211	0.166	3.358	0.120	3.495	0.083	3.619	0.052	3.731	-----	-----	-----	-----	-----	-----
23	0.391	2.826	0.322	2.979	0.259	3.128	0.202	3.272	0.153	3.409	0.110	3.535	0.076	3.650	0.048	3.753	-----	-----	-----	-----
24	0.431	2.761	0.362	2.908	0.297	3.053	0.239	3.193	0.186	3.327	0.141	3.454	0.101	3.572	0.070	3.678	0.044	3.773	-----	-----
25	0.470	2.702	0.400	2.844	0.335	2.983	0.275	3.119	0.221	3.251	0.172	3.376	0.130	3.494	0.094	3.604	0.065	3.702	0.041	3.790
26	0.508	2.649	0.438	2.784	0.373	2.919	0.312	3.051	0.256	3.179	0.205	3.303	0.160	3.420	0.120	3.531	0.087	3.632	0.060	3.724
27	0.544	2.600	0.475	2.730	0.409	2.859	0.348	2.987	0.291	3.112	0.238	3.233	0.191	3.349	0.149	3.460	0.112	3.563	0.081	3.658
28	0.578	2.555	0.510	2.680	0.445	2.805	0.383	2.928	0.325	3.050	0.271	3.168	0.222	3.283	0.178	3.392	0.138	3.495	0.104	3.592
29	0.612	2.515	0.544	2.634	0.479	2.755	0.418	2.874	0.359	2.992	0.305	3.107	0.254	3.219	0.208	3.327	0.166	3.431	0.129	3.528
30	0.643	2.477	0.577	2.592	0.512	2.708	0.451	2.823	0.392	2.937	0.337	3.050	0.286	3.160	0.238	3.266	0.195	3.368	0.156	3.465
31	0.674	2.443	0.608	2.553	0.545	2.665	0.484	2.776	0.425	2.887	0.370	2.996	0.317	3.103	0.269	3.208	0.224	3.309	0.183	3.406
32	0.703	2.411	0.638	2.517	0.576	2.625	0.515	2.733	0.457	2.840	0.401	2.946	0.349	3.050	0.299	3.153	0.253	3.252	0.211	3.348
33	0.731	2.382	0.668	2.484	0.606	2.588	0.546	2.692	0.488	2.796	0.432	2.899	0.379	3.000	0.329	3.100	0.283	3.198	0.239	3.293
34	0.758	2.355	0.695	2.454	0.635	2.554	0.575	2.654	0.518	2.754	0.462	2.854	0.409	2.954	0.359	3.051	0.312	3.147	0.267	3.240
35	0.783	2.330	0.722	2.425	0.662	2.521	0.604	2.619	0.547	2.716	0.492	2.813	0.439	2.910	0.388	3.005	0.340	3.099	0.295	3.190
36	0.808	2.306	0.748	2.398	0.690	2.492	0.631	2.586	0.575	2.680	0.520	2.774	0.467	2.868	0.417	2.961	0.369	3.053	0.323	3.142
37	0.831	2.285	0.772	2.374	0.714	2.464	0.657	2.555	0.602	2.646	0.548	2.738	0.495	2.829	0.445	2.920	0.397	3.009	0.351	3.097
38	0.854	2.265	0.796	2.351	0.739	2.438	0.683	2.526	0.628	2.614	0.575	2.703	0.522	2.792	0.472	2.880	0.424	2.968	0.378	3.054
39	0.875	2.246	0.819	2.329	0.763	2.413	0.707	2.499	0.653	2.585	0.600	2.671	0.549	2.757	0.499	2.843	0.451	2.929	0.404	3.013
40	0.896	2.228	0.840	2.309	0.785	2.391	0.731	2.473	0.678	2.557	0.626	2.641	0.575	2.724	0.525	2.808	0.477	2.892	0.430	2.974
45	0.988	2.156	0.938	2.225	0.887	2.296	0.838	2.367	0.788	2.439	0.740	2.512	0.692	2.586	0.644	2.659	0.598	2.733	0.553	2.807
50	1.064	2.103	1.019	2.163	0.973	2.225	0.927	2.287	0.882	2.350	0.836	2.414	0.792	2.479	0.747	2.544	0.703	2.610	0.660	2.675
55	1.129	2.062	1.087	2.116	1.045	2.170	1.003	2.225	0.961	2.281	0.919	2.338	0.877	2.396	0.836	2.454	0.795	2.512	0.754	2.571
60	1.184	2.031	1.145	2.079	1.106	2.127	1.068	2.177	1.029	2.227	0.990	2.278	0.951	2.330	0.913	2.382	0.874	2.434	0.836	2.487
65	1.231	2.006	1.195	2.049	1.160	2.093	1.124	2.138	1.088	2.183	1.052	2.229	1.016	2.276	0.980	2.323	0.944	2.371	0.908	2.419
70	1.272	1.986	1.239	2.026	1.206	2.066	1.172	2.106	1.139	2.148	1.105	2.189	1.072	2.232	1.038	2.275	1.005	2.318	0.971	2.362
75	1.308	1.970	1.277	2.006	1.247	2.043	1.215	2.080	1.184	2.118	1.153	2.156	1.121	2.195	1.090	2.235	1.058	2.275	1.027	2.315
80	1.340	1.957	1.311	1.991	1.283	2.024	1.253	2.059	1.224	2.093	1.195	2.129	1.165	2.165	1.136	2.201	1.106	2.238	1.076	2.275
85	1.369	1.946	1.342	1.977	1.315	2.009	1.287	2.040	1.260	2.073	1.232	2.105	1.205	2.139	1.177	2.172	1.149	2.206	1.121	2.241
90	1.395	1.937	1.369	1.966	1.344	1.995	1.318	2.025	1.292	2.055	1.266	2.085	1.240	2.116	1.213	2.148	1.187	2.179	1.160	2.211
95	1.418	1.929	1.394	1.956	1.370	1.984	1.345	2.012	1.321	2.040	1.296	2.068	1.271	2.097	1.247	2.126	1.222	2.156	1.197	2.186
100	1.439	1.923	1.416	1.948	1.393	1.974	1.371	2.000	1.347	2.026	1.324	2.053	1.301	2.080	1.277	2.108	1.253	2.135	1.229	2.164
150	1.579	1.892	1.564	1.908	1.550	1.924	1.535	1.940	1.519	1.956	1.504	1.972	1.489	1.989	1.474	2.006	1.458	2.023	1.443	2.040
200	1.654	1.885	1.643	1.896	1.632	1.908	1.621	1.919	1.610	1.931	1.599	1.943	1.588	1.955	1.576	1.967	1.565	1.979	1.554	1.991

[a] k' is the number of regressors excluding the intercept.

Reprinted, with permission, from *Econometrica* 45(8): 1992-1995.

Table C.4   Models with no intercept (from Farebrother): Positive serial correlation

DURBIN-WATSON ONE PER CENT MINIMAL BOUND

N	K=0	K=1	K=2	K=3	K=4	K=5	K=6	K=7	K=8	K=9	K=10	K=11	K=12	K=13	K=14	K=15	K=16	K=17	K=18	K=19	K=20	K=21
2	0.001																					
3	0.034	0.000																				
4	0.127	0.022	0.000																			
5	0.233	0.089	0.014	0.000																		
6	0.322	0.175	0.065	0.010	0.000																	
7	0.389	0.253	0.135	0.049	0.008	0.000																
8	0.469	0.324	0.202	0.106	0.038	0.006	0.000															
9	0.534	0.394	0.268	0.164	0.086	0.031	0.005	0.000														
10	0.591	0.457	0.333	0.223	0.136	0.070	0.025	0.004	0.000													
11	0.643	0.515	0.394	0.284	0.189	0.114	0.059	0.021	0.003	0.000												
12	0.691	0.568	0.451	0.341	0.244	0.161	0.097	0.050	0.018	0.003	0.000											
13	0.733	0.617	0.503	0.396	0.298	0.212	0.139	0.083	0.043	0.015	0.002	0.000										
14	0.773	0.662	0.552	0.448	0.350	0.262	0.185	0.121	0.072	0.037	0.013	0.002	0.000									
15	0.809	0.703	0.598	0.496	0.400	0.311	0.232	0.163	0.107	0.063	0.032	0.011	0.002	0.000								
16	0.842	0.741	0.640	0.541	0.447	0.358	0.278	0.206	0.145	0.094	0.056	0.028	0.010	0.002	0.000							
17	0.873	0.776	0.679	0.583	0.491	0.404	0.323	0.249	0.184	0.129	0.084	0.050	0.025	0.009	0.001	0.000						
18	0.901	0.808	0.715	0.623	0.533	0.447	0.366	0.292	0.225	0.166	0.116	0.075	0.044	0.023	0.008	0.001	0.000					
19	0.928	0.839	0.749	0.660	0.572	0.488	0.408	0.333	0.265	0.204	0.150	0.105	0.068	0.040	0.020	0.007	0.001	0.000				
20	0.952	0.867	0.780	0.694	0.609	0.527	0.448	0.374	0.304	0.241	0.185	0.136	0.095	0.062	0.036	0.018	0.006	0.001	0.000			
21	0.976	0.893	0.810	0.727	0.644	0.564	0.486	0.413	0.343	0.279	0.221	0.169	0.124	0.087	0.056	0.033	0.017	0.006	0.001	0.000		
22	0.997	0.918	0.838	0.757	0.677	0.599	0.523	0.450	0.381	0.316	0.257	0.203	0.155	0.114	0.079	0.051	0.030	0.015	0.005	0.001	0.000	
23	1.018	0.942	0.864	0.786	0.709	0.632	0.558	0.486	0.417	0.352	0.292	0.237	0.187	0.143	0.104	0.073	0.047	0.027	0.014	0.005	0.001	0.000
24	1.037	0.964	0.889	0.813	0.738	0.664	0.591	0.520	0.452	0.387	0.327	0.270	0.219	0.172	0.131	0.096	0.067	0.043	0.025	0.013	0.004	0.001
25	1.056	0.984	0.912	0.839	0.766	0.693	0.622	0.553	0.486	0.421	0.361	0.304	0.251	0.203	0.160	0.122	0.089	0.062	0.040	0.023	0.012	0.004
26	1.073	1.004	0.934	0.863	0.792	0.722	0.652	0.584	0.518	0.454	0.394	0.336	0.283	0.233	0.189	0.148	0.113	0.083	0.057	0.037	0.022	0.011
27	1.089	1.023	0.955	0.886	0.817	0.749	0.681	0.614	0.549	0.486	0.426	0.368	0.314	0.264	0.218	0.176	0.138	0.105	0.077	0.053	0.034	0.020
28	1.105	1.040	0.974	0.908	0.841	0.774	0.708	0.643	0.579	0.517	0.457	0.400	0.345	0.294	0.247	0.204	0.164	0.129	0.098	0.071	0.050	0.032
29	1.120	1.057	0.993	0.929	0.864	0.798	0.734	0.670	0.607	0.546	0.487	0.430	0.376	0.324	0.276	0.232	0.191	0.154	0.120	0.091	0.067	0.046
30	1.134	1.073	1.011	0.948	0.885	0.822	0.759	0.696	0.635	0.574	0.516	0.460	0.405	0.354	0.305	0.260	0.217	0.179	0.144	0.113	0.086	0.062
31	1.147	1.088	1.028	0.967	0.905	0.844	0.782	0.721	0.661	0.602	0.544	0.488	0.434	0.383	0.334	0.288	0.244	0.205	0.168	0.135	0.106	0.080
32	1.160	1.103	1.044	0.985	0.925	0.865	0.805	0.745	0.686	0.628	0.571	0.516	0.462	0.411	0.362	0.315	0.271	0.230	0.193	0.158	0.127	0.100
33	1.173	1.117	1.060	1.002	0.944	0.885	0.826	0.768	0.710	0.653	0.597	0.542	0.489	0.438	0.389	0.342	0.298	0.256	0.218	0.182	0.149	0.120
34	1.185	1.130	1.075	1.018	0.961	0.904	0.847	0.790	0.733	0.677	0.622	0.568	0.516	0.465	0.416	0.369	0.324	0.282	0.243	0.206	0.172	0.141
35	1.196	1.143	1.089	1.034	0.978	0.923	0.867	0.811	0.755	0.700	0.646	0.593	0.541	0.491	0.442	0.395	0.350	0.308	0.268	0.230	0.195	0.163
36	1.207	1.155	1.102	1.049	0.995	0.940	0.886	0.831	0.777	0.723	0.669	0.617	0.566	0.516	0.467	0.421	0.376	0.333	0.292	0.254	0.218	0.185
37	1.217	1.167	1.116	1.063	1.010	0.957	0.904	0.850	0.797	0.744	0.692	0.640	0.590	0.540	0.492	0.446	0.401	0.358	0.317	0.278	0.241	0.207
38	1.228	1.178	1.128	1.077	1.026	0.974	0.921	0.869	0.817	0.765	0.713	0.663	0.613	0.564	0.516	0.470	0.425	0.382	0.341	0.302	0.265	0.230
39	1.237	1.189	1.140	1.090	1.040	0.989	0.938	0.887	0.836	0.785	0.734	0.684	0.635	0.587	0.540	0.494	0.449	0.406	0.365	0.325	0.288	0.252
40	1.247	1.200	1.152	1.103	1.054	1.004	0.954	0.904	0.854	0.804	0.754	0.705	0.657	0.609	0.562	0.517	0.473	0.430	0.388	0.349	0.311	0.275
45	1.289	1.247	1.204	1.160	1.116	1.071	1.026	0.981	0.936	0.890	0.845	0.800	0.755	0.710	0.666	0.623	0.581	0.539	0.499	0.459	0.421	0.384
50	1.325	1.287	1.248	1.208	1.168	1.128	1.087	1.046	1.004	0.963	0.921	0.880	0.838	0.797	0.756	0.715	0.675	0.636	0.597	0.559	0.521	0.485
55	1.356	1.321	1.286	1.250	1.213	1.176	1.139	1.101	1.063	1.025	0.987	0.948	0.910	0.872	0.833	0.796	0.758	0.721	0.684	0.647	0.611	0.576
60	1.383	1.351	1.319	1.285	1.252	1.218	1.183	1.149	1.114	1.078	1.043	1.008	0.972	0.936	0.901	0.865	0.830	0.795	0.760	0.725	0.691	0.657
65	1.408	1.378	1.348	1.317	1.286	1.254	1.222	1.190	1.158	1.125	1.092	1.059	1.026	0.993	0.960	0.927	0.894	0.861	0.828	0.795	0.762	0.730
70	1.429	1.401	1.373	1.345	1.316	1.286	1.257	1.227	1.197	1.166	1.136	1.105	1.074	1.043	1.012	0.981	0.950	0.919	0.888	0.857	0.826	0.795
75	1.448	1.423	1.396	1.369	1.342	1.315	1.287	1.260	1.231	1.203	1.174	1.146	1.117	1.088	1.058	1.029	1.000	0.971	0.941	0.912	0.883	0.854
80	1.466	1.442	1.417	1.392	1.367	1.341	1.315	1.289	1.262	1.236	1.209	1.182	1.155	1.127	1.100	1.072	1.045	1.017	0.989	0.962	0.934	0.907
85	1.482	1.459	1.436	1.412	1.388	1.364	1.340	1.315	1.290	1.265	1.240	1.214	1.189	1.163	1.137	1.111	1.085	1.059	1.033	1.006	0.980	0.954
90	1.497	1.475	1.453	1.431	1.408	1.385	1.362	1.339	1.315	1.292	1.268	1.244	1.220	1.195	1.171	1.146	1.121	1.097	1.072	1.047	1.022	0.997
95	1.510	1.490	1.469	1.448	1.426	1.405	1.383	1.361	1.338	1.316	1.293	1.271	1.248	1.225	1.201	1.178	1.155	1.131	1.108	1.084	1.060	1.037
100	1.523	1.503	1.483	1.463	1.443	1.422	1.402	1.381	1.359	1.338	1.317	1.295	1.273	1.251	1.229	1.207	1.185	1.162	1.140	1.118	1.095	1.072
150	1.611	1.598	1.585	1.571	1.558	1.544	1.530	1.516	1.502	1.488	1.474	1.460	1.445	1.431	1.416	1.402	1.387	1.372	1.357	1.342	1.327	1.312
200	1.664	1.654	1.644	1.634	1.624	1.613	1.603	1.593	1.582	1.572	1.561	1.551	1.540	1.529	1.519	1.508	1.497	1.486	1.475	1.464	1.453	1.442

Reprinted, with permission, from *Econometrica* 48(6): 1556-1563.

Table C.5   Models with no intercept (from Farebrother): Positive serial correlation

DURBIN-WATSON FIVE PER CENT MINIMAL BOUND

N	K=0	K=1	K=2	K=3	K=4	K=5	K=6	K=7	K=8	K=9	K=10	K=11	K=12	K=13	K=14	K=15	K=16	K=17	K=18	K=19	K=20	K=21
2	0.012																					
3	0.168	0.006																				
4	0.355	0.105	0.004																			
5	0.478	0.248	0.070	0.002																		
6	0.584	0.358	0.180	0.050	0.002																	
7	0.677	0.462	0.275	0.136	0.037	0.001																
8	0.754	0.556	0.371	0.217	0.106	0.029	0.001															
9	0.820	0.635	0.460	0.303	0.175	0.085	0.023	0.001														
10	0.877	0.706	0.539	0.385	0.251	0.143	0.069	0.019	0.001													
11	0.927	0.768	0.610	0.460	0.326	0.211	0.120	0.058	0.016	0.001												
12	0.972	0.823	0.674	0.530	0.397	0.279	0.180	0.101	0.049	0.013	0.001											
13	1.012	0.872	0.731	0.593	0.464	0.345	0.241	0.154	0.087	0.042	0.011	0.001										
14	1.047	0.916	0.783	0.651	0.525	0.408	0.302	0.210	0.134	0.075	0.036	0.010	0.001									
15	1.079	0.953	0.829	0.704	0.583	0.467	0.361	0.266	9.185	0.118	0.066	0.031	0.008	0.001								
16	1.109	0.992	0.872	0.752	0.635	0.523	0.418	0.322	0.237	0.164	0.104	0.058	0.028	0.007	0.000							
17	1.136	1.024	0.911	0.797	0.684	0.575	0.472	0.376	0.288	0.211	0.146	0.093	0.052	0.025	0.007	0.000						
18	1.160	1.055	0.946	0.837	0.729	0.624	0.523	0.427	0.339	0.260	0.190	0.131	0.083	0.046	0.022	0.006	0.000					
19	1.183	1.082	0.979	0.875	0.771	0.669	0.570	0.476	0.388	0.307	0.235	0.171	0.118	0.075	0.041	0.020	0.005	0.000				
20	1.204	1.108	1.010	0.910	0.810	0.711	0.615	0.523	0.436	0.354	0.280	0.213	0.156	0.107	0.067	0.037	0.018	0.005	0.000			
21	1.224	1.132	1.038	0.942	0.846	0.751	0.657	0.567	0.481	0.400	0.324	0.256	0.195	0.142	0.097	0.061	0.034	0.016	0.004	0.000		
22	1.242	1.154	1.064	0.972	0.879	0.787	0.697	0.609	0.524	0.443	0.368	0.298	0.235	0.178	0.130	0.089	0.056	0.031	0.015	0.004	0.000	
23	1.259	1.175	1.088	1.000	0.911	0.822	0.734	0.648	0.565	0.485	0.410	0.339	0.274	0.216	0.164	0.119	0.081	0.051	0.028	0.014	0.004	0.000
24	1.275	1.194	1.111	1.026	0.940	0.854	0.769	0.685	0.604	0.525	0.450	0.380	0.314	0.254	0.199	0.151	0.110	0.075	0.047	0.026	0.012	0.003
25	1.290	1.212	1.132	1.050	0.967	0.884	0.802	0.720	0.641	0.563	0.489	0.419	0.353	0.291	0.235	0.184	0.140	0.101	0.069	0.044	0.024	0.011
26	1.304	1.229	1.152	1.073	0.993	0.913	0.833	0.753	0.676	0.600	0.527	0.457	0.390	0.328	0.271	0.218	0.171	0.130	0.094	0.064	0.040	0.022
27	1.318	1.245	1.171	1.094	1.017	0.940	0.862	0.785	0.709	0.635	0.563	0.493	0.427	0.365	0.306	0.252	0.203	0.159	0.120	0.087	0.060	0.037
28	1.330	1.260	1.188	1.115	1.040	0.965	0.889	0.815	0.741	0.668	0.597	0.529	0.463	0.400	0.341	0.286	0.236	0.190	0.148	0.112	0.081	0.055
29	1.342	1.275	1.205	1.134	1.062	0.989	0.916	0.843	0.770	0.699	0.630	0.562	0.497	0.435	0.376	0.320	0.268	0.221	0.177	0.139	0.105	0.076
30	1.354	1.288	1.221	1.152	1.082	1.011	0.940	0.869	0.799	0.729	0.661	0.595	0.530	0.468	0.409	0.353	0.301	0.252	0.207	0.166	0.130	0.098
31	1.365	1.301	1.236	1.169	1.101	1.033	0.964	0.895	0.826	0.758	0.691	0.626	0.562	0.501	0.442	0.386	0.333	0.283	0.237	0.195	0.156	0.122
32	1.375	1.313	1.250	1.185	1.120	1.053	0.986	0.919	0.852	0.785	0.720	0.656	0.593	0.532	0.474	0.418	0.364	0.314	0.267	0.223	0.183	0.147
33	1.385	1.325	1.264	1.201	1.137	1.072	1.007	0.942	0.876	0.811	0.747	0.684	0.623	0.563	0.504	0.449	0.395	0.344	0.297	0.252	0.211	0.173
34	1.394	1.336	1.277	1.216	1.153	1.091	1.027	0.963	0.900	0.836	0.774	0.712	0.651	0.592	0.534	0.479	0.425	0.374	0.326	0.280	0.238	0.199
35	1.403	1.347	1.289	1.230	1.169	1.108	1.046	0.984	0.922	0.860	0.799	0.738	0.678	0.620	0.563	0.508	0.455	0.404	0.355	0.309	0.266	0.225
36	1.412	1.357	1.301	1.243	1.184	1.125	1.064	1.004	0.943	0.883	0.823	0.763	0.705	0.647	0.591	0.536	0.483	0.432	0.384	0.337	0.293	0.252
37	1.420	1.367	1.312	1.256	1.199	1.141	1.082	1.023	0.964	0.905	0.846	0.787	0.730	0.673	0.618	0.564	0.511	0.460	0.412	0.365	0.321	0.279
38	1.428	1.376	1.323	1.268	1.212	1.156	1.099	1.041	0.983	0.925	0.868	0.811	0.754	0.698	0.644	0.590	0.538	0.488	0.439	0.392	0.347	0.305
39	1.436	1.385	1.333	1.280	1.225	1.170	1.114	1.058	1.002	0.945	0.889	0.833	0.778	0.723	0.669	0.616	0.564	0.514	0.466	0.419	0.374	0.331
40	1.443	1.394	1.343	1.291	1.238	1.184	1.130	1.075	1.020	0.965	0.909	0.854	0.800	0.746	0.693	0.641	0.590	0.540	0.492	0.445	0.400	0.357
45	1.476	1.432	1.387	1.341	1.294	1.246	1.197	1.148	1.099	1.049	1.000	0.950	0.900	0.851	0.802	0.753	0.706	0.658	0.612	0.567	0.523	0.480
50	1.504	1.464	1.424	1.382	1.340	1.297	1.253	1.209	1.164	1.120	1.075	1.029	0.984	0.939	0.894	0.849	0.804	0.760	0.717	0.674	0.631	0.590
55	1.528	1.492	1.455	1.417	1.379	1.340	1.300	1.260	1.219	1.179	1.138	1.096	1.055	1.013	0.972	0.930	0.889	0.848	0.807	0.766	0.726	0.687
60	1.549	1.516	1.482	1.447	1.412	1.376	1.340	1.303	1.266	1.229	1.191	1.153	1.115	1.077	1.038	1.000	0.962	0.923	0.885	0.847	0.810	0.772
65	1.568	1.537	1.505	1.474	1.441	1.408	1.375	1.341	1.307	1.272	1.238	1.202	1.167	1.132	1.096	1.061	1.025	0.989	0.953	0.918	0.882	0.847
70	1.584	1.555	1.526	1.497	1.467	1.436	1.405	1.374	1.342	1.310	1.278	1.245	1.213	1.180	1.147	1.113	1.080	1.047	1.013	0.980	0.947	0.914
75	1.599	1.572	1.545	1.517	1.489	1.461	1.432	1.403	1.373	1.344	1.313	1.283	1.253	1.222	1.191	1.160	1.129	1.098	1.066	1.035	1.004	0.972
80	1.612	1.587	1.561	1.536	1.509	1.483	1.456	1.429	1.401	1.373	1.345	1.317	1.288	1.259	1.230	1.201	1.172	1.143	1.113	1.084	1.054	1.025
85	1.624	1.600	1.576	1.552	1.527	1.502	1.477	1.452	1.426	1.400	1.373	1.347	1.320	1.293	1.266	1.238	1.211	1.183	1.155	1.128	1.100	1.072
90	1.635	1.613	1.590	1.567	1.544	1.520	1.497	1.472	1.448	1.423	1.399	1.373	1.348	1.323	1.297	1.271	1.245	1.219	1.193	1.166	1.141	1.114
95	1.645	1.624	1.603	1.581	1.559	1.537	1.514	1.491	1.468	1.445	1.422	1.398	1.374	1.350	1.326	1.301	1.277	1.252	1.227	1.202	1.177	1.152
100	1.654	1.634	1.614	1.593	1.573	1.551	1.530	1.508	1.487	1.465	1.442	1.420	1.397	1.374	1.352	1.328	1.305	1.282	1.258	1.235	1.211	1.187
150	1.720	1.706	1.693	1.679	1.666	1.652	1.638	1.624	1.609	1.595	1.580	1.566	1.551	1.536	1.521	1.506	1.491	1.476	1.461	1.445	1.430	1.414
200	1.759	1.748	1.738	1.728	1.718	1.708	1.697	1.687	1.676	1.666	1.655	1.644	1.633	1.622	1.611	1.600	1.589	1.578	1.567	1.556	1.544	1.533

Reprinted, with permission, from *Econometrica* 48(6): 1556-1563.

Table C.6   Models with no intercept (from Farebrother): Negative serial correlation

DURBIN-WATSON NINETY FIVE PER CENT MINIMAL BOUND

N	K=0	K=1	K=2	K=3	K=4	K=5	K=6	K=7	K=8	K=9	K=10	K=11	K=12	K=13	K=14	K=15	K=16	K=17	K=18	K=19	K=20	K=21
2	1.988																					
3	2.761	0.994																				
4	2.871	1.836	0.582																			
5	2.857	2.178	1.267	0.380																		
6	2.844	2.320	1.655	0.917	0.266																	
7	2.828	2.398	1.871	1.283	0.690	0.197																
8	2.805	2.453	2.008	1.521	1.017	0.537	0.151															
9	2.783	2.483	2.110	1.687	1.251	0.823	0.429	0.120														
10	2.762	2.501	2.181	1.816	1.427	1.044	0.678	0.350	0.097													
11	2.742	2.511	2.231	1.913	1.569	1.218	0.881	0.567	0.291	0.080												
12	2.723	2.516	2.268	1.987	1.682	1.364	1.049	0.752	0.481	0.245	0.068											
13	2.705	2.518	2.296	2.044	1.771	1.484	1.193	0.911	0.649	0.413	0.210	0.058										
14	2.688	2.517	2.316	2.090	1.843	1.582	1.316	1.051	0.797	0.565	0.358	0.181	0.050									
15	2.672	2.515	2.332	2.126	1.902	1.664	1.419	1.172	0.931	0.703	0.497	0.314	0.158	0.043								
16	2.657	2.512	2.344	2.155	1.950	1.732	1.506	1.276	1.049	0.829	0.624	0.439	0.277	0.139	0.038							
17	2.644	2.508	2.353	2.179	1.990	1.789	1.580	1.367	1.153	0.944	0.743	0.557	0.391	0.246	0.124	0.034						
18	2.631	2.504	2.359	2.199	2.024	1.838	1.644	1.445	1.244	1.045	0.852	0.669	0.501	0.351	0.220	0.110	0.030					
19	2.618	2.499	2.364	2.215	2.053	1.880	1.699	1.513	1.324	1.136	0.951	0.773	0.605	0.452	0.316	0.198	0.099	0.027				
20	2.607	2.494	2.368	2.228	2.077	1.916	1.747	1.573	1.395	1.216	1.040	0.868	0.704	0.550	0.410	0.286	0.179	0.090	0.025			
21	2.596	2.489	2.370	2.239	2.098	1.947	1.789	1.625	1.457	1.289	1.120	0.955	0.796	0.644	0.502	0.373	0.260	0.162	0.081	0.022		
22	2.585	2.484	2.372	2.249	2.116	1.974	1.825	1.671	1.513	1.353	1.193	1.034	0.880	0.731	0.591	0.460	0.341	0.238	0.148	0.074	0.020	
23	2.575	2.479	2.373	2.257	2.131	1.998	1.858	1.712	1.563	1.411	1.258	1.107	0.957	0.813	0.674	0.544	0.422	0.313	0.218	0.136	0.068	0.019
24	2.566	2.474	2.373	2.263	2.145	2.019	1.886	1.749	1.607	1.463	1.318	1.172	1.029	0.888	0.753	0.623	0.502	0.389	0.289	0.201	0.125	0.062
25	2.557	2.470	2.373	2.269	2.156	2.037	1.912	1.782	1.647	1.510	1.371	1.232	1.094	0.958	0.826	0.699	0.578	0.465	0.360	0.267	0.185	0.115
26	1.073	1.004	0.934	0.863	0.792	0.722	0.652	0.584	0.518	0.454	0.394	0.336	0.283	0.233	0.189	0.148	0.113	0.083	0.057	0.037	0.022	0.011
27	1.089	1.023	0.955	0.886	0.817	0.749	0.681	0.614	0.549	0.486	0.426	0.368	0.314	0.264	0.218	0.176	0.138	0.105	0.077	0.053	0.034	0.020
28	1.105	1.040	0.974	0.908	0.841	0.774	0.708	0.643	0.579	0.517	0.457	0.400	0.345	0.294	0.247	0.204	0.164	0.129	0.098	0.071	0.050	0.032
29	1.120	1.057	0.993	0.929	0.864	0.798	0.734	0.670	0.607	0.546	0.487	0.430	0.376	0.324	0.276	0.232	0.191	0.154	0.120	0.091	0.067	0.046
30	1.134	1.073	1.011	0.948	0.885	0.822	0.759	0.696	0.635	0.574	0.516	0.460	0.405	0.354	0.305	0.260	0.217	0.179	0.144	0.113	0.086	0.062
31	1.147	1.088	1.028	0.967	0.905	0.844	0.782	0.721	0.661	0.602	0.544	0.488	0.434	0.383	0.334	0.288	0.244	0.205	0.168	0.135	0.106	0.080
32	1.160	1.103	1.044	0.985	0.925	0.865	0.805	0.745	0.686	0.628	0.571	0.516	0.462	0.411	0.362	0.315	0.271	0.230	0.193	0.158	0.127	0.100
33	1.173	1.117	1.060	1.002	0.944	0.885	0.826	0.768	0.710	0.653	0.597	0.542	0.489	0.438	0.389	0.342	0.298	0.256	0.218	0.182	0.149	0.120
34	1.185	1.130	1.075	1.018	0.961	0.904	0.847	0.790	0.733	0.677	0.622	0.568	0.516	0.465	0.416	0.369	0.324	0.282	0.243	0.206	0.172	0.141
35	1.196	1.143	1.089	1.034	0.978	0.923	0.867	0.811	0.755	0.700	0.646	0.593	0.541	0.491	0.442	0.395	0.350	0.308	0.268	0.230	0.195	0.163
36	1.207	1.155	1.102	1.049	0.995	0.940	0.886	0.831	0.777	0.723	0.669	0.617	0.566	0.516	0.467	0.421	0.376	0.333	0.292	0.254	0.218	0.185
37	1.217	1.167	1.116	1.063	1.010	0.957	0.904	0.850	0.797	0.744	0.692	0.640	0.590	0.540	0.492	0.446	0.401	0.358	0.317	0.278	0.241	0.207
38	1.228	1.178	1.128	1.077	1.026	0.974	0.921	0.869	0.817	0.765	0.713	0.663	0.613	0.564	0.516	0.470	0.425	0.382	0.341	0.302	0.265	0.230
39	1.237	1.189	1.140	1.090	1.040	0.989	0.938	0.887	0.836	0.785	0.734	0.684	0.635	0.587	0.540	0.494	0.449	0.406	0.365	0.325	0.288	0.252
40	1.247	1.200	1.152	1.103	1.054	1.004	0.954	0.904	0.854	0.804	0.754	0.705	0.657	0.609	0.562	0.517	0.473	0.430	0.388	0.349	0.311	0.275
45	1.289	1.247	1.204	1.160	1.116	1.071	1.026	0.981	0.936	0.890	0.845	0.800	0.755	0.710	0.666	0.623	0.581	0.539	0.499	0.459	0.421	0.384
50	1.325	1.287	1.248	1.208	1.168	1.128	1.087	1.046	1.004	0.963	0.921	0.880	0.838	0.797	0.756	0.715	0.675	0.636	0.597	0.559	0.521	0.485
55	1.356	1.321	1.286	1.250	1.213	1.176	1.139	1.101	1.063	1.025	0.987	0.948	0.910	0.872	0.833	0.796	0.758	0.721	0.684	0.647	0.611	0.576
60	1.383	1.351	1.319	1.285	1.252	1.218	1.183	1.149	1.114	1.078	1.043	1.008	0.972	0.936	0.901	0.865	0.830	0.795	0.760	0.725	0.691	0.657
65	1.408	1.378	1.348	1.317	1.286	1.254	1.222	1.190	1.158	1.125	1.092	1.059	1.026	0.993	0.960	0.927	0.894	0.861	0.828	0.795	0.762	0.730
70	1.429	1.401	1.373	1.345	1.316	1.286	1.257	1.227	1.197	1.166	1.136	1.105	1.074	1.043	1.012	0.981	0.950	0.919	0.888	0.857	0.826	0.795
75	1.448	1.423	1.396	1.369	1.342	1.315	1.287	1.260	1.231	1.203	1.174	1.146	1.117	1.088	1.058	1.029	1.000	0.971	0.941	0.912	0.883	0.854
80	1.466	1.442	1.417	1.392	1.367	1.341	1.315	1.289	1.262	1.236	1.209	1.182	1.155	1.127	1.100	1.072	1.045	1.017	0.989	0.962	0.934	0.907
85	1.482	1.459	1.436	1.412	1.388	1.364	1.340	1.315	1.290	1.265	1.240	1.214	1.189	1.163	1.137	1.111	1.085	1.059	1.033	1.006	0.980	0.954
90	1.497	1.475	1.453	1.431	1.408	1.385	1.362	1.339	1.315	1.292	1.268	1.244	1.220	1.195	1.171	1.146	1.121	1.097	1.072	1.047	1.022	0.997
95	1.510	1.490	1.469	1.448	1.426	1.405	1.383	1.361	1.338	1.316	1.293	1.271	1.248	1.225	1.201	1.178	1.155	1.131	1.108	1.084	1.060	1.037
100	1.523	1.503	1.483	1.463	1.443	1.422	1.402	1.381	1.359	1.338	1.317	1.295	1.273	1.251	1.229	1.207	1.185	1.162	1.140	1.118	1.095	1.072
150	1.611	1.598	1.585	1.571	1.558	1.544	1.530	1.516	1.502	1.488	1.474	1.460	1.445	1.431	1.416	1.402	1.387	1.372	1.357	1.342	1.327	1.312
200	1.664	1.654	1.644	1.634	1.624	1.613	1.603	1.593	1.582	1.572	1.561	1.551	1.540	1.529	1.519	1.508	1.497	1.486	1.475	1.464	1.453	1.442

Table C.7   Models with no intercept (from Farebrother): Negative serial correlation

DURBIN-WATSON NINETY NINE PER CENT MINIMAL BOUND

N	K=0	K=1	K=2	K=3	K=4	K=5	K=6	K=7	K=8	K=9	K=10	K=11	K=12	K=13	K=14	K=15	K=16	K=17	K=18	K=19	K=20	K=21
2	1.999																					
3	2.951	0.999																				
4	3.221	1.967	0.586																			
5	3.261	2.462	1.359	0.382																		
6	3.235	2.682	1.878	0.983	0.268																	
7	3.198	2.776	2.177	1.459	0.740	0.198																
8	3.166	2.817	2.347	1.776	1.158	0.576	0.153															
9	3.133	2.837	2.448	1.983	1.465	0.937	0.460	0.121														
10	3.101	2.847	2.514	2.121	1.684	1.224	0.773	0.375	0.098													
11	3.071	2.847	2.560	2.220	1.842	1.441	1.035	0.647	0.312	0.081												
12	3.043	2.843	2.592	2.294	1.961	1.607	1.244	0.885	0.549	0.263	0.069											
13	3.017	2.836	2.612	2.349	2.054	1.737	1.410	1.082	0.764	0.471	0.225	0.059										
14	2.992	2.828	2.626	2.391	2.177	1.842	1.544	1.244	0.984	0.666	0.409	0.195	0.051									
15	2.969	2.818	2.635	2.432	2.185	1.928	1.656	1.379	1.104	0.837	0.585	0.358	0.170	0.044								
16	2.948	2.808	2.640	2.447	2.231	1.997	1.749	1.494	1.237	0.985	0.743	0.517	0.316	0.150	0.039							
17	2.927	2.797	2.643	2.466	2.269	2.055	1.827	1.591	1.351	1.114	0.883	0.664	0.461	0.281	0.133	0.035						
18	2.908	2.787	2.644	2.480	2.299	2.102	1.893	1.675	1.451	1.227	1.007	0.796	0.597	0.413	0.251	0.119	0.031					
19	2.890	2.776	2.643	2.492	2.324	2.142	1.948	1.746	1.538	1.327	1.118	0.915	0.721	0.539	0.372	0.226	0.107	0.028				
20	2.874	2.766	2.641	2.500	2.344	2.176	1.996	1.807	1.613	1.415	1.217	1.022	0.834	0.656	0.489	0.337	0.204	0.096	0.025			
21	2.858	2.756	2.638	2.506	2.361	2.204	2.036	1.861	1.678	1.492	1.305	1.119	0.937	0.763	0.598	0.446	0.307	0.185	0.087	0.023		
22	2.842	2.746	2.635	2.511	2.375	2.228	2.071	1.907	1.736	1.561	1.384	1.207	1.032	0.862	0.700	0.548	0.408	0.280	0.169	0.080	0.021	
23	2.828	2.736	2.631	2.515	2.387	2.249	2.102	1.947	1.786	1.621	1.454	1.285	1.118	0.954	0.796	0.645	0.504	0.374	0.257	0.155	0.073	0.019
24	2.814	2.727	2.627	2.517	2.396	2.267	2.128	1.983	1.831	1.675	1.516	1.356	1.196	1.038	0.884	0.736	0.596	0.465	0.345	0.237	0.143	0.067
25	2.801	2.717	2.623	2.518	2.404	2.282	2.151	2.014	1.871	1.723	1.572	1.420	1.267	1.115	0.966	0.821	0.683	0.552	0.430	0.319	0.218	0.132
26	2.789	2.709	2.618	2.519	2.411	2.295	2.171	2.042	1.906	1.766	1.623	1.478	1.331	1.186	1.042	0.901	0.765	0.635	0.512	0.399	0.295	0.202
27	2.777	2.700	2.614	2.519	2.416	2.306	2.189	2.066	1.938	1.805	1.669	1.530	1.390	1.250	1.111	0.975	0.842	0.714	0.592	0.477	0.371	0.274
28	2.766	2.692	2.609	2.519	2.421	2.316	2.205	2.088	1.966	1.839	1.710	1.577	1.444	1.309	1.176	1.043	0.914	0.788	0.667	0.553	0.445	0.346
29	2.755	2.684	2.604	2.518	2.425	2.325	2.219	2.107	1.991	1.871	1.747	1.621	1.493	1.364	1.235	1.107	0.981	0.858	0.739	0.625	0.517	0.416
30	2.745	2.676	2.600	2.517	2.428	2.332	2.231	2.125	2.014	1.899	1.781	1.660	1.537	1.414	1.290	1.166	1.044	0.924	0.807	0.695	0.587	0.485
31	2.735	2.668	2.595	2.515	2.430	2.339	2.242	2.140	2.035	1.925	1.812	1.696	1.579	1.460	1.340	1.221	1.102	0.986	0.872	0.761	0.654	0.552
32	2.725	2.661	2.590	2.514	2.432	2.344	2.252	2.155	2.053	1.948	1.840	1.729	1.616	1.502	1.387	1.272	1.157	1.043	0.932	0.823	0.718	0.617
33	2.716	2.654	2.586	2.512	2.433	2.349	2.260	2.167	2.070	1.970	1.866	1.759	1.651	1.541	1.430	1.319	1.208	1.097	0.989	0.882	0.779	0.678
34	2.707	2.647	2.581	2.510	2.434	2.353	2.268	2.179	2.086	1.989	1.889	1.787	1.683	1.577	1.470	1.363	1.255	1.148	1.042	0.938	0.836	0.737
35	2.699	2.640	2.576	2.508	2.435	2.357	2.275	2.189	2.100	2.007	1.911	1.813	1.713	1.611	1.507	1.404	1.299	1.196	1.093	0.991	0.891	0.794
36	2.690	2.634	2.572	2.506	2.435	2.360	2.281	2.199	2.113	2.023	1.931	1.837	1.740	1.642	1.542	1.442	1.341	1.240	1.140	1.041	0.943	0.847
37	2.683	2.627	2.567	2.503	2.435	2.363	2.287	2.207	2.124	2.038	1.950	1.859	1.765	1.670	1.574	1.477	1.379	1.282	1.184	1.088	0.992	0.898
38	2.675	2.621	2.563	2.501	2.435	2.365	2.292	2.215	2.135	2.052	1.967	1.879	1.789	1.697	1.604	1.510	1.416	1.321	1.226	1.132	1.039	0.947
39	2.667	2.615	2.559	2.499	2.435	2.367	2.296	2.222	2.145	2.065	1.982	1.898	1.811	1.722	1.632	1.541	1.450	1.358	1.266	1.174	1.083	0.993
40	2.660	2.609	2.555	2.496	2.434	2.369	2.300	2.229	2.154	2.077	1.997	1.913	1.831	1.746	1.659	1.570	1.482	1.392	1.303	1.213	1.124	1.036
45	2.628	2.583	2.535	2.484	2.430	2.374	2.315	2.253	2.190	2.124	2.056	1.986	1.914	1.841	1.767	1.691	1.614	1.537	1.459	1.381	1.302	1.224
50	2.600	2.559	2.516	2.471	2.424	2.374	2.323	2.269	2.214	2.157	2.098	2.037	1.975	1.911	1.847	1.781	1.714	1.646	1.578	1.509	1.439	1.370
55	2.575	2.538	2.500	2.459	2.417	2.373	2.327	2.280	2.231	2.180	2.128	2.075	2.020	1.964	1.907	1.849	1.790	1.730	1.669	1.608	1.546	1.484
60	2.553	2.519	2.484	2.448	2.409	2.370	2.329	2.286	2.242	2.197	2.151	2.103	2.054	2.004	1.954	1.902	1.849	1.796	1.742	1.687	1.631	1.576
65	2.534	2.503	2.470	2.437	2.402	2.366	2.329	2.290	2.250	2.210	2.168	2.125	2.081	2.036	1.990	1.944	1.896	1.848	1.799	1.750	1.700	1.650
70	2.516	2.487	2.458	2.427	2.395	2.361	2.327	2.292	2.256	2.219	2.181	2.142	2.102	2.061	2.020	1.977	1.934	1.891	1.846	1.802	1.756	1.710
75	2.500	2.473	2.446	2.417	2.387	2.357	2.325	2.293	2.260	2.226	2.191	2.155	2.118	2.081	2.043	2.005	1.965	1.926	1.885	1.844	1.802	1.760
80	2.486	2.461	2.436	2.408	2.380	2.352	2.323	2.293	2.262	2.231	2.198	2.165	2.132	2.098	2.063	2.027	1.991	1.954	1.917	1.879	1.841	1.803
85	2.473	2.449	2.425	2.399	2.374	2.347	2.320	2.292	2.263	2.234	2.204	2.174	2.143	2.111	2.079	2.046	2.012	1.979	1.944	1.909	1.874	1.838
90	2.460	2.438	2.415	2.391	2.367	2.342	2.317	2.291	2.264	2.237	2.209	2.181	2.152	2.122	2.092	2.061	2.030	1.999	1.967	1.935	1.902	1.869
95	2.449	2.428	2.406	2.384	2.361	2.338	2.314	2.290	2.264	2.238	2.212	2.184	2.157	2.129	2.101	2.073	2.044	2.015	1.986	1.956	1.926	1.895
100	2.438	2.418	2.398	2.377	2.355	2.333	2.310	2.287	2.264	2.240	2.215	2.190	2.165	2.139	2.113	2.086	2.059	2.031	2.003	1.975	1.946	1.917
150	2.363	2.349	2.336	2.322	2.308	2.294	2.279	2.265	2.250	2.235	2.220	2.204	2.188	2.173	2.156	2.140	2.124	2.107	2.090	2.073	2.056	2.039
200	2.317	2.307	2.296	2.286	2.276	2.265	2.255	2.244	2.233	2.222	2.211	2.200	2.189	2.177	2.166	2.154	2.142	2.131	2.119	2.108	2.094	2.082

Appendix D
Guide to ACF/PACF Plots

The plots shown here are those of pure or theoretical ARIMA processes. Here are some general guidelines for identifying the process:

- Nonstationary series have an ACF that remains significant for half a dozen or more lags, rather than quickly declining to zero. You must difference such a series until it is stationary before you can identify the process.

- Autoregressive processes have an exponentially declining ACF and spikes in the first one or more lags of the PACF. The number of spikes indicates the order of the autoregression.

- Moving average processes have spikes in the first one or more lags of the ACF and an exponentially declining PACF. The number of spikes indicates the order of the moving average.

- Mixed (ARMA) processes typically show exponential declines in both the ACF and the PACF.

At the identification stage, you do not need to worry about the sign of the ACF or PACF, or about the speed with which an exponentially declining ACF or PACF approaches zero. These depend upon the sign and actual value of the AR and MA coefficients. In some instances, an exponentially declining ACF alternates between positive and negative values.

ACF and PACF plots from real data are never as clean as the plots shown here. You must learn to pick out what is essential in any given plot. Always check the ACF and PACF of the residuals, in case your identification is wrong. Bear in mind that:

- Seasonal processes show these patterns at the seasonal lags (the multiples of the seasonal period).

- You are entitled to treat nonsignificant values as zero. That is, you can ignore values that lie within the confidence intervals on the plots. You do not have to ignore them, however, particularly if they continue the pattern of the statistically significant values.

- An occasional autocorrelation will be statistically significant by chance alone. You can ignore a statistically significant autocorrelation if it is isolated, preferably at a high lag, and if it does not occur at a seasonal lag.

Consult any text on ARIMA analysis for a more complete discussion of ACF and PACF plots.

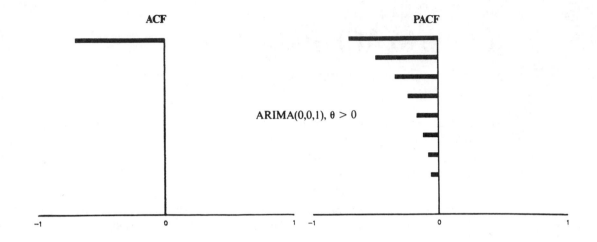

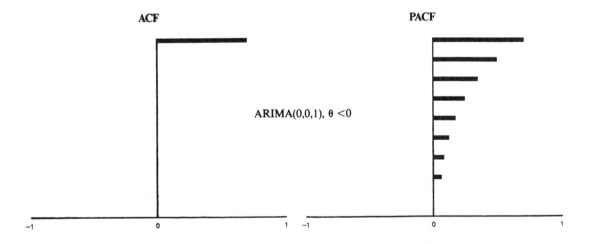

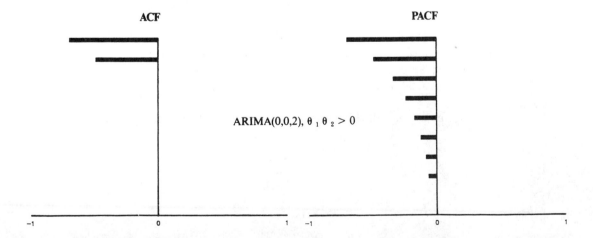

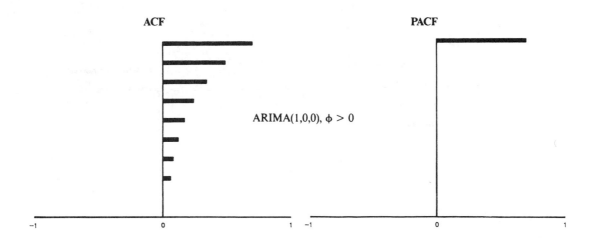

ARIMA(1,0,0), $\phi > 0$

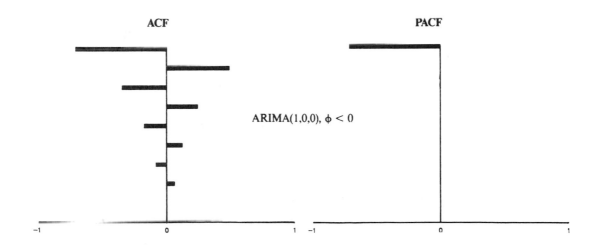

ARIMA(1,0,0), $\phi < 0$

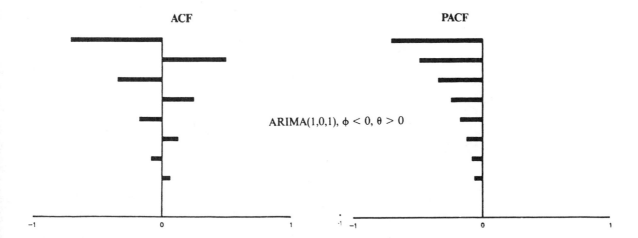

ARIMA(1,0,1), $\phi < 0, \theta > 0$

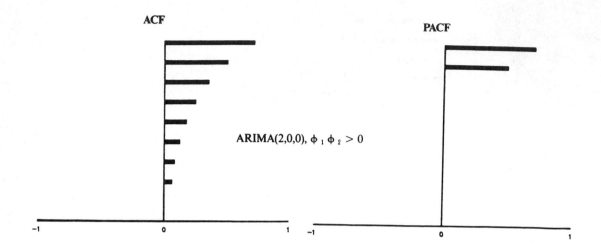

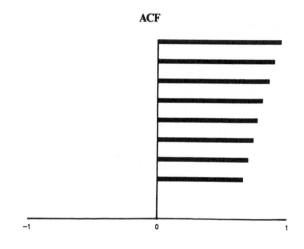

ARIMA(0, 1, 0) (integrated series)

Bibliography

Berenson, M. L. and D. M. Levine. 1992. *Basic business statistics, concepts and applications*. Engelwood Cliffs, N.J.: Prentice Hall.

Cronbach, L. J. 1951. Coefficient alpha and the internal structure of tests. *Psychometrika*, 16:3, 297–334.

Guttman, L. 1945. A basis for analyzing test-retest reliability. *Psychometrika*, 10:4, 255–282.

Hicks, C. R. 1982. *Fundamental concepts in the design of experiments*. 3rd ed. New York: Holt, Rinehart and Winston.

Kristof, W. 1963. The statistical theory of stepped-up reliability coefficients when a test has been divided into several equivalent parts. *Psychometrika*, 28:3, 221–238.

_____. 1969. Estimation of true score and error variance for tests under various equivalence assumptions. *Psychometrika*, 34:4, 489–507.

McGraw, K. O. and S. P. Wong. 1996. Forming inferences about some intraclass correlation coefficients. *Psychological Methods*, 1:1, 30–46.

Milliken, G. A. and D. E. Johnson. 1992. *Analysis of messy data*. Vol. 1, *Designed experiments*. New York: Chapman and Hall.

Novick, M. R. and C. Lewis. 1967. Coefficient alpha and the reliability of composite measurements. *Psychometrika*, 32:1, 1–13.

Searle, S. R. 1987. *Linear models for unbalanced data*. New York: John Wiley and Sons.

Searle, S. R., F. M. Speed, and G. A. Milliken. 1980. Population marginal means in the linear model: An alternative to least squares means. *The American Statistician*, 34:4, 216–221.

Shrout, P. E. and J. L. Fleiss. 1979. Intraclass correlations: Uses in assessing reliability. *Psychological Bulletin*, 86: 420–428.

Winer, B. J., D. R. Brown, and K. M. Michels. 1991. *Statistical principles in experimental design*. New York: McGraw-Hill.

Index